Dancing with the Modernist City

Dancing with the Modernist City

Metropolitan Dance Texts around 1900

Wesley Lim

University of Michigan Press
Ann Arbor

Published in the United States of America by the
University of Michigan Press
Manufactured in the United States of America
Printed on acid-free paper
First published July 2024

A CIP catalog record for this book is available from the British Library.

Library of Congress Cataloging-in-Publication Data

Names: Lim, Wesley Ben, author. | Michigan Publishing (University of
    Michigan), publisher.
Title: Dancing with the modernist city : metropolitan dance texts around 1900 /
    Wesley Lim.
Description: Ann Arbor [Michigan] : University of Michigan Press, 2024. |
    Includes bibliographical references (pages 285–300) and index.
Identifiers: LCCN 2024002408 (print) | LCCN 2024002409 (ebook) |
    ISBN 9780472133307 (hardcover) | ISBN 9780472039692 (paperback) |
    ISBN 9780472904563 (ebook other)
Subjects: LCSH: Dance—Social aspects—History and criticism—
    19th century. | Dance—Social aspects—History and criticism—20th
    century. | Sociology, Urban—19th century. | Sociology, Urban—20th
    century. | Cities and towns—Social aspects—19th century. | Cities and towns—
    Social aspects—20th century.
Classification: LCC GV1588.6 .L56   2024 (print) | LCC GV1588.6 (ebook) |
    DDC 306.4/8409034—dc23/eng/20240326
LC record available at https://lccn.loc.gov/2024002408
LC ebook record available at https://lccn.loc.gov/2024002409

DOI: https://doi.org/10.3998/mpub.11571914

The University of Michigan Press's open access publishing program is made possible
thanks to additional funding from the University of Michigan Office of the Provost
and the generous support of contributing libraries.

Cover illustration: Loïe Fuller appearing in an advertisement for the Folies-Bergère,
a music hall and revue theater. Illustration by PAL (1893). Courtesy of Bibliothèque
nationale de France.

Contents

Acknowledgments

This book has been a long time coming, and there is a village to thank. First, I would like to sincerely thank my acquisitions editor Christopher Dreyer at the University of Michigan Press, who immediately understood and supported the vision of the project on our first meeting at the German Studies Association. I also express my gratitude for the three anonymous reviewers, who thoroughly engaged with the project and provided critical yet constructive feedback throughout the process.

Thanks to Katie LaPlant for overseeing the project until the end; Delilah McCrea and Daniel Otis for their meticulous attention in editing; Kevin Rennells for his great assistance during the production stage; and finally Devon Thomas for their indexing work.

Sections of this book have appeared in previous forms: the Kessler chapter as "From Spectator to Practitioner: Transforming Harry Graf Kessler's Dance Aesthetic," *KulturPoetik. Zeitschrift zur kulturgeschichtlichen Literaturwissenschaft* 13, no. 2 (2013): 197–217; and the Malte chapter, "Bridging Gesture, Gesticulation, and Early Modern Dance: Rilke's *Veitstänzer* in *The Notebooks of Malte Laurids Brigge*," *Dance Chronicle* 39, no. 3 (2016): 279–98. I greatly appreciate the meticulous work of the editors, Juliane Blank and Lynn Matluck Brooks, respectively, and also the anonymous readers for their generous feedback.

Beginning at Vanderbilt University as a dissertation, this project has undergone significant transformation at Colorado College, Miami University, and the Australian National University. It spans a period of about seventeen years, although my engagement with dance and movement began years before. Throughout the years, numerous institutions have awarded me generous funding for travel to do research in libraries and archives and to attend conferences. The Berlin Program for Advanced German and European Studies Dissertation Research Fellowship at the Free University (FU) from 2008 to 2009 gave me access to resources, ample time to contemplate ideas and write, and an incredible network of other scholars to learn from. I am indebted to Karin Goihl for connecting me with the researchers in Tanzwissenschaft at the FU. Yvonne Hardt's seminar on *Tanzlesen* (Reading Dancing) and Gabriele Brandstetter's dance research colloquia were essential in shaping my research. Thanks also to the Akademie der Künste Berlin for allowing me to view the August-Endell-Sammlung. Vanderbilt University graciously provided me with much support: the Gisela Mosig Graduate Research Fellowship funded my first year-long exchange in Berlin in 2005, and I also received the Max Kade Graduate Summer Research Award. Colorado College granted me funds for image reproduction rights in earlier articles. Miami University awarded me the GRAMELAC Archival Research Grant, and most recently the Australian National University generously granted me RSHA conference travel funding, an OSP sabbatical leave to support the revision of this manuscript, and SLLL Strategic Research Funding to cover the costs of indexing.

In addition to various institutions, many individuals have been instrumental in inspiring and guiding me through the entire book-writing process. Opening my eyes to modernism and helping me to draw on my experience as a dancer, my Doktormutter Meike Werner encouraged me to research dance and literature in her fin-de-siècle seminar in 2005. She cued me into the *Veitstänzer* and Malte, and then sent me to study abroad in Berlin. These seeds germinated and now bear the fruit of these productive interminglings regarding the city and urban space. I am grateful for the chat about dance that I had over coffee with Lucia Ruprecht when she presented at a conference on dreams at Vanderbilt. I'll always cherish the coffee with Michael Cowan in Montreal as I was preparing for my qualifying exams. Mila Ganeva encouraged me to begin the manuscript-revising process and gave me incomparable advice on how to navigate academic book publishing. Nicole Thesz meticulously read parts of my manuscript and graciously relayed her experience publishing her own recent book at the time. Cathie Grimm offered her generous conversations and inspirational cat content during my revision. I prize the conversations I had with Tani Sebro about dance and its decolonization. Sheila Johnson has closely read through many of my drafts over several years—I appreciated her printing out my work on physical paper, writing comments in pen, and then sending them to me in Australia. I would like to thank members of the ANU Screen Working Group (Katharina Bonzel, Kate Warren, Fabricio Tocco, Gemma King, Monique Rooney, and Leslie

Barnes), who kindly and critically read one of my last chapters. My ANU Germanist colleagues are without doubt the loveliest group of people to work with: Katie Sutton has tirelessly read my numerous drafts and proposals and has instilled me with much wisdom, patience, and tenacity when it comes to publishing; Maureen Gallagher has swiftly read through my work and given me a steady stream of hilarious cat content to get me through revisions. I owe Catherine Travis and Kath Bode my deepest gratitude for their mentorship and guidance. Josh Brown and Thomas Nulley-Valdes have been invaluable colleagues, who have supported me and given me mental strength while writing this book. And I am eternally grateful for the encouragement and the caring ethos of Mariana Ivanova, Erik Jensen, Maurice Gattis, Mahmoud Hussein, Tas Skorupa, Scott Mersch, Wayne Herbert, and Anthony Vaughn.

I would like to thank those who provided me with critical feedback, much-needed prodding, and generative discussions in numerous conferences, colloquia, and courses over the years: Kentucky Foreign Language Conference, University of Kentucky, Lexington (April 2008); Berlin and Modernism, University of the South, Sewanee, TN (September 2008); the Louisville Conference on Literature and Culture since 1900, University of Louisville, Louisville, KY (February 2009); Berlin Program Colloquia (2009); Anna Leo's Dance History course, Emory University, Atlanta, GA (March 2011); Protest and Reform in Wilhelmine German Culture 1871–1918, Institute of Germanic and Romance Studies, University of London (September 2012); the panel "Pedestrian Crossings: Walking in Philosophy, Literature, and Art," German Studies Association, Denver, CO (October 2013); DAAD Faculty Summer Seminar "Rethinking Performance in Theory and Practice," University of Chicago (2017); and the meeting of the German Studies Association of Australia, Wellington, New Zealand (November 2018).

I am deeply indebted to the Dance and Movement Studies Program at Emory University. Their inclusive program welcomed me, even though I had no previous dance training. Here I developed both my practical and critical inquiry in dance. Learning voraciously by taking endless technique classes, I put my dance education first. Anna Leo's dance history course opened me up to the world of semiotic dance and cultural analysis; Lori Teague introduced me to the Laban efforts; and George Staib's criticism of my first ballet helped me question and complicate my own choreography. I also thank my other dance instructors (Greg Catellier, Sheri Latham, Tara Shepard Myers, and Wayne Smith), the Emory Dance Company, and the American College Dance Association for being so fundamental in my dance education.

I am grateful to my parents, Sally and Benny Lim, who allowed me to explore my interest in movement through figure skating. From 1992 to 1995, they drove me to the Crystal Ice Palace at 5 a.m. for freestyle sessions, brought me chorizo-and-egg tacos for breakfast, and financed a very expensive sport: ice time, lessons, equipment, costumes, and competitions. Figure skating, of course, germinated later into dance technique courses at Emory. I am blessed to have an older and artistically inclined brother, Kenley Lim, who as a part-time DJ at gender-diverse nightclubs in Dallas at the time, encouraged me to pursue dance and to go to my first Love Parade.

I would like to thank the cities of Berlin and Paris for their plenitude of visual and experiential stimuli. My flânerie through their urban streets influenced me to also see them as the authors in my study did. Going on Jugendstilarchitekturspaziergänge, visiting museums, riding all the U-Bahn lines for fun, watching people in public, dancing at parties that wouldn't exist a couple years later, swimming in Teufelsee, Kaulsdorfersee, and Müggelsee, and drinking copious amounts of Club-Mate contributed to the thinking-through and success of this book.

Finally, I would like to express gratitude to my partner Sebastian Herold, who has been along with me on many Berliner Spaziergänge since 2009. You've read through my work for years, been through the highs and lows of the academic lifestyle, and patiently waited a very long time for stability. And I am glad that you can now join me in spotting cockatoos, rainbow lorikeets, and kangaroos.

Introduction

Strolling through the streets of Paris at the end of the nineteenth century, an urban observer happens on an advertisement for the Folies-Bergère, a music hall and revue theater (fig. 1). Illustrated on this poster is a slim, captivating woman; her posterior is exposed, and she is on her tiptoes in heels, coyly looking back at the spectator. Her flowing hair creates the impression that she is in motion, and her body is draped in a billowing material. One could perceive the diaphanous fabric portrayed with bold, expressionist strokes as being separate from her body, but on the other hand she seems to wear the textile as a second skin or even an·appendage, creating a cinematic superimposition.

The woman on the poster is an eroticized representation of the US-American dancer Loïe Fuller, who actually had a stockier frame. Fuller came to Europe around 1900 to perform in variety acts such as the skirt dance, in which she maneuvered a large piece of fabric around her body in choreographed patterns. To further her reach and create a greater impression, she manipulated poles attached to the drapery. In the theatrical setting, colored-light gels beamed onto her draping material, which functioned as a canvas. While the poster advertisement (1893) by PAL (Jean de Paleologue) reflects a more seductive image than her real appearance, the artist seems to combine two striking elements that form a dynamic tension: dance movement and city space. Dance scholar Ann Cooper Albright identifies a rough city skyline in the upper left corner in the splotchy design of the fabric.[1] PAL renders the lighting effects onto her fabric as an expressionistic (stylistically early for the time) metropolitan cityscape combined with her sensual dancing body. One might also discern a slight but colorful, kaleidoscopic effect. Based on this representation, is the city giving her the strength and opportunity to per-

Fig. 1. A seductive representation of Loïe Fuller on an advertisement for the Folies-Bergère, a music hall and revue theater. She seems to meld with the fabric.

form? Or does she create the urban space herself? One aspect seems certain: PAL's advertisement interweaves the dancing body and the projection of a city space as if they had almost become a single entity. Concerning the amalgamation of dancing body and space, Margareta Ingrid Christian's *Objects in Air: Artworks and Their Outside around 1900* investigates similar ideas about how the external space surrounding artwork—often considered to simply be air—creates aerial environments, which can be considered their own aesthetic categories.[2] These artistic organisms auratically reach beyond their physical confines and become incorporated into their own milieu or *Umgebung*.[3] This phenomenon clearly happens to Fuller in the poster.

To take a step back from viewing the image in isolation: such posters found their home among a sea of advertisements in the urban environment. To increase visibility and attract attention, many identical posters were lined up next to each other. The perceptions of the average modern individual in the city had to come to terms with the various kinds of dynamic stimuli overwhelming their senses—bombarding advertisements, bustling traffic, hordes of pedestrians, ubiquitous electronic signage, and distracting window displays. Most could attain what sociologist Georg Simmel refers to as a blasé attitude.[4] By blocking out superfluous stimulation that distracted them from their ultimate goal—catching a train or arriving at work on time—the urban citizen might not see PAL's Loïe Fuller poster. The image theoretically functions as a consumerist enticement by attracting predominantly heteronormative men to attend her performance at the Folies-Bergère, although she did cater to all kinds of viewership. However, some citizens who had more time on their hands and an aesthetic gaze could disengage from the temptations of capitalist society. In the mid-nineteenth century, the French poet Charles Baudelaire typified the term *flâneur* as an idle, wealthy, male who aesthetically read the city during his urban strolls.[5] This sociological type went on long, seemingly aimless walks through the city, observing everyday objects and events on the surface, paying attention not to their utility but to their fleeting aesthetic values. Furthermore, interpreting the writings of cultural theorist Walter Benjamin, contemporary sociologist David Frisby recognizes that the production of texts was also a characteristic of the flâneur.[6] Indeed, these kinds of citizens could create representations of their urban experience in their writing and artwork.

In addition to PAL and Fuller, German-speaking writers and European artists in this study, such as August Endell, Harry Graf Kessler, Rainer Maria Rilke, Alfred Döblin, Else Lasker-Schüler, Segundo de Chomón, and the Skladanowsky brothers Max and Emil, flocked to Berlin, Paris, and other cities to experience the bustling city life, to meet other artists and thinkers, and to write and create. They were all forced to physically and visually negotiate the changing urban space on a daily basis. Berlin was and remains notorious for perpetually reinventing itself. Thus, their new, developing perception further shaped their imaginations when conceiving of movement in their literary, artistic, and cinematic representations. These writers, artists, and filmmakers indulged in flânerie and documented in diaries and letters their experiences of watching early-twentieth-century dancers perform distinct movement styles, including Ruth St. Denis's exotic dances, Vaslav Nijinsky's abrupt and angular movements, and Loïe Fuller's skirt dance—in various spaces such as cabarets, *Varieté* (venues for multiple, short, entertaining acts), and even on city streets. These cases challenged the traditional nineteenth-century institution of theatrical dance—ballet with its storybook and heteronormative, hierarchical narratives—by drawing from the practices and ethos of *Varieté* to demonstrate a variety of emerging modern-dance aesthetics. *Varieté* in particular represented the perceptions of the modern individual in the bustling city. The convergence these writers saw in the unexpected encounters of the moving body interacting with its urban environment and in experimental dance performances gave rise to forms of writing that interwove the two motifs.

Known mostly as an architect, Endell became interested in architecture not through formal training, but via his studies in philosophy, literature, art history, and phenomenology. Thus, he not only designed structures, he wrote critically about architecture. His "The Beauty of the Metropolis" (1908) describes pedestrians walking in a square whose aggregate, swirling movement takes on dancerly dimensions. Strikingly, his depiction aesthetically parallels Loïe Fuller's performances in which her surrounding space and drapery costume seem to absorb her as she moves. Kessler was an intellectual diarist whose privileged connections with the elite allowed him to comment on art, literature, politics, and dance in his journals. He attended balls and noted in his diaries how the costuming of women transformed them into "exotic" beings. Primarily known as a poet, Rilke also drew from the visual, such as during his time at the artist colony in Worpswede and with the French sculptor Auguste Rodin in Paris. In *The Notebooks of Malte Laurids Brigge* (1910), he sets the stage by portraying his protagonist Malte, who observes and closely follows a man in the streets of Paris who repeatedly makes abrupt movements. The Austrian author Stefan Zweig commented that noisy public places disturbed Rilke so much that hours after leaving the area, he would still be unsettled.[7] On the other hand, during walks Rilke noticed the most insignificant things and ascribed meaning to them.[8] Döblin's earlier texts serve as precursors to *Berlin Alexanderplatz*, in which the city space functions more as an active character. Working as a physician in Freiburg, Regensburg, and Berlin, Döblin developed a keen interest in the body in his literary work, which took on cinematic aesthetics called *Kinostil*. His short story "The Dancer and the Body" (1910) chronicles the brief life of a young dancer who begins to experience seeing and dancing with her own body during a stay in an urban hospital. Lasker-Schüler, like Rilke, was also known as a poet. However, she turned to drawing as an alternative to writing. Intellectual and artistic café life played a large role in her conceptualizations of the city in her writings and drawings. In a scene from her novel *My Heart* (1912), the author characterizes a café that transforms into an oriental dancer. Chomón's hand-painted color frames of serpentine dance films added to a choreography of attraction reflecting the perpetual stimuli of a *Varieté* performance. And the Skladanowsky brothers filmed Berlin from numerous panoramic angles. In their first cinematic short, Max films Emil kicking his right leg to the side with the Berlin skyline in the background.

In this study, I argue that these writers, artists, and filmmakers created *metropolitan dance texts* incited by a modernist, flâneur-like, and sometimes queer gaze—breaking away from the historically male, heteronormative view. Their urban encounters with the dancing body inspired a deviation from the actual event, often engaging with its reimagination. Much like PAL's advertising featuring Fuller in an abstracted cityscape, the most fascinating aspect of these representations is their setting in the urban space: in a square, at a ball, in the streets, in a café, in a hospital, and in the cityscape of Berlin and Thebes. The metropolitan space does not function simply like a traditional theatrical stage, as many critics have characterized it, but more like a dynamic entity that interacts with and profoundly stimulates the individuals' dancerly movements—making fluid the bounds between outside and inside. Furthermore, in this new visual genre the representations of urban space sometimes become an active agent and "dance" with the protagonist engaging with a posthumanist mode. This dehierarchicalization of the human and nonhuman creates a new ethics and a shifting of agency by valuing the poetic space as another entity.

Dance, Movement Culture, and *Varieté* in the City around 1900

This section first situates the practice of early-twentieth-century dance, its cognate movement modalities, and the variety theater within the bustling metropolis. It sets the stage for these dancers in the city before showing how they inspired writers, artists, and filmmakers to experiment with representations of the moving body. Like many of his generation, the illustrator PAL had moved to Paris at the turn of the century to seek work. Urban metropolises around 1900 were a dynamic setting that allowed artists and intellectuals from all over the world to come together. Pioneers of early-twentieth-century dance,[9] such as Loïe Fuller, Isadora Duncan, and Ruth St. Denis, all from the United States, and Vaslav Nijinsky from Russia, who danced with the Ballets Russes, toured European cities, including Berlin, Paris, Vienna, Munich, and London, among others. They dazzled and perplexed viewers with their experimental modern dance, which broke away from the form of ballet or *danse d'école*. Many of them also danced in the *Varieté*,[10] the venues for short, entertaining acts that focused on the spectacular and mirrored the experience of living in a bustling city. These variety theaters were often situated in metropolitan centers—for example, Berlin's Wintergarten in Friedrichstraße and the Folies-Bergère in Paris.

Cognate Movement Forms to Dance

During the late nineteenth and early twentieth century, popular German culture turned its attention to other movement forms besides dance for the lay individual to explore: activities concerning physical health such as nudism, gymnastics, and movement pedagogy in schools. Coming to the fore were modalities such as eurhythmics, a movement system inspired by music that was conceptualized and developed by Émile Jaques-Dalcroze (1865–1950), and the Delsarte System developed by François Delsarte (1811–1871), which concentrated on expressing inner emotions through gesture. The latter form was introduced to the US and influenced the movement styles of both St. Denis and Duncan.

Historian Karl Toepfer describes some of the early nude dancers, such as Adorée Villany, Gertrud Leistikow, and Olga Desmond, as well as the well-known developers of expressionist dance Rudolf Laban and Mary Wigman into the 1920s. He argues that through imagery and photographs, not necessarily live performances, the layperson could attain greater access to the spirit of the dancing body. His study addresses many publications that included numerous images, demonstrating the prevalence of German body culture through the Wilhelmine and Weimar Periods as they contributed to the idea of modernity. Like the divergent aesthetics of early-twentieth-century dancers, generalized nudist culture (*Nacktkultur*) also projected "an ambiguous political identity," because the body could signify both a return to the primal instinct as well as "an unprecedented condition of nakedness." According to Edward Ross Dickinson, "The idea that the (relative) nakedness in modern dance performance was not erotic nudity but authentic, 'natural' nakedness—just like in Greek statuary—was absolutely ubiquitous in the discussion of the dance, ultimately becoming an outright cliché."[11] One can see both the erotic and natural qualities in PAL's poster of Fuller.

This shift from dance to more generalized movement for the everyday person demonstrated how the self could change and actively cultivate itself through these varied practices; whether through nature, nudism, or exercise, the individual engaged with a common German physical culture from 1890 until 1936.[12] Early-twentieth-century dancers found themselves in this context and contributed greatly to it. The modern movement practices outlined here were, of course, often in defiant response to the tradition of ballet and drew from practices of the *Varieté*.

Ballet and Modern Dance

Beginning in the fifteenth and sixteenth centuries in Italian Renaissance courts, ballet developed its codified movement vocabulary in France in the seventeenth century under Louis XIV and later flourished in the 1850s in Russia.[13] The ballets of the nineteenth century maintained a tradition based on systematized terminology in French and Italian that corresponded to specific positions and movements. The dances' well-known narratives allowed each performer to portray an easily discernable role, through categories such as gender, nationality, or otherworldliness. Ballets often included recognizable costumes and background sets, creating a familiar or fantastic atmosphere. Early-twentieth-century dancers desired to break free from the strictures of this court and bourgeois model, and they developed drastically different styles. In contrast to ballet, which focused on an antigravitational dynamic, symmetrical form, lightness, elongated lines, and an erect back, modern dance generally worked with the gravitational pull to the floor, focusing on breath, contractions of the torso, and self-expression.[14]

Of the American modern dancers to come to Europe, Fuller performed before the others in this study. Having no traditional dance training, she began as an actress before becoming associated with the skirt dance on the US vaudeville stage. After moving to Europe and escaping the puritanical and conservative American crowd, her performances evolved onto a larger scale. By maneuvering highly voluminous fabric extended by poles in circular, dynamic patterns, she entranced audiences. Fuller also experimented with colorful lights that illuminated her draping textile during the performance. This staging and choreography created the illusion of her body disappearing, and evoked an abstract materialization and posthumanism, which degendered the female body. Her famous performances, such as the *Serpent Dance* (1891) and *Fire Dance* (1896), inspired many imitators, who performed serpentine dances like Fuller's in short films at the beginning of the twentieth century. Other artists created representations of her movement in other media, such as in literature, posters, sculptures, and film. While Fuller's career began in the US, she flourished in Europe with performances in Berlin's Wintergarten. She had, however, an even more profound influence in Paris, performing at Comédie-Parisienne (later called Théâtre de l'Athenée), Folies-Bergère, and Théâtre des Arts.

In contrast to Fuller, Duncan did have formal dance training. Vehemently opposed to the strictures of ballet, her dances were inspired by Greek classicism. She often performed in a loose, draping tunic, abandoning the confining corset and dancing barefoot, executing natural movements such as simple hops and skips. Duncan advocated for whole-body movement emanating from the solar plexus, a network of nerves in the abdomen; she believed the spirit was firmly rooted in the body, not in a transcendental being. Claiming that nature was the "original source of all dance,"[15] she founded a dance school at the edges of Berlin in Grunewald in 1904 to further her movement and philosophical practices. She had debuted in Munich in 1902 and in Berlin in 1903, performing in the Volkstheater and Theater des Westens, respectively,[16] and she often danced to the music of Schubert, Chopin, Brahms, and Strauss.

St. Denis's movement studies began with American Delsarte technique, but she quickly became enraptured by Orientalism after having seen a cigarette advertisement depicting the Egyptian goddess Isis. Gaining extensive experience in American theater before coming to Europe, she drew from the glittering spectacle of vaudeville. German audiences particularly appreciated both her and Duncan's dancing because of their nonacademic performances.[17] In 1906 she choreographed and performed *Radha*, drawing from Hindu mythology. In this dance, fitting for the *Varieté* stage, St. Denis wore a skirt with a bare midriff, a jeweled bodice, bangles on her arms, and bells on her ankles. Despite the glitz of her performance, she wanted her dance to be viewed as art. Unlike Duncan, St. Denis conceptualized the body as a means to escape the physical in order to enter a spiritual realm. From 1906 to 1909 she toured throughout Europe, traveling in 1906 from Paris to Berlin, performing *Radha*, *The Incense* (1906), and *The Cobras* (1906) in the Komische Oper and the Wintergarten-Varieté. St. Denis met and engaged in conversations with intellectuals and other artists, such as Max Reinhardt, Harry Graf Kessler, and Hugo von Hofmannsthal.

Nijinsky came from Russia, but he had an equally modernist take on the body and dance movement. In performances such as *The Spirit of the Rose* (1911), *Afternoon of a Faun* (1912), and *The Rite of Spring* (1913), he embodied animalistic-human and often queer roles with an antiballetic vocabulary: abrupt, angular, and vibrating movements with turned-in feet. Nijinsky belonged to the Ballets Russes, a ballet company from Russia founded in 1909 and lead by Sergei Diaghilev. Under Diaghilev's direction, the dancers freely experimented with new movement, deviating drastically from traditional ballet. The director initiated numerous collaborations with composers such as Igor Stravinsky and Claude Debussy and visual artists like Léon Bakst. His company performed in venues such as the Théâtre des Champs-Élysées, Théâtre du Châtelet, Théâtre National de l'Opéra in Paris, and Theater des Westens in Berlin.

Although the movement styles of Fuller, Duncan, St. Denis, and Nijinsky may not have constituted a unified aesthetic, these early-twentieth-century dancers embraced the freedom to dance on their own terms and experimented with nonballetic movements, costumes, stagings, and themes. Their positioning in major metropolitan cities and ability to tour throughout Europe created a wide and intricate network of potential connections, influences, and collaborative projects with other artists and intellectuals. For instance, at the 1900 Paris Exposition, all three of the American modern dancers mentioned above encountered and drew inspiration from each other, while still developing their own ideas.[18]

Varieté: Bridging Ballet and Modern Dance

The road from ballet to modern dance was not completely direct; it also took cues from *Varieté*, or variety theater. Dance studies scholar Claudia Balk and others have pointed out that *Varieté* dancers led the path to what became modern dance, yet the research done in tracing this lineage has been marginalized.[19] Some considered the dances of *Varieté* performers to be trivial and purely for entertainment.[20] However, many of the trailblazers of early-twentieth-century dance, such as Fuller, St. Denis, and Duncan began their careers in variety theater.[21] In his book *Das Varieté*, Wolfgang Jansen cites Arthur Kahane, who says that it was not the performances of the Wiesenthal sisters who began the rebirth of dance out of ballet, but others like the *Fire Dance* of Fuller, or the dances of Duncan.[22] Gunhild Oberzaucher-Schüller has named the American group of Loïe Fuller, Isadora Duncan, Maud Allen, and Ruth St. Denis as the "prime movers" who began the modern dance movement in middle Europe.[23] Claiming the aesthetic of the *Varieté* to most accurately characterize the early European phase of Ruth St. Denis,[24] she problematizes the line between what constitutes a variety theater performance and the new modern dance. Instead of classifying the dances of St. Denis as purely *Varieté* or modern dance, the early-twentieth-century dancers did not observe strict boundaries, experimenting with continuous changes and resisting any specific categorization.

Critics find it difficult to define *Varieté*.[25] Arthur Moeller-Bruck calls it a prostitute art form that can't be considered art because it embodies Dionysian drives.[26] Ernst Günther characterizes it as mass entertainment whose gene-alogy derives from both the theater and the circus.[27] Oberzaucher-Schüller complicates St. Denis's position as a dancer, who almost always performed in *Varieté* yet wanted to show that her dance was also an art form, a religious exercise, with rhythm being the meaning of dance.[28] St. Denis's costumes also reflected the variety-theater style—skin-baring, colorful, and glittering. She used this venue as an avenue to perform, develop her style, and make contacts with artists and intellectuals. Performance opportunities during this time period were mostly limited to the *Varieté*, opera, theater, and ballet, which were still highly regarded or relatively popular compared to the unheard-of modern dance.

Varieté, like the circus, had multiple moments of interests taking place on a stage, as in a theater. Its short, multifarious acts attracted the constant attention of the audience but revolved around no unified theme.[29] The differ-ent, visually appealing performances switched quickly from one to the next, with little transition time. The *Varieté* could be symbolically captured in the image of the kaleidoscope: "a permanently changing and colorful game."[30] This characterization recalls PAL's depiction of Fuller given in the opening of this chapter (fig. 1). Maintaining freer production guidelines, variety theater allowed other kinds of dance and performance styles to emerge outside of the theater, including skirt dances, serpent dances, cakewalks, cancans, fandan-gos, polkas, waltzes, gymnastics, erotic dances, juggling, animal acts, magic tricks, acrobatics, and sketches.[31] One could argue that because of the open performance guidelines, more experimental pieces could be performed under the guise of *Varieté*. These spectacular displays often presented women wear-ing non-Western costumes and performing Oriental-inspired dances, which led to a large heterosexual male following.[32] These influences from countries in the East arose from colonization, the European fascination with Oriental-ist literature, world exhibitions, and archeological digs.[33]

Peter Jelavich characterizes the German *Varieté* as mostly a low- but also high-end type of entertainment. While the former, sometimes called *Tingelt-angel*, often consisted of performances on a small, raised stage attached to a restaurant or bar where women sold "naughty" postcards,[34] the latter catered to members of the international star circuit such as Loïe Fuller and the Five Barrison Sisters, at commercial establishments like the notable Wintergar-ten, which was used as a vaudeville hall starting in 1887.[35] Although most commonly associated with the lower class because of its entertainment factor, the middle class began attending more *Varieté* performances than theater. To relieve the stress of the monotonous workday combined with perpetual exposure to the traffic, advertisements, shop windows, and sounds of their growing urban environs, they desired a form of entertainment that corresponded to their shortened and fragmented attention spans. *Varieté* served such purposes; it bridged vaudeville artistry with bourgeois society.[36] This performance genre quickly gave rise to the cabaret, which maintained a "middle-ground between [the] mindlessness of popular variety shows and the incomprehensible esoterism of the avant-garde."[37] The Weimar revue and cabaret scene boasted a variety of performers: Celly de Rheidt and her nude dance troupe; Anita Berber, with her androgynous appearance, cocaine-induced performances, and eventual suicide; Josephine Baker's both modern and "primitive" banana dance; the Tiller Girls' precision, which embodied a Taylorist choreography of labor; and Valeska Gert's grotesque parodies of, for example, the Tiller Girls.

The accessibility and objectification of women at these performance establishments ushered in the idea of a *Konsumgesellschaft* (consumerist society) that one could compare to the many *Warenhäusern* (department stores) that had become established in Berlin.[38] The *Varieté* offered a place where guests, particularly heteronormative men, could observe and quickly survey the "goods" on display. This situation led to the idea of buying and consuming products, perpetuating the life of the heterosexual male gaze. Since one could eat, drink, and relax at the variety theater, audience members were not usually involved in intellectual work, but rather were simply amused by the various acts.[39] Not necessarily the main attraction, the performers at these venues were sometimes pushed into the periphery—while the audience themselves could be just as important as the dancers. Although trying to stay spectacular and maintain the focus of the audience, *Varieté* created a similar environment in which the stage performances could be marginalized in comparison to the socializing.

Dickinson argues that some modern dancers, such as Duncan, were fixated on the classical Greek past because of its remarkable cultural prestige among the upper and middle classes, who subscribed to its politically progressive values.[40] Also, at the time, variety theater was not considered a respectable art form, particularly because of its connotations of the sensuous corporeal, the consumptive male gaze, and pleasure—in direct opposition to the Kantian idea of disinterested aesthetic reflection.[41] While this performance form originated outside of the middle class and was deemed immoral, it was eventually accepted, first as a subculture and later as a part of popular entertainment.[42] Modern dance was able to eventually appeal to a mass audience because it did not reflect the middle- or upper-class taste for ballet or that of the lower-class *Varieté*. As a result, besides dancing in the Wintergarten and Folies-Bergere, Fuller, Duncan, and St. Denis were able to make the leap into "high" art, appearing in such venues as the Theater des Westens, the Krolloper, and the Komische Oper.[43] Nijinsky and the Ballets Russes bypassed the variety-theater circuit, because they had immediately been invited to perform in theater and opera venues.

Andrea Haller has investigated how Simmel's essays "Die Berliner Gewerbeausstellung" ("The Berlin Trade Exhibition") from 1896 and "Die Großstädte und das Geistesleben" ("The Metropolis and Mental Life") from 1903—which theoretically describe the mode of perception of the modern individual in the city—parallel the aesthetic experience of watching early short films.[44] Noticing shared terminology such as "overstimulation," "shock," and "excitement" from both areas, Haller extrapolates her argumentation to other modern manifestations, such as trade shows, department stores, storefronts, and of course the *Varieté*. More specifically, Kristen Hylenski's study connects the variety theater movement aesthetic with the fragmented perception of the modern individual. Through an analysis of Frank Wedekind's dance poems "Tingel-Tangel" (1897), "Grand Ecart" (1910), "Modernes Mädchen" (1911), and "Junges Blut" (1912), she demonstrates that the depicted *Varieté* dancers represent the perpetual motion, speed, and ephemerality of modernity, and they successfully control it through flexibility, while paradoxically also providing a refuge and distraction for the early-twentieth-century citizen.[45]

If the form and style of variety theater represent the consumerist experience of modern individuals in the bustling city, which also fed back to them, then my intervention is to ask, Could the aestheticized view of the flâneur in the urban space also be symptomatic of or intrinsically intertwined with the new modern dance? And, further, what are the effects of the new and developing metropolis in the world of dance, and how is this represented in modernist writing and other artistic productions?

Writers and Filmmakers in the Dancing City

Kessler, Endell, Rilke, Döblin, Lasker-Schüler, Chomón, and the Skladanowsky brothers flocked to cities like Berlin and Paris to experience bustling city life, to meet other artists and thinkers, and to write and create. They knew, or knew of, each other, some more than others, and their aesthetic confluences remain apparent. The narrator in Lasker-Schüler's *Letters to Norway* or *My Heart* writes about how Döblin supposedly diagnoses her with thyroid issues, but believes rather that she simply longs for the café life. Both authors had written for Herwarth Walden's literary newspaper *Der Sturm* and frequented the same café scene in Berlin. Rilke, along with his lover at the time, Lou Andreas-Salome, had met Endell in the summer of 1897 in Wolfratshausen. And years before, in 1882, Nietzsche had fallen in love with Andreas-Salome. In 1901 Kessler and the Belgian architect Henry van de Velde had seen Fuller perform her *Serpentine Dance* in Berlin. They both designed the Nietzsche Archive in Weimar and wanted to fulfill the philosophy of the Nietzschian *Übermensch* in architectural form;[46] the architect Endell followed the same idea. And much of Döblin's early writing style is based on developments in early film. And both Chomón and the Skladanowsky brothers worked with experimental moving pictures. While some of the connections and constellations here are less salient than others, they all clearly shared an interest in the aestheticized, moving body and the dynamic stimuli of the city; many were also profoundly influenced by Nietzsche's philosophy, such as the dancing figure Zarathustra, who projected a bodily becoming, creativity, and the exploration of kinetic expression.

Dancers, artists, and authors latched on to Nietzsche's conceptualization of the Dionysian from *The Birth of Tragedy* (1872), which drew from Greek drama and opposed the Apollonian drive.[47] The latter—characterized by orderliness, individualism, and rationality—contrasted with the former's power of the unconscious and the collective. While individuality was associated with the twentieth-century modernist self, it was, according to Susan Jones's reading of Nietzsche, "rooted in pain and conflict. The pain of individuation constitutes the pain experienced by the individual's desire to return to the communal and unconscious drives of the Dionysian."[48] These tropes are still intimately interwoven in the works of authors and dancers at the time.

Some of these writers documented their experiences of watching various forms of early-twentieth-century dance in diaries and letters. In an atelier in Montmartre—a bohemian district in Paris—Rilke attended a performance by a Spanish dancer,[49] who probably inspired his poem "The Spanish Dancer." In addition to witnessing dances by St. Denis,[50] he also supposedly encountered, in the streets of Paris, a real *Veitstänzer:*[51] an individual with a neurological condition that causes abrupt and unexpected movements that resemble a dance. In "Dancers," the doctor and author Döblin characterizes a fictitious experience of witnessing two vastly different dancers: a herculean woman and an emaciated, expressionist dancer.[52] The protagonist in Lasker-Schüler's *Letters to Norway* or *My Heart* between 1911 and 1912 also attended the Wintergarten *Varieté*, various cabarets, and a performance of the Ballets Russes. Chomón filmed dancers and variety theater performers. Max and Emil Skladanowsky were themselves showmen at *Varieté* and toured throughout Europe with their dissolving magic-lantern display. Of all the authors and artists in this study, Kessler, as documented in his extraordinarily extensive diaries, engaged the most with early-twentieth-century dancers by attending their performances and rehearsals. Because of his diplomatic disposition and personal connections, he not only became personally acquainted with dancers, he even collaborated with Nijinsky and Sergei Diaghilev, founder and impresario of the Ballets Russes, on the ballet libretto for *The Legend of Joseph*. These encounters in the authors' writing range the gamut from verifiable documentation, as in Kessler's diaries, to texts of questionable authenticity, such as Döblin's piece. Perhaps more important to remember here, however, is the profound effect of dancing on their literary and visual imagination. Dance studies scholar Kate Elswit also draws from this distinction, when she terms the diverse perception of spectators watching the same Weimar dance performance as an "archive of watching";[53] many of the reactions seemed exaggerated. The writers' interaction with these dancers in this study, even if fictitious, incited them to depict dance and the dancerly form in their literary and essayistic work. And the dance they perceived could very well have been exaggerated by the sole, subjective view of the writer. This phenomenon then further questions the relation between dance and the written word. Since dance was and still is notoriously difficult to adequately render into written form,[54] the authors highlight their own perspective and agenda by experimenting with words, literary structure, and succinct form to represent this exciting new movement form, similar to how PAL creatively portrayed a colorful Fuller dancing with the cityscape in his poster.

The powerful influence of the dancing body on their visual economy would inevitably affect their "gestural imaginary," as Lucia Ruprecht refers to it. Reading the imaginary in connection with the realistic, she states:

> This relationship is hinged between (mis)match, escapism, and powerlessness on the one hand, and creativity, performativity, and empowerment on the other hand; between failing to confront reality, and bringing-about that which is experienced as real in the first place. As a realm that includes but also surpasses individual projections, it is the motor of form-giving and even knowledge-producing practices.[55]

This "second world" allows authors to recognize, modify, enhance, or completely change representations, which provide a creative step beyond the "archives of watching." No longer are writers simply describing what they have seen; rather, they occupy an alternative space of contemplation and germination before creating their dance texts. The authors in this study were not the only ones writing about or documenting dance around 1900. Other writers whose works thematicized dance, the *Varieté*, cabaret, and performances in their prose, poetry, theory, and visual work[56] included Hugo von Hofmannsthal's "On Pantomime" ("Über die Pantomime") (1911), Frank Wedekind's dance poems, Thomas Mann's *Tonio Kröger* (1903), Robert Müller's *Tropen* (1915),[57] Otto Julius Bierbaum's *Stilpe: ein Roman aus der Froschperspektive* (1897), Gerhart Hauptmann's *Und Pippa tanzt!* (1905), Klaus Mann's *The Pious Dance* (1926), Paul Zech's poem "Berlin, halt ein" (1914), and numerous short serpentine-themed dance film scenes in studios such as the Edison, Biograph, Lumière Pathé, Gaumont, and Méliès.

Besides attending performances and collaborating with dancers, these authors had to learn to deal with living in urban metropolises. Kessler, Endell, and Rilke were able to maintain comfortable lifestyles because they had access to familial wealth and had lived in other cities before moving to Berlin and Paris. They often traveled between cities for work, intellectual and artistic exchange, and leisure, especially Kessler. Others, like Döblin, Lasker-Schüler, and the Skladanowsky brothers, struggled to stay afloat financially. After Döblin's father abandoned his mother, she moved the family from Szczecin (Stettin) in present-day Poland to Berlin; it was not until after the author opened his private medical practice in Kreuzberg in 1911 that he attained a more bourgeois existence. Lasker-Schüler moved from Elberfeld with her husband, physician Berthold Lasker, but divorced him in 1912 and was left penniless; she relied on friends for financial support thereafter. Max and Emil Skladanowsky grew up in the proletariat *Kiez* of Pankow and Prenzlauerberg with their father Carl, a tradesman. Despite these variations in socioeconomic status, all these writers and filmmakers maintained a keen eye for observing their metropolitan surroundings. They preserved their social awareness, and the city helped cultivate their modernist, aesthetic seeing through acts of flânerie. They seemed to acquire a flâneur-like gaze in dealing with everyday, metropolitan tasks and events on the surface. While Baudelaire's definition of a flâneur privileges the white, upper-class, heteronormative male, I am more interested in drawing the conceptual and aesthetic details from his way of seeing and adapting them to the readings of my writers, artists, and filmmakers, who had relatively diverse backgrounds and lifestyles. Therefore, I would like to expand this definition to the feminine and queer realm, as Deborah Parsons has done,[58] and also to the working class. I will address the discourse surrounding the flâneur in greater depth in the next chapter.

This study also includes the perspectives of two queer figures: Lasker-

Schüler and Kessler. Lasker-Schüler often dressed in men's attire and took on literary and artistic personas of male, Orientalized figures: Tino of Bagdad and Prince Jussuf. Kessler created close bonds with other queer collaborators, such as Nijinsky and Diaghilev. In *Queer Phenomenology*, Sara Ahmed investigates how bodies move and interact with their surroundings and other people in space; these bodies are influenced by their backgrounds, and negotiate—conforming to or deviating from—lines of whiteness and heteronormativity.[59] Lasker-Schüler and Kessler deviate from hegemonic, heteronormative practices and successfully carve out a social and imagined queer space to productively exercise their creativity. Penny Farfan's *Performing Queer Modernism* argues that queerness was paramount in forming modernism and modernist performances by providing an alternative social and cultural space for subversive, experimental, and imaginative practices to develop, and by allowing individuals to act out queer experiences and sexual identities.[60] By being out of line with normative practices, Kessler and Lasker-Schüler opened up new spaces and paths of inquiry for future queer generations.

Literature, dance, and modernism have already formally undergone scholarly treatment: Gabriele Brandstetter's *Tanz-Lektüre* (1995) is a foundational work in dance studies that uses critical theory and interdisciplinary approaches to examine representations of dance in theater, visual arts, and literature from the early twentieth century and the avant-garde. Originally written in German, the book has since been recognized for its enduring contributions: an English translation, *Poetics of Dance*, appeared in 2015. Felicia McCarren's book *Dance Pathologies: Performance, Poetics, Medicine* (1999) investigates the connections between nineteenth-century French literature and culture, dance history, feminist performance theory, and psychoanalysis. Michael Cowan's *Cult of the Will: Nervousness and German Modernity* (2008) engages with theory, literature, and cultural history to examine how through performative practices, nervous individuals could regain autonomy in a chaotic modernity. Alexandra Kolb's book *Performing Femininity: Dance and Literature in German Modernism* (2009) addresses the interconnections of choreography with German literature from 1900 to 1933 from a feminist perspective. Susan Manning's and Lucia Ruprecht's collection *New German Dance Studies* (2012) provides new dance histories in clusters—Weimar culture and its afterlife, East German dance, and contemporary conceptual dance—and presents a transatlantic perspective from a theoretically wide range of humanistic disciplines. Susan Jones's *Literature, Modernism, and Dance* (2013) focuses on the reciprocal relationship between dance and (mainly British) literature. Kate Elswit's study *Watching Weimar Dance* (2014) draws from dance, theater, and performance studies by analyzing the reception and spectatorship of performances from 1916 and 1932. Lucia Ruprecht's *Gestural Imaginaries: Dance and Cultural Theory in the Early Twentieth Century* (2019) investigates dance through a gestural lens and its related discourses to shed light on movement in the social, aesthetic, and ethical realm of dance around 1900. Susan Funkenstein's *Marking Modern Movement: Dance and Gender in the Visual Imagery of the Weimar Republic* (2020) examines both the synergistic relationships between Weimar artists and dancers and the resulting aesthetic representation of the female dancing body in painting, sculpture, watercolors, drawings, sketches, woodcuts, and photographs. Alys George's *The Naked Truth: Viennese Modernism and the Body* (2020) focuses on the often overlooked corporeal as a prime cite of modernity in Viennese body culture through a range of media. Megan Girdwood's *Modernism and the Choreographic Imagination: Salome's Dance after 1890* (2021) analyzes many artistic representations of Salome and their interconnected influences. Sonia Gollance's *It Could Lead to Dancing: Mixed-Sex Dancing and Jewish Modernity* (2021) investigates the transgressive and acculturating spaces of social dance for Jewish men and women around 1900.

Work has also been written analyzing the city space and architecture as being as tactile and interpretable as the moving body. Andrew Webber's *Berlin in the Twentieth Century: A Cultural Topography* (2011) addresses the artistic imagination of authors and artists who represented shifting (psycho)topographies in their textual, visual, and performance art, paying particular attention to the intermeshing of inside and outside spaces. And while Janet Ward's *Weimar Surfaces* (2001) addresses more of its attention to reading the urban space on its surfaces as translating into the commodification and perpetual mimesis of capitalism, it focuses on the signifying power of architecture in the metropolis. And most recently, Margareta Ingrid Christian's *Objects in Air: Artworks and Their Outside around 1900* (2021) investigates how the external space surrounding works of art creates aerial environments, which deserve to be read as new aesthetic categories. These three works engage with the urban space as a tangible and interpretable entity.

Framework and Argument

Although these and other scholars have covered much territory, their work has not addressed the connections between German textual dance representations and the city space as a central and dynamic element. In *Dancing with the Modernist City*, I focus precisely on the metropolis as an agent, which actively engages with the dancing body in written, visual, and cinematic depictions. My study fills this gap in scholarship by demonstrating how the authors', artists', and filmmakers' perceptions of the city space paralleled their interaction with dance and dancerly movement around 1900. I argue that the convergence these writers saw between the unexpected encounters during their urban strolls and experimental dance performances gave rise to forms of writing, visual arts, and filmmaking that interwove the two motifs. In this study, I bring together works of both well-known and lesser-known German-speaking authors and European artists into an English-speaking context by carefully examining them through close readings. Working at the intersection of cultural history, German literary studies, dance and performance studies, and theoretical inquiry, this book is intended not only for readers from these fields, but for researchers of urban cultures and turn-of-the-century special-ists. I provide detailed analyses of a diverse body of material, generally from 1896 to 1914, including essays, novels, short stories, poetry, newspaper articles, photographs, posters, drawings, and early film. I have selected this period of time because it proves to be a formative, rich period that illuminates the com-plex process of urban citizens acquiring new sensibilities in the dynamically changing social and aesthetic environment of the metropolis before concerns turned to the beginning of World War I. While most of my material consists of written texts, I would like to stress the highly visual—almost cinematic—nature of their depictions, which in some cases daringly dip into the moving image. As a result, my understanding of "text" also includes images, sculpture, architecture, posters, drawings, early film experiments, and the like. Addi-tionally, unless otherwise noted, the translation of German texts into English are my own.

While *Dancing with the Modernist City* draws mostly from the dance and dancerly idiom, given the figures in the study, it also blends in significantly with a performative lens because of the experimental nature of their per-formances and the authors' engagement with imagined space in the literary and textual depictions. Richard Schechner has characterized performance studies as being "sympathetic to the avant-garde, the marginal, the off-beat, the minoritarian, the subversive, the twisted, the queer, people of color, and the formally colonized."[61] In regard to this characterization, my study fits under many of these rubrics, and, therefore, requires engagement with both dance studies and performance studies. Since this book also mainly involves German-speaking, modernist authors and artists from the early twentieth century, the focus on the city leans heavily but not exclusively toward Ber-lin. Stephen D. Dowden and Meike G. Werner argue, however, that since "the place of modernism" follows the artist and writer, it is not necessarily restricted to national borders because they often traveled and maintained a nomadic lifestyle.[62] As such, Rilke's profound connection with Paris—much like Benjamin's—remains justified within this study even though the Austrian author's relationship to Berlin is not as strong.

Forms of Metropolitan Writing

In this book, the style of the texts derives from earlier genres, yet still maintains a concentration on metropolitan phenomena. Martina Lauster identifies the often-overlooked sketches from the mid-nineteenth century (sometimes called *Physiologies*) that depicted the social body in both a visual and verbal form. Under the umbrella of journalistic writing, this amorphous genre featured drawings of everyday citizens in their milieus with descriptions that could lead to many different ideological agendas of contemporary society at the time.[63] This journalistic practice continued, flourishing from the 1830s to the 1950s precisely because it geographically focused on bustling urban areas of London and Paris, but it developed differently later in Berlin around 1900. According to historian Peter Fritzsche, journalists ventured into the city to write about their experiences in a genre called *Skizzen* or *Momentbilder*; instead of trying to capture the entirety of their encounters, these snapshots succinctly depicted specific urban moments in text.[64] He also notes that this genre, which found its home in mass-circulated newspapers, interested intellectuals and proponents of the avant-garde because of its subversive and countercultural potential against bourgeois tradition.[65] Therefore, the genre seems to invite all types of thinkers and artists—intellectuals, journalists, and early filmmakers—to participate in metropolitan observation. It also parallels the carving out of space for modern dance from the *Varieté* and ballet scenes.

Authors wrote in a style similar to the feuilleton, a short genre that often reflected on the development of modern urbanity at the beginning of the twentieth century. This form runs in the same vein as sketches or *Physiologies*, but not necessarily with a corresponding illustration. Susanne Scharnowski argues that Heinrich Heine's *Briefe aus Berlin* (1822) is the proto-form of the feuilleton, which draws from the form of the letter and the seriality of travelogues.[66] In contrast to the journalist, whose texts focused on writing as a commodity, the author or feuilletonist composed with a more artistic flair and without thematic limitations; freedom of topic, style, and political sensibility characterized this genre.[67] Its stylistically open form allowed writers to engage with and express their subjectivity, associations, thoughts, and affect.[68]

And the feuilleton's seriality related to the temporality and ephemerality of daily experiences in the metropolis.[69] We will see this particularly well in Lasker-Schüler's *Letters to Norway* or *Mein Herz*. Despite the variation in terminology between sketches, feuilleton, and *Momentbilder*, they all engaged with the perception of the individual in a city space.

On the one hand, this written form maintained macro, organic, and spectacular views of the cityscapes; on the other, they detailed perspectives of metropolitan structures such as buildings and advertising pillars (*Litfaßsäule*). In their writing, both critics at the time and contemporary scholars characterized the city as a process[70] or organism[71] with theatrical[72] or performative[73] qualities. In his book *Miniature Metropolis: Literature in an Age of Photography and Film*, literary scholar Andreas Huyssen recognizes another genre, called the "metropolitan miniature," identifying it as a prominent but overlooked literary form. Frequently found in the feuilleton section of a newspaper, this written form dealt with "the micrological experience of metropolitan space, time, and life at that earlier stage of modernization when new shapes and scales of urban modernity emerged at accelerated speed but did not yet penetrate the totality of national, social and political space."[74] Writers were still trying to come to terms with the new environment, and therefore were more fixated on understanding the new aesthetics before later needing to grapple with its social and political implications. Miniatures refrained from realistic plot lines and depiction, lacked developed characters, cultivated highly visual and cinematic representations, and remained keenly perceptive of how the external urban stimuli effected the individual's inner life.[75] Drawing from architectural discourses, Huyssen posits the critic Sigfried Giedion's notion of *Durchdringung* (interpenetration), which was enacted through utilizing glass, steel, and ferroconcrete to prevent "borders between inside and outside, above and below, public and private, street and interior, fixed and fluid space."[76] Thus, a "new understanding of architectural space expanded to include traffic, rail lines, trains, stations, and urban movement in general. It opened up the closed city to the circulation of air, movement, and dynamism."[77] Through the performative and organismal representations of Berlin and Paris and combined with Huyssen's understanding of urban space and movement, I will further build on this work by incorporating the dimension of the dancing body and the cities' dancerly traits into the writings of the authors, artists, and filmmakers in this study.

Both writing *about* dance in commentary, reviews, letters, and writing dance texts—a genre that stylistically resembles a dancerly form and often tries to visually represent it—were difficult endeavors at the time, since they demanded the rendering of transient and temporal phenomena into written form. According to dance scholar Sabine Huschka, this predicament stemmed from the experience of watching early-twentieth-century dance, which caused a need to recalibrate the senses.[78] Writers suffered not only from a crisis of their perception but also from a dilemma in their writing: words essentially could not adequately represent a lived experience. The most famous example might be Hugo von Hofmannsthal's *Sprachkrise* in his "Lord Chandos Letter." Dance researcher Gabriele Wittmann argues that even though dancing is not writing, poetry can stylistically awaken the reader's kinesthetic empathy by allowing the reader to feel what the dancer feels.[79] However, it is not just dance movement that can create empathy, but also objects and structures: the dance critic John Martin broadens these fields to the everyday environment—his main examples are rock formations and architectural masses.[80] Combining the lenses of Martin and Wittmann, the writers in this study perceive and depict the intermingling of dancerly movement of pedestrians and urban structures in their texts in a visual language that awakens the reader's kinesthetic empathy.

If one writes about the dancing body, then it is also important to read the space in which the movement happens. The Austro-Hungarian dancer, choreographer, and theorist Rudolf von Laban established ways of perceiving space: less as a malleable object and more through movement and positioning with levels, orientation, place, and distance. He conceptualized a dynamic interaction between space and bodies: "Alongside the movement of bodies in space, there is the movement of space in bodies."[81] Laurence Louppe argues that space does not become alive until we activate it through movement.[82] This ethos, within the realm of contemporary dance studies, provides a lens with which to view dance texts, precisely because the authors' literary depictions no longer take place on a traditional stage, but rather in all types of urban areas. While the Western theatrical space acculturates the dancing body, contemporary dance always seeks, not to reproduce these representations, but to produce its own spatialities and to become its own agent.[83] In a similar spirit, the authors depict their protagonists as embracing and being embraced by their urban topographies and their social surroundings in order to espouse a modernist and poetic experimentation with movement.

This hybridization contributes to ideas of liminal states, particularly when a dancing figure amalgamates with a nonhuman entity. The concept of performance has generally been considered a "centrally human practice," but the posthumanist condition reimagines the body, viewership, and performance by reconceptualizing traditionally conceived positionality; as a result, it becomes a dynamic system of interdependent parts.[84] This dehierarchicalization, then, demands a redefining of these elements. Posthumanism aims to decenter hegemonic Western cultural binaries—body/mind, self/other, culture/nature, global/local, human/animal, human/machine—by showing that humans are continually involved in constituting themselves in various forms through interdependent processes.[85] While much posthumanist thought has derived from Donna Haraway's "Cyborg Manifesto," which addresses more hybridity of machine and organism,[86] the examples in this study demonstrate a wide range of combinations, including the embodiment of space. Scholarly attention in this field has also been examining modernism. In terms of modernist literature, Derek Ryan reads the possibility of carving out an ethics surrounding posthumanism and the genre's experimental nature by focusing on non-anthropocentric perspectives.[87] Ryan draws from Jacques Derrida's reading of D. H. Lawrence on an ethics of "unrecognizability" in *The Beast and the Sovereign*, in which Derrida writes that justice needs to be established with the most dissimilar and the unrecognizable other: an ethics not revolving around humans.[88] Ruben Borg believes that modernist intellectuals such as Virginia Woolf embraced perspective exceeding the limits of human experience and engaging with alternative ways of existing in the world.[89] We see this also, for example, in Rilke's *Dinggedicht* (poem of things) genre. Strands of these thoughts clearly manifest themselves in the interwoven depictions in this book, through the lens of dance.

Building on Huyssen's miniature genre and the concept of interpenetration, I argue that the writers and artists in this study create *metropolitan dance texts* incited by a modernist, flâneur-like gaze, shaped by their gender and queerness, which allows them to depict dancing figures through use of their "gestural imaginary" not necessarily on a traditional stage, but essentially anywhere in the metropolitan environment. They integrate renderings of dancing bodies, which the writers and artists may have encountered at dance performances or during everyday events, and intimately intertwine them with macro and micro metropolitan elements. These literary depictions question traditional conceptualizations of space and performance, since the urban environments often begin *dancing* with the dancer, lending clear agency to the nonhuman and redefining hierarchical states. In some cases, the aesthetic realm of dance and the social space of the everyday city coalesce. In addition to the posthumanist interpenetration between moving bodies and surroundings, this genre highlights the visual, the episodic unexpectedness of urban encounters, and sometimes kinesthetic empathy—by making the protagonist and the reader feel like they embody the dancer and the movement. While flânerie is commonly associated with strolling through a city, I am retaining the writers' aesthetic mode, regardless of whether they or their protagonists are wandering the streets. Instead of falling into the trap of consumerism, as Walter Benjamin has suggested,[90] these dance representations stay in the social and aesthetic realm, but begin building a new ethics that destabilizes ideas of the dancer and cityspace. Working with Lauster's claims that Benjamin's characterization of the flâneur relies exclusively on his readings of Baudelaire and Poe and dismisses sketches as a rich, cognitive source for conceptualizing the individual's experience in a metropolitan space,[91] I embrace dealing with the various backgrounds, perspectives, and imaginative faculties possessed by my authors, artists, and filmmakers, and I seek to further reconceptualize the idea of the flâneur with a posthumanist and queer gaze. Therefore, the macro and micro views of the modernist city take on agency to be equal to or even to overpower their human dancers.

Chapters

While *Dancing with the Modernist City* can be read in its entirety from cover to cover, readers interested in specific authors or topics can immediately proceed to these chapters. Chapter 1, "Perceiving the City as Dancing Entity: Conceptions of Writing the Metropolitan Dance Text," establishes the performative lens on Berlin and Paris around 1900 by analyzing written depictions by German observers. Given the plethora of urban stimuli, authors had to create succinct genres—*Skizzen*, *Momentbilder*, feuilleton, metropolitan miniature—that could encompass the highly visual and aesthetic experience of the modern individual in the city. At the time, writing about dance and creating dance texts were both difficult undertakings because of the struggle to represent fleeting moments in written form. The authors and artists in this study maintained a modernist flâneur-like gaze during their strolls in the city and perceived dancing bodies comingling with the urban spaces; through their experiences, they created the metropolitan dance text.

Chapter 2—"Swirling Affinities: Endell's and Fuller's Architecture, City Space, and Dance," compares the whirling movement aesthetics of Endell's architecture and writing with Fuller's dances and representations. His "The Beauty of the Metropolis" lays out the author's agenda for programmatic change in viewing urban landmarks and space in Berlin with a beautiful aesthetic. A sitting flâneur watches pedestrians in a square, whose amassed movements create a dancing entity. Similarly, Fuller's performances, which involve twirling a long, continuous piece of fabric around her body, create a hypnotic and indelible image. Her dances inspire artists to design posters and architects to build structures in her likeness, which adopt the shape of her dancing body and the energy of the city space. As Fuller's and Endell's ideas of dance and architecture intertwine, their depictions of dancing bodies and urban space begin coalescing and become indistinguishable.

Chapter 3, "From Spectator to Practitioner: Developing Harry Graf Kessler's Queer Dance Aesthetic," provides an alternative overview of early-twentieth-century dance through the single, queer perspective of the intellectual and diplomat Kessler. Attaining a modernist flâneur-like gaze through his attendance at balls, his perception veered toward aestheticizing the everyday. After watching the performances of Fuller, St. Denis, and Nijinsky, he developed a "queer sublimity"—a term Brett Farmer defines as a queer utopian space with limited heteronormative materiality. Kessler began seeing vacillating dichotomies in their dancing: intellectualization and eroticization, masculine and feminine, animal and human. The count was not only motivated to chronicle his experiences and interactions with these dancers, he was inspired to collaborate with Nijinsky and Diaghilev in creating the ballet libretto *The Legend of Joseph* (1914) with a distinctly queer aesthetic. Thus, Kessler transformed from an arts patron into an active practitioner of dance who could express his own sexuality.

Chapter 4, "Bridging Representations of Gesture, Gesticulation, and Early-Twentieth-Century Dance in the City: Rilke's *Veitstänzer* in *The Notebooks of Malte Laurids Brigge*," looks at the aesthetic influences of gesture and space on his literary depiction of a man with *Veitstanz*, a neurological disease that causes the sufferer's body to perform erratic gestures and movement. St. Denis's *Radha*, Michel Fokine's *The Spirit of the Rose* featuring Nijinsky, Rodin's *Porte de l'Enfer* and *Danseuses Cambodgiennes*, and Rilke's live encounter in Paris with a *Veitstänzer* help him to recognize the vitality connected with fragmented gesture. Rilke's protagonist Malte follows the man as they both traverse the streets. Paris, therefore, becomes a performative and dynamically changing urban entity. With the metropolitan stimuli perpetually antagonizing the *Veitstänzer*, the man first demonstrates communicative and willful gestures, which suddenly transform into uncontrollable gesticulations, highlighting the posthumanist agency of the sickness. Rilke aims for his protagonist and the reader to eventually aestheticize these movements as the moving body transitions into early-twentieth-century dance.

Chapter 5, "Documenting the Demise of Ballet and the Emergence of Modern Dance in the Hospital: Döblin's Early Texts on Dance and Space," establishes Döblin's conceptualization and employment of urban space as an active stimulus in an early work titled "Modern," in which an unemployed seamstress succumbs to her own sexual desire and out of guilt presumably commits suicide in a city fountain. His text "Dancers" demonstrates his knowledge of both historical and contemporary dance practices around 1900, from the dominant male gaze of hierarchical ballet to the emerging explosive, expressionist dance. Döblin's movement and spatial imagination further seek representation in the short narrative "The Dancer and the Body," which chronicles the life of a female dancer whose posthumanist body begins to rebel and maintain a separate existence from her; the girl is sent to a university clinic to seek treatment. The metropolis has created a thriving hospital environment full of probing doctors who document the volatile movements of her body and the dancer's eventual suicide. While the doctors are probably excited that their urban hospital can house a modern specimen for scientific research, Döblin is mostly captivated by her expressionistic movement aesthetic.

Chapter 6, "Cabarets, Cafés, and Cities: The Birth of Early-Twentieth-Century Dance in Lasker-Schüler's Writing and Drawings," first examines the author's conceptualization of dance and space in her oeuvre. It focuses on her epistolary prose work *My Heart*—derived from *Letters to Norway*—which captures the coffeehouse scene as a social and emotional location in Berlin around 1900. In one letter, she depicts how the Cafe Kurfürstendamm transforms into an Oriental dancer, highlighting a fantastical, posthumanist aesthetic of melding dance and architecture. This work also features some of her drawings, which she believes express herself better than words. Lasker-Schüler often draws Thebes as an Orientalist cityscape, and integrates human figures (or parts of them) that become absorbed into the space. Like Endell and Fuller, her writing and drawings depict not only a transcendent, dancerly realm but a domain that becomes beautifully enveloped by the city. Both become malleable and dynamic images.

Chapter 7, "From Drawings to Early Cinema: Lasker-Schüler's Protocinematic Images and the Experimental Films of Chomón, and the Skladanowsky Brothers," draws from the end of chapter 6 by looking at Lasker-Schüler's drawing of her own alter ego Abigail-Jussuf in a benevolent robe embracing Thebes. Evoking photographic superimposition, spirituality, spectacularism, and transformation, this image's proto-cinematic characteristics reflect a desire to transition into photography and early film experiments. Chomón's trick transformation and color films of a serpentine dancer further the posthumanist mode in Lasker-Schüler's image. And the Skladanowsky's six-frame film fragment of Emil—kicking to the side while standing on a rooftop with the Berlin skyline in the background—explores the moving body and the city. This chapter chronicles the affinities of their representational practices, which are bringing the metropolitan dance text into other media besides written form.

The coda ties these authors' and filmmakers' works together to show how these representations of dance not only demonstrate an aesthetic shift from nineteenth-century bourgeoisie balls and ballet into experimental, early-twentieth-century dance, they also challenge the notion of traditional theater space by staging dances in and with the city. These metropolitan dance texts underscore their highly visual nature with a posthumanist, flâneur-like, sometimes queer gaze; they stage unexpected urban encounters, and often evoke a kinesthetic empathy from the protagonist and reader. Furthermore, they establish how the city was not only the setting for writers to watch the performances of dancers but became a performative stage, one that sometimes, strongly interacted with their literary dancers and sometimes absorbed the dancing figures. In other words, in these literary dances, the urban space can also *dance* with the dancers, engaging in interpenetration and creating a new ethics by giving nonhuman entities agency. These authors were wholly concerned with and aesthetically stimulated by coming to terms with not only the urban stimuli but also the new, modern dance. Thus, their experiences amalgamated into the same aesthetic entity and manifested themselves in their metropolitan dance texts.

The space of modernism in the city and in the gestural imaginaries of the authors and filmmakers in this study create both a productively empowering and frighteningly destructive realm in which human dancers are no longer the sole dancers in the metropolitan dance texts. Every part of the urban space—conceptualized and built by humans—has on both a macro and micro level varying degrees of agency to engage with and sometimes dance with the human. In these texts, the dancer no longer takes center stage but instead shares the space with the city. These modernist aesthetics decentralize the human and seriously consider the potential agency, contribution, and life of urbanity in all its related forms.

One

Perceiving the City as Dancing Entity

Conceptions of Writing the Metropolitan Dance Text

The current of circulating blood gets fiercer day by day fertilizing the community in all articulations, [. . .] impelling the aim of an indistinctly perceived new, city organism. Day by day Berlin pushed its outposts a bit farther out. Day by day the boom swelled its street music more strongly and flashed lights full of new ideas. The pace of the development came so quickly that the pathways of earlier and deliberate logic were mostly abandoned and brought on volatility, thus creating difficult problems.[1]

Around 1910 Max Osborn, a critic and journalist for the *Vossische Zeitung*, characterized Berlin as a living organism or body (*Stadtorganismus*), using images of circulating blood not only to imply the constant development and interconnectedness of a metropolis but also to demonstrate a working system whose various parts contribute substantially to Berlin's changing existence. This bustling, urban image indiscriminately considers all visual stimuli. Osborn's word usage, particularly "street music," "lights," "pace," and "volatility," evokes images of lively, unchoreographed movement being performed by the city itself in a posthumanist lens. The street melody accompanies the piece while the lights illuminate the set, and the tempo continues to erratically and unpredictably change. This performance scene could probably have been seen not only on a theatrical stage, but also in the urban space of Berlin. Osborn wrote for commercial enterprises like the department store *Kaufhaus des Westens* (*KaDeWe*), and he was aware of the importance of presenting Berlin in a flattering and lively manner. These poeticized activities and movements were generated by the booming industry, which in turn caused more individuals to move into the city to pursue their professional work, resulting in a large urban expansion. This brought on overcrowding and unsanitary condition in the workers' areas. Although Berlin was known more for its factories and commerce, it also introduced commercial department stores, and entertainment districts such as Friedrichstraße. All kinds of city dwellers traversed the city on foot or took the growing lines of public transportation. This bustle served not only as the dynamic backdrop, it incited many journalists and writers to observe Berlin both more pragmatically and as an aesthetic spectacle.

Osborn's writing could fit under the rubric of *metropolitan dance text*, since the metropolis seems to enact performative vitality. This keen urban observer and artistic critic creates an "establishing shot" of Berlin around 1900. Born on February 10, 1870, in Köln, he studied philology, literature, and art history in Heidelberg, Munich, and Berlin, receiving his PhD in 1893. Later on, he began to focus more on architecture, urban planning, and Berlin's cultural historical, economic, and social development. In some ways, his background, pathway, writing style, and subject matter—the vibrancy and beautification of industrial Berlin—resemble Endell's aesthetic program, as we will see in the next chapter.

This chapter maintains a performative lens while providing historical background on Berlin and Paris around 1900. It sets the stage and traces the written representations of the urban space from the perspective of German observers, who first maintain macro, organic, and spectacular views of the cityscapes, and second offer detailed perspectives on metropolitan structures such as buildings and advertising pillars (*Litfaßsäule*). Both critics at the time and contemporary scholars today characterize the city as theatrical and performative, as a process. The modern individual at the turn of the century, following Georg Simmel's conceptualization, had to come to terms with the multiple stimuli of metropolitan life by developing a blasé attitude. According to Peter Fritzsche, journalists ventured into the city to write about their experiences in a genre called *Skizzen* or *Momentbilder*, which succinctly depicted specific urban moments. Writers began composing texts, which Andreas Huyssen terms "metropolitan miniatures," which often appeared in the feuilleton section of newspapers. This genre tackled the newness of the urban experience in short texts that highlighted the visual, avoiding realistic plots, and remaining hypercognizant of how outer stimuli affected the inner life of a metropolitan citizen. Given these discourses, I build on these views and propose to further push the reading of the urban environment by applying a dance perspective, and interpreting the city itself as both a dancing entity and a space for dance. This chapter provides a short history of dance, addresses its conceptualizations, and problematizes the relationship between dance and written text. The writers Kessler, Endell, Rilke, Döblin, and Lasker-Schüler and the filmmakers Chomón and the Skladanowskys maintained a flâneur-like gaze during their urban strolls and perceived dancing bodies comingling with urban spaces. Through these experiences, they composed the genre of the metropolitan dance text. This form highlighted the visual, the episodic unexpectedness of urban encounters, the posthumanist interpenetration between moving body and surroundings, and often the kinesthetic empathy related to the narrative's protagonist, the author, and the reader. Their texts introduced a dancerly element to the metropolitan experience, demonstrating an interweaving of two seemingly different worlds.

Berlin Cityscape

According to Max Osborn, before Berlin became an industrial *Weltstadt*, the important buildings in past decades had been castles, palaces, and churches—symbols of ruling authorities.[2] The nineteenth century reflected the increase of the bourgeoisie, who placed more importance on parliament and administrative buildings, universities, educational and research institutes, and museums.[3] The following century turned to architecture that at first seemed secondary, such as train stations, industrial buildings, office buildings, and department stores, but these structures nevertheless came to the fore.[4] This progression reflects the significant increase in population, the rise in daily traffic in comparison to the past, and the growth of commercialization. This sudden influx caused everyday buildings to be more commonly identified with dynamic movement as more and more structures were erected to fit modern, industrial needs. Osborn continues by describing Berlin's mass development as expanding not only upward and outward but also inward, to take into account the need for space by increasing density of neighborhoods. His depiction from the opening of this chapter creates the image of a small, urban topographical map, which continues to grow *up*, *out*, and *in* as if it were a phenomenon observable from afar.[5] Evolving at great speed, the city lacked a logistical vision and plan for erecting buildings; Osborn echoes this observation when he characterizes Berlin's growth as a threatening, ominous confusion. An outside, encompassing perspective also invites one to recognize Berlin's growing posthumanist structures, organic body, and perpetually driving movement as aesthetically resembling a performance.

In addition to the booming machine industry and the hordes of pedestrians strolling the streets, this metropolis also began widely capitalizing on the use of electric current. Whereas before, gas had been the source of energy, electricity was used to light lamps and the large signs surrounding areas like Friedrichstraße. The *Vossische Zeitung* from 1900 described lively illuminations timed to both flash bright colors as part of a working system and to combat the darkness.[6] The poeticizing radiance is highlighted by its springing nature, which emphasizes the "dancing" light's dynamic, organic movement, similar to that of a performer.

The art critic and publicist Karl Scheffler, author of the most famous survey of the city, *Berlin. Ein Stadtschicksal* (1910), comments that the city's fate was "always to become and never to be."[7] He also claims that this metropolis lacks cultural urbanity and remains the "capital of all modern ugliness."[8] His negative characterization points to frustration with the inability to definitively classify Berlin, and it also demonstrates a pessimistic view of the future and the repercussions of modernity. This metropolis may not have had comparable, long-standing landmarks like those in Vienna, Paris, or London, but one could argue that Berlin's depiction as an eternally evolving process was its most redeeming and enduring characteristic. Besides providing a variety of activities and outlets for its citizens, the metropolis also bombarded them with information and created an even larger gap between social classes. The sudden influx of individuals also crowded living quarters, forcing as many as six to eight families to live together in one apartment. Literary scholar Lothar Müller summarizes some of the common viewpoints of Berlin in comparison to other capital cities in Europe:

> Measured against London, a classical industrial metropolis with a sense of tradition, Berlin seemed an economic-industrial center brutal and uncultivated in the American style. Measured against Paris, the organically beautiful city, Berlin appeared artificial and ugly. The contrast was between an urban culture of poetry and one of prose— Paris, even as a modern metropolis, was capable of poetry; Berlin was hopelessly prosaic.[9]

Despite many of these unfavorable conceptions and poetry's hegemonic valuation over prose in association with Berlin, the city was also the breeding ground for experimental literary production and early-twentieth-century dance; both were immensely influential in the arts at the time. If Berlin were a perpetually evolving process, then it can be likened to a performance because both deal with the transient existence of a temporal phenomenon.

Active Bodies: The *Litfaßsäule*

Moving away from a more macro view of the city, this section focuses on the comparatively smaller yet still legible architectural structures within the metropolis. The large number of cafés, display windows, advertisements, and *Litfaßsäulen* (advertising pillars) were placed strategically to be seen by city dwellers and to attract business. If parks, gardens, and kiosks were supposed to invite people to linger, then the hordes of people rushing onto the bus and streetcars caused them to hurry. With decorative wrought-iron crowns and colorful images, the green, two-meter tall *Litfaßsäule* were meant to visually attract people, while their roundness added to their ease of readability (fig. 2).[10] The curved, bowing nature of the *Litfaßsäule* itself and the highly ornamented, organic depictions of women in print complemented each other and augmented the other larger buildings being erected in the art nouveau style, or *Jugendstil*. Metropolises such as Berlin, Paris, Vienna, Munich, Prague, and Brussels aimed to create entire cityscapes with this particularly ornate, architectural style: department stores, metro stations, building facades, home furnishings, and even silverware and glass pieces.

In the 1850s, the Berlin printer Ernst Litfaß first conceived of and erected these tall structures, on which posters, advertisements, and notices could be neatly organized.[11] At his death in 1874 he had a legacy of 150 pillars, which turned into 1,500 by around the turn of the century.[12] One short vignette describes people from different social classes perusing the same *Litfaßsäule*: upper-class women looking at the opera and theater programs, a petty bourgeois family also reading the theater program, and a group of workers viewing training courses for carpentry and bricklaying.[13] The pillars were accessible and catered to all kinds of people for different purposes, yet they united all individuals spatially. One feuilletonist recalls that the *Litfaßsäule* collected "the debris that otherwise floated aimlessly in the ocean of the street."[14] Not only were the citizens of Berlin reading the texts and gleaning information, they could also read the *Litfaßsäule* as a posthumanist, living, architectural body within the urban space. They emerged in Paris starting in 1868, when the printer Gabriel Morris won a competition for exclusive rights to advertise in the city. He drew inspiration from the German version, yet renamed them *colonnes Morris* for the French context. Litfaß was a pioneer during his time, melding art and industry; his text "Reiseskizzen nach Paris" (1854) reflects the style of genre in Heine's "Briefe aus Berlin" and attests to his time in Paris cultivating the eye of a journalist or flâneur, who could systematically glean detail from visual events.[15] Gifted at networking and building relationships, Litfaß's personality resembled Kessler's. His design also took inspira-

Fig. 2. The first *Litfaßsäule* in the courtyard of Ernst Litfaß's printing shop in Adlerstraße. Lithograph, 1855.

tion from the *Harrissäule* in London (1824) by George Samuel Harris, which consisted of eight-sided columns on wheels, lit from the inside.[16] These pillars became a symbol of disorder as well as a medium through which artists experimented with new fonts, bright colors, and flashy layouts.[17] They began looking like giant exclamation points,[18] and they "screamed" their "thick letters" and danced a "never-ending Cancan."[19] As soon as *Litfaßsäulen* were being used not only to simply communicate information but as an artistic medium, their size seemed to associate them posthumanistly with bodies in the urban cityscape. Their ostentatious colors and flashy fonts allowed them to assume even more expressive, human-like attributes. Although the pillars contained seemingly static posters and ads, the art nouveau style and vibrant colors added to their organic movement, and, it could be argued, contributed to their ability to dance. While some interpreted the pillars as an eyesore in a sea of other visual stimuli, others read them as the incarnation of perpetual dancerly dynamism. For example, Osborn notes the importance of the poster as a medium for the *Litfaßsäule* because it created new possibilities for ornamental and colorful expression, featuring large, comprehensible images with energetic colors and sweeping lines.[20] By combining the general need to distribute artistically expressive information, the poster and the pillar fused to not only communicate knowledge but to enlighten the public about art and to blend in with the other *Jugendstil* architectural bodies such as metro stations and facades.

Osborn's description recalls the serpent dance of the American modern dancer Loïe Fuller. During her performance, she swirled long drapes extended by bamboo poles and rotated her body and arms to create the impression of perpetual motion. Given the dance's likeness to art nouveau and her countless representations in posters of this same style, Fuller was also called "danced art nouveau" (*Getanzter Jugendstil*).[21] Affectionately called "movement images" (*Bewegungsbilder*),[22] posters depicting Fuller captured only one moment in time, but nonetheless communicated the illusion of successive movement through color and body positioning. The large advertisements functioned in two ways: first, to encourage spectators to come see her performance, and second, to allow pedestrians to marvel at the poster's beauty, as if Fuller's representation were actually dancing, thereby demonstrating the desire to see kinetic movement. Yet this poster is not the only object that can be regarded as moving; the entire *Litfaßsäule* with its loud fonts and designs, and on an even larger scale, all architectural forms—particularly in *Jugendstil*—within the entire cityscape of Berlin, are moving and performing.

Parisian Cityscape

While Berlin had been developing quickly around 1900, Paris had undergone most of its more dramatic architectural changes from about 1853 to 1870, when Baron Haussmann imposed structural regularity and efficiency. He enforced consistency of building facades, split streets, created geometrical patterns, and directed transportation to monuments; this uniformity contributed to the city's beauty.[23] David Jordan believes these changes also contributed to the life of the boulevard (*la vie Parisienne*) creating an *esprit de boulevard* and a physical space for the boulevardier—one who frequents the streets.[24] The writing of both Stefan Zweig and Karl Scheffler maintain this spirit as urban German-speaking observers. In his memoirs *The World of Yesterday*, Zweig reminisces about the lure of the street and his "naive and yet wondrously wise freedom of existence" in Paris during his twenties:

It was not easy to stop once you had started strolling, for the street drew you on magnetically; it was a kaleidoscope, constantly disclosing something new. If you were tired you could sit on the terrace of one of the ten thousand cafés and write letters on stationery which was supplied free of charge, and at the same time have the street vendors trying to sell you their entire stock of baubles and gadgets.[25]

In this depiction, the streets act less as a stage and more as an active post-humanist agent that envelopes Zweig into its lively throngs and perpetually engage his senses. Interestingly, his depiction does not recall an intellectualization and abstraction of events and objects, but rather surrounds him with an abundance of consumer distractions, recalling the need for a Simmelarian blasé attitude.

In Scheffler's book *Paris. Notizen*, he assumes the perspective of a train approaching Paris by describing first the journey, the border, and then the city itself—in some ways, not unlike the opening of Walter Ruttmann's *Berlin: Symphony of a Great City* (1927). Scheffler acquires a macro view of the city, which then slowly continues through introducing many architectural styles and individual artists. The author characterizes the city as traditional and organic, and unlike Berlin, which is continually becoming, Paris relies on what it has already become.[26] From a wider view he portrays the city as "a clearly divided organism" that "begins to breath as if it were a living being."[27] Similar depictions of nature and posthumanism, as we will see in the next chapter, find their way into Endell's characterization of Berlin street scenes. Scheffler was deeply committed to German impressionism[28] and, therefore, maintained an aesthetic interpretation of Paris.

In contrast to Zweig, who came to be surrounded by the temptation of consumption, Scheffler maintains a critical perspective: "Paris engages with what Kant calls 'the intellectual interest of beauty' [and] fantasy moves the image into the light of a higher, spiritual meaning, and thus begins the duplicity of watching and thinking, that belongs to complete aesthetic enjoyment."[29] The urban observer no longer merely feels the transcendental elevation of beauty, but also tries to intellectually interact with the phenomenon. Scheffler's observation will resonate throughout with the rest of the authors and thinkers in my study, who perceive the stimuli in their metropolitan surroundings, and who attempt to understand their effects on their bodies and to give them literary representation in writing their metropolitan dance texts. Furthermore, Scheffler renders the Parisian atmosphere as "theatrical,"[30] as if "the city becomes a huge stage."[31] He therefore progresses from describing Paris as an awakening organism to a performative entity on a stage.

From Process and Performativity to Dance

Fritzsche characterizes the metropolis in this way: "Again and again in the history of modern thought, cities have been a challenge to clarity of vision: the details, in themselves decipherable, do not come together to make a full picture."[32] In trying to encompass an entire view of the city, the details impede. Modernity has created a fragmented life, in which maintaining focus becomes nearly impossible. The growing population and erected buildings have physically changed the cityscape, allowing for more anonymity and encounters for its citizens. Fritzsche calls Berlin and other metropolises "an incalculable, ongoing process" filled with "unfamiliarity and flux."[33] If one views Berlin as constantly evolving, then it is likened to a performance involving temporality and the spectatorial presence. Although most experimental dance performances at the time were choreographed, they involved modern movement vocabulary and themes that had not yet been codified as in ballet. These new performances similarly reflect the "unfamiliarity" that Fritzsche uses to describe Berlin. This lack of design resembles the process of improvisation, in which movements are performed within given parameters but are nevertheless spontaneous. The building of structures cannot be completely impulsive; however, a pedestrian's scurrying off to a rendezvous could entail a bit of surprise. Fritzsche's observations imply an outsider's view of these processes as an aestheticized stage.

Given the organic and performative nature of the city, dance scholar Gabriele Klein correspondingly asserts the city's artistic disposition as a process: cities are works of art comprised not just of objects; they are also living sculptures maintained by humans in motion.[34] Her perspective implies that if artists can create paintings, sculptures, music, buildings, and dances, then their cumulative work should constitute art on a large scale. Klein also states that metropolises are dynamic works of art, implying movement, life, continuation, and transience. In the urban space, one not only admired paintings in a museum or dance performances in the theater, but also the architecture in the streets. Nearly every facet, whether beautiful or ugly, could be aestheticized, even sports.[35] By creating the metaphor of a city as sculpture, Klein likens the space to a pliable and rather slow process that imitates the human form. Alluding not just to sculptures but also to bodies moving in space, she states that both these posthumanist elements shape a performance and thus create an artwork. In the absence of a designated inner or outer space in her definition, the city space transgresses the boundaries of a performance—suggesting it could happen anywhere. With people, objects, and structures maintaining positions within the urban expanses, the cityscape is both part of the stage and an active agent in the performance.

Theater studies scholar Erika Fischer-Lichte uses the term "autopoetic feedback loop" and "co-presence" to describe the dynamic interaction between a performer and an observer.[36] Applying this idea further, Matthias Bauer illustrates the performative, urban space when he describes how, since the modern city often incorporates open spaces for individuals to move, it also prompts them to see others and the collective. As such, the space allows for "gazes and gestures, actions and reactions" to occur and creates a "performative dimension"; all citizens in the metropolis, therefore, have the possibility of being watched as if on a stage.[37] Bauer brings out the modern tendency to be acutely aware of one's surroundings, observing that what could transpire on stage could also happen literally anywhere in the city, always making it a veritable *Schauplatz*. His observations address the performative aspects of the citizens' environment, because the observers often have a stake in all the events and phenomena around them. Unlike a traditional performance in which the line between the audience and those on stage is clearly drawn, the modern city dweller takes part in the action and becomes a performer by default. Bauer's concept of the urban space also conceives of the actors mainly as people, while Osborn considered the architectural structures and ambience as the prime movers. However, I acknowledge the validity of both objects and people in a posthumanist turn as dynamic beings in a highly performative space.

The Metropolitan Dance Text Through Flânerie

For Berlin and Paris to be characterized both as a stage *and* as a moving aesthetic entity itself—with its many citizens, buildings, vehicles, and streets that represent the performers or objects—there must also be spectators in order to complete this notion of a performance. This section outlines different views on the condition of modern individuals who have to learn about their new urban surroundings, and on the subset of the flâneur who can aesthetically perceive movement in the metropolis. The changing cityscape affected the fin-de-siècle observers, who were inundated with numerous stimuli, by shaping their minds to become attuned to an aestheticized environment.

In his essay "The Metropolis and Mental Life" ("Die Großstädte und das Geistesleben") from 1903, Georg Simmel delves into the sociology of the modern citizens whose greatest challenge involves heightened sensitivity to their surroundings.[38] Urban stimuli constantly bombard the citizen, overloading their senses; yet after a certain point, the brain grows accustomed to this activity. Soon, however, the repetitiveness bores and overexcites them, and only new stimulation can catch the individuals' attention, thus eliminating their blasé attitude. This desensitized state helps citizens cope in a dizzying world of agitation, yet it dulls their senses to the everyday. The writings of journalists at the time seemed stylistically to reflect this bewildered and overstimulated perception. The fact that they selected these specific moments from many others and rendered them into words demonstrates their importance to the writers.

While Simmel details the experience of the general individual, and of authors, artists, and filmmakers, I will discuss a more particular sociological type that emerged because of the modern city: the flâneur. Traditionally conceived, this well-dressed bachelor or widower was typically suspended from social obligation.[39] He engaged in the activity known as flânerie, which consisted of strolling around, usually in an urban environment, without a plan or purpose, and observing his surroundings. Most noted in the works of Charles Baudelaire in the *Paris Spleen* collection from 1869, the flâneur or poet portrayed a vision of the public sphere and spaces of Paris. Keith Tester argues that for Baudelaire, the poet is unmistakably a man who can collect aesthetic meaning and maintain an individual, existential security from the brimming hordes of people—the visible public—of the metropolitan environment of the city of Paris.[40]

During the poet's quest for meaning, the metropolis serves as the flâneur's thriving space for art and existence, while the privacy of his home bores him.[41] Baudelaire notes that the poet is able to be away from home and yet feel *at* home anywhere; he is at the very center of the world, and yet is not seen by the world.[42] His home is then in the city, where he could critically engage his psyche and continue his livelihood. Since the poet is at the center, he creates his own world by abstracting and aestheticizing his environment. Everyday objects that have a certain significance for the masses suddenly take on new meanings in the poet's mind. In fact, his own definitions of these new concepts change continually, just like his metropolitan surroundings. Maintaining his anonymity while observing people and structures remains paramount, for it allows him to analyze them in their natural state, unbeknownst to them. He can traverse the cityscape under the guise of a passerby, his head spinning with intrigue from the urban stimuli. An aestheticizing of the moving, interacting bodies in space therefore creates the notion of a performance.

Tester continues his characterization of the flâneur: "Defining [. . .] the meaning and [. . .] order of things [. . .] implies a connection between the intuited fluidity of things in the environment of the city and the physical negotiations of the space and other bodies carried out by the poet during his walks in crowds."[43] The fluidity of his experiences causes him to think even more quickly, not only because of the dynamic bodies and objects he is watching but because the flâneur is moving in the same space as the performers he is observing. Unlike a poster on a *Litfaßsäule* that creates the illusion of movement despite remaining in one place, the pedestrians and objects in the city space are constantly in motion. The flâneur has to both rely on the action on the streets to glean information, and be responsible for navigating his own body through space.

The flâneur's observations do not consist of simply looking, but studying and analyzing his surroundings.[44] Although his environment remains familiar, he can read scenes differently each time and reap new meaning. Bruce Mazlich from 1994 suggests that "while the flâneur is presented as a native of his locality, he is actually an individual caught in the act of attempting to regain and keep his native's mastery of his environment."[45] Since his knowledge of the area is also perpetually changing, he too must continue to read his surroundings on a daily basis to keep abreast on its newness. Mazlich writes that the flâneur is like an explorer who has to claim his territory and "transform the display of empire into a spectacle which can be mastered."[46] Since the environment and stimuli in the city are constantly undergoing changes, marking a "territory" in the land maintains importance. However, not only is the geography evolving but the meaning that the flâneur has adopted is also in flux. The area that he explores will forever need to be remapped.

Pricilla Parkhurt Ferguson too notes the abstraction with which the flâneur reads his surroundings: "The flaneur is entertained, not distressed, by the ever-changing urban spectacle. [. . .] He reads the city as he would read a text—from a distance."[47] The spectacle is a dynamic process within the city, consisting of a multitude of stimuli inundating the flâneur's faculties. By keeping his distance, he stays less emotionally involved and remains objective in his experiences. This level of abstraction allows him to pull away from "narrative" and to observe his surroundings aesthetically. Although he could be concentrating on a small detail in the city, he would also pull back and try to create a bigger picture, allowing the performance to take place.

Not only does the flâneur need the metropolitan space, but he needs to generally be outside to conduct his analysis. Flânerie loses its distinction in the second half of the nineteenth century as it moves toward the interior space. However, Ferguson also states, "If, by chance, the flâneur turns up at the theatre, it will not be for the drama on stage but for the crowded, bustling 'street scene' in the corridors where the real drama takes place. With the shift to the interior, the flâneur is on his way from [a] public to a private personage."[48] Assuming this role, for example, is Harry Graf Kessler, a well-connected intellectual who wrote an exhaustive and detailed diary about his daily experiences, which included going to balls and social events. In his entries, he not only described attendees but commented on events with a critical distance. The city space perpetually revitalizes the flâneur by providing him a space to analyze; but with the advent of the department store and the commoditization of goods, his ability to stay objective begins to slip as he succumbs to the pressure of consumerism.[49] He no longer creates meaning in his own world, but falls victim to and adopts the social conventions in front of him. I would argue, however, that the authors in this book were often able to maintain an aestheticized view even if located in an interior space such as a café or hospital.

David Frisby identifies moments in Walter Benjamin's writing that characterize the flâneur as a modern individual who studied people, social types, and constellations; this individual not only read the city's architecture and spatial configurations, but also read the city as a text, much like Franz Hessel.[50] Frisby continues by illuminating another aspect of the flâneur's activities:

> The *flâneur*, and the activity of *flânerie*, is also associated in Benjamin's work not merely with observation and reading but also with *production*—the production of distinctive kinds of texts. [. . .] the *flâneur* can also be a producer, a producer of literary texts (including lyrical and prose poetry as in the case of Baudelaire), a producer of illustrative texts (including painting), a producer of narratives and reports, a producer of journalistic texts, a producer of sociological texts.[51]

Frisby's insight reveals one of the greatest and most provocative problems for the flâneur and the modern individual in the metropolis at the turn of the century: the desire to capture an experience through the medium of text. Trying to grasp minute details in a lived event remained a daunting task, given the numerous facets of small, fragmentary experiences.

Frisby's interpretation suggests that almost any writer or journalist who wrote about their surroundings could have been a flâneur. Baudelaire was not the only one producing literary texts based on his experience in the metropolitan area; Kessler, Rilke, Döblin, Lasker-Schüler, Endell, the Skladanowsky brothers, Chomón, and others were also highly influenced and inspired by the dynamic urban spaces and constant movement enveloping their senses. Besides literary text production, newspapers and reportage reached even more city dwellers, who read them daily.[52] These texts trained readers in how to navigate their own city and guided them to sensational sights.[53] The writings of the journalist and flâneur—as Frisby suggests, these character types can be one and the same—not only spread their knowledge of the city, but attempt to recreate lived experience to other citizens. Fritzsche notes the uniqueness about each report:

> The attention to, and even celebration of, diversity and difference tended to undermine a coherent vision of the city. On-site reports, behind-the-scene investigations, and portraits of specific places and passing events put the accent on the singular and did so at the expense of more generic patterns. What physiognomies lost in universality they gained in detail: *Skizzen*, *Momentbilder*, and other snapshots of city places and city people over the course of a single day collected little more than moments and incidents.[54]

These collections of unique experiences characterize the flâneur's multifaceted experience in the metropolitan space. Treating certain moments in time like images, these *Momentbilder* could appear linked together, creating the illusion of dynamic movement as in film; I pick up this cinematic mode in the final chapter. In synthesizing their own experience within the space, journalists or flâneurs must first be able to remember the scene as best as possible; they must perpetually cultivate their "gestural imaginary," interpret their own senses, and be able to recreate and adapt in writing not only the content but also the feeling during the experience.

While the discourse in this chapter refers to the flâneur as a wealthy, male individual, I am more interested in drawing the conceptual and aesthetic details of this way of seeing and applying them later to the readings of my authors, artists, and filmmakers, who come from relatively diverse socioeconomic backgrounds, lifestyles, gender expressions, and sexualities. Therefore, I would like to expand this definition to the feminine and queer realm, as Deborah Parsons has done,[55] and also to the working class. While Endell, Kessler—who was homosexual—and Rilke more or less fit under this conventional conceptualization, Döblin and the Skladanowsky brothers—from working-class backgrounds—and Lasker-Schüler, who barely scrounged enough money to live in Berlin and maintained a queer existence, are still able to attain a modernist, flâneur-like gaze, which dramatically influenced their artistic production.

In his book *Miniature Metropolis: Literature in an Age of Photography and Film*, Andreas Huyssen identifies the literary form of the metropolitan miniature, which had always been in plain view yet was never classified. Often published in the feuilleton section of a newspaper, this genre concerned "the micrological experience of metropolitan space, time, and life at that earlier stage of modernization when new shapes and scales of urban modernity emerged at accelerated speed but did not yet penetrate the totality of national, social and political space."[56] Since writers were still trying to come to terms with the new environment, at the time, they were more fixated on aesthetics. Their miniatures avoided realistic plot and description, lacked developed characters, maintained highly visual and cinematic representations, and remained thoroughly aware of the external urban stimuli's effect on the individual's inner life.[57] Huyssen pulls from the architectural discourse by introducing Sigfried Giedion's idea of *Durchdringung* (interpenetration), which was achieved through using glass, steel, and ferroconcrete to prohibit "borders between inside and outside, above and below, public and private, street and interior, fixed and fluid space."[58] Thus, a "new understanding of architectural space expanded to include traffic, rail lines, trains, stations, and urban movement in general. It opened up the closed city to the circulation of air, movement, and dynamism."[59] Through Huyssen's understanding of space at the time and its integration into the miniature form, I further build on his work by incorporating the dimension of the dancing body and posthumanism. The authors and writers in this book create metropolitan dance texts based on a flâneur-like gaze shaped by their various gender expressions and socioeconomic backgrounds. While flânerie is commonly associated with strolling through a city, I am retaining the aesthetic mode, which these writers maintain, regardless of whether they or their protagonists are wandering the streets. Instead of falling into the trap of consumerism, these dance representations stay in the aesthetic and social realm but also begin carving out a new ethics. They integrate renderings of dancing bodies, which they may have encountered at dance performances or in everyday life, and intimately intertwine them with metropolitan elements in order to often highlight the agency of the nonhuman. Interpenetration plays a key role in these author's dance depictions, as some are set in city squares, streets, hospitals, and cafés. Due to the fluidity of these spatial representations, these metropolitan dance texts also waver between aesthetic and social realms.

From Dance Theory to Dance Text

This section draws from the metropolitan miniature and explores conceptualizations of dance in creating a framework to understand metropolitan dance texts: the episodic unexpectedness of urban encounters, posthumanist interpenetration between moving body and surroundings, the difficulty of writing about dance, and often kinesthetic empathy by making the protagonist and the reader feel like they embody the dancer and the movement. I will subsequently apply this to the readings throughout the remaining chapters.

The exciting urban experiences of Endell, Kessler, Rilke, Döblin, Lasker-Schüler, Chomón, and the Skladanowskys evoke correspondingly vibrant portrayals in their writing and films, both of the metropolis and of the moving body. In their urban encounters, they are confronted with figures whose maneuverings range from simple walking in a city square or at a ball, in the case of Endell's and Kessler's works; to sharp and abrupt gestures, as portrayed in Rilke's and Döblin's writing and the Skladanowsky's film; and, in greater contrast, to Lasker-Schüler's and Chomón's depiction of a free-flowing, boundless body. These scenes can arguably be considered "metropolitan dance texts" to the extent that an observer—either the reader, viewer, or protagonist—witnesses a moving body interpenetrating the urban space. In characterizing this kind of movement, dance scholar Gabriele Brandstetter and anthropologist Christoph Wulf remark that all dances involve the staging and performance of the moving body in rhythmic sequences; expressing their interaction with other humans and the world, they communicate, represent, and articulate differing histories and cultural conditions.[60]

By employing movement and bodies, dance essentially communicates interpretable knowledge to the spectator. Just as choreographers convey an idea or express emotion to an audience through their dance works, the authors and filmmakers in this study similarly compose metropolitan dance texts out of their own words, phrasing, syntax, or camera angles to create representations of urban elements and the moving body. Their works are regarded as "modernist" texts not only in respect to their depiction of the metropolitan setting but also in assuming stylistic qualities such as those embodied in the metropolitan miniature. Their artistic production can also be considered more like the new "free," "modern dances" taking place at the beginning of the twentieth century, which reject the conventions of the nineteenth-century ballet and also integrate aspects of the *Varieté*.

In Brandstetter and Wulf's definition, dances are staged and performed, but arguably these notions are lacking in the seven authors' and filmmakers' renderings. Naturally they "stage" and "choreograph" their own metropolitan dance texts, but most readers, onlookers, and protagonists of the text encounter relatively *unexpected* scenes. Some of the scenes, arguably, assume this model of the unstaged performance—Endell sits himself comfortably at a café to observe a colorful display of people moving within a square; Kessler eagerly watches the female ball guests in their costumes; Malte encounters the *Veitstänzer* in the streets of Paris; the doctors study Ella's bizarre symptoms in the hospital; Lasker-Schüler's narrator suddenly begins dancing with Minn on the Islam stage; Max films Emil in a test shot performing an impromptu kick. The protagonists and readers, in a sense, are viewing less a choreographed dance and more an impromptu performance. This distinction brings up a vital difference between a staged and an unscripted dance—that of authentic feeling, about which philosopher Susanne K. Langer states, "It is *imagined feeling* that governs the dance, not real emotional conditions. [. . .] Dance gesture is not real gesture, but virtual. The bodily movement, of course, is real enough; but *what makes it emotive gesture* [. . .], is illusory [. . .]. It is *actual movement*, but virtual *self-expression*."[61] Langer essentially addresses the masking of true feelings by creating the illusion of real ones. The captivating nature of a dance piece is often so powerful and moving that the onlooker gives little regard to the "virtual" emotions. However, the way these seven writers and artists portray dance leaves no illusion about the dancers' emotions. In fact, the staging of these "unexpected performances" creates even *more* authenticity for both the protagonists and the reader of these texts. These remarkable events connect with Fritzsche's understanding of the city dweller's preparedness for surprises within the urban space. By expecting the unanticipated, writers could immediately absorb, interpret, and later create metropolitan dance texts based on specific encounters in and around the city.

The creation of this genre emerged from the authors' own compelling experiences in the city, which incited them to not only thematisize dance, but more importantly to situate dance in and among the urban landscape and structures. Furthermore, the moving body thoroughly engages with and reacts to the city as a stimulus, and vice versa. As dance scholar Sabine Huschka remarks, "The avant-garde tendencies in literature and art are inspired by dance as a form of distinct sensuality and dynamic kinetics, since they both mystically, concretely, and yet abstractly shape the energy of the emerging modernity."[62] No exceptions to this trend, the figures in this study had written texts or produced films concerning their own encounters with dance and movement in their respective cities. Endell's text "The Beauty of the Metropolis" ("Die Schönheit der großen Stadt") recounts his experiences of observing modern architectural structures as well as moving groups of people. He serves as a prime example of an author who was inspired by a new way of seeing Berlin since his programmatic work encouraged others to perceive this city in an aesthetic light. His cinematic lens highlights his urban encounters in small vignettes in which the everyday and the dancerly can co-mingle and interpenetrate.

Writing about dance, however, remained inherently difficult, according to Huschka, "For it encounters an underdeveloped space, that—interweaving with the area of the senses pertaining to one's own body—is foreign to one's capability to speak."[63] Huschka summarizes some of the difficulties of representing dance that various writers and intellectuals around 1900 experienced, especially when encountering dance performances in the metropolis. To "translate" and find the most accurately corresponding adjectives and syntax to describe a movement sequence can present such hardships that the result is often catastrophe. In fact, "language will never be able to access this unreachable area of dance"[64] because it encounters the problem of reducing "a dynamic, spatial-temporal event to a verbal equivalent."[65] This detachment exists between language's relative precision and the deficient vocabulary from which the new modern dance suffers. To complicate this situation productively, Elswit's idea of an "archive of watching" displays a pluralist view of performances, still recognizing that each—whether accurate or exaggerated—is a reflection of personal perception. Furthermore, Ruprecht's "gestural imaginary" posits the creative power of taking visual stimuli and artistically altering their form and content. Scholars have therefore shifted their attitudes toward dance representations, from being a handicap to being an empowering freedom of multiplicity.

Early-twentieth-century dancers such as Isadora Duncan, Ruth St. Denis, Loïe Fuller, and Vaslav Nijinsky from the Ballets Russes desired an emancipation from the *danse d'école* hegemony by embracing a freer body through experimental movement and representation. This drastic change confronted the viewers with a set of foreign movement vocabularies, leaving them in a void without the necessary tools to understand and interpret the new dance. With the performance breaking free from the balletic conventions and the codification of describing dance, the audience lacked sufficient vocabulary to identify new movements. And unlike ballet, with its elaborate sets and costumes, many modern dances are performed on barren stages, or as Brandstetter has noted, in places away from the conventional theaters: museums, ateliers, gardens, etc.[66] Not only did viewers have to come to terms with the new movement style, they had to interpret the costumes, spatial ambience, and *mise en scène* as integral aesthetic entities; this paradigm shift created many difficulties, yet also exciting opportunities for authors to write about the freer modern dance and its surroundings. Endell, Kessler, Rilke, Döblin, Lasker-Schüler, Chomón, and the Skladanowskys worked on their own specific ways of depicting the interpenetration of dance and city space. Essentially a new kind of language had to be developed to discuss dance: "In the process, one went from the idea of a general untranslatability to one of a new language that had to be found, in order to be able to verbally capture movement."[67] The untranslatability of perceiving movement into text leads to an alternative, as, for example, that developed by Gabriele Wittmann, who realizes that the entities of dance and writing are not the same and therefore raises possibilities instead of the limitations for depicting and writing about dance.

Wittmann's investigation stems from the question, "Is there language that can kinesthetically express or recreate the momentum of dance?"[68] She first considers the possibilities of dance critique, but finds it deficient in describing the actual dance; these kinds of texts also use too few adjectives and metaphors, and so, unfortunately, convey an insufficient sense of movement within the text.[69] She next turns to poetry—particularly by poets from the end of the nineteenth and beginning of the twentieth century who were inspired by dance—and ascertains that the atmosphere, the depicted images, and the rhythm of the dance are related, but not necessarily the kinesthesia.[70] In this instance, her observation brings one closer to reproducing the feeling of the dance, as in Rilke's "Spanish Dancer" ("Spanische Tänzerin") and arguably the other texts discussed in this book. Although poetry with its rhyme and meter may come closest to conveying dance movement, other prose texts can have a similar ability, such as in the scene with Malte and the *Veitstänzer*.

Wittmann continues to argue that as children humans develop a "sense of movement" (*Bewegungssinn*), which corresponds to understanding fundamental movements such as falling, turning, and stabilizing, etc. Subsequently, when one watches a dance performance, not only do we perceive visually, we sense the movement as well.[71] She later coins the concept of "mimetic sense" (*mimetischer Sinn*) to mean a state of watching others in which "we slip, in a way, *into the skin* of another being. In our imagination—or wherever this process occurs—we ARE this other being."[72] Although she was not the first theorist to discuss the degree to which an observer "becomes" or assumes some of the feelings of a dancer performing, Wittmann mentions a key aspect for helping to understand not only how Rilke in the atelier or Döblin in the theater felt as they observed dance, but also for how they portray the protagonists in their texts who watch dance. In many of the works discussed in this study, particularly *The Notebooks of Malte Laurids Brigge* and "Die Tänzerin und der Leib," a main character is confronted by a scene involving dancerly movement in which an emotional connection *is* or *is not* expressed throughout the duration of the observation. The greatly thematisized *mimetischer Sinn* hints at a crucial component of watching dance that the authors undoubtedly had felt themselves and that remains a prominent characteristic of metropolitan dance texts.

Wittmann's argument concludes that poetry is the most appropriate type of writing to recreate the kinesthetic experience of observing a live dance because of its aural, recitative, and performative component.[73] Her support of poetry lies behind the similar ephemerality of both media; they tend to be shorter in duration and demonstrate transient elements of being "performed." Wittmann essentially likens poetry to music, given its sounds, rhythm, and fleetingness, and music parallels dance in regard to its temporality. Dance and poetry are similar in that they can be performed numerous times, but every execution produces a unique occurrence. Therefore, although it is not the case with all the texts in this study, prose texts that liken lyric—*The Notebooks of Malte Laurids Brigge* and *Letters to Norway/Mein Herz*—can arguably be perceived as dance texts in their own right, particularly because Rilke and Lasker-Schüler are mostly regarded as poets. Yet, as this study will argue, while poetry might be the genre closest to the form and content of a dance, other forms of media such as photography and film can also assume this role.

The nineteenth century proved to be a developmental period regarding the physiological mechanisms of one's spatial orientation. In 1820 the physiologist Thomas Brown ascertained that "our muscular frame was not merely a part of the living machinery of motion, but was also truly an organ of sense."[74] Moreover, in 1880 the neurophysiologist Henry Charlton Bastian coined the word "kinesthesia" after demonstrating the connection of the cerebral cortex to the muscles' sense of three sensations—pain and fatigue, weight and resistance, and movement and position.[75] Originating from *kine*, Greek for movement, and *aesthesis*, for sensation, the original use of the word "kinesthesia" dealt with "the muscular sense of the body's movement."[76]

The term "kinesthesia" emerged at the end of the nineteenth century, as did the term "empathy"—Greek for *empatheia*—which originated in 1873 and was named *Einfühlung* by German aesthetician Robert Vischer. Later it was translated into English by Edward Titchener in 1909. In analyzing the experience of viewing art, Vischer describes the sensation of moving into the object being observed and assuming its dimensions and demeanor.[77] This visualization allowed the viewer to inhabit the body of another person or object and to appropriate the corresponding kinesthetic sensation.

Empathy and kinesthesia began drawing attention in dance circles through the *New York Times* critic John Martin, whose writings appeared from the 1930s to 1960s. Formulating a theory of dance expression, he argued that while observers are watching a dancing body, they feel similar kinesthetic sensations, a process called "inner mimicry," much like Wittmann's "mimetischer Sinn." Martin's observation not only takes into account dance movement, but more broadly pedestrian motions and even objects:

> Since we respond muscularly to the strains in architectural masses and the attitudes of rocks, it is plain to be seen that we will respond even more vigorously to the action of a body exactly like our own. We shall cease to be mere spectators and become participants in the movement that is presented to us, and though to all outward appearances we shall be sitting quietly in our chairs, we shall nevertheless be dancing synthetically with all our musculature. Naturally these motor responses are registered by our movement-sense receptors, and awaken appropriate emotional associations akin to those which have animated the dancer in the first place. It is the dancer's whole function to lead us into imitating his actions with our faculty for inner mimicry in order that we may experience his feelings.[78]

The viewer's recognition of and identification with another moving body forces the onlooker's body to also "dance," yet Martin begins his argument with describing relatively "static" objects such as architecture and rock formations. These objects, therefore, take on a posthumanist perspective by approaching the agency of the dancer. Although these massive bodies do not "move," they still provide an area for either expansive or encroaching space and allow themselves, regardless, to be read as affective phenomena. Despite his use of natural or urban masses as a transition into the moving, dancing body, his remarks point to his broad interpretation of kinesthetic empathy. For a growing metropolis like Berlin, therefore, Martin's view—and I will adopt this perspective as well—would pertain not only to the dancing bodies, but to the space and urban structures *themselves* who are also dancing: *Litfasssäule*, the streets, cafés, squares, and hospitals. The metropolitan dance texts thoroughly engage with the interpenetration between dance and the city exuding intense kinesthetic empathy.

Laurence Louppe draws on the work of Rudolf Laban, who establishes ways of perceiving space. Seeing it less as a malleable object, it deals more with movement and positioning in space: levels (high, intermediate, low), orientation (lateral, perpendicular), place (vertical, horizontal, lateral, sagittal), and distance. He conceptualizes a dynamic interaction between space and bodies: "*Alongside the movement of bodies in space, there is the movement of space in bodies.*"[79] Louppe perceives space as "an affective partner, almost able to change our states of consciousness."[80] Instead of bodies ruling the space, their posthumanist perceptions evoke a leveling out of the embedded hierarchy, and charging both human bodies and the environs with emotion potential. In addition, even though the levels and orientation of which Laban speaks are essentially invisible, according to Dominique Dupuy, "To dance is to render space visible."[81] This means, however, that space does not become alive until we activate it through movement.[82] Louppe proposes further that space also seems to be "the exteriorisation of the 'inner landscape,' a purely poetic space whose articulation with objective space is only transitory, analogous to an imaginary spatial resonance and unable at any moment to actualise itself completely."[83] She suggests that in the act of dancing, space becomes a fleeting visualization that only lives through enacted movement in the immediate and small reverberating space around it. These characterizations convey a dynamic, dehierarchicalized, and affective relationship between moving body and space. This ethos, within the realm of contemporary dance studies beginning primarily with Laban, provides a lens with which to view the metropolitan dance texts. While Louppe fundamentally looks at the "invisible" space to be enlivened through the body, she also makes a distinction between "space" and "place." The latter could be specific places, as in "topographical poetics" such as Trisha Brown's site-specific studies *A Man Walking Down the Side of a Building* (1969) or *Roof* (1970). But the topography has a profound influence on the staging and choreography of movement in the metropolitan dance texts, precisely because they no longer take place on a traditional stage. While Western theatrical space, through the image of a chessboard, had acculturated the dancing body to lines, planes, and geographical shapes, essentially imparting an "interiorizing" of the architecture, contemporary dance always sought not to reproduce these representations but to produce its own spatialities and to become its own agent.[84] Margareta Ingrid Christian's study *Objects in Air* similarly investigates how artwork auratically reaches beyond their physical confines, creating aerial environments, which can be considered their own aesthetic categories.[85] In a very similar dancerly spirit, the authors depict their protagonists embracing and being embraced by their urban topographies and their social surroundings in order to espouse a modernist experimentation with movement.

While Wittmann argues that poetry as a dance text might be the closest genre that kinesthetically recreates the experience of live dance, many other dance scholars turn not only to texts of various styles (literature, performance critiques, newspaper articles, etc.) but to other types of media. These include film, photographs, and interviews with choreographers, and have been termed "remembering texts" (*Erinnerungstexte*) by some scholars.[86] While the transience and singular phenomena of dance do not allow it to be properly recorded, scholars attempt to recreate the dance as much as possible. While being able to watch the same performance in order to discuss or write about dance remains an ideal for some scholars—its nature makes this feat impossible. Instead, they have to piece together as much of the performance as is attainable through other media and through their cultivated "gestural imaginary"—keeping Elswit and Ruprecht in mind here—to recreate or create a different manifestation of the dance. While the scenes that Endell, Kessler, Rilke, Döblin, Lasker-Schüler, Chomón, and the Skladanowsky brothers depict do not necessarily correspond to live encounters with dances but more to creations of their own imagination, the authors' metropolitan dance texts comprise one part of a body under the larger term *Erinnerungstexte*. Although such scripts and media remind one of past performances, dance texts also assume the role of a "translator," as Janine Schulze points out.[87]

Inspired by Benjamin's understanding of the word "translation," Schulze argues that dance texts also function as translations, which aim at referring to the original. Translations should, therefore, be viewed as an interpretation and a large component of the entire artistic project that affords variability and allows the translated text to live longer in other contexts.[88] The notion of the text's continuous life demonstrates, as Benjamin argues, a transformation and renewal of the original.[89] Instead of considering the shortcomings of a dance text, which will only come close and never actually *become* live dance or have the same aesthetic impact, Schulze's interpretation of Benjamin supports the empowering independence of the dance text as a medium in its own right. Although they can refer to a phenomenon or performance in the past—even if fictitious—they should justifiably be judged and analytically interpreted as a genre on its own and within the writers' fictional realities.

This chapter has set the stage for the rest of the book by applying first a performative and second a dance lens to written and filmic representations of Berlin and Paris around 1900. German observers perceived the cityscape with macro and organic views as well as more micro ones by focusing on individual urban structures and landmarks. Given the plethora of stimuli in the city, the writings of urban observers could not convey the magnitude of such experiences and instead focused on shorter *Momentbilder* to encapsulate their experiences. Andreas Huyssen identifies the "metropolitan miniature" as a written form often appearing in the feuilleton section of newspapers. This genre tackled the newness of the urban experience in small texts highlighting the cinematic, avoiding realistic plots, and remaining hypercognizant of how outer stimuli affected the inner life of a metropolitan citizen. Additionally, the authors in this study maintain a modernist flâneur-like gaze during their strolls in the city, and perceive dancing bodies comingling in urban spaces. These spaces and objects gain agency, making a case for the nonhuman. As a result, they compose metropolitan dance texts: a genre that highlights the visual, the episodic unexpectedness of urban encounters, posthumanist interpenetration between moving body and surroundings, and often kinesthetic empathy related to the narrative's protagonist, the author, and the reader. Their texts introduce a dancerly element to the metropolitan experience, demonstrating a colliding and interweaving of two seemingly different worlds.

Two

Swirling Affinities

Endell's and Fuller's Architecture, City Space, and Dance

On viewing an image of the Loïe Fuller Theater, one notices how its small windows and entry remain secondary to its pervasively sweeping and fantastical ornamentation, which organically consumes most of the building's surface areas. With curvy lines resembling sensual water imagery and crashing waves, these natural connotations of *Jugendstil* iconography convey a sense of perpetual movement, paradoxically embodied in a static architectural object. Situated in Paris, the Loïe Fuller Theater, inspired by the dancer herself and built by Henri Sauvage (and later modified by Pierre Roche), was part of the World Exposition in 1900 (fig. 3). Atop the entrance stands a life-sized statue of Fuller in her long, draping costume, which inspired the wavelike facade fully encompassing the building. Georges Teyssot's essay "The Wave: Walter Benjamin's Lost Essay on *Jugendstil*" traces Benjamin's ideas of *Jugendstil* through his written fragments, which sketch the idea of an "open-air architecture"—the bourgeois interior entering the exterior, creating a hybridized representation with the wave as the key aesthetic feature.[1] Similarly, in Munich architect August Endell created an asymmetrical, mythical, wavelike "sea creature" displayed on the outer facade of the photography atelier Elvira. Like the Loïe Fuller Theater, this swirling, spectacular image dwarfs the entrance and windows and seems to envelope the building. Drawing from this idea of "interpenetrating" interior and exterior spaces, this chapter explores the swirling aesthetic affinities between Endell's and Fuller's conceptualizations of dance, architecture, and city space.

Although there is no evidence that Endell attended dance performances

Fig. 3. Loïe Fuller Theater, built by Henri Sauvage (and later modified by Pierre Roche). Courtesy of the Helen M. Danforth Acquisition Fund

in general while he was living in Berlin or Munich, his aesthetic transition closely parallels the movement qualities and philosophy of Fuller, who began touring Europe around 1900. Cynthia Novack's term *movement environment* essentially characterizes a permeation of various dance movements influencing each other and creating an atmosphere "implicitly perceived and understood by everyone."[2] Thus, even though Endell and Fuller may never have met or known of each other's existence, they both demonstrate affinities to aestheticized, modern movement, and abstract conceptualizations of space. During her famous serpentine performances, Fuller donned a long, draping textile that covered her entire body except for her head. Grasping two rods connected to the fabric, which elongated her reach, Fuller then rotated her body and swung her arms in the air, creating designs as colorful lights illuminated her from the wings and below. Her performances inspired many artists and architects associated with *Jugendstil* or art nouveau to create posters, sculptures, and buildings in her likeness—embodying the dynamism of her flowing fabric. Departing significantly from her common association with the variety theater, scholarship also discusses how Fuller's dances not only desexualized the female body, but also evoked a posthumanist aesthetic, abstracting her form so that she appeared to *become* natural elements or beings, such as a fire, a lily, or a butterfly.[3] Contemporary viewers of her performances, such as Stéphane Mallarmé, were thrilled to leave the mimetic realm of representation and read Fuller's dance as a "hieroglyph" with enigmatic meaning that inspired one to read, see, and even write differently.[4] Similar to Endell's urban depictions, Fuller's performances also evoked a marked abstraction and enforced a new kinesthetic on its viewer.

In this chapter, I explore and compare the discourse concerning Fuller's performances and her artistic representations with Endell's aesthetic program in "The Beauty of the Metropolis" (1908). His didactic approach begins with his critique of romantic ideas, leading into the influence of impressionism, and then finally to the description of street scenes. Instructing readers to observe based on their emotions and not necessarily their intellect, his impressionistic and visual vignettes thus reflect the genre of the "modernist miniature":

> [an] antiform [that] resists the laws of genre as much as a systemic philosophy or urban sociology, [and] cross[es] the boundaries between poetry, fiction, and philosophy, between commentary and interpretation, between language and the visual. But as form it is firmly grounded in the micrological observation of metropolitan space, time, and life at the earlier stage of modernization.[5]

This highly visual and proto-cinematic form not only highlights the depiction of the city but embraces the fragmented perception of a modern city dweller in the urban space. Endell's miniature "In Front of the Café," in which pedestrians lose their individuality and begin impressionistically forming swarms and swirls as in the *Fotoaltier* Elvira, could also be regarded as a dance text. It both bolsters his architectural phenomenology and stylistically resembles the posthumanist performances of Fuller. It is similar to live dance. Gabriele Brandstetter defines a genre of the dance text, which sees

> dance dramaturgy as a succession and climax of movement elements; the contrast between controlled and released gesture, between disci-

pline and ecstasy as models of discovering and losing oneself as an individual; the duality of nature and culture, of movement and stasis, of the ephemeral versus the eternal in the transitory process of signification and designification.[6]

While most of the scholarship on Fuller has focused on her performance aesthetics, femininity (or lack thereof),[7] proto-cinematic representation,[8] and technological prowess in the theater, few studies have critically addressed her use of space in depth—particularly within the context of the metropolis and with Endell's architectural phenomenology—in both her performances and artistic representations of her.

Given Endell's intensely visual language and proto-cinematic representation of urban movement in "The Beauty of the Metropolis," Endell's modernist miniatures, particularly "In Front of the Café," can be regarded as a metropolitan dance text. I argue that it allows the urban observer to also understand and interpret the new phenomenon of early-twentieth-century dance, particularly Fuller's aesthetic. More specifically, I trace how his architectural phenomenology strongly resembles the discourse concerning Fuller's performances with fabric and light. Dance around 1900 saw a myriad of different movement styles, by performers such as Isadora Duncan, Ruth St. Denis, and Vaslav Nijinsky. Furthermore, Endell's metropolitan dance text coupled with Fuller's performances at the *Varieté* and artistic representations of her in art and architecture—in a Folies-Bergère poster by PAL from 1893 (fig. 1) and her own Fuller Theater at the World's Fair in Paris in 1900 (fig. 3)—highlight their elastic conceptualization of space and dance. These experimental depictions are similar in some ways to the kinesthetic empathy associated with modern dance. Moreover, I argue that Endell's and Fuller's work question traditional ideas of dance not only by staging movement in the urban space but by demonstrating their interconnected and liminal fluidity. Humans and objects not only perform dancerly movement in the metropolitan space, but the dynamic energy of the city also, in return, *dances* with them—they become absorbed into and interpenetrate each other, rendering both almost indecipherable. They engage with Christian's idea of how artworks reach beyond their own physical confines and into the space and air around them, creating an aestheticized aerial environment.[9] In these representations, art and space maintain an equal partnership; rather than dance dominating the aesthetic atmosphere, the invisibility of the space is suddenly made visible and granted agency.

Endell's Aesthetic Program

Born in 1871 in Berlin, Endell first began studying philosophy but after moving to Munich expanded into literature, art history, and aesthetics. During his years there, from 1892 to 1901, he became more interested in applied arts and architecture and met with avant-garde circles. He not only become acquainted with Stefan George and the poet's followers during the mid-1890s, he met Hermann Obrist, who was known for modern embroidery and influenced the intricacies that Endell would apply in his own facade detailing. He was influenced by impressionist painters as well as by contemporary sociologists and members of literary circles, including Georg Simmel, Lou Andreas-Salomé, and Rainer Maria Rilke.[10] Endell visited the lectures and seminars of the psychologist Theodor Lipps, who had been developing an *Einfühlungstheorie*—a theory of empathy.[11] In a letter to his cousin Kurt Breysig in 1897, Endell wrote, "I sense everything. I put line to line without a care about nature. The only guiding light is the impression I wish to achieve. [. . .] For me these are form images which elicit emotional responses, and nothing else."[12] In contrast to other architects of the time who received formal training in drawing and design, his approach to architecture focused on the overall response of the observer and was influenced by his studies in philosophy and phenomenology. When Endell opened his Schule für Formkunst in Berlin in 1904, he referenced his way of learning about architecture: namely, for students to base their technique not on academic pedagogies, but on unmediated feelings.[13] Besides designing book illustrations and decorative pieces for art magazines like *Pan* and *Dekorative Kunst*, Endell created decorative designs for wall reliefs, textiles, carpets, window glass, and lamps.[14] While his most distinguished work was probably the photography atelier Elvira in Munich from 1897, whose facade depicted fantastical, dragon-like ornamentation, less is known about Endell's philosophical work.

In his first essay, "On Beauty," written in 1896—twelve years before he wrote "The Beauty of the Metropolis"—Endell expressed two of his ambitions: first, "We have to learn to see, and we have to learn that form and color bring forth certain feelings of which we become genuinely aware."[15] Second, he wanted to express his view of fine art and to close the gap between the artist and the audience, because he feared the layperson considered art to be too intellectual. In learning about and recognizing these new aesthetic ways of seeing, one was to look at an object or phenomenon not for its function, but instead for its optics and affect. Endell's perspective was similar to Wilhelm Wundt's argument concerning the focus on sensuous form and deemphasizing content,[16] which strongly influenced Harry Graf Kessler's own intellectual thought. Endell further argued that one will find "an endless source of extraordinary and unimaginable pleasure [. . .]. It is indeed a new world that emerges [. . .]. It's like an intoxication, like a frenzy that comes over us [. . .]."[17] This new way of seeing was not necessarily focused as much on the intellectual; rather, it was intended for the everyday person at the time. Endell's aesthetic concepts were influenced by the French impressionist painters, who heavily informed his perspective on observing natural and urban phenomena.[18] The goal for much of Endell's work was to create beauty that could influence the individual psyche.[19] These principles, brought forth in his earlier work, flourished in the modernist miniatures of "The Beauty of the Metropolis," which thoroughly depict his aesthetic program and were further developed by using urban structures and spaces as examples.

Two years later, in 1898, the journal *Dekorative Kunst* published an article by Endell called "Formenschönheit und dekorative Kunst." The piece contains a table of adjectives, with examples such as "sober" and "tender" on the left and "disgusting" and "wild" on the right. These attributes correspond to feelings a viewer could have when observing architecture.[20] Zeynep Çelik Alexander claims that Endell's affective theory had less to do with the eighteenth-century understanding of physiognomy—"the assumption that an inner character pressed its marks upon the face"—and had more in common with the late-nineteenth-century idea of pathognomy, which implied that emotional expression was influenced by one's surroundings.[21] According to Alexander, Endell's architectural phenomenology of combining "mathematical rigor and lived experience" seems to maintain an opposing relationship between these two elements.[22] Incidentally, Loïe Fuller's work embodied a similar dichotomy in some ways: her fluid, feminine movements and shapes contrasted with her traditionally masculine knowledge of light, science, and technology.

Before turning to "The Beauty of the Metropolis," one should first consider the facade of the Atelier Elvira in Munich, which was Endell's first attempt to realize his affective theory.[23] A feminist couple had commissioned him to overhaul their photography studio and living space. The massive, asymmetrical ornamental relief on the facade created quite a stir since critics regarded the haphazard design as lacking discipline. Endell himself comments that over the largest window, functioning as a shadowy mass, was "a heavy, uniform ornament that fills the irregular free space."[24] As a result, the facade seems to explode and exude a senseless, inharmonic, and tormenting effect.[25] The academic architect Johannes Otzen described the monstrosity as a self-absorbed, decadent *Übermenschornamentik*: "Modern architecture exaggerated scale, it had studied Nietzsche with profit, the superman haunts its structures, and all sound judgment of reality is lost. Relaying total arbitrariness, the superman ornamentation represents no architectural function and is subordinated to personal whim."[26] Concerning the representational intent of the ornament, the contractor for the photo atelier Joseph Hartwig recalls, "Endell explained its form and structures to me as relating to nature, to the peach pit, the fluttering bands or waves that ripple on the shore, etc."[27] The hybrid animal design and mixed vegetative forms moved beyond logical representation and into a more abstract realm.[28] In fact, as Stacy Hand brings to light, "rather than an ornament that serves to augment or embellish architectonically created space, we have one that creates its own space, in the form of an optical illusion, as if it were to literally establish the existence of that second world, the world of the visible, as artefact of perception."[29] In other words, instead of being in space, Hand argues, the amorphous object *becomes* space, crossing the lines of what normally constitute both. The ornament's organic ability to create space relates strikingly with the architect's "In Front of the Café." Despite the criticism, Endell's bold design forges in the direction of a modernist style and demonstrates the widespread philosophies of Nietzsche seeping into intellectual realms, including literature and dance. While "character, *convenance*, and decorum" dictated the social order of buildings of previous centuries, Endell's style maintained that form and space affected the lived experience of architecture.[30]

Endell's phenomenology manifests itself not only in theoretical writings and physical architectural structures, but also in his modernist miniatures. Published in 1908, "The Beauty of the Metropolis" is divided into various sections, including "Denouncing of the Era" ("Die Anklage gegen das Zeitalter"), "Renunciating Today" ("Die Abkehr vom Heute"), "The Love of Here and Today" ("Die Liebe zum Heute und Hier"), "The Metropolis" ("Die große Stadt"), "The City as Landscape"[31] ("Die Stadt als Landschaft"), and "The Street as a Living Essence"[32] ("Die Straße als lebendiges Wesen"). As these titles suggest, Endell begins by lamenting how his contemporaries view the world by constantly looking to the past and reveling in romantic notions.[33] By critiquing modern society, he gives himself a platform from which to continue building his aesthetic theory. Endell then proclaims a devotion to the present day and depicts the paradox of Berlin: "what is astonishing is that the metropolis, despite all its ugly buildings, despite its noise, despite everything that deserves criticism in it, is, for those who want to see, a wonder of beauty and poetry, a fairy tale more colorful and manifold than any tale told by a poet," and it also "embraces in its streets thousands of beauties, numerous wonders, an endless richness that lays exposed before everyone's eyes and yet is barely noticed."[34] By embracing the here and now, Endell proposes the possibility of seeing beauty in Berlin, which many critics had historically depicted as a prosaic, industrial city. Inspired by the impressionistic idea of trying to depict "The Veils of the Day" such as fog, mist, sun, rain, and dusk, Endell uses these "veils" as a means to give color, life, and movement to otherwise dirty, empty urban structures and scenes. As Alexander Eisenschmidt writes, "Endell's notion of the city aspired to its rethinking, rather than its remaking," and his theory "sought to engage with rather than modify the existing city."[35] Instead of changing the metropolis of Berlin by creating new, beautiful buildings, the existing structures were to be observed as possessing a new kind of beauty. These thoughts resonate similarly with the aesthetic effect of Fuller's dancing. In a small leather notebook, Fuller had jotted down some aphorisms, which resonate strikingly with Endell's perspective: "It is not what you see, but how you see that counts."[36]

Endell's modernist miniatures, a collection of concise, urban impressions, first begin with beautified urban structures—"The Romanesque Church," "The Iron Bridge," "Friedrichstraße Train Station." They culminate in large expansive areas—"Unter den Linden," "Potsdamer Platz," "In Front of the Brandenburg Gate." After Endell imbues these static urban architectural structures with the "veil" and colors, he intensifies his depiction by infusing the open spaces with the dancerly, aesthetic movement of people and crowds to create an even greater feeling of a living, dynamic system, exemplifying Rudolf von Laban's and Laurence Louppe's conceptualization of an active and activated space. In each of Endell's concise descriptions, he abstracts from the actual function of the everyday scenes that he witnesses and aestheticizes them by emphasizing their color, form, and movement.

Essentially, his readings of these places and buildings progress successively. First giving the reader a detailed look at a rather insignificant urban structure, he then moves on to larger bird's-eye views of metropolitan squares. In the last section of his text, called "The Street as a Living Essence," and in a miniature called "In Front of a Café," Endell characterizes an unnamed square in Berlin as people move in and out of the area. His enchantment with the scene emerges as the moving pedestrians do not seem to resemble people but rather abstracted forms that group together and later break apart as in a dance. Helge David accurately describes Endell's text:

> In the current of permanent presence, Endell tries to take pleasure
> in the impressionistic transience of the visible through a moment of

contemplation. He revels in a new slowness without wanting or being able to restrict the speed of modern life. The visible is momentary and is movement. The metropolis of the present has rid itself of its high ideals and establishes itself new every day.[37]

Being in a city of constant flux and perpetual becoming, the bombarding stimuli encourage the preservation particularly of striking and memorable moments, which Endell achieves. The idea of ceaseless movement relates remarkably, as we will see later, with Fuller's aesthetic. In his writing, Endell tries to capture the visual impressions of his daily life, similar to the journalists of around 1900, as discussed by Peter Fritzsche:

> The attention to, and even celebration of, diversity and difference tended to undermine a coherent vision of the city. On-site reports, behind-the-scene investigations, and portraits of specific places and passing events put the accent on the singular and did so at the expense of more generic patterns. What physiognomies lost in universality they gained in detail: *Skizzen*, *Momentbilder*, and other snapshots of city places and city people over the course of a single day collected little more than moments and incidents.[38]

Similar to Endell, journalists strolled about the city until they encountered a newsworthy event. They attempted then to recreate and capture it in a written form called *Momentbilder*, which resembles Huyssen's miniature. Since recording routine events daily was virtually impossible for Endell, he collected impressions that furthered his goal of encouraging his contemporaries to observe Berlin as aesthetically beautiful. In addition to his programmatic agenda, his snapshot from "In Front of the Café" involving pedestrians moving in the square establishes an alternative aesthetic beyond the idea of an urban "performance": it calls to attention the dynamic movement, form, and color of a metropolitan dance text.

Encountering Dance in the Urban Space and Writing a Dance Text

Endell begins his accounts from "In Front of the Café":

> In this regard, among the most astonishing is the life of a square. Across from the ill-fated Romanesque church is a café with a terrace

where I have often sat for hours on summer evenings, and where I never grow tired of watching the colorful play of people's comings and goings.[39]

He places himself as an observer of urban phenomena by watching "the life of a square," which can be read less in terms of its portrayal of daily life, and more about the people's lively display in the narrator's eyes. Accustomed to his daily wanderings about the city, Endell seats himself at this café precisely to watch people come and go within the square. His interest in writing about the urban experiences arises from the heightened sensitivity of the modern individual in the metropolis, according to sociologist Georg Simmel. In his essay "The Metropolis and Mental Life" ("Die Großstädte und das Geistesleben"), Simmel describes the city dwellers' experience as their senses are bombarded by a plethora of dizzying stimuli. Overwhelmed with information, they soon develop a filter—a blasé attitude. This desensitized state helps citizens cope in a dizzying world of agitation, yet it may dull their senses to the everyday.[40] Considering that Endell had attended some of Simmel's lectures in Berlin,[41] his theories probably permeated Endell's thoughts while writing "The Beauty of the Metropolis."

In this respect, he seems to modify the concept of the nineteenth-century Parisian flâneur, who would be walking and observing at the same time. Endell is seated in order to keep a fixed distance so he can observe the square more objectively, instead of being in the midst of the living system. Suspended from social obligation, blending in with other pedestrians, and maintaining anonymity, the nineteenth-century flâneur strolled around the city and aesthetically observed and studied his perpetually changing urban environment.[42] He felt at home in the metropolis and became excited to enter the dynamic space. For the most part, Endell preserves these ideas, yet allows his flâneur to remain seated during this scene. In doing so, he stages the pedestrians and the square as a more traditional dance performance, but allows chance to dictate the movement.

Endell continues with his dance text by critiquing the design of the space and introducing his dancers:

> The square is misguided as architecture, perhaps even worse as a traffic system—as if someone tried to produce the greatest possible number of dangerous crossings—but it is unique as a field over which human figures are distributed. The crowds of the neighboring streets dissolve here in all directions, and the whole place seems covered with individuals.[43]

Endell points to a fault in the planning of this space, calling the square "misguided" in its architectural construction and noting its failure to allow smooth traffic flow; but the square takes on a unifying role as the side streets lead into the main area. Despite his comment regarding the poor architecture, he focuses on the space and the people filtering in because his café view allows him to observe from a greater encompassing distance. In fact, he does not emphasize the pedestrians' individuality but rather their streaming collectiveness and their likeness to a natural phenomenon. Fuller's dances also likened themselves to ideas of nature such as butterflies, fire, and lilies. In doing so Endell abstracts from the everyday appearance of the group and concentrates on their dancerly and posthumanist form.

The dynamic movement, however, furthers his interest even more as the groups of dancers change formations:

> The people move apart from each other. Space stretches between them. With a shifting perspective, the more distant figures seem increasingly smaller, and one clearly feels the vast expansion of the square. All of the people are free from one another; now they move toward one another in dense groupings; now there are gaps; the formation of the space is always changing. Pedestrians push themselves through, conceal one another, detach themselves again and walk freely and alone, each emphasizing, articulating his share of space. The space between them thus becomes a palpable, immense, living entity.[44]

In this scene, visual play ensues between the single people forming groups and the space in the square, creating the sense of constant activity and liveliness. This activity reflects Louppe's idea,[45] drawn from Laban, that space can only become visible through movement: "Alongside the movement of bodies in space, there is the movement of space in bodies."[46] Furthermore, Endell's characterization of the space "stretching" and being able to change formation gives it an agency, redefining its previous passive purpose through activation. In doing so, he unknowingly engages with theoretical dance discourses from his architectural perspective and brings space onto a more equal level with the pedestrians. At times forming tight clumps that then break apart, the pedestrians maintain their individual identity. While free from each other, maintaining their own will, they also remain formed groups. The movement patterns evolve from coalescent formations into the dancers' maneuvering between and momentarily concealing each other. Throughout this energetic description, Endell focuses his attention on the aesthetic play between the people and space, giving no consideration to reading specific individuals.

Essentially, he reads their movements on a higher level of abstraction, instead of everyday utility. While he has seated himself at the café distant enough to see the patterns and arrangements, his separation probably causes him to be unable to distinguish individual faces and gestures.

Endell's staging of his dance text reflects elements of dance, which Gabriele Brandstetter has defined as progressive movement elements reaching a peak.[47] Her characterization fits remarkably well with Endell's "In Front of the Café," concerning the succession and climax of movements. By depicting the perpetual and fluctuating motion of both individual and groups, the ensuing excitement and unpredictability culminate in the space's becoming a living essence—with the causal relationship of movement activating the space. This new, organic entity can only be produced through the work of the dancerly pedestrians, whose perpetual movement transforms the space into another being with which to dance and engage. Thus, the dancing body and the space become intertwined and essentially indistinguishable. The linear and teleological direction of Endell's miniature implies the continually transient nature of dance as a process. This new entity involves a degree of transformation in order to reach this transcendental state, which can only be attained through the equal labor of both the dancing individuals and the space.

His metropolitan dance text relinquishes disciplined control and unleashes an ecstatic expression like his ornamental, dragon-like facade on the Elvira photo atelier. Through this heightened level of abstraction, the dance text demands to be both interpreted and felt. Additionally, Brandstetter notes two further aspects of abstraction, which characterize avant-garde dances and dance texts: "Detaching oneself from a mimetic concept of theatrical performance, and splitting up traditionally established complexes of collaboration between the arts in theater (e.g., stage design and costume design, dance, and music)."[48] "In Front of the Café" certainly moves beyond the communication and the utilitarianism of human interactions and into an abstraction of swirling forms. The "antiform" nature of the modernist miniature seems to call for a reshuffling of theatrical tradition with architecture and venturing into the realm of dance.

While Endell is observing the people in the square with an aesthetic delight from his perch at the café, the pedestrians probably do not think they are being watched. Endell, the sitting flâneur, retains his anonymity and blends in with the rest of the crowd, in order to obtain any position that is to his liking and to maintain an optimal point of observation. The architect desires to watch the moving people in their natural setting while aestheticizing their everyday, dancerly movement. To him, the people are not just pedestrians maneuvering in a square but rather a living entity with its own dynamic life that can be experienced. Other urban observers at the time similarly depicted large metropolitan settings in their writing; for example, the critic Max Osborn in 1910 characterized Berlin as an "organismal city" (*Stadtorganismus*) with a certain tempo and circulating blood.[49] Walter Rathenau described the city as extending its long "black tentacles," in reference to its rapid growth.[50] Urban physiognomists like Anselm Heine observed the cityscape as a panorama of daily scenes: zooming trains, busses, street cars with occupants reading the newspaper.[51] Although Heine's scene could be read simply as a display of the new means of travel, it evokes the notion of perpetual forward motion and an aestheticization of the ways of traversing the urban space. Fritzsche calls Berlin and other metropolises "an incalculable, ongoing process" filled with "unfamiliarity and flux."[52] Osborn, Rathenau, and Heine's metropolitan depictions not only awaken connotations of the city as an organic being, but also highlight aesthetic movement qualities that could resemble dance. Thus, Endell was not writing in a void, but rather in the company of many other urban observers feeling the dynamic and transforming pulse of the city and finding a particular writing style to represent their experiences.

Besides the architectural space of the square and the groups of people in constant motion, Endell adds the effects of the "veils" to his "In Front of the Café," which he earlier outlined theoretically as a means of adding more color and energy to the display:

> What is even more extraordinary is when the sun endows each pedestrian with an accompanying shadow or when the rain spreads a glistening, uncertain reflection underfoot. And in this strange space-life unfolds the swarm of brightly painted trucks, the colorful dresses, everything united, cloaked, embellished with the veils of day and of dusk.[53]

The sun causes the people to cast a shadow, which adds another dimension to their appearance. Meanwhile, the colorful trucks and dresses combined with the pedestrian movement create swirling impressions that are difficult to absorb because of the constant activity. Rather than using traditional stage lighting to illuminate his dance, Endell appropriately applies the sun as a natural source that adds dimensions to the dancers, the space, and surroundings objects. Thus, his metropolitan dance text does not necessarily privilege the moving individuals, but also highlights the dynamic nature of the *mise en scène*, which recalls his architectural phenomenology. By referencing theater and lighting, he highlights the posthumanist agency of the sun, which "endows" the pedestrians with a shadow. By noting the "strange space-life," Endell points to a new, undefined amalgamation of both natural and urban space with everyday movement and "theatrical" lighting. While this miniature illustrates the scene's dance-like nature, it also corresponds to the modern individual's experience in the metropolitan space. The cityscape's dynamics also relate back to Berlin's urban environment filled with an overwhelming excitement that stimulated Endell's gestural imaginary. The use of natural light similarly relates strikingly well to the lighting innovations of Fuller's performances.

In this miniature, Endell clearly establishes an aesthetic perspective, which carries the reader through his personal impressions of a dancing city. It remains true to his phenomenology of championing the overall impression of a dynamic environment as opposed to abiding by academic architectural tradition. His dramaturgical work in the metropolitan dance text "In Front of the Café" stages moving bodies that both inhabit the urban space and have the ability to create another spatial being through dancing. In this way, space and body become more indecipherable. This text and his asymmetrical relief ornament on the Elvira photo atelier represent exemplary instances of intensely visual depictions that do not privilege the human body but instead elevate the agency and visibility of space, and thus reflect Laban's and Louppe's ideas of movement activating spatialities. Endell establishes an alternative aesthetic by highlighting the dynamic movement, color, and spatial engagement of a metropolitan dance text.

Aesthetic Convergence: Endell and Fuller

The rest of this chapter investigates Fuller's dance performances and artistic representations—poster and architecture—and compares them to both Endell's written aesthetics—theoretical and practical—and his architectural work, primarily the Elvira photo atelier. I aim to bring their discourses together to explore their intersections of dance, dance text, and city space.

Since Endell's miniature "In Front of the Café" stylistically resembles a dance text, we can also analyze it as a dance performance. For instance, the *Illustrierte Zeitung* provides a journalistic *Momentbild* of Loïe Fuller, which could arguably be considered a dance text like Endell's; it pays particular attention to the illumination of Fuller's body in the stage lighting and her turning movements:

> What surprises the viewer in her depiction is less the art of dancing itself than the staging of the whole "number," which she performs: the marvelous skillfulness and speed in her movement, with which she performs her serpentine dance.
>
> Before she begins her performance, the hall and stage are enveloped by an impenetrable darkness. The stage introduces a fantastically equipped cave, and through a crevice Miss Fuller enters the scene. Suddenly electric light illuminates her beautiful face. She begins to turn like a spinning top; the folds in her long, white, silk costume—embroidered with snakes and butterflies—elevate themselves and form figures in the swirl of the dance; several of which are shown in our drawings.
>
> The perpetually changing reflexes and colors of the electric light contribute substantially to enhance the effect of the entire performance. The viewer is able to feel transformed into believing that Miss Fuller could be dancing in a diamond atmosphere, thus designating her as a serpentine dancer seems completely justifiable.[54]

While this journalistic text might lack the lyrical and visual beauty of Endell's style, this description and characterization of Fuller highlights key similarities with "In Front of the Café." Her perpetual motion echoes the continuous movement of Endell's groups weaving in and out of each other. The electric light illuminating Fuller further enhances the swirling patterns in her fabric, which reminds one of the flowing shapes in Endell's dance text. Similarly, these patterns reinforce the idea of abstraction, allowing the viewer to feel transported into another transcendent mode of understanding. While Fuller's otherworldly and posthumanist representation resonates with evolving forms that Endell perceives, the journalist depicts being transported into a new belief, eliciting a strong religious connotation and elevating the perspective even higher than Endell's. Both demand a new way of seeing and a new aesthetic to understand more abstract forms and colors. By reading these dance texts together, one can begin establishing a way to interpret not only these forms of early-twentieth-century dance movement, but also to create a written language that describes and relays a lived experience.

While the American dancer Loïe Fuller began her career in vaudeville, she became famous after moving to Europe and joining the *Varieté* circuit in Paris in 1892. Much like Endell, who did not have academic training in architecture, Fuller lacked formal dance instruction, unlike some other early-twentieth-century dancers. She was known for her performances wearing a long, draping textile with elongated wands attached underneath. Grasping these rods, she swung her arms around and swiveled her torso to create various patterns as light from the wings and below illuminated her movement.[55] She even asked herself if her unorthodox depiction was dance: "What is dance? It is motion. What is motion? The expression of a sensation. What is a sensation? The reaction in the human body produced by an impression or an idea perceived by the mind."[56] Abstracting from and negating the historical and social background associated with dance, her ideas instead focus on the feeling and the representation of that sensation, like Endell's aesthetic theory. Both of their concepts relate to the individual's emotion while observing either performance or architecture.

Empathy and kinesthesia began warranting attention in dance circles through the *New York Times* critic John Martin. In writings that appeared from the 1930s to the 1960s, he formulated a theory of dance expression. Martin argued that while observers are watching a dancing body, they will feel similar kinesthetic sensations: a process called "inner mimicry." This phenomenon relates to the physical reaction to all kinds of events: we pucker our lips when we watch someone bite into a lemon, or we yawn when someone around us does.[57] Consequently, Martin's observation not only takes into account dance movement (as with Fuller's performances), but more broadly pedestrian motions and even objects, as in Endell's street scenes:

> Since we respond muscularly to the strains in architectural masses and the attitudes of rocks, it is plain to be seen that we will respond even more vigorously to the action of a body exactly like our own. We shall cease to be mere spectators and become participants in the movement that is presented to us, and though to all outward appearances we shall be sitting quietly in our chairs, we shall nevertheless be dancing synthetically with all our musculature. Naturally these motor responses are registered by our movement-sense receptors, and awaken appropriate emotional associations akin to those which have animated the dancer in the first place. It is the dancer's whole function to lead us into imitating his actions with our faculty for inner mimicry in order that we may experience his feelings.[58]

The viewer's recognition and identification with another moving body forces the onlooker's body to also "dance," yet Martin begins his argument with describing relatively "static" objects such as architecture and rock formations: moving beyond the human. Although these massive bodies do not "move," they indeed do still provide an area for either expansive or encroaching space and allow themselves, regardless, to be read as empathetic phenomena. Despite using natural or urban masses as a transition into the moving, dancing body, his remarks still point to his broad interpretation of kinesthetic empathy. For a growing metropolis like Berlin or Paris, Martin's view would then pertain not only to the dancing bodies in the city space like Fuller's, but also the space and urban structures *themselves*, as in Endell's street scenes. In addition to Martin's overarching principle of bringing together both aesthetic and everyday movements—similar to Fuller and Endell's conceptualization of space and dance—he also blurs the distinction between space and object, since both can evoke emotional responses in a viewer. As a result, Martin perpetuates the fluidity of both ideas and even elevates the agency of the nonhuman.

Fuller's use and conceptualization of space were also in line with emerging and later forms of modern dance. According to Ann Cooper Albright, these embodied

> an acute awareness of the dynamic elasticity of space. Rather than accepting the stage as a static frame (complete with painted backdrop) in which a dancer poses or in which a group of dancers creates a pleasing tableaux, modern dance renders space active. Space can be haunting or inviting. Dancers can puncture it, embrace it, or recede from it. With no more dramatic narrative than the energy of their movement, they can dive through space or be sheltered by it. Indeed, a key difference between music-hall dancing in Paris at the turn of the twentieth century and the kind of expressive dancing that Fuller worked with was this awareness of extending the body beyond one's own kinesphere to engage the space around.[59]

Just as Fuller's dances exuded a palpable energy that interacts with her immediate environment, Endell's dance text "In Front of the Café" emanates a similar radiating vitality into its surroundings. While his work brings to the reader visual representations of pedestrian dancers creating and interacting with a new essence, Fuller creates her vigor through physical performance for her viewer. Throughout the rest of my analysis, I further probe her use of space, particularly as she is portrayed in the urban landscape.

While at the beginning of Fuller's career, her fabric featured prints of snakes or butterflies and her limbs were exposed, later she used more material, which was not printed and encompassed her whole body except her head. Unlike in previous centuries of academic dance such as court dances and ballet, which maintained idealistic goals by achieving aesthetically pleasant gestures, poses, and gracefully connected steps, Fuller's dance aimed at perpetual motion during her entire performance.[60] Rhonda Garelick characterizes her dancing: "Overall, Fuller's innovations tended to dissolve the shape of her body into a whirl of fabric and light, devoid of most corporeal as well as social or historical specificity; she was no longer a dancer performing a role, or even a dancer dancing, but somehow a force of performativity itself, mutating into vast and ephemeral decorative forms."[61] Fuller's textiles and movement transform into performative shapes, which evoke Endell's metropolis manifesting itself as beautiful, dynamic systems. Fuller's style offered a new way of interpreting her own performances: "I have never studied, and I don't believe the ancient Greek dancers ever studied how to move their feet, but danced with their whole bodies—with their head and arms and trunk and feet. I believe that they studied more the *impression* that they wished to convey by their dancing than the actual way of dancing."[62] Additionally, Fuller's dances were more characteristic of impressionism than of the expressionistic *Ausdruckstanz*.[63] Dance scholar Gabriele Brandstetter characterizes Fuller as "a dancer of metamorphosis" whose dances are inherently related to both motion and emotion as sensed by the viewer.[64]

Fuller's focus on her overall impression, her connection to impressionism, and the evocation of emotion through movement resonate strikingly with Endell's aesthetic theory. Furthermore, Fuller was not a trained dancer in the academic sense; in fact one questioned if she was even a dancer. Similarly, the disregard for tradition that critics believed Endell reflected in his work was due to his lack of formal training in architecture. Because Fuller's upper body was developed from maneuvering the heavy poles, Penny Farfan reads her as queerly masculine. Her uncanny performance itself also leads to an unsettled a set of binaries.[65] Because of her queer identity, Fuller was able to experiment with her costuming, lighting, and movement to create a vacillating indeterminacy on par with its kinesthetic space. Agreeing with Farfan, Susan Potter's reading of Fuller's public sexuality based on conflicting characterizations by Cooper and Garelick also expresses an "incoherent sexual category that was at this cultural moment in the process of uneven emergence."[66] Contemporary cinematic depictions of Fuller have also continued in highlighting a queer aesthetic. The Fuller biopic *The Dancer* (2016) shows her developing queer identity through her tireless or torturous work ethic and flirtation with Isadora Duncan.[67]

As a result of both Endell's and Fuller's unorthodox backgrounds and comparable *movement environments*, both embraced an impressionism not connected necessarily to historical lineage but one expressly felt through lived, embodied, and transcendental experience. Their paths easily led them to reconceptualize traditional practices in dance, architecture, and space, demonstrating their penchant for experimental forms of depiction and modernity.

Enveloping Fuller in the City

I now examine the interconnectedness between Fuller's and Endell's aesthetics and their "performance" spaces through more concrete examples: the *Varieté*, the poster, and finally through architecture. Fuller performed many of her dances in the variety theater scene in Paris at the Folies-Bergère, which often consisted of short acts with no unified theme and aimed to sustain the fleeting attention of the audience. Since the multifarious, visually appealing performances constantly switched with little transition time, the visualization of the *Varieté* could be captured in the image of the kaleidoscope: "a perpetually-changing and colorful game."[68] Similarly, Simmel's depiction of the city dweller's adapting to constant stimuli in the dynamic urban landscape provides a similar kind of experience at the variety theater, which replicates the metropolitan experience on a microcosmic scale. With freer production guidelines, the *Varieté* allowed other kinds of movement forms to emerge outside the theater—skirt dance, serpent dance, cakewalk, cancan, fandango, polkas, waltzes, gymnastics, erotic dances, juggling, and sketches.[69] Many early-twentieth-century dancers like Loïe Fuller, Ruth St. Denis, and Isadora Duncan began their careers in variety theater. One could argue that because of the more open performance standards, more experimental pieces could be performed under the guise of *Varieté*.

Given the accessibility and objectification of women through the male gaze, their performances linked them to the emerging *Konsumgesellschaft* or consumerism in Berlin.[70] The variety theater acted like a shop window, offering a place to quickly survey displayed items, thus leading to the idea of buying and consuming products. Much like the bustling city, which was experiencing drastic advances in technology, an influx of immigrants, and changes in the urban landscape, the modern individual was also becoming an observer and a consumer, developing like the city. Theodor Adorno scrutinizes this culture industry, which functions primarily as entertainment, creating sameness and homogeneity derived from a standard formula.[71] He warns that it denies individuality and critical engagement, demanding conformity to the economic enterprise or risking being forever sidelined as an "eccentric loner."[72] Yet in many ways, the trope of the intellectual, artist, and author being on the fringes suggests that they often run counter to and remain critical of mainstream society.

While relaxing, drinking, and eating at the *Varieté*, one was usually not involved in analytical or intellectual work, but was simply amused by the various acts.[73] Sometimes marginalized, the performers were not necessarily the main attraction: the audience themselves also drew attention. However, unlike the consumption associated with the variety theater, Fuller's performances created a more mysterious atmosphere, which isolated the audiences' attention by offering an indelible image of intellectual abstraction. Instead of using constant, low lighting like most *Varieté* acts did, she began in complete darkness—as noted by the journalist from the *Illustrierte Zeitung*—and performed as an abstract being while the lights were turned on. One could liken her performance to an urban phenomenon that Endell's mind perceived after abstracting an encounter during his flânerie through the city. Given the perpetually changing understanding and fluid boundaries of the city—in which outside could be inside and vice versa, echoing Webber[74] and thus engaging with Giedeon's idea of interpenetration[75]—Fuller's performance does not take place within a strictly traditional theater performance space, but rather in a more social environment. She distinguishes herself from other acts because the darkness rouses the viewer's attention, differentiating her from the sea of stimuli effecting the modern viewer. Instead of assuming a recognizable role, Fuller emerges as an abstract entity whose energy reverberates not only into the stage space but into the audience. Albright argues that while Fuller drew from her experience in popular entertainment, she never seemed to abide by either the "flesh-market mentality of the one or the middle-class aestheticism of the other. Instead, she played across these genres while developing an approach to movement that was truly her own."[76] Albright's characterization portrays Fuller's queer body and existence as allowing free experimentation of form regardless of the seemingly binary viewership. Fuller distinguishes herself from her *Varieté* surroundings and establishes her own movement aesthetics, but on a much grander scale she integrates her performances *into* a perpetually changing urban environment. Similarly, Endell's square in Berlin contrasts itself with the other stimuli because it catches his attention, and more conspicuously locates its movement not only in the metropolis but as part of the urban landscape—keeping in mind the macro and micro views of the city mentioned in chapter 1. As a result, both the pedestrians and Fuller dance in the city while their performance spaces interact with them: as if becoming sewn into the fabric of the metropolis by activating the space with their movement.

To incite interest in the *Varieté*, posters became one popular means of advertising during the late nineteenth century. After moving to Paris in 1892, poster artists such as Henri de Toulouse-Lautrec, Jules Chéret, and PAL were inspired to feature representations of Fuller in their work. Her depiction by the Romanian-born poster artist Jean de Paléologue, better known as PAL, in 1893 conveys her variety-theater sensuality and illustrates her emerging modernist aesthetic (see fig. 1). While the poster's vibrant colors catch the attention of passersby among the sea of other ads, they also reflect the vast array of stimuli that one encounters at the *Varieté*. Atypical of a showgirl, Fuller maintained a sturdy, androgynous frame and donned a draping fabric, which covered most of her body. Yet PAL's poster and countless others portray her as a slim seductress whose hair harmoniously flows in the air like her textile. French artistic posters like the one of Fuller operated with seduction as their key advertising strategy.[77] Garelick and Brandstetter agree that while these poster depictions of Fuller do not correspond to her physical appearance, the aesthetic effect connected to watching her dancing overwhelmingly left the viewer with an enraptured, intoxicated impression. Thus, the posters designers convey Fuller's captivating impression as embodying a flirtatious and hypersexualized woman.[78] Film scholar Tom Gunning argues that her sensual performance was able to speak to all viewers, regardless of class and training.[79] Potter's study of Fuller also opens up the viewership of Fuller's dances beyond the heterosexual, male purview and into a homosocial and lesbian gaze as she performed for women in salons and private gatherings, which deemphasized the dancer's eroticism.[80] Despite the seeming lack of sexual connotations, her performances, nevertheless, would "sustain the possibility of women's erotic interest," actually helping to exercise their visual pleasure.[81] Thus, the overall emotional impression of her dances aimed to reach a wide audience and were largely open to personal interpretation.

Furthermore, in her close reading of the poster, Albright notes that the serpentine design "evokes [. . .] a winding road (something along the lines of a Technicolor version of Oz's 'yellow brick road'). This poster almost provokes the viewer into searching for various images about the abstract splotches of color. I find it hard to resist seeing, anachronistically, a twentieth-century urban skyline in the upper-left-hand corner of the spiral."[82] Just as a *Varieté*-goer might become entranced with this poster, Albright similarly gives in to the temptation to analyze it and look for recognizable images. The urban iconography does come through as a spiraling street with a vaguely discernible metropolis. Building on Albright's argumentation, in this instance, PAL blends Fuller with the cityscape, creating a hybrid posthumanist depiction. The dancer gives life to the city by swinging her arms and allowing the light projections to illuminate not only her body but also her fabric, thus creating the hazily distinguishable metropolis. If we read this poster in the context of Endell's aesthetic theory, then one recognizes that PAL's city does not appear as an easily definable entity, but rather as an overall impression. Interestingly, this skyline is not represented with curving lines like Fuller's drapery, but rather with straight, fragmented shapes and even expressionistic strokes that reveal a kaleidoscopic effect, reminiscent of the symbol for the *Varieté*. Albright notes, "Fuller was able to create the magic [of her performances] in the midst of a conscious and deliberate use of technology. She engaged the expressive possibilities of stage lighting by dancing with, rather than simply in the midst of, color and light."[83] PAL seems to not only (un)consciously and expressionistically imprint the metropolis on her fabric, but also the experience of perceiving her performance, and most importantly he depicts her dancing body as being a part of this urban space. Furthermore, if we apply Garelick's argument concerning how French poster artists did not literally depict Fuller, but rather the *impression* from her performance, of an erotic woman swinging a diaphanous fabric, then we could interpret PAL's representation of Fuller similarly. While he did feel an intoxicating sensuality from her dance—manifested in her slim, womanly figure—he certainly, and most importantly for this chapter, experienced the effects of modernity, which manifested themselves as fragmented, colorful shards resembling a skyline. PAL's poster functions as a striking example of how Fuller's dancing and use of light leaves an impression on the artist that results in his representing the metropolis as folding into a dancer or vice versa; either way, the dancing body and urban space become melded together. In contrast to the industrial city, which becomes swirling shapes in Endell's depiction, in PAL's poster Fuller's whirling fabric and lighting transform into a *Varieté* girl who posthumanistically fuses into an abstracted, expressionistic representation of the city.

While it may seem implausible to suggest that Endell saw this particular poster while in Berlin, since it probably appeared only in Paris during its initial posting, the architect was undoubtedly situated in an urban space saturated with multiple stimuli as he wrote his modernist miniatures in "The Beauty of the Metropolis." During the architect's flânerie, he certainly encountered many posters plastered on buildings and advertising columns (*Litfaßsäulen*). Since they were not necessarily designed to be closely observed and analyzed, as in a museum and gallery setting, artists and advertisers' posters used bold shapes, brilliant colors, the flattening of space, and much less detail, thus often focusing on a single image.[84] The June 9, 1893, issue of the journal *Le Mirliton* features an illustration by Theophile-Alexandre Steinlen on its cover (fig. 4). The image depicts a man, who might be a flâneur, on a Montmartre street, observing a poster by Henri de Toulouse-Lautrec of Aristide Bruant, which advertises Bruant's cabaret. Instead of featuring the poster, Steinlen's illustration highlights the act of observing in a metropolitan space, suggesting to the reader the importance of interpreting the city with a flâneur-like gaze. While Ruth Iskin considers it implausible that this drawing reflects reality, since the Bruant posters hung among a sea of other posters, not in isolation,[85] it is possible to imagine Endell walking the streets of Berlin and reading the streets for aesthetic meaning. According to the architect's theory, a sea of posters publicizing *Variété* and cabaret could lose its purpose as advertising, transforming into a giant swirl of perpetually moving, colorful shapes like Fuller's dances. While it is impossible to prove if Endell ever saw Fuller's performances or encountered her posters during his walks, their affinities are apparent. Her depiction as literally a part of the dancing skyline and Endell's metropolitan dance text in the city bring their interpretation of urban movement and modernity much closer together, because their representations curiously and experimentally delve into each other's fields. Both his dance text and PAL's poster demonstrate the indistinguishability of dance and urban space and activate the agency of the nonhuman.

In addition to posters of Fuller that covered the Parisian urban space, the dancer commissioned the Loïe Fuller theater to be built by Henri Sauvage (with amendments by Pierre Roche) as part of the World Exposition in 1900. Situated along the Rue de Paris among theaters and cabarets, her building served as a museum and a theater in one structure, again, occupying a liminal space. Its design embraced her serpentine dance's art nouveau style with a swirling fabric pattern and ornamentation; atop the theater stood a statue of the costumed Fuller with her arms outstretched as if to take flight (fig. 3). Brandstetter notes that "In its integration of construction and ornament it resembled August Endell's Atelier Elvira (Munich 1898). Every detail reflected the spirit of Loïe Fuller's dances; the pavilion seemed to translate her serpentine dance into architecture."[86] His ornamental dragon, and stylistically by extension his dance text, share affinities with Fuller's serpentine

Fig. 4. The June 9, 1893, issue of the journal *Le Mirliton* cover image by Theophile-Alexandre Steinlen depicting a man, who might be a flâneur.

building and reflect its spirit. Both focus less on function and more on the affective opulence, seductive fervor, and fantastical imagination of their creations. Thus, not only does Fuller's theater become the architectural structure of a serpentine dance, but it brings her performance aesthetics and overall impressionism closer to Endell's aesthetic theory. Architecture, dance, and space collide and form a posthumanist restructuring.

Situated as a featured building at the fair, the pavilion and, by extension her dancing, become a part of the microcosm of a densely populated urban area, further extenuated by the blurring of boundaries concerning performance spaces and the performativity of the individual. According to Albright,

> No longer were performers found only on theatrical stages or in the circus. At the dawn of celebrity culture and the ascendance of the dandy, both men and women became increasingly aware of their public personas [. . .] By bringing the theatricality of electrical lighting out into the streets and constructing an endless variety of fantasy sets to the average pedestrian, the Paris exposition of 1900 built an enormous stage upon which anyone could play. The whole experience bordered on the phantasmagoric.[87]

Similar to the *Varieté* sphere but on a much larger scale, the exhibition created a performative stage both inside and outside the urban space. The invention and wide use of electricity, functioning as an alternative illumination to the sun, allowed the modern city dweller to not only bask in the amazement of Fuller's indoor variety performances, but to bring her whirling theater out into the streets. Thus, electricity extended her visual reach to more easily mesh itself among the other exhibition buildings and more prominently into the urban landscape. Much like PAL's poster and the *Varieté* space, both Fuller and the artistic representations of her situate the dancer as not only moving *in* the city but also *with* the city space, by imbuing it with her energy: thus, making the dancing body and space indistinguishable. Similar to the way Endell illuminates the changing dimensions of "In Front of the Café" using the sun, the Currents describe the numerous ways in which Fuller's pavilion is illuminated:

> The completed Loïe Fuller Theater, a strange little building, had an air of narcissism about it, totally devoted as it was to the dancer and her reflection in art. Its facade was wrapped in folds of plaster that called to mind her draperies in motion, and it was topped by a life-size statue, which looked like a great bird about to take flight. All this was the work of Pierre Roche, and so were the curved bas-relief figures of two dancing girls that entwined the entrance. At night the white stucco exterior became ablaze with light, shining up from below. Inside, during the day, sunlight steaming through stained-glass windows gave a kaleidoscopic effect. In the evening, a similar effect was created by electric lights. The stage was quite small, with the auditorium having room for only two hundred seats.[88]

Much like Fuller's dances, which demanded the integration of light to create their magic, this depiction emphasizes the use of illumination to bring life to the theater. Natural light during the day created a kaleidoscopic image reminiscent of the *Varieté* setting as well as the abstract metropolis in PAL's poster; both of which, in general, represent the perceptive mode of an urban individual around 1900. These different lighting effects also point to the performative nature of a static building. Despite its fixed presence, the flowing, swirling design purposefully creates the illusion of movement. Thus, the theater's facade coupled with the contrasting lighting effects combine to form different "dances," which not only perform but emanate into and become part of the organic city space and continue the paradoxical and posthumanist vacillation between the natural and artificial. To connect Endell and Fuller once again: while his architectural view of "In Front of the Café" turns into a vibrant metropolitan dance text, Fuller's dancing inspired the construction of her theater; they share an affinity in wanting to create representations in comparable fields and in interacting with the metropolis.

Sauvage and Roche were not the only architects commissioned to create a structure for the 1900 exposition; Endell was to have completed his own. After finishing the Elvira photography studio in Munich, he wrote to his cousin Kurt Breysig on April 13, 1899, telling him about his next commissioned project: "a pavilion of iron and glass" for the World's Fair in Paris, for an "iron foundry in Luxemburg."[89] He was excited about the pay and the new work, which consisted of an "iron construction artistically formed on a 7x7-meter base, 12–14 meters high. Something stupendous could be made [. . . .] I often thought I was all finished. Now that [feeling] has gone away. I have regained confidence.'"[90] However, by December 1899 it appeared that the commission had failed, and the structure was never realized. If Endell's pavilion had been built, he might even have met Fuller; given her connection with architects and artists of the time, it's a distinct possibility. Nonetheless, Brandstetter's observation of Fuller's theater, and by extension Fuller's actual dancing, show that she was stylistically closer to Endell's aesthetic project. Its pervasive integration into the urban landscape provides a lens for also viewing early-twentieth-century dance. Like Fuller's *Varieté* performances, PAL's poster of her, and Endell's "In Front of the Café," Sauvage's and Roche's Fuller Theater is deeply rooted in and actively engaged with its metropolitan environment, to the extent that its dancing movement becomes indistinguishable from its surroundings. Dance, architecture, and space essentially become one and the same as dehierarchialized entities.

In an essay related to the conceptual construction of the Fuller Theater,

Simmel in "The Berlin Trade Exhibition" (1896) theoretically analyzes the transience of exhibitions. Structurally similar to the *Varieté* in which short acts of disparate themes were strung together, expositions seem to also densely pack as much representation as possible into an object or set of objects. His essay focuses particularly on the physical structures built specifically for these world exhibitions, which were not necessarily constructed to last:

> [T]he imagination of the architect is freed from the stipulation of permanence, allowing grace and dignity to be combined in their own measure. [. . .] [T]he attraction to the transient forms its own style and, even more characteristically, does this from material that doesn't appear as if it was intended for temporary use. And in fact the architects of our exhibitions have succeeded in making the opposition to the historical ideal of architecture not a matter of absurdity or lack of style; rather they have taken the point last reached in architecture as their starting-point, as if only this arrangement would allow its meaning to emerge fully against a different coloured background and yet be seen as part of a single tradition.[91]

Instead of negatively viewing the transience of architectural structures at a world exposition, Simmel embraces the situation, which creates a unique opportunity for unbridled creativity. These academically and historically divergent designs, in retrospect, are sometimes even remembered better than permanent structures. Through their outlandish imagery and striking descriptions they create an enduring mythology. In fact, the idea of freeing the creative spirit from tradition resonates strongly with Endell's and Fuller's focus on their work's overall impression—a prominent effect of Nietzsche's influence. Perhaps we mourn the loss of Fuller's theater and Endell's ornamental dragon because of their aesthetic daringness. We are compelled to either imagine how they would look had they survived until the present day, or to rely on photographs. Stacy Hand notes of this phenomenon, "There is a certain irony to the fact that the Elvira photography studio in Munich is only known through photographs."[92] Since the structures are no longer standing, we can only rely on memory, which in turn seems to make them more memorable than standing structures. In many ways, the sentiments of transient architectural structures fit strikingly with conceptions of dance as a transient phenomenon and Schulze's idea of the *Erinnerungstext*.[93] Theorists often view dance as a medium that lacks permanence due to its fleeting, ephemeral nature as a process.[94] Susan Foster writes that dance's transient quality could be characterized as disappearing just "as rapidly as it presented itself."[95] And for André Lepecki, "from the moment the question of dance's presence began to be formulated as loss and temporal paradox, dance was transformed into hauntology and taxidermy—and choreography cast as mourning."[96] While Fuller's theater was always meant to be temporary, it did stand as an aesthetic object in the urban landscape, to be admired and observed. However, after a dance like Fuller's is performed and experienced by an audience as a material object, it disappears at the conclusion. The dance only survives as fragmented memories and in other representations, or *Erinnerungstexte*[97]: film, photography, dance text. Photographs or discourse can merely recount the decadent exterior of the Elvira photo atelier. Like Endell's architectural phenomenology and dance text, Fuller's swirling theater inches closer toward the realm of dance—given its attempt to create an impression similar to her actual dances, and its transient existence.

Even though Endell and Fuller never met, their *movement environments* and similar backgrounds allowed them to share comparable modern movement aesthetics and conceptualizations of space. They entered their respective fields not through a traditional academic route, but rather with a focus on an overall impression, privileging the feelings and emotions perceived from viewing either their performances or architectural structures. Furthermore, Endell's works—the asymmetrical, ornamental facade of the Elvira photography atelier and his modernist miniatures in "Beauty of the Metropolis," particularly "In Front of the Café"—not only demonstrate modernist, architectural phenomenology, they create a metropolitan dance text and thereby engage with Fuller's performances. Her uncanny *Varieté* acts, her artistic representations in PAL's poster, and her own theater exhibit her engagement with architecture. They also underscore how her queer existence manifested itself in new aesthetically modern and uncanny objects. Fuller's and Endell's curiosity and desire to move beyond their own fields of knowledge meant that both figures delved inadvertently and fruitfully into the terrain of the other. Moreover, their work depicts dancers who not only dance in the urban space, but most importantly, whose movement and bodies become absorbed and dance with the cityscape. The urban space is first rendered visible through movement and granted agency to interact with the dancing body, highlighting the activeness of the nonhuman and creating a new ethical space. While dance theorizing by Laban and Louppe and modern movement practices have astutely been aware of the active and affective nature of space as partner, this chapter has brought this to light in a German studies context.

In Endell's case, his dancers create another spatial entity through their dancing. In Fuller's depictions, her performances not only become part of the *Varieté* setting, but represent the changing environment and perception of the individual. PAL's poster depicts Fuller physically joining the expressionistic representation of a city skyline, and the Loïe Fuller Theater dances as a physical structure in the Parisian streets. Reflecting a flâneur-like gaze on the aesthetic potential of the moving body in the urban space, Endell's and Fuller's conceptual ideas and artistic representations of dance and architecture interpenetrate with the episodic unexpectedness of urban encounters and contribute to the genre of the metropolitan dance text.

Three

From Spectator to Practitioner

Developing Harry Graf Kessler's Queer Dance Aesthetic

The diarist Harry Graf Kessler eagerly documented his experiences with various dance forms in European metropolises around 1900. Growing cities like Berlin and Paris functioned as cultural centers of intellectual and creative exchange, forming inspiring melting pots and social meeting places.[1] These metropolitan hubs attracted many artists, such as the pioneers of American modern dance and the Ballets Russes. In contrast to nineteenth-century balls and ballets, their liberating dances greatly influenced how Kessler perceived the early-twentieth-century dance movement. As a representative of a new generation, he wanted to understand the emerging experimental dance and to begin a written aesthetic discourse concerning the new movement form.

Nietzsche's philosophy played an influential role in encouraging Kessler as an evolving individual, an *Übergangsmensch*,[2] to develop his own perception. Similarly, the poetry of French symbolist Henri de Régnier inspired Kessler's reflection on developing his own aesthetic sense focusing on perceiving common objects and events anew—devoid of their traditional meaning—while establishing a subjective connection with them. Kessler began putting his theory into practice when he attended social balls, which, for him, assumed a modern, aesthetic meaning beyond that of the nineteenth-century tradition. Kessler also started to theorize about a *Tanzrhythmus* that would speak to the senses of spectators, bringing them to a mystical level of consciousness. As balls continued, dancers from around 1900 such as Loïe Fuller, Ruth St. Denis, Isadora Duncan, and Vaslav Nijinsky from the Ballets Russes began touring metropolises in Europe demonstrating experimental movements, ranging from the free and flowing to the fragmented and angular body, from animalistic to human characteristics, from human to abstract materialism, and from masculine to feminine qualities. These avant-garde dance methods challenged the proper character of balls and ballets and fascinated Kessler, particularly the practices of St. Denis and Nijinsky. These two dancers engaged his developing aesthetics and queer identity, which helped him escape into an intellectual and creative realm. In this chapter, I argue first that based on Kessler's experience with nineteenth-century balls and then with the liberating dances of Fuller, St. Denis, and Nijinsky, his perception underwent a fundamental change, resulting in his refined aesthetic sensibilities, his intellectualization and eroticization of the dancing body. Second, I argue that these developments allowed him to conceptualize and collaborate in creating the dance *Josephslegende*, demonstrating his transformation from an outside observer into an active practitioner who infused a decidedly queer perspective in his piece. According to Penny Farfan, queerness was essential to modernism's ability, first, to thrive as a mode practiced on a stage by experimenting freely with texts, staging, music, and dance movement;[3] it helped modernism. Second, queerness created a space for everyday social interactions with other queer artists and intellectuals in the city. Queer performances opened up possibilities for imagined and critical contexts for creative individuals to develop their own identities.[4]

There are few published critical case studies on the aesthetic reception of early-twentieth-century dance from a single, developing, queer perspective—like that of the cosmopolitan flâneur Kessler—and this chapter help fills this gap. Rather than providing a purely historical background of dance at the time, this chapter describes critical discourse related to early-twentieth-century dance and recognizes the profound aesthetic effects of dance on intellectuals at the time, while also providing an alternative outlet for creative queer culture, as seen with Fuller in chapter 2. Furthermore, it sets the stage for the chapters to follow, regarding how the cosmopolitan city space, emerging dance forms, and dancers of the time influenced the writings of Rilke, Döblin, and Lasker-Schüler, and the films of Chomón and the Skladanowsky brothers.

Background of Harry Graf Kessler

On September 5, 1901, the poet Richard Dehmel explained to his friend Count Harry Graf Kessler, "You will write the memoirs of our times. That is the right path for you at this moment: you must get to know all people, in all circumstances, that mean anything. I envy our grandchildren because they will be able to read it."[5] Dehmel's comment essentially encapsulated Kessler's occupation as a diplomat and quintessential cosmopolitan gentleman. In Kessler's obituary from the 1938 émigré journal *Maß und Wert*, Annette Kolb depicted Kessler as the ultimate European because of his German, French, and English ancestry and upbringing. She praised not only "the sharpness and delicacy of his artistic sensitivity," but also his personality, which magnetically attracted the best and brightest—the intellectual elite—who formed his company wherever he went.[6] Kessler documented his life experiences in his meticulously recorded diaries on over 15,000 pages covering a fifty-seven-year period.[7] His comprehensive journals are a rich source of information about twentieth-century thought for scholars of art, literature, and politics by virtue not only of his differentiated insights, but because of his remarkable memory and his familiarity with a vast number of prominent people—estimated to be more than 40,000.[8]

Born in 1868, Kessler belonged to a generation—like the other artists and intellectuals in this study—that fervently read Nietzsche: "Within us a secret messianism originates. The deserts, which belong to each messiah, were in our hearts; and suddenly from above the desert Nietzsche appeared like a meteor."[9] Nietzsche's ideas changed Kessler's morals and forever influenced his developing intellectual thought. Kessler poetically depicted this drastic transformation:

> Our generation was certainly the first one that was deeply influenced by Nietzsche. At first our feeling was a mixture of pleasant fright and marveling admiration in front of the monstrous fireworks of his spirit, in which one piece after the other of our moral ammunition went up in smoke. The raw climate of the century necessitates another healthiness and hardship of the soul instead of the soft and romantic, German Biedermeier. The balance between human and social environment, which had destroyed the cataclysm of the nineteenth century, had to be established again through humanities' adapting to the new world, which more radically repressed the older one.[10]

In a series of striking images, Kessler illustrated the transformation from the older into the newer generation whose weapons and protective armament go up in smoke. Like Endell with his overtly ornamental dragon on the Elvira photo atelier or Fuller with her mesmerizing *Serpent Dance*, Kessler was eager to unleash his own creative potentiality. Leaving behind their past contentment, this generation became enthusiastic about the changing future, a key feature of the count's figure of Joseph in the libretto *Josephslegende*.

Furthermore, Nietzsche was also interested in dance, which surfaced in many of his philosophical works. Pervading ideas from *The Birth of Tragedy* (*Die Geburt der Tragödie*), in which Nietzsche expressed unleashing humanity's Dionysian side, could also notably characterize Kessler's thought:

> Humanity expresses itself by singing and dancing as a member of a higher community. It has unlearned how to walk and speak and is on its way dancing in the air. Enchantment speaks from its gestures. Much like how the animals speak and the earth bears milk and honey, something supernatural tinges out of humanity.[11]

As we will see, Kessler's experience with the dances of Fuller, St. Denis, and Nijinsky opened his thought and elevated the count's intellect to a mystical level. Departing from Apollonian orderliness, Nietzsche cast a spell on Kessler and his generation, who reveled in the thought of profound affect.

Kessler's Developing Aesthetics

In 1893 Kessler started his traineeship in the Amtsgericht Spandau and delved into Berlin salons and balls. Originally based on eighteenth-century French models, the societal events of Wilhelmine Germany established their own form. Unable to continue due not only to the war but to other emerging forms of entertainment, such as cinemas, cafés, and nightclubs, the salons soon vanished.[12] As long as they continued salons and balls still, however, provided the quickest avenue for a young, sociable gentleman to establish contact with other diplomats, politicians, and artists in a city setting.[13]

Kessler's first exposure to dance occurred in the context of social balls—creating space for both the nobility and the bourgeoisie to gather: "The nineteenth-century ballroom was the perfect setting in which ladies and gentlemen, attired in the latest fashions, could exercise their considerable dancing abilities and, more importantly, demonstrate their mastery of polite behavior, which was required for acceptance into genteel society."[14] These social dances were not seen as critically engaging artworks, but rather as a measure of whom one knew. Balls gauged one's ability to "perform" a role from an etiquette manual.[15] In other words, "conduct was [. . .] codified during this period."[16] Despite adhering to these strict codes, dances like the waltz and polka also led to repetitious movement and contact, opening a "libidinous reservoir."[17] Kessler associated this with a freeing of the body, and he wanted to delve into the realm of being able to "feel," to sense aesthetically, and to think intellectually about dance.

Additionally, Kessler acquired "the ability to view social events as a detached observer whose sensitive eye could make fine distinctions in gestures and costumes and whose imagination could provide the smallest nuance with an abstract meaning."[18] In other words, by objectifying his surroundings, Kessler began to obtain the aptitude of the flâneur—less like the nineteenth-century Parisian type in the streets and more in everyday situations, creating his own unique meaning of observing moving bodies from the perspective of a particularly dancerly aesthetic.[19] Therefore, on a larger scale, to Endell in "The Beauty of the Metropolis," while pedestrians and architectural structures transformed into dynamic shapes and colors, to Kessler ball guests and their costumes morphed into aesthetic objects on a smaller scale. Nonetheless, like the *Varieté* performances and architectural structures of Fuller, the ball belonged to the fabric of a perpetually changing city. While developing this new ability to see, Kessler started to theorize aesthetically about the objects and stimuli around him. He became interested in developing an aesthetics in which a phenomena's beauty was not defined by society, but rather by a feeling originating in the observer.[20] Of course, Endell's own architectural phenomenology and Fuller's dance aesthetics focused on the overall impression and emotions rather than being based on academic knowledge—both in a similar vein to Kessler's conceptualization.[21] Furthermore, the count's desire to acquire this lens can be attributed to his queerness: since he was not there to take part in the marriage market, he tended to be rather bored at balls, and therefore needed an aesthetic outlet to explore his creativity.

While Kessler did attend numerous balls, given his highly social nature and aristocratic status, the movement form of ballet was also on his mind. Academic ballets originated from the aristocratic court and highlighted graceful steps and orderly movements in geometrical patterns; thus, they were representative of the court's political life and social hierarchy. When it became passé for male dancers to perform aristocratic principles on stage, these values were relegated almost solely to performances by women; as a result, female dancers were largely subjected to the male gaze and became further disenfranchised.[22] For example, romantic ballets such as *La Sylphide* maintained a heterosexual male perspective of obtaining the elusive object of desire: a sylph. While the protagonist James performed traditionally masculine ballet movements such as high jumps and virtuosic pirouettes, the nameless sylph—wearing a white, romantic tutu symbolizing the immaculate—embodied the *femme fragile* whose dance steps in pointe shoes exhibited a lofty and ethereal effortlessness. However, during the late nineteenth century, ballet went into decline. Alexandra Kolb suggests that around 1900 German and Austria did not have a prominent ballet company; theaters restaged historical ballets such as *Giselle* at second-rate quality, reducing their serious and elite status to "light and often erotically infused entertainment."[23] As an *Übergangsmensch*, Kessler found himself in this environment straddling the decline of ballet and the rise of both the *Varieté* and early-twentieth-century dance.

In attempting to expound his new thought, Kessler first published the essay "Henri de Régnier," engaging with the poetry of the French symbolist of the same name in the 1895 issue of *PAN*, a modernist art and literary magazine. In the beginning of the essay he described how "compared to a dream, reality is shallow"[24] ("im Vergleich zum Traum ist die Wirklichkeit schal"[25]). By contrasting reality with dreams, he demonstrated how fantasy could lead to a freeing boundlessness. Kessler further characterized Régnier: "his perceptions, his drives, his instincts are not his individual property, but rather presupposed by his ancestors or from his surroundings."[26] Kessler implied that Régnier's feelings and instincts were not a product of his own discovery, but rather were shaped by his social environment. Lacking his own unique way of seeing, the French poet perpetuated the meaning of how others sensed and interpreted the world. Resorting to a "turning away from the world," ("Abkehr von der Welt,"), Kessler did not want to turn his back on the world, but rather to reevaluate it with a "refined sensibility" ("verfeinerte Sensibilität"[27]). Endell professed a similar disengagement with the current world and sought to perceive it more aesthetically, allowing the overall impression to penetrate the viewer's emotions. The architect desired a rethinking of Berlin as being beautiful, instead of trying to change the city itself. In both Endell's and Kessler's cases, once the mind and senses had been attuned to this new perception, they could gain more freedom while creating more meaning.[28] The influential ideas of Nietzsche and Régnier together demonstrated key aspects of Kessler's changing aesthetic, which were enhanced in interpreting both everyday motions and dance movement.

Before publishing in *PAN*, Kessler used his diaries as an "idea workshop for the essay" ("Ideenwerkstatt für den [Régnier] Essay"), furthering his aesthetic inquiries.[29] In an entry on February 14, 1895, Kessler's thoughts entered the flâneur's aesthetic realm, abstracting from the utility of everyday movement and creating personal meaning:

One wanted to declare the raw and characterless movements of the actor or the leapfrogs from ballet as art.[30] For my part the way in which a girl places her feet while dancing or how a young officer holds his horse between his thighs gives me a joy that, in this way, none of the so-called orthodox works of art can. I find in such movement, of which a drawing, for example—even done by the Japanese—can only provide a snapshot, a secret beauty, an unconscious style, which enchants me more than all the perfection of fixed forms.[31]

While Kessler's description brings together traditional dance and theater, he applies a different lens addressing pure movement. He begins with conventionally aestheticized movement forms like ballet, but shifts his focus to smaller, erotic details: the girl's feet while dancing might point to a foot fetish, and the officer clutching a horse between his legs points to homoerotic or even phallic imagery. By focusing less on the entire human body and concentrating more on pure, momentary movement of the extremities, these two depictions abstract from the event's utility. His fixation on the erotic quality of these body parts alludes to a sexualization he would detect in St. Denis's dancing and later thematicize in his *Josephslegende*. Here one can observe the aesthetic ideas that Kessler developed in the Régnier essay: recalibrating the mind to see objects and events with fresh eyes while establishing new emotional connections with them. Movements—like the girl's feet and the officer clutching the horse—resonated more with Kessler than the more traditional dance forms. The "unconscious style" refers to his aesthetization of everyday movements since the girl and officer do not realize they are performing beautiful movements for the count. His depiction strikingly resembles Endell's metropolitan dance text "In Front of the Café," in which seemingly banal pedestrians turn into impressionistic dancing swirls of liveliness. The former utilitarian signification of pedestrians, feet, and thighs is erased, replaced by boundless aesthetic and erotic meaning.

That he is enchanted much more by movement than by the static form of drawing or photography exemplifies his desire to move into a different medium; we will see the same impulse with Lasker-Schüler's drawings. Furthermore, as we see in the next chapter, Rilke perceives the everyday stimuli similarly when he interacts with Rodin's work and depicts the isolated body parts of the *Veitstänzer*. Despite being captivated by his new perceptual mode, Kessler struggled with his "orthodox," traditional aesthetics of theater and ballet. On the brink of discovering a "secret" aesthetic current—which his character Joseph in *Josephslegende* would later embody—the count continued to push the tide even further through his social interactions with dancers and artists in the city.

Kessler as a Flâneur of Social Balls

Kessler regularly watched and participated in social balls during the 1890s. On February 4, 1894, he described a masked ball in the Palast Hotel:

> I at first dressed up as black-and-white Pierrot, later in a red topcoat with white court shoes. Danced until five in the morning.[32] Lovely costumes: Frau v. Mutzenbecher as a black and white Pierrette, the Greindl lady as Marie Antoinette, the old Fürst Radziwill as a Bedouin, Koscielski in black top coat, court shoes, red stockings and a tie, Peñalver as a gypsy, Loën as a pharaoh, Michel Königsmarck, Lafaille u Winterfeldts as cooks with electrically-glowing noses.[33]

In addition to describing upper-class society, he emphasizes not only their elaborate and sometimes Orientalizing garb but his superfluous need for two outfits. Dancing in costume brings sophistication and playful anonymity, even though he can still recognize each individual. Kessler's journal is littered with shorter entries describing his experience at balls, especially on weekends. These events played a large role in his social life and functioned as an open *Schauplatz* because he could talk with people, watch others, and be observed himself. Similar to the environment at a *Varieté* like the Folies-Bergère, ball attendees themselves were the main attraction. While Kessler's activity at balls affectively applies a performative lens in a more private yet socially enclosed space, his flâneuresque perspective also relates more to an aesthetic view of the metropolis. Matthias Bauer illustrates the performative, urban space when he described the modern city as:

> A place where the collective attention of observers focuses, because at this location something new happens and manages to be viewed. To speak of scenes of collective attention does not only imply that there is more than one viewer because the observed event happens in an open and accessible space. Rather such a scene incorporates the coordination of gazes and gestures, actions and reactions, so that a performative dimension ensues. Since the act of knowing—that one's actions virtually occur on a stage—is also brought to consciousness, one as an agent—even the passive viewer—remains watched as well. However,

the observers know that they are present at a performance playing a role as part of a staging that demonstrates, exemplifies and manifests something.[34]

Bauer brings out the modern tendency of being acutely aware of one's surroundings and observing that what could appear on stage could also happen literally anyplace. Thus, the city transforms into a constant *Schauplatz*. His observations address the performative aspects of the citizen's environment, because observers often have a vested interest in all the phenomena around them. Unlike a traditional performance with clearly demarcated lines between audience and performer, the modern individual takes part in the action, becoming involved by default. While Bauer's interactive web of connections relates more to the observer's experience in the metropolis, Kessler's view still retains these attributes in the ball setting.

The count, however, desired an intellectual outlet that would allow his senses to observe his surroundings anew, as demonstrated in the Régnier essay. While observing people, he not only noticed the performative dimensions of their interactions, but he acquired an aesthetic eye by abstracting from the guests' socializing and dancing, much as the flâneur Endell did with the pedestrians and architectural structures in the streets of Berlin. On November 26, 1897, Kessler described a casual acquaintance—Asta Freifrau von Pachelbel-Gehag-Ascheraden, the wife of estate entailment head and chamberlain Carl Freiherr von Pachelbel-Gehag-Ascheraden—who liked dancing for others:

> Afterwards went to Berlin with the Pachelbels; she goes and leaves again from Rathenow. She's been dancing for 15 years as often as she can and doesn't shy away from exertion; she certainly looks for beautiful women and allows herself to be admired; maybe to make her husband jealous and also perhaps to receive confirmation from gallants concerning her beauty since she questions it.[35]

Kessler's depiction clearly demonstrates the dance's performative aspects based on the woman's demeanor. By using movement both to make her own husband jealous and to affirm her beauty, Pachelbel's solo reminds one of Fuller's and St. Denis's emancipatory dances, which presented liberating movement foreign to German audiences. As Bauer had mentioned, the boundaries of this dance are also lost as the onlookers are implicated in the performance: Pachelbel, her husband, the women, and Kessler himself become "dancers." Such a constellation will be brought more to the fore when we consider Rilke's *Veitstänzer* in the next chapter. Nevertheless, Kessler's reading of her dance utilizes his analytical abilities, which he did not engage during the earlier balls. The count is interested in the way in which Pachelbel could become her own individual—free from the dance etiquette books. At the masked ball, he merely described the attendees, their attire, and the dancing taking place. During Pachelbel's dance however, Kessler presents his own reading regarding the purpose of dance—still within the social context—and demonstrates his awakened interests through her freer dance. Instead of belonging to a ballet company and following the choreography of a heterosexual, male director, she dances on her own accord an as empowered woman.

Kessler's affinity to moving bodies in public, coupled with his desire to see less traditional styles of dance, manifested itself on February 8, 1898, while attending a grand court ball in Berlin:

> The Grand Duchess of Hessen stuck out from the rest again, perversely beautiful in a gold-worked brocade sheath, embroidered thickly with violet jet pearls.[36] She resembles a *bayadére* [Indian temple dancer]. The suggestive way she pulls her head and upper body back when she stops dancing; but all the while, even in the most extreme lasciviousness of her movements, she never appears inelegant. She is truly an enchanting creature.[37]

Kessler observes the Grand Duchess of Hessen's resemblance to an exotic, Orientalized Indian temple dancer as she notoriously flaunts her flashy attire. She does not fit into mainstream ball society in which, according to one etiquette book: "To be eccentric in dress, or even to be unusual, is impossible to her, as it would be, of course, painful, if she has delicate sensibilities."[38] Additionally the duchess's body movements do not exemplify etiquette rules, which require "dignity of carriage"[39] and would denounce a head "swinging to the right and left."[40] The duchess knowingly challenges these traditions and at the same time correspondingly attracts Kessler's attention.

His fascination particularly with the female dancing body can be partially attributed to what Brett Farmer termed "queer sublimity": "diva worship emerges here as a practice of resistant queer utopianism: [. . .] the transcendence of a limiting heteronormative materiality and the sublime reconstruction, at least in fantasy, of a more capacious, kinder, queerer world."[41] This might seem to particularly be the case with Kessler, since open homosexuality was against the law in Wilhelmine Germany. He would practice his intimate expression in his private diary and within his circle of friends and acquaintances. Female dancers had been generally relegated to the heterosexual male gaze, and the queer gaze directed at women's performances could work to create an idealistic, imagined world for Kessler to inhabit. From a postcolonial perspective, however, his depiction exoticizes this "enchanting creature" as a *bayadére* and others her body and presentation. Farmer draws from traditional ideas of Western romanticism—a delirious feeling of religious transcendence that goes beyond experience and cognition—and connects it to queerness: a "categorical rupture, a breaching of conventional subjective boundaries that encounters and imagines the obscene or excluded otherness of discursive normativity."[42] In this vein, romanticism shares many tropes with modernism, to which Farfan argues queerness contributed greatly. Kessler's viewing of Pachelbel and the grand duchess awakens the possibility that the idolatry wasn't directed at just one female dancer, but many other performers. Such an emergence allowed other queer observers to embrace this sense of emancipation.

Like Pachelbel, the duchess moves with an erotic freeness as demonstrated by her throwing her head and upper body back as she dances. Dance scholar Gabriele Brandstetter recognizes this bending backward as *cambrure*, tracing its origins to the dancing maenads, the female followers of Dionysus.[43] On ancient Greek vases the maenads were often depicted in a similar back-bent position, which represents an irrational, uncontrollable hysteria. Brandstetter notes a corresponding development concerning solo female dancers at the turn to the twentieth century, who also performed variations on the *cambrure* during their dances: Isadora Duncan, Ruth St. Denis, Grete Wiesenthal, and Mary Wigman.[44] Aware of her free, natural body, the grand duchess liberates herself from the stifling corset. Kessler is enchanted by the duchess' attire and in particular by her seductive movements. She similarly practices the fashionable late-nineteenth- and early-twentieth-century obsession of Orientalism, which would capture Kessler's attention in St. Denis's dancing.

Following his observation of the grand duchess and further developing his view of dance, Kessler published the essay *"Kunst und Religion"* (1899) in *PAN*'s fifth issue. One of his arguments focuses on the effect of dance on the senses:

> The dance joins the internal state to the powerful sensation of bodily muscles and nerves. [. . .] The dance rhythm does not aim for a certain feeling like beauty of joy, rather dance elevates only particular emotions to which the soul is most strongly drawn, toward strength

and clarity and shapes itself according to the sensations of the body. Therefore, dance is able to house every shade of personality carrying it away into abundant feelings from beat to beat to the unattainableness of mysticism and love.[45]

Kessler notes the power of dance on the observer's entire body. The dance's rhythm does not lead to a single emotional response, it continues based on the sensations and perceptions of the spectator, strikingly echoing Endell's architectural phenomenology and Fuller's impressionistic approach to interpreting her dances. Kessler believes that this *Tanzrhythmus* echoes throughout the dance. Indeed, his idea of reaching beyond the bounds of reality correlates with Nietzsche's thoughts on how humans could sound "something supernatural" ("etwas Übernatürliches") while dancing and singing.[46] The duchess's aura intensifies Kessler's appetite for more dance, causing him to develop theories about movement and rhythm in his essay. Her performance corresponds to Régnier's influence on the count in that it both explores a new realm of movement and fosters the ability to aesthetically perceive stimuli anew. "*Kunst und Religion*" also echoes queer sublimity because of their related religious connotations. Kessler's experiences of perceiving particularly while watching female dancers perpetually whets his appetite to see more performances. By seeing them dance, he would temporarily escape the hegemonic heteronormativity of the ball scene and enter an unexplored and sensual, imagined realm, one to which he would eventually contribute creatively.

Loïe Fuller: Kessler's Intellectual Abstraction

Loïe Fuller and other dancers like Ruth St. Denis began the movement away from the ballet aesthetic and into the "free dance."[47] Since dance in the United States resisted experimentation due to its "legacy of Puritan anti-theatrical prejudice,"[48] these early-twentieth-century dancers laid their roots in Central Europe, particularly in Germany, planting the germ that later became *Ausdruckstanz*—a dance based on physical movement that represented feelings.[49] While the previous chapter presented the background on Fuller's movement aesthetics, here I show Kessler's experience of watching her dancing.

Although he first saw Fuller on February 29, 1892, in New York while traveling around the world, his next encounter with her proved more memorable.[50] Kessler and his friend Henry van de Velde, the Belgian *Jugendstil* architect, became reacquainted with Fuller's dancing during her performance in Berlin on December 7, 1901. Kessler detailed her performance:

> In the evening went with Van de Velde to see Sada Yacco and Loïe
> Fuller. Van de Velde quite accurately depicts Loïe Fuller: This is the
> realization of everything we have sought with Neo Impressionism.
> In connection with the small story line, which forms the basis of the
> dance (A burning woman in sunlight): I would like to know if this
> is the beginning or the end of this artwork. In short, it is complete,
> and yet it seems to me that there would still be a possibility for fur-
> ther development. Sado Yacco played the geisha and kesa[51] again with
> complete tenderness and command of her artform.[52]

Van de Velde's observation implies that neo-impressionism remains a concept seeking actualization, and Fuller's dance embodies the fulfillment of his
imagination's wish. His and Kessler's agreement on naming her the realization of the emerging style demonstrates their incessant desire to match a
concept with a live instance. Developed by Georges Seurat and Paul Signac,
neo-impressionism's pointillism technique reacted to impressionism's direct
color mixture on the palette or canvas. Pointillism used primary colors in the
form of small, defined dots to create scenes with scientific exactness.[53] Van
de Velde refers to Seurat's later work, such as *Le Cirque*, depicting an acrobat,
a ringmaster, and a woman on a prancing horse, and to Seurat's emphasis
on dynamic, linear expression. Seurat was probably inspired by the famous
poster designer Jules Chéret, who had depicted Loïe Fuller in various renderings. Van de Velde and Kessler must have also been keenly aware of how
Fuller's costume and movement style resembled the architectural form of
Jugendstil, as both dancer and art nouveau style utilized curves to create an
organic, natural appearance. The style was also van de Velde's hallmark, as
evidenced in his custom furniture for Kessler.[54]

Additionally, Kessler notices a prominent quality in early-twentieth-
century dances: the lack of plot. Without a solid, developed narrative, Fuller's
dance embodies the development of an organic idea. She demonstrates perpetual motion instead of the consciously held poses of nineteenth-century
ballet. Rather than noticing her movement, Kessler portrays her as a woman
burning in sunlight: a poetic and even posthumanist abstraction, consistent
with his new aesthetic way of seeing. In much the same vein as Endell's perceptions, Kessler sees Fuller being "painted" by different colors of light and
tries to find a verbal description corresponding to the dance. The count no
longer sees large draping material being waved around with a colored light
projection, but rather a transformed, impressionistic image.

Although Kessler is preoccupied with characterizing Fuller's dance, he notices Sada Yacco's delicate and subtle movement. In her autobiography *An Unfinished Life*, Ruth St. Denis remarks that Yacco remained the "antithesis of the flamboyant, overblown exuberance" of "American acrobatics."[55] Renowned mostly as an actress, in her dances Yacco expressed both her theatrical ability and her exotic appeal.[56] While balls were generally characterized as entertaining social events that demanded little intellectual work—except for when Kessler watched the dances of Pachelbel and the grand duchess—Kessler and van de Velde read Fuller's dance with intrigue and productive confusion, which created a desire to experience more types of experimental movement. Kessler attested to his eagerness to thematicize Fuller's dance in his diary by both describing and interpreting the performance. Although her dance provided Kessler with a desired abstraction from reality, St. Denis's performances captivated him to an even greater degree.

Ruth St. Denis: Kessler's Intellectual and Erotic Fascination

While St. Denis was performing in Berlin in 1906, she not only mesmerized the general public but also Kessler, with whom she had close contact for about a month during her stay. Their short but fascinating bond marked the beginning of Kessler's deeper involvement with dance, which moved beyond basic observation. Born near Somerville, New Jersey, in 1879, St. Denis was brought up on the teachings of François Delsarte, who believed that movement could communicate emotion more adequately than language; thus her own choreography aligned with her dance movements, corresponding to an emotional state.[57] Like Fuller, she began as a skirt dancer, but later, according to an often-told and mythologized story, she realized her calling as a dancer through spiritual revelation: while on tour in 1904 with the DuBarry Company, she encountered a poster advertising Egyptian Deities cigarettes in a store window, which depicted Isis and ancient Egypt.[58] St. Denis's interests eventually shifted from Egypt to India[59] as she meticulously studied cultural artifacts through literary sources and photographs. However, with her American, white, middle-class, bourgeois background, she could not create authentic Indian culture.[60] Her cultural appropriation exemplified Edward Said's concept of Orientalism: a familiar-strange dichotomy in which the West interprets the East within an imagined geography as primitive, childlike, and mysterious.[61] During the late nineteenth and early twentieth century in American and Europe, the "exotic" came into vogue in high-art contexts, professing a utopian view of yearning for the splendor of classical civilization and offering "an antidote to the chaotic urban conditions that threatened the middle and upper classes."[62] Having used similar terminology to describe the grand duchess, Kessler fits in with this background, which helped shape his interpretation and description of St. Denis's dancing. On October 29, 1906, he relayed his experience of watching her:

> Wrote to Hofmannsthal about St. Denis, whom I saw on Saturday with Schröder.[63] I have now seen her again in one of her truly great things and have had the most powerful impression that dance as an art has ever given me. An Indian temple dance, completely naked, but nevertheless in a fairy-tale-like dress made of dark golden jewels. How the lines of the nude meld with the folds and its heavy grace, so that sometimes the robe and sometimes the body of the girl seem to disappear, and yet both are equally effective in their richness and grace; [it] is truly like a *bayadère*. The essence of the *bayadère*, consisting of just two poles: an animal-like beauty and mysticism, without any intermediate scale of intellectual or sentimental tones being present. The sexless divinity and the simple sexual woman, with the contrast heightening—with the greatest potency—the unified effect of both. She is an American, and it is very striking and subtle how she is able to combine the asexuality of her race with the almost animalistic, subhuman sexuality of the Oriental woman.[64]

Kessler considers her dance to be art rather than simple *Varieté*, thus pulling St. Denis into the more artistic ranks of early-twentieth-century dance and corresponding to the aim of her entire aesthetic project. His description describes the flashy costumes of *Varieté* and also expresses the qualities of a higher art. Similar to Fuller's *Serpent Dance* as described by Brandstetter, St. Denis's performance also retains qualities of abstract materiality yet still expresses some feminine sexuality. Entering the realm of the posthumanist, Fuller's image could be recognized as a woman dancing, but her long, draping costume drew more attention to the dance's material significance and less to her gender. Although Kessler interprets St. Denis's dance in a similar way, he describes her body paradoxically as "completely naked, but nevertheless in a fairy-tale-like dress" ("ganz nackt, aber doch in einem märchenhaften Kleid") and as "sexless divinity and the simple sexual woman" ("geschlechtslose Gottheit und blos-geschlechtliches Weib"). His depiction deliberately resists a clear representation because his mind constantly oscillates between these two oppositions, yet he feels strongly and perceives these sensations in correspondence with his own body. It seems that he, on the one hand, can see with a "male gaze,"[65] recognizing what could be erotic for a traditionally heterosexual man, but at the same time can disengage and recognize her dance depiction as abstractly material because of his queerness. St. Denis's dance makes him feel the *Tanzrhythmus* about which he theorized in "*Kunst und Religion.*" Kessler also calls her a *bayadère*, reminding us of his fascination with the Grand Duchess of Hessen and his penchant for Orientalized dances. Instead of falling completely prey to Orientalism, he designates her as having prudish American roots. Thus, he is not wholly seduced by her image, implying that her depiction is not authentic, but rather a vacillating hybrid of appropriated ideas. If the performance of the grand duchess begins his generalized diva worship, St. Denis's performance ignites and further catalyzes his growing aesthetic sensibilities and analytical abilities in an imagined queer space.

By viewing St. Denis's dance as a new art form that productively challenges his expectations of dance, Kessler is forced to reflect more often about his own experiences. In contrast to his rather short entries on Fuller, Kessler seems completely enraptured by St. Denis's performance as he tries to precisely articulate his sensual interpretation of her dance in a longer, more developed entry. Her dance's paradoxical representations express a level of abstraction, creating a less tangible idea. Seeing more early-twentieth-century dance and noting each dancer's particular movement style allows him to better read and interpret dance. St. Denis's dances allow him to openly exercise and experiment in a sensually queer and intellectual space, which further develops his identity.

Instead of remaining a quiet observer of dance, Kessler came into contact with St. Denis and learned about her movement aesthetics. His queer fandom evolves, therefore, from merely watching her performances to actually engaging her in conversations in artistic circles. On November 16, 1906, he wrote:

Miss Smedley invited me to dine with Ruth St. Denis in the Lyceum Club. Even dressed for a social occasion she has a very striking appearance: a very small head on a very long, slender body, flexible and erect like a riding crop. But above the still quite young face, appearing barely twenty-six or twenty-seven, almost gray hair. She says serious, deep things and then suddenly childish naïvetés. She says she would like to dress even the doormen in her theater in Indian costumes, so that the audience gets in the mood from the moment they enter. And she says that the repetition, the continual, monotonous repetition accounts for the power and magic of Oriental art, the patient, lulling, repetition, until the viewer forgets himself as if hypnotized and surrenders his spirit completely to the spirit of the artwork.[66]

Having been captivated by her performance, Kessler has little trouble seeking St. Denis's company, given his extensive connection with Berlin's artistic community. He leaps at the opportunity not only to satisfy his own curiosity but to begin his choreographic inquiries as a practitioner. Since he does not know St. Denis well—as the citation implies—Kessler can still only judge her body and movement. Likewise, his idea of her remains largely influenced by her stage aura and not necessarily by her personality. The count's impression of St. Denis's dualistic nature from her dancing also seems to permeate her appearance and personality—he notes the dancer's further polarities: young face vs. gray hair, and intellectual vs. naïve comments. Thus, he draws less of a distinction between her performance and her pedestrian aura. His observation is further bolstered when St. Denis desires that the doormen also be dressed in costume: this rather innocent remark, however, moves in the direction of life as dance and dance as life. Thus, while Loïe Fuller's theater penetrates the city as a dancing structure, on a smaller scale, St. Denis's comments suggest the power of dancing moving into the city.

St. Denis's desire for a theatrical atmosphere—the monotonous, repetitious ambience combined with oriental magic—demonstrates a prime example of Kessler's reverberating and trancelike *Tanzrhythmus*, in which the body perceived sensations based on the dance rhythms, which can be compared to the individual feeling associated with Endell's architectural phenomenology. St. Denis, like Fuller, provide Kessler with performances that had never been seen by a German audience.[67] These dances offer new stimuli to further the bounds of his perception, helping him to escape the everyday and further indulge in a privileged version of queer sublimity.

While balls and *Varieté* entertained audiences, St. Denis's dance hypnotized its attendees, arguably taking them to another level of consciousness—or to the "unattainableness of mysticism and love" ("Unerreichbaren der Mystik und Liebe"), as Kessler explains. When she wants the observer to give "his spirit completely to the spirit of the artwork" ("seine Seele ganz in die Seele des Kunstwerks"), St. Denis expects them to become part of the performance, creating a profound connection between them and establishing the dance rhythm. St. Denis's goal, therefore, is to create a hypnotic world—through her repetitive, lulling movement—which transcends the stage and involves the audience's empathy: much like the performances of Fuller and the work of Endell.

Kessler's conversation with St. Denis at the Lyceum Club continues:

> She speaks very clearly and precisely about her art. [. . .] But while inventing a new dance she must always wait for inspiration to get the details. "I am often very long over one thing, till I find exactly what I have in mind. I was two years over *Radha*. Because the moment you cut away from tradition, you have to be *all* yourself, or else you're a hybrid, you're nothing."[68]

Clearly, in her own speech, St. Denis tries to distinguish herself from the *Varieté* dancers with whom she performs; she wants to branch into the new modern dance by explicitly explaining to Kessler her choreographic method. He even mentions how she talks about her art—moving beyond the entertaining *Varieté* and into a newer form requiring deep reflection. Interestingly, she recognizes how, by cutting away from tradition, "you have to be all yourself, or else you're a hybrid, you're nothing." St. Denis implies that the only way to maintain individuality involves being completely new while abandoning the old. In a similar vein, Kessler's changing aesthetic—involving intellectual reflection as well as sexuality—upholds many of her sentiments about perceiving stimuli in a new way. However, in contrast to St. Denis, he seems to perpetually perceive and prize the hybridity in all of the performances of dancers around 1900.

As St. Denis performed more often in Berlin, Kessler's exposure to her dance intensifies, as does his queer diva worship. After another performance, he praises her even further, on November 18, 1906:

> Went with the Gerhart Hauptmanns and the Ludwig von Hofmanns to the matinee of Ruth St. Denis in the Theater des Westens. The moment when she awoke out of the lotus flower and stood up was like a spring. I have never seen an art that so completely radiates outward like budding flowers, soft green, and the fresh, pure April sky as her movements at that moment. She is the first great dancer, a genius of movement.[69]

Once again Kessler considers St. Denis's dancing as an art and not just a *Varieté* act. His personal conversations with her, in turn, make him more interested in her work. To feed his fascination he informs himself about her movement philosophy. By interpreting a moment in her dance as "like a spring" ("wie ein Frühling"), Kessler recognizes St. Denis's inclination toward the natural body. Freeing the nineteenth-century body from its stifling etiquette, corsets, and traditional gender depictions, dancers around 1900 could read their own bodies in a natural state, and they experimented without boundaries. One could therefore also interpret Kessler's desire to perceive his surroundings without preconceived meaning as a return to nature.

After comparing St. Denis to natural beauties, Kessler recalls a comment made by Gerhart Hauptmann's wife about St. Denis's dancing: "Grete Hauptmann said correctly that Otero [a Spanish dancer and courtesan; W.L.] has a flexible and beautiful body, but here [with St. Denis] you have the intellect as well, that can make something out of the material."[70] ("Die Grete Hauptmann sagte richtig, die Otero habe einen eben biegsamen, schönen Körper, aber hier komme der Intellekt dazu, der aus dem Material Etwas mache."[71]) Grete Hauptmann's comment embodies not only the essence of Kessler's aesthetic goal but also one of the purposes of modern dance as a whole. While a *Varieté* performance would only keep an audience member engaged for a short period, and the balls were places of amusement and social interaction, St. Denis's dances have proven to have longer-lasting, profound effects that demanded intellectual reflection on Kessler's part and incited further discourse in his journal.

After citing Grete Hauptmann's comment about St. Denis's dance engaging the intellect, Kessler continues by describing the ensuing balance yet constant play, which he experiences through his senses:

She danced at the end almost naked, without being either chaste or unchaste. She is both at the same time in the Greek way. She has the most beautiful back that you have seen, but during her dance it affects the eye and the sexual instinct so equally that she almost keeps the balance. Perhaps this is not psychologically accurate, but [there is] some such balance in which the naked sensuality is kept in check, or so I think. There are evidently whole categories of feelings that do not flow into sensuality in the narrowest sense (individual restraints) and that exert an anti-sexual attraction (diversion). This alternating between the different sensualities is perhaps the actual enjoyment of art. The instinct to save yourself from the one in the other [is] the most frequent motive behind creating art.[72] Sexual arousal and artistic pleasure: parallel conditions that replace each other; creating art of transition between the two, in which an equal status is alternatively sought.[73]

By watching the lotus dance, Kessler has not only derived new meaning by interpreting her dance as spring, but he examines his own senses and how his feelings change as a result of experiencing her dance. This process of first feeling and then analyzing these perceptions embodies Endell's architectural phenomenology. This entry typifies Kessler's diaries as an "idea workshop" ("Ideenwerkstadt"), demonstrating his desire to work through characterizing his senses in writing. Besides inspiring him to judge familiar objects and events anew, St. Denis's dance has a profound impact on his senses, bringing him to perceive both a "balance" ("Gleichgewicht") as well as an active play—"sexual arousal and artistic pleasure" ("Sexuelle Erregung und Kunstgenuss")—via his sensual faculties. Whereas before he had simply mentioned vacillation between contrasting qualities, now he characterizes them as a dynamic game that plays with his senses. Kessler would recognize a similar duality in Nijinsky's dances and thematicize it in his own libretto *The Legend of Joseph* (*Josephslegende*). Interestingly, he does not indulge himself completely in just one sense, the sexual, but rather finds a balance. He can both recognize the enjoyment of her dance and access his "libidinal reservoir" to a much greater extent than through the balls. St. Denis's dances awaken Kessler's perception of sexuality in art and opens up a new part of himself that was perhaps previously untapped—in order to explore his own sexuality and develop his queer identity. St. Denis's dance incites a dynamic process of sensual play and *Tanzrhythmus* that perpetually affects Kessler's feelings and engages his intellect. While Endell uses his *flâneuresque* perspective to perceive dance movement in the streets of Berlin, Kessler goes beyond mere observation. The city gives him the ability to develop his modernist aesthetic and maintain his cosmopolitan connections not only in the ball setting but among live performances and in critical conversations with St. Denis and his intellectual circle. Through his group of friends and intellectuals and her captivating performances, the count not only carves out a physically queer space, but also an intellectual space to develop his own queer aesthetics.

Furthermore, Kessler's developing aesthetics find profound resonance in St. Denis's performances and her own movement philosophies. His queer sublimity associated with her dances takes a step beyond being a mere observer and into the realm of more analytical discussion. Kessler's desire to see a balance between the sexual and the intellectual, embodied in St. Denis, represents his longing for his own developing queer identity, which he is able to realize in his collaboration with the Ballets Russes.

The Legend of Joseph: Kessler's Collaboration with the Ballets Russes

After his engaging meetings with St. Denis, Kessler's burning desire to work with dancers and to learn more about the process of collaboration reached a high point during his dealings with Sergei Diaghilev, artistic director of the Ballets Russes, and Diaghilev's lover and muse Vaslav Nijinsky. According to Karl Schlögel, Diaghilev wanted to create a cult of beauty cultivating men, not women, creating a homoerotic "Resonanzraum" (resonance chamber).[74] With music by Richard Strauss and set design by Léon Bakst, their work together resulted in the dance *The Legend of Joseph*. Kessler was not only able to exercise his queer fantasy of watching and idealizing dancers, he was able to work with highly influential queer artists.

On May 21, 1910, the *Vossische Zeitung* wrote a preview greatly anticipating the Ballets Russes:

> In the Theater of the West the first guest performance begins today with the great Russian Ballet at 8 o'clock. The most extraordinary aspect of this ensemble is the star: a man, barely 20 years young named Nijinsky—the most brilliant dancer not only of the Russian Theater but surely the strangest and most interesting dance artist of the present day. In regard to lightness, expressiveness, and flexibility none of the celebrated prima ballerinas of St. Petersburg and Moscow rival Nijinsky.[75]

This citation already notes the extraordinary and unique talent of the male dancer Nijinsky, whose prowess overshadows that of the ballerinas at the time. In contrast to a long-standing tradition of ballet, which always highlighted the female dancer, the Ballets Russes held Nijinsky's modern and virtuosic dancing in high regard.

Kessler enjoys watching male forms such as that of Nijinsky. Alex Ross comments, accordingly, on the count's sexuality:

> There were many tensions behind the calm exterior of the globe-trotting connoisseur. Kessler was attracted to men and made little attempt to conceal that attraction behind alliances with women. He responded in erotic terms to boxing matches in London's East End; chatted up a teen-age Belgian sailor; and, by 1907, was in a relationship

with a svelte young racing cyclist named Gaston Colin, who achieved immortality when he was sculpted by Kessler's good friend Aristide Maillol ("Le Cycliste," Musée d'Orsay). Adopting a freewheeling attitude toward sexuality, Kessler foresaw that German mores would undergo a revolution in the nineteen-twenties.[76]

In contrast to Ross's observations, John Derbyshire maintains that Kessler's "rather guarded, detached [writing] style" lacks interiority and that the diaries do not provide direct evidence of his homosexuality.[77] Taking both of these views into consideration, I believe both could be accurate: on the one hand, his proclivity toward younger men is apparent, and on the other, his writing does try to stay more objective by not expressly communicating personal feelings. Nonetheless, on some level, Kessler felt comfortable with his sexuality since he dealt largely in creative and aesthetic fields. Given both Kessler's and Diaghilev's diplomacy, stature, and homosexuality, it would seem natural that the count and the duo would be able to collaborate. Ramsay Burt ascertains that "during the period 1909–13, Nijinsky was undeniably involved in a homosexual relationship with Diaghilev, and it therefore seems reasonable to take into consideration where it is relevant and useful at looking at his work."[78] Thus, addressing Nijinsky's choreographic and Kessler's librettist work would be important in ascertaining the (un)conscious (sexual) desires of both, particularly because of their openness about their queer identities: a safer space for unbridled creativity. The count's penchant for the young male (body) and the impresario's proclivity for the budding Nijinsky certainly influenced their decision to depict Joseph in *The Legend of Joseph*. Before Kessler even met the duo, Hugo von Hofmannsthal wrote to the count from Paris on March 16, 1912, about his dealings with them:

> I arrived last Saturday morning from Berlin and since Saturday evening have lived with no one but Diaghilev and Nijinsky in fact, evenings in the theater, lunching with them, sitting and speaking from lunch until the theater again—and hardly sleeping at night but still happy—composing ballets for them of which now two, a tragic antique one, and a macabre one in costumes of Carpaccio, have now been drafted and fixed, enriched and modified, brought so far in this hotel room and on Nijinsky's sickbed that it now almost seems to me that the music has already been composed, the sets designed, and as if there could be nothing more beautiful. The tragic subject is Orestes and the Furies, a ballet of thirty-five minutes. The draft is going to

Strauss, who is supposed to compose music for it. [. . .] This naturally does not at all preclude, Harry, that we would do a third. [. . .][79]

The third ballet, *The Legend of Joseph*, eventually becomes Kessler's project because he wants to prove his artistic independence from Hofmannsthal. The Austrian writer had discredited much of the work that Kessler had contributed to *Rosenkavalier* and wished to give the count another chance for collaboration, but Kessler would work primarily without Hofmannsthal's help.[80] Despite these later developments, the count's entry documents the first contact that at least in the beginning would lead to a working partnership between Kessler and Hofmannsthal as they collaborated with Diaghilev, Nijinsky, Strauss, and others.

Hofmannsthal's conversations with Diaghilev and Nijinksy also preceded the Ballets Russes' first performance in Paris, which was noted as having been well received. Kessler had personally invited Rodin to a rehearsal,[81] and composers such as Igor Stravinsky and Maurice Ravel also attended. Kessler described the main ballet piece *The Afternoon of a Faun* (*L'après-midi d'un faune*), which portrays a sexually charged faun who interacts briefly with nymphs, and in the end manages to snatch one of their scarves, with which he masturbates—however, the interpretation of the ending is widely contested. Penny Farfan reads this ballet via a queer lens: by circumventing the rigid dichotomies of male-female, human-animal, and homosexual-heterosexual, the faun also bypasses the nymphs to seek pleasure by himself.[82] This was Nijinsky's first opportunity to choreograph for the company; some of the members were resistant to the unnatural and stiff choreography. While Debussy's dreamlike, languid music plays and the dancers move in "profile" resembling reliefs or images on Greek vases, the faun's abrupt and angular movements are in juxtaposition with the serene atmosphere. Kessler described Nijinsky's dancing on May 27, 1912, during a private rehearsal:

After the prelude from "Daphnis et Chloé" by Ravel, Nijinsky's "Afternoon of a Faun" comes on: archaic, stylized gestures that accompany Debussy's music; Nijinsky modulates the half animalistic, half sentimental desire so harshly with his young body that it comes across as tragic; one has a look, half frightened half captivated, into the natural origins of a tragedy. The momentum of Nijinsky's performance indeed overwhelms the delicate, complicated music of Debussy and Bakst's kitschy tableau is disruptive. But despite this disharmony, the impression retains a kind of resurrection of antique paganism.[83]

Kessler first characterizes Nijinsky as a never-before-witnessed half-animalistic and half-sentimental hybrid. This polarity is reminiscent of St. Denis's *Tempeltanz* as Kessler tries to depict her mixture of body and fabric. Both of their indeterminacies point toward queerness, which Kessler perceives and identifies with. Since Nijinsky's dance lacks a predictable concept, Kessler's approach involves relating his own knowledge from his experience of watching Fuller and St. Denis to the representations of the performance. The juxtaposition of Nijinsky's sharp movement and Debussy's impressionistic music creates a disharmony, which Kessler regards productively as it reminds him of a rebirth of antiquity. Despite this dissonance, Kessler believes they still create a unified impression. Nijinsky's dance evokes sensations of both terror and enchantment, establishing the pervading *Tanzrhythmus*. These feelings reverberate through Kessler's body and maintain his interest for the remainder of the dance while transporting him to a mystically queer realm. This modern aesthetic furthers the ways in which Kessler could conceive of the dancing body by coupling it with contrasting music and scenery.

After the Ballets Russes' performance in Paris, they traveled to Berlin, and Kessler noted their reception in Berlin on December 10, 1912:

> Russian Ballet. First performance of "Afternoon of a Faune" here. Entire Berlin there. [. . .] Wild success, so much so that it had to be repeated. Only [Oskar] Bie turned around and whispered: "I didn't find anything special about it." However, I found it more captivating than in Paris. The faun: half animal, that foreshadows human, that senses what it means to be human, an animal that compares itself with the others, the first flash of reflection and with that also tragedy and also humor; but predominantly tragedy. One believes, to feel in all of Nijinsky's movements, that it is an animal that is ashamed of his nakedness (fall of mankind). Extreme concentration of expression; only a genius can have such a command in the sparingness of means.[84]

Reverting back to his previous observation from the Paris performance, Kessler builds on Nijinsky's animal/human duplicity or queerness. This posthumanist duality embodied in the faun is reminiscent of the comments regarding not only Loïe Fuller's *Serpent Dance*, in which she wavers between being a woman and a figure of animated drapery, but also St. Denis's *Tempeltanz*. In all three cases, the spectator cannot forget that each phenomenal body is a human dancer performing, but the sheer act of the semiotic body, through costuming and dancerly movements, enchants the audience into thinking that what they perceive is real. Choosing the mythical creature of the faun—

half man and half goat—results in Nijinsky's pluralist representation. While animalistic drives are inherent in the human being, his striking costuming and movement communicate a greater carnal presence and visual preoccupation with the sensual. Although the count only refers to the animal/human dichotomy, his observations allude to a vacillation between feminine and masculine: Burt recognizes these qualities in Nijinsky's dancing, which possesses "sensuality and sensitivity (conventionally feminine) with extraordinary strength and dynamism (conventionally masculine)."[85] In regard to Kessler's perception and feeling, these three dances instill a *Tanzrhythmus* that leads to an "unattainableness of mysticism" ("Unerreichbaren der Mystik").

Furthermore, in addition to fragmented, stylized gestures and displaced stillness, Hanna Järvinen argues that through the two-dimensional body positioning and movement, which erases or flattens space in the traditional theater space, Nijinsky's aesthetic destabilizes the audience's perspective, demanding their constant attention.[86] His approach contrasts with those of Endell and Fuller, who both relished activated space as an anthropocene entity. By identifying Nijinsky's "extreme concentration of expression," the movement style confronts Kessler's aesthetic and forces the count to recognize both the dancers' arduous work and the way Nijinsky limits the dancers' range of motion. The count's keen assessment echoes Lucia Ruprecht's observation: instead of virtuosity associated with tremendous leaps and endless pirouettes, Nijinsky's mastery was devoted to the painstaking performance of detailed and minute movements.[87]

The Afternoon of a Faun was not the only modern piece by the Ballets Russes that forever changed the face of twentieth-century dance and influenced Kessler's own work; *The Rite of Spring* (*Le sacre du printemps*) was even more significant. Stravinsky's atonal and violent music established a precultural mood, while the turned-in, angular, heavy choreography of Nijinsky defied the institution of ballet. A key to the crisis of modernism, according to Brandstetter, is the melancholic longing for a primitive culture; artists and choreographers staged this imagined primitivism, which they had never known.[88] And through a gestural lens, Ruprecht reads a productive mode of impairment by using punctuation and interruption as key aesthetics,[89] as opposed to perpetual flow as found in Fuller's dance and Endell's metropolitan dance text. Reminiscent of Nietzsche's Dionysian side, the dance depicts the sacrifice of a young girl to the god of spring while surrounded by tribesmen. Kessler attended the premiere in Paris on May 29, 1913. He noted in his diary:

> In the evening the premiere of *The Rite of Spring*. A completely new choreography and music. Nijinsky's dancing style as different from

Fokine's as Gauguin's from———.[90] A thoroughly new vision, something never before seen, enthralling, persuasive, is suddenly there, a new kind of wildness, both un-art and art at the same time. All forms laid waste and new ones emerging suddenly from the chaos. The public, the most elegant house I have ever seen in Paris—aristocracy, diplomats, the demimonde—was from the beginning restless, laughing, whistling, making jokes. Here and there some stood up. Stravinsky, who sat with his wife behind us, raced outside like possessed after scarcely five minutes. Suddenly a stentorian voice cried out from the gallery, "Okay, whores of the sixteenth (the Sixteenth Arrondissement, that of the elegant world), are you going to shut up soon!" The reply came from a loge: "Voila those who are ripe to be annexed." At the same moment D'Annuzio and Debussy in Astruc's loge got into a quarrel with a neighboring loge, screaming into their faces, "What a bunch of imbeciles!" [. . .] And above this crazy din there continued the storm of salvos of laughter and scornful clapping while the music raged and on the stage the dancers, without flinching, danced fervently in a prehistoric fashion. At the end of the performance, the monde and demimonde went at it until a frenetic applause triumphed so that Stravinsky and Nijinsky had to come on stage to take repeated bows.[91]

Kessler's enthrallment and knowledge of dance continued to grow as he witnessed this scandalous and groundbreaking piece, which utilizes completely new, modern choreography and dissonant music. A striking image of a rising modern aesthetic, the piece "deserted" all previous forms and emerged suddenly from chaos. The audience—displaying a wide range of both raving excitement and utter repulsion—reacts even before the end of the piece, attesting to the shocking and contentious performance; these highly divergent reactions mirror the reactions that Malte and the waiters received with the *Veitstänzer* in the following chapter. Kessler seems more interested in the audience reaction than in the dance itself. This dance undoubtedly opened his eyes to an experimental aesthetic, which provided him with a range of influences in conceptualizing his own work.

Kessler followed the Ballets Russes while they toured, gaining key insights into their aesthetic use of the moving body, music, and set design. Even before the company's premiere in Paris, Kessler—who conceptualizes the libretto for *The Legend of Joseph*—began his collaboration with Diaghilev and Nijinsky, composer Strauss, and the set designer Bakst. In 1928 Kessler incidentally reminisced about the origins of the ballet libretto, which seems to reflect a mythic sensibility similar to St. Denis's encounter with the Egyptian cigarette ad. During a late dinner in Paris, the count describes how Diaghilev expressed interest in creating a biblical ballet in Venetian costume. While sitting in the restaurant, the count observes the wealthiest Muslim prince, Aga Khan, who had just realized that he had forgotten his bejeweled turban in the car, and also a couple dancing a tango; this scenario stylistically inspired the opening scene to *The Legend of Joseph*, which featured a decadent banquet scene.[92] Interestingly, the count's depiction seems to be connected to a dream world—he recounts waking up at 5 a.m. to write down the main parts of the whole ballet.[93] The project became a Europe-wide affair as Kessler traveled between London, Berlin, Munich, Paris, and other cities to work with his Russian dancers and German composer. He met in London with Diaghilev, Nijinsky, and Bakst on July 10, 1912, to first relay the conception, motivation, and gestures of each character while Nijinsky choreographed corresponding movements.[94] After conveying his ideas to Strauss in Garmisch concerning the music, Kessler received feedback from not only his collaborators but also Lady Ripon, a patron of Diaghilev who was responsible for bringing the Ballets Russes to debut in London's Covent Garden in 1911.[95] Kessler wrote:

> Before breakfast [I] read a part of *Joseph* to Lady Ripon's relief. She had been nervous for months concerning the subject because Joseph is a "strange character" and she feared that Nijinsky could become ridiculous. She told me afterward she was put to ease; the character is being redone and wouldn't be able to shock anyone.[96]

Her comments probably moved the depiction of Joseph into a less experimental (perhaps even less homoerotic and queer) realm, yet still remained modern. As this was Kessler's first work, he probably showed trepidation and was eager for approval from those in his intellectual circle.

The ballet's plot tells the story of the biblical Joseph from the book of Genesis. Kessler states that Joseph is a graceful, wild, and pious—not Christian or intellectual, but rather possessing the morals of his people—shepherd boy, who tastes like an apple about ready to ripen and whose voice is still changing.[97] His piousness gives him light feet so he can fly above his people, a depiction that strongly references Nietzsche's *Übermensch*. According to Kessler, Joseph expresses his dance on three levels: first, as a noble child regarding the morals of his people; second, as a powerful and exhilarated hero; and finally, as the discoverer and creator of a new, distant, and bright world.[98]

Joseph's aura radiates a supernatural luminosity, a mystic duality that vacillates between being childlike and becoming focused on the future.[99] Living in a world saturated with power and opulent beauty, Pothiphar's wife cannot love, live, or feel until Joseph's dance awakens her senses; she wants his secret. While embracing him in a motherly way during his sleep, she is overwhelmed by passion and kisses him. According to Kessler, Joseph's purity as a boy is tarnished by her advances. As a result, she feels angry and ashamed and orders her husband to execute the boy. In the last scene, the boy shines even more radiantly as the wife darkens and dies.[100] Joseph's dance represents "a cleaner, purer world" filled with joy and exuberance that at the same time retains a mysterious solitude.[101]

Kessler's depiction of a youthful, childlike Joseph mirrors his affection for younger men; in fact, the count's comment about the boy's ripeness strikingly alludes to forbidden fruit and the fall of man. It is as if the count wants to consume his own creation, but realizes that he cannot, and he similarly denies Pothiphar's wife's satisfaction. The secret, which Joseph possesses and she wants to know, resembles the one that Kessler himself tries to unlock on seeing the girl's feet and the officer's thighs clutching a horse.[102] Through training from watching the dances of Fuller, St. Denis, and Nijinsky, the count is able to recognize a new aesthetic, queer world in which eroticism and intellectualism alternate, yet coexist; however, Pothiphar's wife wants direct consumption instead of intellectual reflection, and is denied Joseph. Instead of portraying a seductress tempting a heterosexual man, Kessler reverses these roles, depicting an innocent boy who does not seem to be aware of his own mystical power and budding sexuality. The posthumanist and queer nature of dance—human-material with Fuller, human-animal and masculine-feminine with Nijinsky, and sexual-intellectual with St. Denis—manifests itself in Joseph's childlike-future or past-becoming dichotomy. In essence, he takes from these binary characteristics and recasts them with a subversive queer perspective.

Kessler relays the boy's mystery to Strauss while in Garmisch on August 4, 1912:

I stressed that Joseph was a *dreamer*. The atmosphere of *the magical* (transitioning to that of the miraculous, in part contrasting with it) must envelop the entire conclusion from the moment of Joseph's nakedness. This moment of Joseph's disrobing must be the high point of the work for both eye and ear, a very powerful effect and shift in the mood[. . . .][103]

In congruence with the Régnier essay—"compared to a dream, reality is shallow"[104] ("im Vergleich zum Traum ist die Wirklichkeit schal"[105])—Kessler wants his dreaming protagonist to transport himself and his audience into a mystical realm, perhaps a queer sublimity. He departs, to an extent, from St. Denis's eroticism and uses Joseph's nudity instead to symbolize reaching a higher level of consciousness. According to Laird Easton, Joseph had become the Nietzschean *Übermensch* or rather *Überkind* because of his youth and his focus on the future.[106] Kessler hoped that the piece would be interpreted as modern und symbolic.[107] If Joseph embodies Nietzsche's *Übermensch*, or at least demonstrates strong ties to this idea, then one might also read the ballet's symbolism with Kessler's own biography. The count deeply wants to branch out intellectually in his established artistic circles and to learn about varying aspects of art, arts administration, and politics. He is constantly involved in projects through his own personal connections, and he continually learns to see more aesthetically by watching the early-twentieth-century dance pieces of Fuller, St. Denis, and the Ballets Russes. Kessler's dance, therefore, relates closely to his own life—representing the perpetual striving for and developing of his artistic, collaborative, and analytical prowess. However, even though Kessler's intentions in his writing seem to insist on Joseph's nonsexual and transcendental nature, the erotic, homosexual gaze still manifests itself, as did the heterosexual gaze on St. Denis's dancing. If Joseph, the secret bearer of new knowledge and the future, symbolizes Kessler, then one could read Pothiphar's wife as a diva who wants to learn from him. In many ways, this portrayal reverses and subverts the power dynamic with queer sublimity—the homosexual male does not idolize the female performer, as with the grand duchess and St. Denis; it's the other way around. Kessler places Joseph, and in some ways himself, as the focal point of the ballet. Despite this, I think one can still use the term "queer sublimity" because there is an escape into another vast, unknown space open to imaginative and queer opportunities. The notion of queer sublimity seems to negate the importance of gender, instead simply reducing both to a humanist level.

Although the role of Joseph was choreographed by Nijinsky and was to be danced by him, his marriage to dancer Romola de Pulszky betrayed his homosexual relationship with the master Diaghilev, who fired him.[108] The experimental and expressive movements of Nijinsky were replaced by those of the introspective Leonid Massine, as Kessler commented on March 25, 1914: "very nice specifically the internal rumination, the power of a religious ecstasy. He is the exact opposite of Nijinsky; entirely intimate like a Russian folksong, nothing like Nijinsky's brilliance and superhuman power. He grabs one's attention through deep sensitivity."[109] While the premiere on May 14, 1914, at the Paris Opera was a "brilliant social event" due to Kessler's masterful ability to gather aristocrats and artists, the piece was generally not well received by the press because it did not meet the expectations created by the hype. Although Massine's dancing was praised on the whole, the scenery and music met with mixed reactions. The libretto was strongly criticized as being pretentious, unintelligible, and too laden with symbolism, as the critic Arthur Pougin remarked.[110] Perhaps the lack of understanding was due to the large number of collaborators being overly ambitious.[111] Schuster summarizes the piece, stating "Josephslegende is a late representative of the turn-of-the-century with its contradictory mixture of historicism, eclecticism and individual moments of modernity, that materialize in Joseph's expressionistic dance."[112] Although Kessler may have overconceptualized and sought too much help for his project, his connections within the artistic community in the metropolises of Berlin, London, and Paris allowed him to witness seminal early-twentieth-century dance pieces that demonstrated a range of experimental aesthetics that shaped his own queer and artistic identity.

I would like to suggest that Kessler's queerness finds liberal and freeing expression in *The Legend of Joseph*. His exposure to the interactions of Diaghilev and Nijinsky, while they were still lovers, created a desire to channel and thematicize the count's own sexual desire in his libretto. Kessler's diaries allude to a penchant for young men, and his ballet similarly allows the erotic—seemingly veiled in intellect—to reach its (sexual) climax. One could read Joseph's denial of Judith's actions as a lack of desire for the female form. The increase in intensity until Joseph's naked reveal could also point to a desire for a new, subversive homosexual male gaze.[113] While the female form in *Varieté* blatantly refers to the sexual consumption of women by heterosexual men or perhaps lesbians and homosocial heterosexual women, Kessler imbues his ballet with a more homoerotic, modernist view of the body: nudity as a form of naturalness as well as eroticism, and youth with a focus on the future and naiveté. Both nakedness and childlike innocence easily slide into the homosexual gaze of both sexual desire and embodiment, just as St. Denis's dance wavers between an intellectualization through materiality and her seemingly nude body. Taking pleasure in the male dancing body around 1900 can be imagined through homosexual men; only they and heterosexual women could relish the "spectacle of male sexuality."[114] Therefore, Kessler's libretto seems to pull from a range of dual posthumanist and queer paradigms (animal and human, sexuality and abstraction, masculine and feminine) as established in the dances of St. Denis and Nijinsky; it recasts Joseph and *The Legend of Joseph* with a decidedly queer perspective and reversal of queer sublimity. Nijinsky would have found these aesthetics agreeable to his own as he choreographed the piece. As Burt states, "For Diaghilev and Nijinsky as homosexual men, this marginal position [. . .] enabled a limited but contained expression of homosexual experience. Nijinsky's homosexuality was signified purely through ambiguities within the stories, and through qualities of costume and décor."[115] I think, however, that this view could be further complicated: Nijinsky's costuming and dancing could also be pointing toward a queerness and a desired indeterminacy, rather than a more fixed form that would communicate homosexuality at the time. Among likeminded men of his generation, Kessler probably felt at ease with the duo synthesizing, processing, and thematicizing the new dance aesthetics that he witnessed, which allowed him a safe space to integrate his own developing queer identity into the ballet. And as Farfan has already mentioned, such groups allowed the formation and experimentation of queer identities both on stage and in everyday life.[116]

While Endell's flâneuresque perspective allows the architect to perceive dance movement in the streets of Berlin, Kessler's view affords him the perception of a flâneur at balls and in other social settings. His developing aesthetic sensibility, however, goes beyond mere observation and enables him to tap into the city's artistic social scene; the metropolis gives the count the opportunity to develop his modernist aesthetic and expand his cosmopolitan contacts beyond the nineteenth-century ball setting among live dance performances and through critical conversations with dancers and in intellectual circles. While Endell's work seems to strongly hint at an abstracting of intertwining dancerly movement from a more outside perspective, Kessler throws himself into the creative process intimately as a practitioner. Both perspectives, abstract and personal, reflect the varying levels of access and background knowledge that went into his productive manifestations of dance.

In the Régnier essay, Kessler desires a "turning away from the world."[117] He wants to perceive familiar objects, people, and events in his surroundings with fresh eyes and devoid of any inherited meaning. We see that by abstracting and reading movements aesthetically, Kessler developed a penchant for the liberated, erotic body in dance. The performances of the Grand Duchess of Hessen, Fuller, St. Denis, and Nijinsky provide him with much more than just a display of dance movement. Their dances demonstrate motions that the count had never witnessed, and they align aesthetically with Kessler's new way of seeing: both intellectualization and eroticization, in St. Denis's case, of the dancing body and through dichotomies that queerly and posthumanistically vacillate between animal and human, sexuality and abstraction, masculine and feminine. Through watching these dances in the city, Kessler revels in queer sublimity and fandom: he wants to become a part of dance culture, and his privileged upbringing permits him to make his dreams come true. Essentially, Kessler's conversations with St. Denis offer him new stimuli that extend the limits of his perception, sparking his interest in collaboration and furthering his diva worship. By widening the scope of his interpretation of movement in general, the dances of Fuller, St. Denis, and Nijinsky also help him engage intellectually with early-twentieth-century dance. In particular, his collaboration with Diaghilev and Nijinsky brought out a distinctly queer perspective in the count's libretto, which further subverts the idea of queer sublimity. Ultimately, his heightened enthusiasm for the moving body inspires him to not simply remain an outside observer, but to become an engaged practitioner in creating *The Legend of Joseph*.

After World War I, Kessler continued his artistic pursuits. Through his social and artistic connections, he had an enchanting encounter with the African American dancer Josephine Baker. On February 13, 1926, the Austrian theater director Max Reinhardt invited Kessler to the librettist Karl Vollmoeller's home, where she was relaxing nude—save for a pink muslin apron—with other female dancers. Kessler describes her as dancing like an ancient Egyptian figure, in a childlike and playful manner: "A bewitching creature, but almost quite unerotic. Watching her inspires as little sexual excitement as does the sight of a beautiful beast of prey."[118] This characterization is a further reflection of the vacillating dichotomies he perceived with St. Denis and Nijinsky. On seeing her in the arms of another girl dressed as a boy in a dinner jacket, the utter queerness of the pair inspires Kessler to propose a show for them based on the Song of Solomon, with ancient and modern music, half jazz and half Oriental.[119] Kessler remained steeped in queer society and was inspired to create correspondingly eclectic performances into the 1920s.

Four

Bridging Representations of Gesture, Gesticulation, and Early-Twentieth-Century Dance in the City

Rilke's Veitstänzer *in* The Notebooks of Malte Laurids Brigge

"We came to a crossing, and the man ahead of me raised one leg and hopped down the steps to the street. [. . .] The steps on the other side he cleared in a single bound. But scarcely was he up on the pavement than he again drew up one leg a little and hopped up high on the other foot, then did it again and again."[1] Walking through the streets of Paris, the protagonist Malte notices a man with an erratic gait. The man's repetitive and jerky movements, characterized as a "choreography of restlessness"[2] by Eric Santner, initially resemble everyday gestures governed by his will, but later evolve into uncontrollable gesticulations showing signs of a brewing grave illness. At the end of the scene, the man falls to the ground, overpowered by the unpredictable and angular movements. Critics have convincingly suggested that the man suffers from *Veitstanz* (St. Vitus's dance or Huntington's chorea),[3] a progressively degenerative neurological disease characterized by involuntary, irregular, and abrupt movements of the extremities, face, and trunk.

This mysterious scene from Rainer Maria Rilke's prose work *The Notebooks of Malte Laurids Brigge* (*Die Aufzeichnungen des Malte Laurids Brigge*) highlights characteristics, such as the city setting and the observation of urban phenomena, that pervade much literature written around the turn of the twentieth century. Some scholars believe that Rilke's stays in Paris compelled his breakthrough into modernism.[4] In particular, this scene highlights performative dimensions of the metropolis and a range of bodily movements: gesture, gesticulation, and dance. The man's disjointed and jolting gait, which causes him to "stick out," also relates aesthetically to the works of dancers around 1900. While elaborate set designs and large dance casts characterized the nineteenth-century spectacle of ballet, modern dances of the twentieth century took place in minimalist spaces, often with solo performers.[5] Dancers such as Isadora Duncan, Ruth St. Denis, and Vaslav Nijinsky reinvented gesture not "by recovering a cultural code, but by delving deeply into a rhetoric and practice of discovering precultural energies."[6]

Informed by discourses on the flâneur and the metropolis, the work of Giorgio Agamben and Andrew Hewitt, and Rilke's writings on dance, I investigate the social, aesthetic, and pathological implications of using St. Vitus's Dance as a metaphoric device. Like Endell in "The Beauty of the Metropolis" and Kessler at balls and in other social environments, the flâneur was able to read aesthetic meaning from everyday events in the metropolitan space.[7] Agamben notes that, in certain social settings, the nineteenth-century bourgeoisie would lose control of their gestures, resulting in an outbreak of tics and Tourettism.[8] The term "bourgeois," I believe, here indicates members of an educated middle class of relatively comfortable means in non-working-class professions; the intellectuals, at least, could be assumed to hold a critical eye to the nature of their metropolitan circumstances and experiences. Hewitt maintains that their gesticulations could be aestheticized through the choreography of modern dance.[9] There remains, however, no particular *literary* depiction that bridges the gesticulation of an everyday individual and Western European dance aesthetics from around 1900, within the context of urban space. But one certainly can cite aesthetically varied, emerging modern characteristics in the dances of St. Denis, Nijinsky, and others, and scholars such as Hewitt and Michael Cowan have identified multiple examples of the nervous and fragmented individual in literature.

In this chapter, I first situate Rilke amid the stimuli of Paris, which had a profound influence on his writing. His poem "Spanish Dancer" was probably inspired by his experience watching a dancer in a Montmartre atelier, and in it he integrates representations of both dance and space. Second, I demonstrate that Rilke's *Veitstanz* in *The Notebooks of Malte Laurids Brigge* provides us with a hybrid, posthumanist depiction connecting the realms of dance and space on a performative and dynamically changing urban stage. This scene can be read as a metropolitan dance text highlighting a symbolic dancerly battle between gesture and gesticulation that is liberated from the traditional theater and dance space and situated in city streets. While the performance begins with simple, everyday gestures conveying willful desires, the nonhuman agency of the metropolitan environment and disease causes these movements to escalate into a chaotic and confusing struggle, ending in the victory of the *Veitstanz*. Malte empathizes and becomes thoroughly intertwined kinesthetically with the man's movement. Rilke creates this metropolitan dance text to represent the modern body and psyche; he chronicles its critical transition from communicative gesture to aesthetic fragmentation and the spatial shift from theater stage to urban space.

As I outlined in chapter 1, "Perceiving the City as Dancing Entity: Conceptions of Writing the Metropolitan Dance Text," I conceptualize the metropolitan space in all its macro and micro characterizations—from minute, fleeting details of an individual or object to grander, impressionistic views of cityscapes. Thus, I characterize the generalized idea of Simmel's "stimuli,"[10] whether visual, aural, olfactory, or tactile, and whether expressed through human movement or via objects such as buildings, streets, or public transportation, in terms of both a corresponding detailed or aggregate view interacting with or interpenetrating the dancing body. Therefore, the role of the human as dancer is deemphasized while the agency of the other stimuli is elevated. The *Veitstanz* thus symbolizes the beginnings of modern dance seeking expression through the body while also creating kinesthetic empathy between Malte and the man. I develop the transition from gesticulation to dance by comparing the *Veitstanz* to other examples in Rilke's writings on dance and the city. In addition to engaging with the urban space nearly every day, the author's dance and gestural imagination was profoundly influenced by encountering an alleged *Veitstänzer* in Paris, by watching both St. Denis and Nijinsky perform, and by interacting with Rodin's work. Rilke channels these experiences into his protagonist Malte, who is forced to learn and write not only about the abrupt and angular aesthetics of the emerging modern dance, but also about the bodily crisis of the everyday citizen in the city.

Simmel's essay's "The Metropolis and Mental Life" ("Die Großstädte und das Geistesleben") describes modern individuals' experience as their senses are bombarded by a vast array of stimuli, in response to which they develop a filter and a blasé attitude. Only something new would catch their attention and take them out of this state; their responses to the everyday are dulled.[11] This phenomenon probably occurred to Endell while he watched street scenes in Berlin, and it certainly pertains to Rilke and his protagonist Malte. While Endell is a "sitting" flâneur and Kessler a flâneur of salons and balls, Malte similarly does not epitomize the flâneur in the nineteenth-century

Parisian sense. Harald Neumeyer concludes that Malte is afraid to be a flâneur.[12] Like Endell and Kessler, Malte (by way of Rilke) learns to see more aesthetically, but instead of gleaning a beautiful impression like Endell or perceiving an intellectual eroticization like Kessler, Malte experiences anxiety. But even though Rilke's protagonist feels safe in the library's confines and often fears leaving home, his circumstances ultimately compel him to see and write about urban events and strangers in the streets. In conjunction with the idea of Huyssen's modernist miniature and the journalistic *Momentbild*, David Frisby illuminates another aspect of the flâneur's activities:

> The *flâneur*, and the activity of *flânerie*, is also associated in Benjamin's work not merely with observation and reading but also with *production*—the production of distinctive kinds of texts. [. . .] [T]he *flâneur* can also be a producer, a producer of literary texts (including lyrical and prose poetry as in the case of Baudelaire), a producer of illustrative texts (including painting), a producer of narratives and reports, a producer of journalistic texts, a producer of sociological texts.[13]

Among his list of genres, one must also include the metropolitan dance text. Frisby's insight reveals one of the greatest and most provocative issues for flâneurs such as Malte, and more generally the modern individual in the metropolis at the turn of the century: the desire to capture an experience through the medium of texts. Encapsulating every minute detail in a lived event could be a daunting task, given the number of facets associated even with a small, fragmentary experience. Yet as we will see, Malte (through Rilke) attempts to create a metropolitan dance text that depicts the emerging modern dance taking over the bourgeois body while integrating the fragmented perception of the modern city dweller in the metropolitan streets.

It is important to situate the *Veitstanz* or St. Vitus's dance historically. Emerging in the early modern period, the condition was characterized with jerky gestural movement. Some commentators interpreted these afflicted individuals as being hot blooded, mad, demonically possessed, or under the influence of witchcraft.[14] However, in the 1500s the Swiss physician Paracelsus contended that these chorea, epilepsy, and other involuntary movements were related to the *spiritus vitae*, neutral forces related to all matter and locomotion that had no symbolic signification.[15] His vitalist philosophy explains that earthquakes as much as the bodily systems of humans and animals are subject to laws of repetition and tremors.[16] Kélina Gotman reads these changes in the perceptual paradigms of these choreomania as a *translatio*: "a passage or shift—literally, *kinesis*, movement, route—between political and intellectual modalities that the narrower concept of 'translation' does not quite capture."[17] Relating to a *translatio* that changed in the nineteenth century from Paracelsus's vitalist reading to an aesthetic lens within urban discourse, Hewitt has looked at social choreography as it derives from the aesthetic,[18] identifying an "aesthetic continuum" of movement from everyday strolling to conventional dance.[19] Part of his study focuses on the "aesthetic gesture" of displaying the body through the act of walking.[20] Similarly, flânerie also typifies the ambulatory movement of the pedestrian in city streets. In response to Agamben's claim that the nineteenth-century bourgeoisie had lost control of their gestures,[21] Hewitt argues that this can only be the case if one distinguishes between gesture ("a willing linguistic articulation") and gesticulation ("a subjection of the body to spontaneous or involuntary movements").[22] He proceeds to blur the line between gesticulation, gesture, and dance:

> Dance fails as gesture through an inability either to begin or to complete the gesture, and it figures a linguistic play that neglects the work of semiotic closure. . . . Dance figures either an aesthetic of interruption or, stated more positively, an openness to discourses that cut across primary lines of communication, confounding hegemonic meanings. . . . This suggests a fascinating possibility that choreography as an aesthetic practice responds to the "loss of gesture" or "destruction of experience" in the bourgeois era; that it emerges both as an uncontrollable chorea, or symptom of the loss of gestural control, and as an attempt to regain control through aesthetization.[23]

Using this lens to analyze Rilke's *Veitstänzer* scene brings out the observed man's complex motions, which on one hand resemble dance movements, yet on the other, are both voluntary gestures and uncontrollable gesticulations resulting from the agency of the sickness. His motions, therefore, reveal an intricate battle between gesture and gesticulation (or human and nonhuman), each fighting for control over the man's body. While his gestures demonstrate his will and desire to complete everyday tasks such as walking, he cannot function normally because of his uncontrollable gesticulations. As a result, Malte and other onlookers are confused by the man's movements in the social and urban setting. Following Hewitt's argument that the aesthetic continuum includes both social communication and modern dance, the description of this man's erratic and abrupt movement in effect creates a modern aesthetic technique that bridges the everyday and dance. Similarly, Felicia McCarren notes that Nijinsky's *L'Après-midi d'un faune* (1912) and *Le Sacre du printemps* (1913) both portray dances "akin to madness," highlighting the artistic representation rather than the malady, and thus commenting on contemporary understandings of madness.[24]

Rilke and Paris

Living in the Parisian metropolis heavily influenced all facets of Rilke's writings, just as Endell and Kessler had been affected by their cities. Rilke's move to Paris in 1902 coincided with the beginning of his work *The Note-books of Malte Laurids Brigge*. The author left his wife and daughter behind in Worpswede to go to Paris, where he began to work on his prose book along with other projects, such as a monograph on Rodin. In many respects, Malte resembles the author, who was also new to Paris and had to struggle to adapt to the crowded, anonymous daily life. In his autobiography *The World of Yesterday*, Stefan Zweig characterizes Rilke as difficult to track down and as someone who lived "secretly," "gently," and "invisibly" in Paris, without a fixed work space or accommodation; as a result of such circumstances and the resulting anonymity, Rilke felt freer.[25] Zweig relates a vignette of how even sitting in noisy public spaces would unsettle Rilke for hours afterward.[26] Recalling moments during their flânerie, he wrote "But it was nicest to walk with Rilke in Paris, for that meant seeing the most insignificant things with eyes enlightened to their meaning. He noticed every detail, and he liked to repeat aloud the firm names on the signs if they seemed rhythmic to him. It was his passion—almost the only one that I ever observed in him—to know every nook and cranny of this Paris."[27] Along the same lines, one can tie Malte's feelings toward and aesthetic perceptions of Paris more directly to the author's.

Most critics see Rilke's relationship to Paris as ambivalent.[28] In his letters, he sometimes describes how beautiful Paris looks, and in other instances expresses a desire to be back in the countryside.[29] Like Rilke, Malte suffers from this pull between forces; the protagonist feels comfortable and safe at home, but at the same time is compelled to explore the streets, where he inevitably encounters strange events. Without question, Rilke finds Paris engaging and helpful for his productivity, as he writes in a letter to the Swedish painter Tora Holmström in 1907:

The demand that this city has on one is boundless and incessant. [. . .] Thus, it does not immediately help one right away and directly with artistic endeavors; at first it initially does not affect the work that one does,—but it continually transforms, enhances and develops an individual, it quietly takes the tools from one's hand, that have been used, and replaces them with others: unspeakably subtler and more precise ones creating thousands of unexpected things, like a fairy, that is interested in seeing a creature take on all kinds of forms, whose possibilities remain hidden within. One has to let Paris, if one is surrounded by it for the first time, take effect like taking a bath, without doing much except feeling and letting it happen to oneself.[30]

Rilke's poetic and metaphoric description of the city's shaping the thinking and writing process relates similarly to the passive absorption of daily activity. The posthumanist stimuli seep into the body as if Paris were an active agent helping him write, and the author becomes a medium through which the city acts. The city can physically "take the tools" out of one's hands. In a sense the writer seems less capable of deciding what to depict in his work, as if he were dependent on unexpected urban experiences. Indeed, it is the author's poetic and aesthetic sensibility that would enable him to relay this process into writing. Recognizing the validity of Rilke's observation that the city is writing itself, with the author being its means of expression, the fragmentary, episodic nonlinearity of his work shines through, and the posthumanistic urbanity takes on significant agency by replacing the writer. The image of letting Paris percolate into the body also shows the emphasis not just on the psyche through sight, smells, and sounds—typical of a flâneuresque experience—but also, most importantly, through the entire corporeal experience. The transference of the daily, metropolitan experience in all its macro and micro effects highlights the primacy of the body as a direct receptacle and as a slowly developing process. This act of eventual transmission manifests itself in the scene with Malte and the *Veitstänzer*. Rilke's comment that the city "continually transforms, enhances and develops an individual" could also be applied not only to Malte as a writer but to the choreography and staging of the *Veitstänzer*'s metropolitan dance text. While the protagonist has to grapple with the boundaries of his aesthetic perception, the man's body and disease seek experimental play with symbolic representations of emotion instead of mimesis, thereby arguably breaking into early-twentieth-century dance.

Rilke's depiction of how the metropolis can create more subtleties and cause the body to exude "thousands of unexpected things" points strikingly to his encounter with the actual *Veitstänzer*'s performance: the excitement incorporated "thousands of dances."[31] Furthermore, Rilke's characterization of the metropolis as a fairy that expresses itself through "a creature [that] take[s] on all kinds of forms, whose possibilities remain hidden within" seems to also relate to the *Veitstänzer* and the hidden aesthetic meaning behind his movements, pointing to the significant reality that the man does not necessarily control his motions, the metropolis largely dictates how the man functions. The city incites a perpetual explosion of autonomous and legible fragments, all harboring various aesthetic meanings not only in terms of Malte's writing but in the physical expression of the *Veitstänzer*. Rilke's depiction of the metropolitan effects on the individual relate as well to Endell's architectural phenomenology and Fuller's idea of allowing the impressionistic stimuli to seep into the body. The more precise transformation of which Rilke speaks correlates with the subtle changes in aesthetic meaning that Kessler felt while watching St. Denis's dancing and the "aesthetics of interruption" that Hewitt purports. This mode of interpenetration and posthumanism similarly exhibits itself in chapter 5 with Döblin's dancer Ella and in chapters 6 and 7 with Lasker-Schüler's drawings.

In a letter to his wife Clara on April 26, 1906, Rilke described his encounter with a Spanish dancer in his friend painter Ignacio Zuloaga's atelier:

> Yesterday was the baptism of Zuloaga's son. I did not have any time to go to church but went for a while to his new atelier in Montmartre where I was surrounded by thirty or forty complete strangers. (I recognized Cottet by his nose and beard since he was by himself, not speaking to anyone.) Everybody was singing and dancing. A Spanish woman, whose essence it was to sing, sang very beautifully in the rhythm of her Spanish blood, the Carmen and Spanish songs; a gitane with a black and colorful shawl, danced Spanish dances. It was rather full of atmosphere in the mid-sized atelier, in which one crowded. (But the spectators surrounding Goya's dancer were even more cramped.) Zuloaga was endearing and nice with his pride and his gleaming smile.[32]

Although his encounter with the Spanish dancer does not occur in the streets, it nonetheless takes place in an unconventional, urban performance area: an atelier, where Zuloaga presumably worked on his art. The staging of dances and performances outside of the theater space around 1900 was an appealing idea, according to Gabriele Brandstetter:

First, the choice of *performance space* was closely related to turn-of-the-century theater and dance reform. Alternative theater spaces and stage designs were seen as free from the burden of the nineteenth-century illusionist theater tradition. The recourse to ancient amphitheaters, festival halls, rotundas, and all forms of experimental avant-garde theater architecture is not the only indicator of attempts to change the institutional landscape. The conquest of new performance spaces also held similar significance for dance. In addition to concert halls, artists' houses, and park terraces, galleries and museum spaces were likewise turned into stages for modern presentations of movement.[33]

Having grown tired of the conventional nineteenth-century settings for dances, choreographers and dancers sought to venture into different, urban spaces. This experimentation with staging in spaces besides the traditional theater certainly widened the scope of the choreographer's and the viewer's aesthetic regarding how a dance could be produced. While there was a demand to use alternative areas as settings for dances, the space correspondingly invoked its own analysis just as much as the movement of the dancers.

Not only did the dance take place in an atelier, just as significantly Rilke as author is enveloped in a sea of strangers at the performance, and this isolation corresponds to the modern individual's anonymity in the metropolitan streets. One could also assume that Rilke did not necessarily anticipate such a dance performance in an atelier, which intensifies the unexpectedness of the situation. Rilke's text focuses first on contextualizing the space and then further concentrating on the dancing woman, who herself creates a fiery, festive mood. The combination of her singing and dancing casts a spell over the audience that Rilke tries to convey in his letter to his wife. In his writing, he both recapitulates the dance and conveys the aesthetic effect it has on the moving and singing onlookers. In addition, Zuloaga's proud demeanor and smile seem to parallel the mood of the Spanish dancer in the poem "Spanish Dancer" ("Spanische Tänzerin") that Rilke wrote two months later, in June 1906.

Rilke's experience of watching the dancer in the atelier served as a strong catalyst for his portrayal of what he had experienced himself. He does not simply explain the protocol of the dance but instead translates the movements visually, rhythmically, and aesthetically into a poetic dance text:

As in one's hand a sulphur match, whitely,
Before it comes aflame, to every side

> Darts twitching tongues—: within the circle
> Of close watchers hasty, bright and hot
> Her round dance begins twitching to spread itself.
> And suddenly it is altogether flame.
> With her glance she sets light her hair
> and all at once with daring art
> whirls her whole dress within this conflagration,
> out of which her naked arms upstretch
> like startled snakes awake and rattling
> And then: as though the fire were tightening round her,
> she gathers it all in one and casts it off
> very haughtily, with imperious gesture
> and watches: it lies there raging on the ground
> and still flames and will not give in—.
> Yet conquering, sure and with a sweet
> Greeting smile she lifts her countenance
> And stamps it out with little sturdy feet.[34]

Echoing the live atelier performance earlier, Rilke depicts the audience in the poem as surrounding the dancer and her flame and framing the context and the space. The onlookers' close proximity creates not only an intimate mood but also an increasing fervor that begins slowly and intensifies to a grand flourish as the flame is extinguished. The round formation also allows the crowd not only to watch her dancing but also, importantly for Rilke, to convey their reactions gazing on the woman. The end of the dance, in which she demonstrates her control over the flame by smiling and stamping it out, parallels Zuloaga's grin of pride during the atelier performance, which further reflects his control over the dance.

Although the flame was probably not present at the actual performance, this imagery concurrently incites the Spanish woman to dance and demonstrates her power to control the flame. The fire represents not simply the passion of the dancer but also the growing interest of the spectators, whose emotions and co-presence intensify in tandem with the flame's magnitude. Brandstetter notes that:

> Rilke's poem . . . provides an exposition of the most important aspects
> of dance and dance-texts: dance dramaturgy as a succession and climax
> of movement elements; the contrast between controlled and released
> gesture, between discipline and ecstasy as models of discovering and

losing oneself as an individual; the duality of nature and culture, of movement and stasis, of the ephemeral versus the eternal in the transitory process of signification and designification.[35]

The succession and intensification of kinetic elements become a choreographic device in order to create a sense of repetition, variation, and momentum. These techniques command the viewer's interest and cause it to subsequently evolve with the dance's intensity. Rilke attempts to recreate these feelings by using rhyme, allowing the text to be read in a specific rhythm that propels one to the conclusion. Within the poem Rilke does not just create an ambience and describe the dance, he captures the fervent spirit and relationship between the dancer and the nonanthropocentric flame. While the rational dancer represents discipline and the fire stands for burning affect, they both contribute symbiotically to the driving ecstasy. With their combined powers, the woman can manipulate the seemingly untamable fire to reach a climactic state, which undoubtedly and intentionally reverberates with the audience.

"Spanish Dancer" clearly shows strong evidence that the atelier performance probably inspired and helped shape Rilke's thoughts in creating the poem. While his letter to Clara and the subsequent poem based on his experience attest to his presence there, one could further argue that the city of Paris served as a focal point, arousing his imagination to actualize his own literary work. Not only does he decide to write about the dancer, he chooses the genre of lyric over prose to convey his experience. Like many of the unexpected events that Rilke encountered in Paris's expansive urban landscape, his experience in the atelier stands out as a memorable event worthy of documentation, not simply in a letter to his wife, but also in the form of a dance poem.

From Gesture to Gesticulation

The episode involving the man with *Veitstanz* begins as Malte remarks that his fever had become less severe than in the previous days. The remnants of this sickness linger with him as he comments: "Today I did not anticipate a thing; I went out so jauntily, as though it were the most natural, most straightforward of things, something that took me and crumpled me up like a piece of paper and tossed me away."[36] Malte does not have a cheerful attitude when he ventures into the city. After his encounters with the strange cauliflower salesman and the deteriorating walls, his mood is not that of his usual enjoyment of the secluded libraries. Further confused because of his fever, it seems as though he would be even more cautious, but relative to the unexpectedness that one finds in city life around 1900, as proposed by Peter Fritzsche, Malte should have learned that a walk through the streets of Paris entail strange and shocking encounters.

Much like a modern individual experiencing many of these events while meandering through the streets like Malte, he or she was supposed to be prepared for them. During Malte's wandering, he describes the atmosphere and "stage setting" of his surroundings:

> The boulevard Saint-Michel was deserted and vast, and walking up the gentle slope was easy. Casement windows overhead opened with a classy sound, sending a flash flying across the street like a white bird. A carriage with bright red wheels passed by, and, further on, someone was wearing something of a light green colour. Horses in glinting harness trotted along the road, which was freshly washed down and dark. The breeze was brisk, fresh, mild and bore everything up: smells, shouts, bells.[37]

Here Rilke describes the urban scene not only visually but also aurally and olfactorily with the words "smells, shouts, bells" ("Gerüche, Rufe und Glocken"). Rilke's modernist miniature here tries to awaken the reader's senses to recreate the immediacy of a stage setting. Rilke does not involve himself in a long impressionistic view, but rather focuses his perception on his immediate vicinity as an urban dweller in the streets. His succinct sentences aim at recreating the feeling of presentness not by creating classically beautiful, idyllic scenes, but through describing the rather raw, everyday occurrences in the city. As we will see in the next chapter, Döblin uses a similar technique, called *Kinostil*, because of its aesthetic resemblance to the cinematic medium. Rilke's description takes into account the modern individual's change in perception in being more instantaneous and dynamic.

Along similar lines of understanding space, Susan Foster's concept of "frames" deals primarily with how dance sets itself apart from other events, particularly in the more traditional theater setting. Posters or ads in the streets and in magazines could probably lure individuals into a theater, while a program would help focus their attention on a particular dance piece.[38] The lighting, ambience, and layout of the theater were also supposed to contextualize themselves as conditions surrounding an event that was different from the outside world.[39] While Foster's definition of a proscenium theater setting shows a clear delineation between audience and performer, with the focus mostly in one direction and within a boxlike structure, her second type of theatrical setting encapsulates more closely the structure of the *Veitstänzer* scene:

> Theater-in-the-round implies the opposite [of a proscenium setting]: the fact that any viewer can see other viewers watching the dance from other perspectives suggests that all viewing locations are valid and desirable. Equally important, the action in theaters-in-the-round is framed by the audience itself, and this frame is ambiguous. Dancers exiting from the space merge with the audience, while at the same time viewers can watch each other as part of the performance. Furthermore, the action in a theater-in-the-round is usually more physically proximate, and viewers can see dancers sweating and breathing hard.[40]

While her definition may not fit precisely with the construction of Rilke's metropolitan dance text scene, it does capture the viewer's ability to see other observers, be closer to the performer, and maintain an ambiguous and dynamic boundary with the dancers: key aspects in the *Veitstänzer* scene. It differs, however, in that Malte not only has to physically follow the man by walking, but the protagonist has to continually be aware of his perpetually changing urban space, thus demonstrating that the metropolis has a profound impact on the man's performance. Similarly, the dynamic observation of figures and changing of settings is more reflective of how Matthias Bauer understands the performative dimension of the urban space as an open *Schauplatz*.[41]

Malte's interaction with the *Veitstänzer* actually begins indirectly as the protagonist describes the confused reactions of waiters when they see the man pass by on the sidewalk:

> Slickly combed waiters were busy scouring the doorstep. . . . The waiter, who was quite red in the face, gazed closely in that direction for a moment or so; then a laugh spread over his whiskerless cheeks, as if it had been spilled on them. He beckoned the other waiters over, turning his laughing face rapidly from right to left a couple of times, so that while he called them all across he missed nothing himself. There they now all stood, looking down the street, or trying to see, smiling or vexed, whatever the absurdity was that they had not yet made out.[42]

These varying reactions point toward the observers' puzzlement in trying to ascertain and interpret the man's movements. Given the episode's setting in the streets instead of the theater, the first waiter hardly expects an aesthetic performance, but he certainly notices the oddness of the man's movement. Reacting in his everyday social frame of reference, he waves for his colleagues to take a look. The first waiter had probably already seen the man perform a combination of both willful gestures—such as walking, jumping, or carrying his cane—and the abrupt and angular gesticulations associated with *Veitstanz*. Like the waiters, Malte's response to the man's movements does not evidence understanding, but rather confusion. The protagonist's goal for the rest of the scene is to decipher this code in the same vein as Benjamin's conceptualization of the flâneur. While it may seem that the man is the only performer, the waiters and Malte become implicated in the performative space because they are interacting with him, even if not directly, through their co-presence.

Continuing his walk in the streets, Malte begins to focus on the individuality of the man whose gestures have raised so many eyebrows:

> I supposed that, as soon as I could see better, there would be some unusual and striking figure in view, but there proved to be no one else ahead of me but a tall, lean man in a dark greatcoat, wearing a soft black hat on his short, ash-blond hair. I could see to my satisfaction that there was nothing at all ridiculous either in this man's clothing or in his behaviour, and was already trying to look past him, down the boulevard, when he tripped over something. Since I was following close behind him, I took care when I came to the spot, but there was nothing there, nothing whatsoever. We both continued walking, he and I, the distance between us remaining the same.[43]

Malte's detective skills have led him to a person whose appearance does not seem particularly strange until the man trips over an undiscernible object. As soon as he gets closer to the *Veitstänzer*, Malte has to be aware of how he himself acts, to make sure that no one, especially the man, notices the protagonist's watching. By remaining anonymous, he will be able to observe the man's performative movements in their "natural" state.

The investigation takes on complexity when Malte notices that the man had not tripped over anything. This puzzling stumble, the first movement that the protagonist can analyze, does not make sense: logically, there must have been an object that caused the man to trip. The everyday act of walking, which normally does not demand constant attention, now becomes the focus. The gesture of tripping implies a loss of bodily control, whether caused by imbalance or an outside force. Hewitt comments, "Stumbling needs to be thought of not as a loss of footing but rather as a finding of one's feet: it is the act in which the body rights itself by a rétraction [Hewitt's spelling] and the mind becomes aware of the operation of measure and balance—'a secret force'—operating in and through the body."[44] Therefore, the stumble heightens the *Veitstänzer*'s awareness of his own positioning and of observers' possible perceptions. At this point, Malte is concerning himself solely with the gesture of extremities as it relates to social communication in the city setting; he has not yet witnessed movement that would indicate a gesticulation or aesthetic framing. After this stumble, the two begin walking almost in tandem as Malte maintains the same distance between them to not call attention to himself. Here is also the first instance in which Rilke depicts their coming together, making it seem as if they are one unit. Malte sets himself parallel to the man, not only in step, but eventually also in feeling. Additionally, using Simmel's lens, the plethora of urban stimuli have caused Malte's attention to focus only on the strange and unexpected, thereby drawing him to the *Veitstänzer* and causing the protagonist to physically pursue the man like a flâneur follows his object of aesthetic meaning. Unlike Endell's observing the crowd and Kessler's watching the early-twentieth-century dancers in a confined space, Malte must actively pursue his dancer and constantly ascertain the ambient geographical surroundings: he must not only evaluate the reactions of other observers but also his own, thus offering a dynamic, performative space.

From this point on, the intensity of their connection builds, and Malte's interpretation of the *Veitstänzer*'s gesture begins to change:

We came to a crossing, and the man ahead of me raised one leg and hopped down the steps to the street, as children who are having fun sometimes hop and skip when they're walking. The steps on the other side he cleared in a single bound. But scarcely was he up on the pavement than he again drew up one leg a little and hopped up high on the other foot, then did it again and again. At this point, you might easily once again have taken the sudden movement for tripping, if you'd concluded that there was some little thing there, the pit or the slippery skin of a fruit, something or other; and the odd thing was that the man himself seemed to imagine there was something in his way, because every time he gave the offending spot one of those looks, part vexed, part reproachful, that people do give at such moments.[45]

Malte's analysis of the man deepens as they approach a different urban structure: a crossing. While this architectural construct, on the surface, seems to be merely an intersection of two roads, it also evokes a range of symbolism—the convergence of two dynamic pathways, those between Malte and the man. Also, in a more antagonistic sense, a crossing could indicate a discordant change of one mental and physical state into another. In other words, Rilke operatively stages the crossing not only as a metropolitan landmark to describe the urban space in which Malte and the *Veitstänzer* move, but as a symbol to further bridge and actively represent their connection in feeling and movement. Using the sidewalk and the street as the stage, Rilke also uses the "imaginary" piece of fruit as a choreographic hindrance to activate the *Veitstänzer*'s symptoms and to further demonstrate the artifice of his performative actions. Throughout his study, the protagonist compares the man's hopping, walking, stumbling, and looking with everyday, communicative gestures; but the incessant repetition of these movements, seemingly occurring without cause, continues to confuse Malte. These motions no longer resemble gestures but begin to veer more in the direction of gesticulation. The man also realizes how observers may be interpreting his actions, and therefore, in effect, performs as if he believes that a foreign object has caused his movements. In this way, the *Veitstänzer* tries to fit into the normative social fabric of everyday metropolitan society by making it appear that his gestures are warranted and have communicative meaning.

Michael Cowan comments specifically on the *Veitstänzer* scene: "Nervous bodies—whose tics, twitches, cramps, spasms, convulsions, and paralyses rendered strikingly visible their refusal to obey the dictates of the will—fulfilled a symbolic function in the turn-of-the-century bourgeois imaginary."[46] He points to the fact that the man's movements become interpretable instead of fulfilling a purely objective purpose. The *Veitstänzer* begins to "stick out," as Santner says, and slowly enters the more creative phase of his illness. And while he still wants to show signs of belonging, the agency and force of the posthumanist *Veitstanz* desperately wants to begin its ecstatic dance.[47]

In addition to the erratic skipping, another gesticulation begins, involving the man's shirt collar:

The collar of his greatcoat was turned up; and however hard he tried to fold it down, now with one hand, now with both, he simply couldn't manage it. These things happen. I didn't find it disconcerting. But then I realized, to my boundless astonishment, that the man's busy hands were in fact describing two movements: one a hasty, secretive motion with which he covertly flapped up the collar, and the other the elaborate, prolonged, over-explicit motion, as it were, with which he was trying to fold it down. This observation so perplexed me that a full two minutes passed before I saw that the selfsame fearful, two-syllable hopping motion that had just deserted the man's legs was now going on in his neck, behind the raised greatcoat collar and his nervously busy hands. From that moment on, I was tethered to him.[48]

As soon as the movement in the *Veitstänzer*'s legs subsides, it begins to manifest itself in his hands, as he unsuccessfully attempts to fix his collar. If the gesture had merely been performed once, Malte would probably not have been interested in the man. But the constant, fragmented iterations at alternating speeds draw attention to the *Veitstänzer*'s unpredictable movements and add to the textures of this metropolitan dance text. Santner also detects this breakdown in understanding: "Malte's own terms of description collapse the distinction between physiology and signification, suggesting that the tic in question is a kind of 'signifying stress' moving through the body, an observation that attaches Malte, a struggling writer, all the more passionately to the man."[49]

Not only does the tic signify stress tied to the man's social situation among other onlookers, but Malte also has to reevaluate the phenomena as he watches. As a result, the protagonist in effect begins framing the situation within a movement or dance aesthetic, incorporated in his wide range of reactions. At times, Malte is astonished and confused as he becomes progressively "tethered" to the man. Using Hewitt's lens, this scene lacks a single semiotic meaning, which opens a discourse and incites an "aesthetic of interruption," in much the same way that Endell and Kessler perceived their own dancing objects. While maintaining clear attempts to communicate social meaning through the use of everyday gestures, the episode actually highlights the impossibility of clarity and instead invites many aesthetic interpretations. Thus, the *Veitstänzer* enters an even more creative realm as the illness battles his gestures.

After having observed the man's movement, Malte discovers visible manifestations of the disease's presence:

I grasped that this hopping motion was wandering about his body, trying to break out here or there. I understood his fear of other people, and myself began warily to check whether passers-by noticed anything. A thrill of cold went down my spine when his legs suddenly made a low, convulsive jump, but no one had seen it, and I decided that I would stumble a little too if anyone did notice.[50]

The hopping movement, which manifested itself first in his legs and then in his hands, actually traverses the man's entire body and reveals that the *Veit-stänzer* is host to an uncontrollable disease. Rochelle Tobias notices a similar phenomenon involving many of Malte's urban encounters with other citizens who appear to be "overflowing or spilling out of themselves. . . . Malte is convinced that the body is a vessel for something larger than itself that once exposed will quickly outgrow or outsize itself."[51] At the conclusion of the novel, she writes, he "pours himself out into his notebooks to become an 'impression that will transform itself' and a text that is the world or landscape of his heart."[52] Tobias's reading of Rilke's poetics concerning the expansion of the self exposes parallels with the *Veitstanz*'s desperation to break out of the man's body. This desire to also break free mirrors the drawings of Lasker-Schüler wanting to transform into film. As Tobias has identified the "transformation" of Rilke at the end of the novel, one could interpret the *Veitstanz* as not only inhabiting and using the man's body to express itself, but also as literally wanting to break out of its confines to spread a new form of movement—that of early-twentieth-century dance.

Indeed, through watching and kinesthetic empathy, which I discuss later in this chapter, Malte is able to learn about the modern movement form's aesthetic fragmentation and experimentalism. Therefore, for Rilke, it seems necessary that the battle between gesture and gesticulation and its eventual transition into modern dance be witnessed not only by the protagonist, but by extension, also by the reader of the metropolitan dance text.

The *Veitstänzer*'s condition enters the realm of gesticulation as soon as he cannot control his movements. The hallmark of the neurological disease, which uses the man's body as a medium to manifest symptoms, remains its unpredictability. Malte does not completely lose himself in the aesthetic, but rather remains quite aware of the prevailing social situation, noting the stigma attached to the *Veitstänzer*'s condition. Within the perpetually changing urban surroundings, the protagonist continues to track the afflicted man's gesticulations by sensitively detailing the ongoing battle with the sickness:

His one fully visible leap was so cannily timed . . . that there was no cause for concern. Indeed, everything was still going well; now and then, his other hand would grip the stick and press it more firmly to him, and instantly the danger was averted once again. Even so, I could not keep my anxiety from growing. I knew that as he walked along, making an infinite effort to appear nonchalant and carefree, the terrible convulsions were gathering within his body; within me, too—I shared the fear with which he sensed them growing and growing, and I saw how he clutched the stick when the spasms began inside him.[53]

The bridging of Malte and the man functions as a leitmotiv that demarcates the increasing intensity of the movements and further intensifies their connection. Experienced in his own condition, the man apparently has ways to suppress his symptoms, and accordingly Malte's mind is momentarily put to rest. The *Veitstänzer* is able to make the disease's jumping appear to be of his own volition, thus demonstrating a relationship between the blending of his willful gestures and the disease's involuntary gesticulation. By incorporating a cane, the man appears to have therapeutically and performatively practiced dealing with his condition in order to fit into normative society. He presses the cane into his back as a method of stabilization to control his disorder. His movement practice suggests similarly what Cowan argues happened around 1900 as physical culture created new mental and physical therapies specifically aimed toward helping people overcome fear; they became motivated to succeed in a chaotic, industrial world and to cultivate their will.[54] Like the man's debilitating condition, which affects all facets of his daily life, Malte is also overwhelmingly consumed by the *Veitstänzer*'s fear of not blending in to daily life. Furthermore, the extent to which the man has learned to performatively use his cane to suppress his symptoms mirrors how he also has to "perform" his movements for Malte, by inadvertently turning himself into a spectacle. The dynamic stage that Malte has created similarly blurs the line again between a socially communicative environment and an aesthetic one.

So far Malte's encounter with the man has been in less-populated, pedestrian areas. As the two enter a busier street scene with more people and traffic, the performative space changes. The urban surroundings and stimuli cause the gesticulations of the *Veitstanz* to act in full force and the performance to reach the pinnacle:

The Place Saint-Michel was busy with large numbers of vehicles and people hurrying to and fro, and often we would be caught between two carriages; . . . we walked out on to the bridge, and all was well. It went well. Now, an element of uncertainty affected his walk, and he would take two paces, then he stood still again. Stood. His left hand gently released its grip on the stick and rose, so slowly that I saw it tremble against the air; he pushed his hat back a little and wiped his brow. He turned his head slightly, and his gaze swept unsteadily across the sky, the houses and the water, without taking any of it in, and then he gave in. The stick was gone, he flung wide his arms as if he meant to fly, and something like a force of Nature broke forth from him and doubled him up and tore him back and set him to nodding and bowing and slung some dancing power out of him and into the crowd. For by now a large number of people had gathered around him, and I saw him no more.[55]

This climactic scene shows the *Veitstänzer*'s downfall as he enters a crowded area. The heightened agitation leaves him more susceptible to potential spectators; even if they are not yet watching him, the mere suspicion of being seen is enough to send the man's entire body into a fit. Their observing triggers a vicious and ever-worsening cycle of fear in the afflicted man, whose concern to hide his condition intensifies his symptoms. His own willing gestures are no match for the disease's uncontrollable gesticulations. Cowan would deem the man unable to regain control of his body through performative therapy, thus undermining his chances for autonomy. Similarly, the perpetually changing cityscape, resulting from their walking together, brings the relationship between the dancing disease and the urban space even more closely together. It is as if the metropolitan area directly affects dance. While the crowd of people who surround the fallen man functions to provide a more formal observation of his movement and concretely reflects Foster's theater-in-the-round setting, the mere suspicion of the *Veitstänzer*'s being watched while traversing the city, toward the beginning of the scene, virtually allows the entire metropolis to operate as the performative stage. This more dynamic understanding of how the urban space continually transforms builds on Foster's conceptualization of framing. Likewise, it broadens Bauer's idea of a *Schauplatz* by adding the dimension of the strolling individual whose surroundings and perception are perpetually changing.

The malady consuming the *Veitstänzer* operates in full force by combining the movements that Malte had witnessed since the beginning of the scene: the fragmented steps integrated with a complete standstill of this "dancer's" feet, adjustments with his hands, letting go of his cane, and a full body surge as if preparing for flight. While observing his movements in isolation, Malte had at times misjudged them to be part of the man's willful gestures. However, these distorted motions in combination reveal the man's inner battle between gesture and gesticulation. The disease not only uses the *Veitstänzer*'s body as a means to express itself via "dancing power" (*Tanzkraft*),[56] it literally seeks to break free and make itself known, even if only to Malte. Furthermore, Rilke uses the bridges not only to further cement Malte's and the *Veitstänzer*'s kinesthetic bond, but also to highlight the perpetually changing urban landscape that both traverse. By deciding to stage the man's demise on a pedestrian bridge, Rilke emphasizes the battle between the disease and the bourgeois gestures, and with that disallows the man from reaching the "other side." This choreographic choice could point to the perpetual push and pull between nineteenth-century bourgeois conventions—both in society and in theatrical dance practices—and, at the turn of the century, the modernist embrace of experimental aesthetics in terms of bodily movements and spatial considerations. While the *Veitstanz* does succeed in expressing itself, it will forever need a human as its vehicle for articulation. After all, early-twentieth-century dance could never have happened without the strong reaction to nineteenth-century traditions, and in that respect it is strangely indebted to it. Similarly, staging the downfall on the bridge demonstrates that the connection between Malte and the *Veitstänzer* cannot continue: the protagonist can only follow him while they are both moving, otherwise the covert investigation must end. The aesthetic enterprise of the man's dancing loses its power on the bridge as soon as Malte loses sight of him. Whether on deserted streets or densely populated boulevards, a myriad of urban stimuli—crossings, bridges, bystanders, trash, vehicles, and overall ambience—are allowed to penetrate and chip away at the *Veitstänzer*'s already vulnerable and progressively declining condition. Decidedly interpenetrating and influencing the man's movements, the city seems, therefore, to be directly responsible for inciting the emergence of a modern dance aesthetic through *Veitstanz*. For this battle to occur, the man, his disease, and the city must be interacting at the same time. The sickness requires his body as a host to symptomatically express itself through abrupt movement. Thus, *Veitstanz* as a posthumanist entity is granted an overpowering agency to take over the man's own willful movements.

Kinesthetic Empathy through Motion and Emotion

Throughout the passage, while the intensity of the *Veitstanz* continues to build, the connection between Malte and the man similarly magnifies. Before having directly encountered the man, and judging only the reactions of the waiters, Malte feels his fear start to develop: "I sensed a touch of fear rising within me. Something was impelling me to cross the street; but I merely started to walk faster."[57] An unseen power compels Malte to investigate the mystery. The walk of the frightened flâneur throughout the changing urban environment seems to be used as a choreographic device to build tension and narrative suspense. Not only does he have to painstakingly watch the man, he has to constantly evaluate his surroundings. After having seen the *Veitstänzer* perform his erratic hand movements, Malte writes, "From that moment on, I was tethered to him."[58] Involving himself and the reader even more, Malte often mentions that his fear increases as the *Veitstänzer*'s gesticulations intensify. The protagonist's connection with him, however, is not solely limited to the man's physical movements, but becomes increasingly enmeshed with the *Veitstänzer*'s actual emotions.

In fact, the protagonist clearly empathizes with the man's movements as they both physically react to the "thrill of cold."[59] By using a street crossing and bridge, Rilke physically and symbolically connects the two because of their respective reactions to the disease's performance and to the responses of others on the urban stage; the protagonist implicates himself in the performance—a "strange urban *pas de deux*,"[60] as Santner characterizes it—by also dancing with the *Veitstänzer*, whose sickness has symbolically transferred itself to Malte's body. Susan Foster would term this phenomenon "movement contagion": "The dancing body's 'contagion' can impel our bodies as outward manifestations of an interiorized psyche, to mimic its movement, and, as a result, feel its feelings. Or it can prompt an active engagement with physicality, enlivening our perception of our own bodies' articulateness."[61] Instead of being a mere observer of the man's gestures, gesticulation, and dance movement, the protagonist slowly embodies the man's physical experience, thus becoming even more aware of his own body. Rilke himself also relays similar thoughts on how Paris can replace the writers' tools with "unspeakably subtler and more precise ones creating thousands of unexpected things."[62] In both cases, early-twentieth-century dance can reinvigorate and awaken the senses to what is already there. In keeping with Endell's and Fuller's focus on an aesthetic object, which should correspondingly have an impressionistic effect on the feelings, Rilke highlights the complexity and richness of Malte's sensual perception and compulsion to understand.

In an Endellian fashion, the protagonist appears both to empathize and to analyze: he regards the *Veitstänzer*'s movements as a strange and unique occurrence worthy of study among the multitude of stimuli in the urban space. Malte then begins decoding the man's performative movements, based on other people's reactions to his dance. He can also empathize with the *Veit-*

stänzer. In a sense, the architectural arrangement of the metropolitan scene—the passersby, the streets and bridges—contributes to the performative urban environment, which further intensifies the man's dance and shows the city's impact on an individual: Rilke's letter to Tora Holmström clearly details these effects. In the next chapter, we see that Döblin's writings pick up on this interpenetration. One could argue that the protagonist has a profound understanding of the man's physical and social situation, without even having spoken to him. This further demonstrates the dancerliness of their encounter, which lacks words and uses the body and urban environment as the sole means of aesthetic communication. The protagonist has based his conclusion purely on the man's involuntary pathological movements, his interaction with the urban space, and Malte's own kinesthetic empathy.

Foster based her work on the concepts of John Martin, the *New York Times* critic whose writing appeared from the 1930s to the 1960s. According to his theory of dance expression, the observer, while watching a dancing body, will feel kinesthetic sensations similar to those of the dancer—a process called "inner mimicry," in which the onlooker in a sense imitates the movements of the dancer.[63] This phenomenon relates to our physical reactions to all kinds of events, Martin claims: we pucker our lips when we watch someone bite into a lemon, or we yawn when someone around us does. Martin clearly connects the everyday realm of gesture and the realm of dance movement. By demonstrating the interconnectedness of gesture and dance movement as both being capable of creating kinesthetic empathy or inner mimicry, the *Veitstanz* serves as a hybrid embodiment of gesture and gesticulation battling each other, further intensified by the urban space, and, as a result, constituting an instance of early-twentieth-century dance.

Martin's argument leads to his depicting the emerging modern dance and creates radically new assumptions regarding movement and motion:

The modern dancer, instead of employing the cumulative resources of academic tradition, cuts through directly to the source of all dancing. He utilizes the principle that every emotional state tends to express itself in movement, and that the movements thus created spontaneously, though they are not representational, reflect accurately in each case the character of the particular emotional state. Because of the inherent contagion of bodily movement, which makes the onlooker feel sympathetically in his own musculature the exertions he sees in somebody else's musculature, the dancer is able to convey through movement the most intangible emotional experience.[64]

By abandoning the stories and spectacle of ballet, modern dance engaged the body in developing a personal narrative. Similarly, by not referring to academic tradition and by moving toward a more emotional state, Martin's theory corresponds strikingly to Endell's and Fuller's approach, since they did not have an academic background in their fields of work and instead focused on the overall impression and the physical response of the body to outer stimuli. Jacob Haubenreich's study, which directly concerns the *Veitstänzer*, also incorporates the empathy of the reader: "These bodily figures function more like symptoms than symbols, participating in a disruption of traditional meaning-making based on a stable symbolic order—a disruption which involves us as readers, who are also swept up in a surge."[65] Thus, the readers bear witness to and kinesthetically involved themselves in the dance's performative immediacy, which becomes alive and renewed every time they engage with the metropolitan dance text.

Rilke's Writings on Dance

The first part of this chapter addressed both the strong influence of the urban space on the *Veitstanz* and the dance's critical transition from communicative gesture to uncontrollable gesticulation. In this next section, I discuss the degree to which Rilke's writings on dance, gesture, and the body, particularly in his letters, were influenced by his encounters in and around Paris, Berlin, and Italy from 1902 to 1910. While performances did engage the author's gestural imagination, creative individuals with whom he had close personal relationships also played a significant role: Hugo von Hofmannsthal, Harry Graf Kessler, and most importantly Auguste Rodin. Rilke certainly was not in a void concerning his encounters with dance movement, because he belonged to a broader social movement that Cynthia Novack calls the *movement environment*. Her term essentially characterizes a permeation of various dance movements that influence each other and create an atmosphere "implicitly perceived and understood by everyone."[66] These experiences seep into Rilke's literary depictions, particularly with the *Veitstanz* scene, and further his aesthetic transmutation of that movement into early-twentieth-century dance.

As discussed earlier, in a letter to his wife Clara on April 26, 1906, Rilke describes a Spanish flamenco dancer he saw in the artist Ignacio Zuloagas's atelier in Montmartre,[67] about whom he would later that year write the poem "Spanish Dancer" ("Spanische Tänzerin"). On February 11, 1907, in a letter to Clara, Rilke tells her about attending a wedding in Capri and describes the dancing of a tarantella.[68] While these two excerpts hark back to traditional styles of dance, they also suggest nonconventional, modern forms. Writing to his friend Lou Andreas-Salomé on July 18, 1903, while at the Worpswede artist colony, Rilke recollects an encounter in Paris: a man stumbles along the streets with an abrupt and unpredictable gait, which presumably inspired the author to depict the *Veitstänzer*. Interestingly, Rilke writes this letter once he has gained some distance from the Parisian encounter; it probably had a profound effect on his thinking and aesthetic and demanded lengthy rumination before he formulated his thoughts in writing. While his letter very closely resembles the literary depiction, it also uses different dance imagery to describe the man's body, in which "the excitement of a thousand dances were."[69] Instead of conceptualizing the *Veitstanz* as an organic whole, this epistolary depiction alludes to the endless frenzy and continual momentum of isolated body parts in creating countless fragmented dances. Where Fuller's dance and Endell's metropolitan dance text "In Front of the Café" focus on the overall impressionistic entirety of numerous continual stimuli affecting the senses, Rilke aims to break down cohesiveness into smaller fragments. The multiplicity and boundless intellectual space created through observing these three dances brings them together precisely because of their seemingly contradictory movement philosophies: the paradoxical nature of modernity and modernism. For Endell and Rilke, the bustling metropolitan atmosphere was able to evoke two stylistically divergent dance depictions. Recalling his own comment about the city writing itself, Rilke began to conceptualize dance as part of an urban environment no longer limited solely to a theater or dance space: essentially, the everyday plight of one man in the dynamically changing city could be seen in an aesthetic and dancerly light.

Another difference between the real and the literary *Veitstänzer* is the order in which Rilke choreographs the movements and interactive looks of passersby. Instead of Malte's indirect discovery of the man through the waiter's strange reaction in the dance text, Rilke first encounters the real *Veitstänzer* through a group of people who are staring at the man, who unsuccessfully tries to pull down his own collar. While the depiction in the letter probably stays faithful to the actual order of events, from a narrative and choreographic perspective, it also seems to reveal too much; the literary version, however, proceeds in a more mysterious fashion, by allowing the curiosity of Malte and the reader to slowly grow and by letting the *Veitstänzer's* unpredictable movements build to a dramatic climax. While Rilke was not able to use his letter to Andreas-Salomé as the finished version, it forms a critical foundation that he would mold and craft into his metropolitan dance text. Even though the author transmutes his personal perspective to the protagonist Malte, Rilke maintains the heightened tension of his text by focusing attention on the enigmatic and dance-like qualities of the *Veitstänzer*.

Like Kessler, Rilke and his wife saw Ruth St. Denis perform in 1906. In a letter written in Berlin to Karl von der Heydt, a banker who helped Rilke during his financial struggles and was also interested in literature, Rilke writes that Clara saw St. Denis perform and reported to him, "It wasn't much different qualitatively from yesterday's performance, but nonetheless striking."[70] And on November 27, 1906, Rilke writes to his wife stating that he had read Hofmannsthal's essay on St. Denis—most likely "Die unvergleichliche Tänzerin" ("The Incomparable Dancer")—and would be sending her, Clara, a copy.[71] In this essay, Hofmannsthal reviews St. Denis's dance *Radha* and formulates in it the basis of his thoughts regarding emerging modern dance. He characterizes the dancer's unconventional, antimimetic, and indescribable dance as an intoxicating linking of gestures.[72] According to Hofmannsthal, she dances in a glittering, see-through costume that hints at her nakedness and points toward endless meaning.[73] The dance rhythm reminds him of an 1889 performance he witnessed in Paris by Cambodian dancers (incidentally, these are the ones Rodin saw and drew, and the same ones Rilke had written about in his letters).[74] In Hofmannsthal's conversation with Rodin, the artist believes that these dancers move "correctly" while European dancers dance "incorrectly," and he bases his judgment on what he describes as feeling with his eyes, like when his ears hear wrong notes.[75] While Hofmannsthal also notes that St. Denis's dance is indescribably beautiful, he remains undecided about whether the audience likes it,[76] a reaction that points again to a modern aesthetic struggling to emerge. Of course, Hofmannsthal is able to characterize her movements, yet by calling her "incomparable," he alludes to her freshness as a new kind of dancing figure. St. Denis's unconventional depiction, indescribable gestures, and dialectic between body and garb probably permeated Rilke's gestural imagination by inspiring him to conceptualize and experiment with the unorthodox *Veitstänzer* whose movements he transforms aesthetically to evoke endless meaning.

Furthermore, as discussed in chapter 3, on October 29, 1906, the cosmopolitan arts patron Harry Graf Kessler, who also knew Rilke, had written about St. Denis to Hofmannsthal, who had not yet seen her perform. Kessler describes her "Indian temple dance," most likely *Radha*, as if she were completely naked but, at the same time, wearing a fairy-tale dress made of black gold. However, in his posthumanist depiction, costume and body seem to blend as she becomes both a genderless, ethereal being and a clearly gendered woman.[77] Kessler clearly senses the dialectic of body vs. object and gender vs. nongender, as well as a hybrid union of such opposites.

The fact that he writes to Hofmannsthal before the author had seen St. Denis dance could point to Kessler's direct influence on "Die unvergleichliche Tänzerin," and therefore also on Rilke. Thus, Rilke may have recognized Kessler's perceived paradoxes in *Radha* and may have wanted to relay a similar dichotomy in his *Veitstänzer*, both as a man dealing with his disease and the agency of the sickness expressing itself using the man's body as a vessel. In the metropolitan dance text, it is deliberately unclear at which point the man's movements are willful and when the disease's gesticulations take over: indeed, the relative power of the two forces wavers throughout the dance depiction. As we saw in the previous chapter, Kessler similarly thematicized an oscillating ambiguity with Joseph, who embodied simultaneously a child-likeness and the future. Both St. Denis's and the *Veitstänzer*'s dancing, therefore, embodies a vacillating, dynamic duality that defies a single, hegemonic interpretation.

After Rilke published *The Notebooks of Malte Laurids Brigge*, dance movement continued to influence his writing and intellect. Aside from having witnessed St. Denis dancing and having read Hofmannsthal's essay, Rilke had also seen Nijinsky perform *Le Spectre de la rose* in June 1911. Rather than referencing nineteenth-century ballet technique, this modern *pas de deux* favored curving, tendril-like arm and hand movements reminiscent of *Jugendstil* or art nouveau. Alluding to the opening of *La Sylphide*, in which James is asleep as the sylph enters the window, *Le Spectre de la rose* reverses the gender roles by having Nijinsky leap into the room as a young woman sleeps on a chair. Additionally, Nijinsky assumes an androgynous role: his traditionally masculine powerful jumping is juxtaposed with a feminized upper body adorned with numerous silk rose petals. On July 4, 1911, having seen Nijinsky's performance, Rilke wrote to his friend and patron Marie von Thurn und Taxis that he wanted to create a work for the Russian dancer—a poem that could be imbibed and then danced.[78] His formulation seems to strikingly relate to his letter to Tora Holmström, whom he advises to let Paris slowly seep into the artist and allow the city to use the body as a means of expression. In both instances the body seems to channel an outside, nonanthropocentric stimulus—a poem or a city—to have a direct effect, through ingestion or osmosis, on itself as a means of transmutation and articulation. Rilke marks the power of these objects, elevating their agency arguably to a poetic and literal level. Harry Graf Kessler noted in his journal on the same day that he was excited to work with Rilke in conceptualizing the piece.[79] However, the project was never realized beyond a list of characters, "Figurines pour un ballet," and two dialogues in German.

While the role reversal, androgynous depiction, and break from nineteenth-century ballet aesthetics in *Le Spectre de la rose* did not directly influence the *Veitstanz* scene, since the ballet was performed after the publication of the novel, these ideas still demonstrate a rupture with the past and would become part of Rilke's gestural and dance imagination. Dance continued to influence his writing, as witnessed by his 1913–1919 exchange of letters with Clotilde Sacharoff.[80]

One of the greatest influences on Rilke's dance and gestural imagination was his relationship with Rodin. Rilke had moved to Paris to write a monograph on the artist. In a letter to his wife Clara on September 2, 1902, the author describes his initial encounter, which involved walking around the artist's property in Meudon, a landscape littered with broken sculpted body parts—hands, arms, legs, and torsos—that had belonged to Rodin's *Porte de l'Enfer* or *Gates of Hell*. Rilke's act of strolling on the grounds certainly evokes not only the image of flânerie in the city and Malte's frightful encounter with the *Veitstänzer*, but also his *literally* noticing fragments (of body parts) in the Benjaminian sense, which could stimulate "thousands of meanings" and "dances." According to Rilke, one could "create new connections from the broken pieces; new, bigger, legitimate unity. And this richness, this endless, continuous invention, this presence of mind, pureness and vehemence of new beginnings, this inexhaustibility, this youth. . . . That is without equal in the history of humankind."[81] Breaking with tradition, Rilke laid out a modern aesthetic reminiscent of the way the sculptural body fragments elicited a response toward unity. He conceived of these separate body parts, therefore, as evoking a new, valid meaning that embraces an infinite and dynamic understanding of the world. Rilke's focus on the body parts of the *Veitstänzer*, particularly on hand and leg articulation, allows for a similar reading, given his previous encounter with Rodin's fragments from the *Porte de l'Enfer*. On the one hand, the man's abrupt gestures point toward the fragmentation of a particular body part; on the other, they demand a new hermeneutic approach to invest them with aesthetic meaning. And certainly a strong influence on the man's fragmented movements is the urban space—its crossings, bridges, pedestrians, trash, and overall ambience— which allow the metropolis and the *Veitstanz* to express themselves as empowered, interpenetrating dancing entities.

Rodin's influence continued to permeate Rilke's aesthetic in relation to body and movement; the author wrote to Clara on October 15, 1907, about his encounter with the artist's drawings, *Danseuses Cambodgiennes*. On seeing Rodin's exhibition at the Salon l'Automne, Rilke became mesmerized particularly by the dancer's hands in the study "Fleurs humaines." In a Rodinesque fashion, the author assigned independent and willful attributes to the hands, which can sleep and awaken. In the dormant phase, they rest on the dancer's lap, and are still. However, on waking, "These fingers spread apart, open, like beams of light or curved like the petals of a rose of Jericho. The enchanted, delighted and anxious fingers, at the end of a long arm, are dancing. And the entire body uses this extreme dance to maintain balance in the air."[82] By likening the hand to a rose of Jericho, Rilke implies that not just ten fingers are moving, but rather a seemingly infinite number. He concentrates on the personification and articulation of the hand whose fingers actually dance. While the focus seems to be on just one part of the body, Rilke understands it as a unity. Whereas the human body as a whole is normally depicted as dancing, he decenters this depiction by imbuing the hands with posthumanist agency. In a rather "unheimlich" fashion, he seems to disembody the fingers and hands by making them appear more as "objects," but then he joins them to the full body again. For the author, the hands and fingers are the main attraction, which in turn dominates the entire "human" body. In regard to the *Veitstänzer*, Rilke also described the man's hand movements in detail as they secretly but incessantly flipped his collar. Similar to the articulated motions of the Cambodian dancer, the man's hand movements in turn migrated to his legs and then eventually throughout his whole body, evoking an unorthodox dance.

In Rilke's monograph on Rodin, he describes the artist's drawing technique as one that involves using contours with "vibrating outlines."[83] Jana Schuster has argued that these multiple contours create the illusion that the subject is actually dancing.[84] Georg Simmel's comments on Rodin's depictions as representative of the "modern Heraclitus-like existence,"[85] which focused on ever-present change and the perpetual flux in the universe. Both the Cambodian dancer's and the *Veitstänzer's* continually fluctuating hand movements attuned Rilke's senses to a more Rodinesque view by focusing on the vitality and agency of living hands; these posthumanist hands as seeming "objects" can have a vigorous life of their own, devoid of a complete human body. Extrapolating further, the act of walking through a continually changing metropolis functions as a catalyst that further incites and interpenetrates the man's fragmented chorea, and that, in turn, adds another intensifying dimension that Rilke and Malte have to account for. In chapter 6, Lasker-Schüler's drawings also draw on Rodin's technique to evoke dancerly movement.

Clearly, Rilke was keenly attuned to his movement environment, influenced by watching performances and through his interactions with Hofmannsthal, Kessler, and Rodin. Being situated in a metropolis and able to travel enhanced his ability to become familiar with and develop his own movement imaginary and aesthetic. His experience with the actual *Veitstänzer* in Paris opened his mind to experimenting aesthetically with everyday occurrences, illness, and dynamic city space. Rilke situated his flâneur Malte on a performative stage; the protagonist is forced to dynamically observe urban stimuli continually effecting the *Veitstanz*. His attendance at St. Denis's performances and his reading of Hofmannsthal's "Die unvergleichliche Tänzerin" exposed him to a new and unconventional presentation of the dancing body and its oscillating existence, both of which he integrated into his *Veitstänzer*. Although his encounter with Nijinsky happened after his novel's publication, gender role reversal and modern movement were already part of the aesthetic influencing his gestural imagination. Above all, Rodin played a vital role in shaping Rilke's intellectual and aesthetic development into modernity by highlighting the hermeneutics of fragmentation. The author's experience with the *Porte de l'Enfer* and *Danseuses Cambodgiennes* honed his skills in recognizing the vitality of details and the aestheticized power of singular body parts, undoubtedly influencing his fragmented depiction of the *Veitstänzer's* extremities. As Rilke had relayed to Holmström: the "boundless and incessant" effect of the city works to "transform, enhance and develop an individual" who creates "thousands of unexpected things."[86] His situation in the metropolis, particularly in Paris, allowed his experience with bodily fragments and movement to transform his aesthetic and manifest themselves in his literary depiction of the *Veitstänzer*.

Interpreting the New Dance Aesthetic

At the end of the *Veitstanz* episode, the man's worst fate has been realized: he has become the concern and spectacle of the crowd. Rilke's term "dancing power" (*Tanzkraft*), along with the description from his letter to Andreas-Salomé describing the real *Veitstänzer's* excitement of "thousands of dances," further point to the dance-like nature and performativity of the man's symptoms. Whereas the sudden, angular movements fail as social communication, Rilke's text shows how they succeed as aesthetic expression and seem to decenter the human perspective by bringing in the vitality of the nonanthropocentric dance. However shocked Malte and the onlookers might be by the *Veitstänzer's* performance, Rilke draws on the possibility that these disjointed and isolated movements might be regarded as inciting a changing aesthetic, from traditional theatrical beauty to fragmentation in the metropolis as a new norm. This transformation is realized in Rilke's depiction of the *Porte de l'Enfer* and *Danseuses Cambodgiennes*.

While Malte has always felt more comfortable in libraries, he recognizes the need to explore the metropolis, and this in turn inspires him to write. Essentially, fear of the unknown in the urban environment spurs the protagonist to deal with and write about the experience of modernity. Harald Neumeyer recognizes Malte's fear of change as resulting precisely from the protagonist's not knowing where it will lead. Malte experiences this change not as a development toward a new way of perceiving, working, or living, but rather as a loss of previously fixed meaning.[87] Despite the protagonist's resistance to this change of meaning, Rilke, as an author, calls into question the perceived repulsiveness of the *Veitstänzer*'s motions, demanding that his protagonist and the reader reevaluate their ways of seeing. Steffan Arndal suggests that learning to see does not begin correspondingly by developing a correct, concentrated, or conscious seeing, but rather through the erasure of learned concepts and reclaiming the original perception of a child.[88] Although the goal of the new way of seeing remains unclear, Malte's rumination, in a section following the man's dance, demonstrates the beginning of his conceptualization.

Malte notes his understanding of Baudelaire's poem, "Une Charogne," in which "There is no choice, and no refusing [of what one sees]."[89] Here, Baudelaire writes about a decaying carcass that the poem's protagonist and his lover encounter during a stroll. David Weir reads the active process of deterioration as creating its own kind of vitality as voracious maggots feast on the dead animal.[90] This juxtaposition is similarly pursued by Malte when he describes a pregnant woman who carries "a twofold fruit: a child, and a death."[91] Weir's comment also reflects a posthumanist mode by noting the agency and decentering of the human perspective. One could also relate "Une Charogne" to the *Veitstänzer*'s life-compromising disease. The decomposing carcass's appearance of being lively as it is consumed represents an example of nonanthropocentric empowerment and Baudelaire's radical aesthetization, which can be seen as similar to the man's performance. The *Veitstänzer*'s debilitating disease devastates his body, while the intensity and strength of his movements create an enlivening vigor for Malte's writing and intellectual development, as well as a new, emerging dance vocabulary. Through usurping the human body, the disease and the urban experience are given a platform to express itself. Yet as Arndal writes, for Malte as well as for Rilke, ugliness remains ugly.[92] While the ugly does not become beautiful in a traditional sense, one could conceive of the man's movements as an aesthetic of fragmentation.

On a grander scale, if we interpret this dance as a symbolic battle between the bourgeoisie's losing control of gesture, as Agamben suggests, and becoming susceptible to involuntary gesticulation, as Hewitt remarks, then one could understand the *Veitstanz* as symbolizing early-twentieth-century dance eagerly emerging from battle and demanding a new aesthetic. This also pushes the idea of what can be conceptualized as a "dancer," since Rilke empowers a posthumanist neurological condition instead of the human psyche to be the source of new dance. In contrast to Fuller, St. Denis, and Nijinsky, who already maintained an experimental and individualistic ethos and could more or less be considered dancers by their movements and the framing of their stage performances, the *Veitstänzer* demonstrates the body struggling to maintain its social and communicative gestures and eventually gives in to the new aesthetic of modern dance. Rilke's metropolitan dance text, therefore, does not just focus on the performativity of his abrupt symptoms, but instead chronicles the progression throughout, displaying the new movement form as a product of the metropolitan experience. In the next chapter, Döblin's protagonist Ella functions in a similar way to Malte and the man. While the level of interpenetration here, in contrast to Endell's and Fuller's representation, is less hybridized, the interaction and causal effects of the metropolitan environment and *Veitstanz* still act as profoundly active agents inciting the man's symptoms. The metropolis—represented by road crossings, bridges, and passersby—has played a prominent role in deciding to express itself through the man's body and likewise through Rilke's metropolitan dance text. The man clearly has applied his various movement therapies to tame his sickness, but the abrupt movements, which are to become aestheticized in early-twentieth-century dance, are ready to be born. Rilke's experience in Paris and in writing about dance and gesture both indirectly and directly inform the *Veitstanz*. As part of the author's movement environment, St. Denis's *Radha* influences the depiction of the *Veitstänzer* by providing a precedent for experimenting with unconventional and dialectic literary depictions. The greatest influences on Rilke's depiction are probably from the actual *Veitstänzer*, Rodin's *Porte de l'Enfer*, and *Danseuses Cambodgiennes*— interactions that clearly demonstrate a focus on the living and aestheticized singular body part.

Agamben comments on the incomprehensibility of gesture: "An age that has lost its gestures is, for this reason, obsessed by them. For human beings who have lost every sense of naturalness, each gesture becomes a destiny.

And the more gestures lose their ease under the action of invisible powers, the more life becomes indecipherable."[93] One can connect this illegibility to both the involuntary gesticulation of a nervous society and the beginnings of modern dance. The *Veitstänzer*'s performance demonstrates Malte's difficulty in distinguishing between these forms as they begin to blend gesture, gesticulation, and dance—similar to St. Denis's indistinguishable body and dress in *Radha* from Kessler's account. Rilke seems to suggest that gestures should not necessarily be easily understood or convey a single meaning, but like dance, should open a window for further boundless interpretation, as he learned from Rodin. In the context of this chapter, therefore, gesture and gesticulation are shown to harbor aesthetic meaning, moving beyond their communicative features.

Additionally, as a frightened yet determined flâneur, not only does Malte have to continually concentrate on the abrupt and unexpected chorea of the *Veitstänzer*'s movements, he has to reevaluate the perpetually changing urban environment while he walks. This metropolitan setting—the passersby, the streets, the bridges—forms a dynamic, interpenetrative performative space and brings the new dance out from its confines in a theater. Not only do the aesthetics of modern dance find representation in the *Veitstanz*, but so does the fragmented perception of the modern city dweller who has to battle with innumerable stimuli in the metropolis. Rilke not only bridges gesture, gesticulation, and early-twentieth-century dance, but also theater and urban spaces.

If the *Veitstänzer* represents the modern body whose own willful gestures have to battle gesticulation, then the resulting fragmented combination of these movement styles demands a new aesthetic, which Malte only just begins to grapple with after observing the man's performance. Similarly, as Judith Ryan has commented, Malte not only learns to see, he has to learn to read the movement.[94] The process of being able to understand and interpret the *Veitstänzer*'s movements arises from Malte's curiosity in observing the man's struggle with gesture and gesticulation. Malte, like Rilke, is implicated in and forced to grapple with the performance that embodies the crisis of the modern individual. While the movement contagion does not affect spectators like the waiters, it fully engages Malte, Rilke, and potentially others (including the reader) to become involved in a developing dance aesthetic, one that is further intensified by and interacts with the metropolis. Malte empathizes and becomes thoroughly intertwined kinesthetically with the man's movement. By having the *Veitstanz* win the battle, in this instance, Rilke lends a voice to early-twentieth-century dance practices and suggests that Malte and the reader take notice of peculiarities of the moving and dancing body. The author also highlights the agency of a nonanthropocentric disease to not only claim power over a human body but to use it to create a new modernist aesthetic: no longer is the human the sole creator of dance; the urban space and other objects can also choreograph. Thus, Rilke brings these object-dancers to the level of the human and also ushers in a new ethics.

Nonetheless, as the ending of the *Veitstanz* on the bridge suggests, the struggle between nineteenth-century bourgeois dance traditions and modernity continues. The next chapter highlights this transition even more explicitly in Döblin's ballerina Ella. Similarly, as Ryan has commented, while Rilke did uphold tradition, he also tried to break away from it.[95] She further remarks that *Malte Laurids Brigge* is "precariously positioned on the boundary between naturalism and aestheticism."[96] Based on Rilke's writings on dance, his literary *Veitstänzer* contributes to the advent of early-twentieth-century modern dance with the metropolitan space and significantly fosters an emerging critical understanding of their experimental aesthetics.

Five

Documenting the Demise of Ballet and the Emergence of Modern Dance in the Hospital

Döblin's Early Texts on Dance and Space

Following the fall of Rilke's unorthodox *Veitstänzer*, this chapter charts the course of a similar demise, but of a more traditional type of dancer. Alfred Döblin's prose text "The Dancer and the Body" (1910) portrays a young dancer's plight: stricken with an illness and an untamable body that begins to have a life and will of its own, the protagonist Ella is brought to a hospital and remains under the strict supervision of medical specialists, who read her symptoms daily and track their findings. The girl's conflict with her body escalates to the point that after she embroiders three figures and dances an unharmonious waltz with her body, she stabs herself in the chest. Döblin portrays an unruly body, quite similar to Rilke's *Veitstänzer*, dealing with the stress of a highly scrutinized life, first as a dancer and second as a hospital patient; both roles force Ella and her "body" to perform in accord with her surroundings. While the narrative hardly describes her dancing, it does intimately depict the effects of the environment on the dancer's behavior and the performativity of herself.

Whereas Endell's and Rilke's depictions of the dancing body were closely tied to the outside urban space, Döblin's dancer performs in an intimate institutional setting, however, it is still intrinsically tied to modernity and the metropolitan environment. Like Malte's discovering the abrupt movements of the *Veitstänzer*, who might be seeking medical treatment, it seems that Döblin continues this narrative trajectory by following his dancer Ella into the hospital. Although the doctors and nurses do not engage with more traditional understandings of flânerie as Rilke, Endell, and Kessler did, they do meticulously study, treat, and document their specimen and her movements as a casualty of modernity. The reader should maintain an expanded understanding of the term *flânerie*, as moving beyond an exclusive focus on events in the streets and looking at how stimuli can profoundly aesthetically change Ella's movements in the interior of the hospital. This chapter analyzes "The Dancer and the Body" in its historical context, alongside Döblin's other writings on feminism, dance, and city space. It first addresses his early writing aesthetics, including his *Kinostil*, which reflects the episodic nature of early cinema and manifests itself in his metropolitan dance texts. Second, his earliest text, "Modern" (1896), programmatically demonstrates an unusually feminist view of Wilhelmine society; this social and political essay bookends a narrative depicting Bertha, an unemployed seamstress, who ostensibly becomes *absorbed* into the urban space at the end of the story. Third, displaying his knowledge of contemporary discourses on dance, in 1912 Döblin published a text—similar in structure to "Modern"—in the literary magazine *Der Sturm* called "Dancers" ("Tänzerinnen"), which bemoans how dance has become solely a woman's domain filled with wooing dances and natural movement; he then exuberantly depicts two dancers: one of whom exudes the abrupt movement qualities of *Ausdruckstanz*.

Although it appears that the city does not play as prominent a role in this last narrative as it does in "Modern," Rilke's *Veitstänzer*, Endell's square, and Fuller's theater, it still has a major impact on modernity and the dancing individual's movement and interaction with the metropolitan space, subverting the nineteenth-century Parisian idea of flânerie. As Michael Cowan puts it: "Attributed to the effects of modernization generally and to modern economic transformations in particular, the neurasthesia of modern culture found its most direct expression in the form of a body that refused to obey the dictates of the will."[1] Becoming clinically sick because of modernity was therefore not unfamiliar, particularly given conflict between the body and spirit in the case of Ella. Through reading these texts as representative of Döblin's dance aesthetic and spatial imagination, I argue that in "Modern" he modifies his characterization of the absorbent and posthumanist city, which causes Bertha to perform. In "The Dancer and the Body," Döblin now manifests the aggregate urban space into a looming and intense pressure put on by the modern doctors, thus provoking Ella to dance. My understanding of the metropolitan space integrates both macro and micro stimuli of all kinds—individuals, objects such as buildings or streetcars, and the spatial environment—as outlined in chapter 1. Like the perpetual dynamics of the productive metropolis and the objective camera view of the streets that documents Bertha's downfall and envelops her in "Modern," the constant observation of the male doctors and female nurses also creates a clinical atmosphere focused on experimentation and scientific discovery. Similar to the flâneur-like gaze surveying the Berlin milieu at the beginning of "Modern," the doctors act as medical detectives who monitor her symptoms and behaviors less as individuals but more as an imposing, aggregate mass—an extension of the metropolitan spatial ethos. Unlike earlier alienist asylums, which were situated in the countryside for patients, the metropolis created the space for university clinics. These were established at the end of the nineteenth and beginning of the twentieth centuries with a focus largely on research: arguably, the dancer was brought to one of these types of urban clinics. Spurred on by modernity, this scientific environment causes a battle to develop even further between Ella's nineteenth-century ballet and her twentieth-century modern body. Like Malte, who watched the *Veitstänzer*'s body progress from gesture to gesticulation and finally to modern dance in the Parisian streets, the doctors witness Ella's balletic body eagerly explode with expression, demonstrating clear impulses of the emerging expressionist dance (*Ausdruckstanz*) taking place in and being caused by the urban hospital environment. Along with his *Kinostil*, the interaction and interpenetration of Döblin's characters with their urban environment, specifically in "Modern" and "The Dancer and the Body," further contributes to the genre of the metropolitan dance text.

Döblin's Aesthetics

During his school days Döblin could not connect with classical culture such as the works of Schiller and Goethe.[2] Instead he preferred the "unliterariness" of Dostoevsky's writings because they dealt with such themes as defiance and rebellion, which propelled him into an uncharted and boundless realm.[3] He was also attracted to the popular arts such as film, which provided a break from classical hegemony. Peter Jelavich describes how Döblin sought to reform the way authors write:

In place of subjective impressions, writers should strive to provide exact descriptions of objects; in place of psychologically motivated plotlines, they should chronicle sequences of events, as if they were medical case notes. "The hegemony of the author must be smashed; the fascination of self-abnegation cannot be pursued far enough. Nor the fanaticism of renunciation: I am not I, but the street, the lanterns, this and that event, nothing more. This is what I call the stonelike style [den steinernen Stil]." Döblin also called this a *Kinostil*, which he equated with "highest concentration and precision" in the depiction of events and "extremes of plasticity and vitality" in the use of language. "The dawdling of storytelling has no place in the novel; one doesn't tell stories, one builds." Döblin demanded "paucity, economy of words" and a "rapid succession of events" recounted "simply, in brief cues." He insisted that "the whole must seem to be not spoken, but rather present."[4] Döblin's concept of a *Kinostil* was based on the aesthetics of the nickelodeons, venues that were disappearing rapidly when he wrote the essay in 1913. [. . .] The young medium reveled in its visual potential, and it explored the physical world: techniques like close-ups and slow-motion photography allowed audiences to see their material environs in completely new ways and brought unobserved details to light. Moreover, early cinema programs consisted of a variety of shorts, lasting three to fifteen minutes, replete with diverse and often contradictory moods and genres. [. . .] What this diverse assemblage shared was a focus on the visual, the object, the physiognomy. When stories were told, they were too short to be more than vignettes that lacked character development.[5]

Jelavich draws from Döblin's ideas in "Berliner Programm" (1913) and connects them with early cinema aesthetics; these concepts manifest themselves in the author's early work and will therefore help us better understand his texts. Even though Döblin began his medical studies in 1900, he developed a sensibility that produced precise, evocative, and lively prose, somewhat resembling medical case notes that highlight a succession of events. Heidi Tewarson maintains, however, that his literary writings were not "case histories lifted from his psychiatric practices," but rather maintained "very specific poetic and philosophical intentions."[6] As Döblin was trained in both medicine and literature, his short stories read like an intriguing and harmonious hybridization of the two, as if a medical study had been given aesthetic attributes. Thus, "The Dancer and the Body" can be seen as deriving, in part, from the doctors' protocol and observations. Döblin's text is an uncanny self-reflection; one could even read it as an attempt to present objective medical facts in an episodic manner, allowing it to take on more characteristics of a modernist miniature, as proposed by Andreas Huyssen.[7] His *Kinostil* and episodes value the objective camera-eye's focus on the visual and the physiognomy not only of the body, but of the cityscape. He alludes to the agency of the nonhuman and the decentering of the hegemonic author: perspectives of the camera and other objects begin to take shape. I use these stylistics to inform my reading of Döblin's dancing women in their urban and clinical spaces.

"Modern"

Döblin's research interest in urban space and its depictions is clearly evident in his novel *Berlin Alexanderplatz* (1929), which dealt extensively with the metropolis as a living organism and as a "microcosm [of the world that] is always in flux, never stable or static, and therefore uncontrollable."[8] Regarded as being just as important as a character, the urban industrial space "comes alive and asserts its uniqueness."[9] Döblin's clear posthumanist interest in depicting the city as such in his writing, however, began long before this prose text. Unlike Rilke, whose bourgeois upbringing supported his existence in Paris at the age of twenty-eight as he engaged with and wrote about the city, Döblin was dependent financially on his mother, who had broken up with her husband and, thus, had been looking for work in the bustling metropolis of Berlin at the turn of the century. Referring to his actual birthplace of Stettin as his "Vorgeburt" (before his birth), Döblin declared that he was born on his arrival in Berlin at the age of ten.[10] He presumably states this to more definitively attach himself with Berlin. At the age of eighteen in 1896, Döblin composed an early text that remained unpublished during his life. Called "Modern: An Image from the Present" ("Modern: Ein Bild aus der Gegenwart"), it begins appropriately with a visual depiction of the metropolitan space: "Bustling people flooded into Leipzig Street. On the sidewalk disorder rushed from all walks of life and professions."[11] His depictions switch between masses and individuals, emphasizing both macro and micro views:

The bank officer trotted heavily with his large leather briefcase, [. . .] drifters, the Germans call them flâneurs with long cigarettes in one hand and twisting a slim walking stick in the other. [. . .] Then one saw at the back on Dönhoffsplatz a hay wagon that was overloaded and unable to move forward. One cart after the other the horsecars lined up until Friedrichstrasse. And at the obstacle, there now a sound! All around thick throngs of people. [. . .] And now the horsecars continue: all in double time. [. . .] The crowd broke up immediately. [. . .] Then they all slowly passed Dönhoffsplatz, step by step.[12]

Similar stylistically, on the one hand, to Rilke's depiction of the *Veitstänzer* scene, Döblin uses succinct, yet image-evocative language to depict the urban activity. He even mentions the flâneur as a sociological type—less an intellectual or artist and more a dawdler—and the story's protagonist becomes one. Gabriele Sander characterizes the narrator's perspective itself like that of the flâneur.[13] Similarly, David Dollenmayer notices the filmic propensity of the prose, which seems to pan "like a camera" over the cityscape, selecting "seemingly random but characteristic details until it reaches the central character."[14] The author maintains an objective camera eye that surveys the urban stimuli, focusing on and alternating between single entities and masses. The laborious line of horsecars, one of which pulls a cart overstuffed with hay, vividly evokes the image of an assembly line operating inefficiently, thus indicating industrialization's emphasis on punctuality and production. Interestingly, Döblin depicts this older form of transportation even though Werner von Siemens had already created the first electrical streetcar, in 1881, and construction of the Berliner U2 had begun in 1896. The author depicts the horses instead of a machine to demonstrate specifically the organismal strain on a creature being treated as a machine that now has to work even harder to maintain its pace.

The image of the overworked animal is then followed by the introduction of the twenty-four-year-old protagonist, who is now unemployed and looking for work. Not having the luxury of being a flâneuse, this working-class woman "had no interest in the urban activity around her and did not look at the shiny window displays. [. . .] Habituation dulls the senses."[15] In Simmel's terms she has already attained a blasé attitude, and instead of looking for aesthetic inspiration in the city like Rilke's Malte, the working-class Bertha is dealing with the harsh reality of trying to find work as a seamstress. Her only comfort is her Catholic faith, but even this is under strain: "Only now and again would she open her bible, she forgot her God in the throngs of life, the hardship of the moment. She would rather chat with her friends in the evening. [. . .] The metropolis, the metropolis is approaching,—Beware, poor soul!—"[16] The narrator's perspective allows him to focus his gaze on Bertha, just as Malte concentrates on the movements of the *Veitstänzer*. The narrator's last comment creates a foreboding image of the metropolis ready to consume Bertha. Döblin views the big city less in its individual parts and more as a brooding, amorphous premonition, as if the cumulative stimuli that create the city (bustling streets, throngs of pedestrians, architecture, and transportation) are embodied into a powerful entity. We have seen how Rilke's urban depiction, particularly of bridges and crossings, created a similar cumulatively intensifying force with which the *Veitstänzer* has to grapple. And while Endell perceives the stimuli in the square—pedestrians and space—as congealing into "a palpable, immense, living entity,"[17] Döblin depicts this collected energy as oppressive instead of liberating.

The narrative portion of "Modern" comes to an end as Bertha's friend drags her along through Berlin: "And they continued on, street after street——Leipzigerstraße—Andreasstraße, from the quarter of the wealthy into that of those who work—or do not; and in every striving for that,—we saw Bertha."[18] The narrator leaves the reader with fragmented, filmic impressions as the protagonist drifts aimlessly like a flâneuse, less in the vein of being an intellectual seeking excitement, and more in the sense of being lost and seeking guidance. Pulling back the focus on Bertha and her predicament, the filmic gaze seems to situate her more prominently as a passive object being absorbed into the "physiognomy" of the urban bustle. Dollenmayer characterizes the city here "in Marxist terms as a place of corruption and exploitation of the working class."[19] By ending the first part of the narrative with a dynamic image, Döblin implies that both Berlin's liveliness and its economic drive continue despite her despair and sickness. "We saw Bertha" ("Wir sahen Bertha") breaks away from the objective eye, pulling the readers into the narrator's programmatic agenda to awaken them to her slow demise.

Before returning to the narrative, Döblin begins a sociological exposition describing the role of women in Wilhelmine society, drawing generously from the study *Woman and Socialism* (*Die Frau und der Sozialismus*) (1883) by August Bebel. Döblin explains that since women have needed to start working because of capitalism, they often must accept even lower wages than men. Because of their meager earnings, some have to resort to prostitution: "And that is the horrible part,——they can save themselves from this bleak life: there is one escape—one escape—prostitution!——————"[20] The repetition reinforces the emphatic, assertive nature of his prose—stylistically similar to the explosiveness of Dostoyevsky's language, which Döblin admired—but the dashes visually reinforce an emotional exclamation, tension, and emptiness associated with the profession of sex work. While Döblin does acknowledge the aristocracy and bourgeoisie in his exposition, his main concern is working-class women; his personal milieu and background allowed him to become keenly aware of their plight. While Bertha does not turn to prostitution per se, the narrator seems to programmatically warn against such a dire decision. Ella, in "The Dancer and the Body," also deals with parallel circumstances. Running antithetical to Wilhelmine norms, Döblin acknowledges bodily desires: "No part of the body must be neglected, under punishment of the worst sicknesses. And whoever dares to defy nature, to suppress his or her 'animal instincts,' will be crushed in this battle."[21] This perspective certainly manifests itself in his early literary prose writing, as we will see.

Following his sociological commentary, we return to Bertha, who has been cooped up in her room and becomes idle due to her unemployment. Döblin uses the atmosphere of the city and the room to reflect her mood as the scene opens: "Tranquility, humid tranquility lay in Bertha's room. Sunken into herself, she sat at the edge of the bed; [. . .] and in her eyes was a dreamy, dull thoughtless tranquility."[22] Her body has probably been resting in bed for a while, and its warmth has dispersed throughout the room, which had probably not been aired out recently. Döblin is keenly aware of the space and Bertha's body as he melds the two together. This depiction also evokes sexual connotations of female arousal, which foreshadow the rest of the scene. The narrator describes the sunset: "Glowing red rays announce the sunset, an image which even the metropolis with its factory smoke cannot destroy."[23] Döblin depicts a rather filmic superimposition in which both images are laid on top of each other, but the city is unable to extinguish the sunset. Döblin again recalls the city as an aggregate mass to which Bertha once belonged, with factory smoke symbolizing modernity's perpetual production. The glowing, natural rays represent her burning sexual desire. While consistent with acknowledging "animal instincts" ("tierische Triebe") and allowing Bertha to similarly experience her own feelings, the ominous power of the city still dominates the situation.

After her lover Gustav arrives and they have sex, Bertha immediately recognizes her sin and begins repenting on her prayer chair: "She is overwhelmed with the sublime magnitude of which she had almost forgotten—, her lost existence."[24] Döblin depicts her faith as an overwhelming, aggregate force, as if he is pitting religion and instinctual desire against each other. The end of the story depicts Bertha fleeing into the city at night:

> —she rushed outside, just get out of the room, in flying haste down the stairs—onto the silent streets. Agitated, rushed, driven out by her imagination—street after street—without looking in which direction—until she stands still, hoarsely panting.
>
> At the water.
>
> The Engelbecken.
>
> [. . .]
>
> She felt she could not withstand the drive that was buried inside her, she had to surrender to it—and she would be dishonored—the damage would be her fate—And here now—suicide—thou shalt not kill——! Oh, how to save oneself from this chaos?

[. . .]

[Manuscript torn] now it swirled again in her brain. In ghostly [Manuscript torn] round dance entangling, hovering, circling around her [Manuscript torn] seducing and confusing her [Manuscript breaks off here].[25]

Much like in the last narrative scene before the sociological exposition in which Bertha's friend drags her into the throngs of Berlin, the protagonist confusingly launches herself into the quiet streets at night. Her agitated state juxtaposes perpetual motion with the reticent streets. While there is no commotion in the city, the space remains a living entity, as in Endell's and Rilke's depictions. The silent streets evoke the image of a city structure bearing witness to a woman's psychological breakdown: as if the streets can speak, but do not. As Döblin's objective camera perspective—"I am not I, but the street"—and impending medical case notes, the streets, as well as the reader, can easily record Bertha's downfall in succinct detail. The author decenters the human by empowering the streets to act. Whereas during the daytime, the streets have to survey all of Berlin's constant activity, at night they can give their undivided attention to the protagonist and remain the sole witness to her undertakings. Dollenmayer states of Döblin's prose style, "he suppresses smooth narrative transitions in favor of abrupt juxtapositions that heighten the psychological immediacy and veracity of the fiction."[26] Of course, these sudden changes in highly visual imagery also imitate cinematic cuts, and thereby rouse the filmic capabilities of his *Kinostil* writing. This filmic style manifests itself in chapter 6 with Lasker-Schüler's writing and drawings. "Street after street" indicates the endless magnitude of Bertha's becoming enveloped into the city, which also beckons her to find a solution to her problem.

One could also interpret the staging of Bertha's confusion in the nighttime metropolis as representing her lonely and disoriented psychological state, highlighting her demise due to the aggregate power that has dictated her life: the surveying streets. In fact, while she does not "dance" per se in the streets, she does perform *in* and *for* the city. The power of the metropolis compels her to stumble out of her room, as if to engage in a sacrificial dance.

The ending brings to light some seemingly intentional ambiguities. Some scholars conjecture that Bertha ends up drowning herself in the pond,[27] given Döblin's emphasis on staging her near a fountain, but the manuscript breaks off. One could read this sudden end more as a dramatic gesture than as the consequence of the manuscript's fragmentary nature. The last page of the text is also torn, to enhance the materiality and performativity of the page and the confused dance. Perhaps Döblin intentionally ripped the text to create corresponding fragmentations to add to the intensity of Bertha's disoriented psychological state. Indeed, the torn last paragraph evokes circular dance images as representative of her bewilderment: "In ghostly [Manuscript torn] round dance entangling, hovering, circling around her."[28] Figures begin circling around her, creating a dizzying atmosphere as she wages what is probably a battle between life and death. Döblin depicts Bertha's unraveling in a circular dance, as paradoxical images that represent both a confining and an emancipating movement. He comments that dance, on the one hand, implies a coordination and timeliness that evoke the ideas of metropolitan productivity and mechanization: a masculine trait. On the other hand, it could also free the body by opening a libidinal reservoir: a traditionally feminine attribute.

Elizabeth Wilson comments on this masculine and feminine dichotomy of the city:

> Yet the city, a place of growing threat and paranoia to men, might be a place of liberation for women. The city offers women freedom. After all, the city normalises the carnivalesque aspects of life. True, on the one hand it makes necessary routinised rituals of transportation and clock watching, factory discipline and timetables but despite its crowds and the mass nature of its life, and despite its bureaucratic conformity, at every turn the city dweller is also offered the opposite— pleasure, deviation, disruption. In this sense it would be possible to say that the male and female "principles" war with each other at the very heart of the city life. The city is "masculine" in its triumphal scale, its towers and vistas and arid industrial regions; it is "feminine" in its enclosing embrace, in its indeterminacy and labyrinthine uncenteredness. We might even go so far as to claim that urban life is actually based on this perpetual struggle between rigid, routinised order and pleasurable anarchy, the male-female dichotomy.[29]

Through Wilson's characterization of the modern metropolis, one can see that Bertha's experience in Berlin has evoked both masculine and feminine qualities. Freed from having a devoted partner such as a husband, she is liberated to have a life in the metropolis. However, since she probably came to the city for work—like Döblin's mother—Bertha is presumably forced to work long hours for a meager wage with little time for diversion. As a result, she becomes part of the masculine "clock watching, factory discipline and timetables" as Döblin depicts her becoming enveloped into the perpetual motion of the city while looking for work. However, once she is unemployed, she dawdles around and seeks, even unconsciously, "pleasure, deviation, disruption" when she is encased in the dampness of her bed and room. The ending—her confused dash through the city to the Engelbecken—could be read, therefore, as a mixture of both masculine and feminine modernity. She becomes a slave to the modern city, first by becoming part of its routinized workforce and then later succumbing to its evening temptations. In the end, the cumulative urban stimuli of the city with its surveying power beckons her out of her home and onto the streets, forcing her to perform movements that reflect her confused state.

Modernity, and by extension, the urban space, have caused her to repress both her Catholic faith and her sexual desire. When Bertha is unemployed, she has time to act on her underexplored appetites, which, however, clash with her religion. By drowning herself in the Engelbecken, she enters a complex realm: on the one hand, suicide is a sin even worse than sex without procreation under Catholicism, but at the same time, modernity both frees and kills her: a sexually liberating death by water. As Tewarson states, "All that matters is the willingness to give up the illusion of self-creation and yield to reabsorption by nature. In effect, Döblin's characters must either accept or long for death."[30] By staging her demise in the city as a presumed suicide, Döblin shows the contradictory effects of modernity on its desperate victim as the aggregate urban space documents her demise through performative movement: Bertha becomes absorbed into the physiognomy of her maker. Döblin's "Modern" demonstrates his developing interest in depicting the working-class woman, the absorbent and cumulative power of the city space, *Kinostil*, and the narrator as flâneur, while alluding to a performative dance in the metropolis. We will see how he integrates these ideas in his "The Dancer and the Body" (1910), and particularly how he develops his understanding of dance and space. Before addressing this text, however, I will first explore Döblin's experience with and knowledge of dance, not just prior to his writing this story, but even after, to continually show how movement and performance practices penetrated his dance and spatial imagination.

Döblin and Dance

Despite sometimes leaving Berlin to further his studies in medicine, Döblin was always brought back to the metropolis by the desire to develop himself intellectually. He befriended Herwarth Walden, who married Else Lasker-Schüler and later became the editor of *Der Sturm*, a magazine devoted to culture and the arts, in which Döblin published his "The Dancer and the Body" and other early works.[31] In 1904 Walden began the Society for the Cultivation of the Arts (Verein für Kunst), which met weekly, and took part in lectures, readings, and concerts that included writers and intellectuals belonging to the Berliner Bohème—artists, philosophers, humanists, cultural critics, architects, and actors.[32] Those who took part included Peter Altenberg, Hermann Bahr, Peter Behrens, Hermann Bang, Peter Baum, Max Brod, Louis Corinth, Richard Dehmel, Alfred Döblin, Julius Hart, Peter Hille, Arno Holz, Harry Graf Kessler, Kaul Krauss, Thomas Mann, Johannes Schlaf, and Frank Wedekind.[33] In October 1911, Döblin published a small text in *Der Sturm* of his experience watching Gertrude Barrison, a notable Austrian variety theater performer, during a reading for the Verein für Kunst. While he had previously seen her dance, Döblin focuses instead on reading her performance. He describes her dramatic "transformation, not change" ("Verwandlung, nicht Veränderung") from the last time he saw her, as if to emphasize the magnitude of this profound and fundamental shift: "She spoke full of sound using all registers: severely, wildly, tenderly, with passion and depth."[34] Döblin characterizes the performative and atmospheric changes that her reading—particularly when she says the word "maturity" ("Reife")—produces in the environs of the small hall of the architecture house where the event takes place:

> A reversal emerged from the severe, lyrical, theoretical, and abrupt into the mass of empiricism, and into the richness of experience, the fall into diffuse life. Here as well: maturity,—I do not, however, want to call that which preceded it immature. There were not six candles like before in the hall, but these two illuminated brightly enough.[35]

The strict, theoretical mass of empiricism breaks into a boundlessness of experience and an unfurling of life: a visual image largely characterizing modernity breaking off from nineteenth-century aesthetic tradition. This liberation and maturity relate not only to Bertha in "Modern" and Ella in "Dancer and the Body," but more broadly to Rilke's *Veitstänzer* and early-twentieth-century dancers such as St. Denis, Fuller, and Nijinsky. Döblin does not relay the contents of her reading, but rather concentrates on their performative effects, which permeate the space with its energy.

Besides being a vigilant spectator of performances, Döblin himself took part in public readings. The literary historian Rudolf Kayser reminisces about a day back in 1913:

In the backroom of a café in Potsdamer Street a curious and small community has gathered. Quite young people, painters, literati, poets—among them Else Lasker-Schüler and the other doctor-poet Gottfried Benn. An agile, small man with reddish goatee and sharp glasses leaps up to the stand, reads in a lively fashion and without tiring from a manuscript called "Conversations with Calypso: On Music." He reads with great passion, half instruction, half declaration, both as a thinker and writer. It is Alfred Döblin.[36]

Given the explosive and expressionistic nature of his work, such acts of reading brought the text even more to life as the author stood in front of an audience to perform his work. Döblin was cognizant of the dynamic nature of performance, which organically transformed into an interest in the dancing body.

"Dancers"

After writing "The Dancer and the Body," the image of the female dancer continues to inhabit his imagination and critical writing about early-twentieth-century dance aesthetics. Ernst Ludwig Kirchner, who created the woodcut image for Döblin's book *The Canoness and Death* (*Das Stiftsfräulein und der Tod*) from 1913, also published an illustration called "Dancers" ("Tänzerinnen") in September 1911 for the cover of *Der Sturm*. This image emerged approximately a year before Döblin's text of the same name, which appeared in the same publication in October 1912. While his text deals with two female dancers, Kirchner depicts a symmetrical image of three variety theater dancers, or perhaps circus performers given the large tent in the background, holding hands as the two on the outside lift their legs, performing a *battement*.[37] Their shoulders and arms do not appear relaxed but rather tense and angular, which is both intentional and a result of the imprecision of woodcut as a medium. Could Kirchner here be trying to subvert normative balletic or *Varieté*-style movement in favor of a transition into expressionist dance? Reacting to Impressionism's atmospherics and rigid academic technique, Expressionism focused mainly on expressing inner emotions through their work but also the performative act of creation. This woodcut could have inspired Döblin to write his "Dancers."[38]

In this essay, he critiques both past and recent forms of dance:

We have had enough of the bad dancers. A dance modality that isn't academic isn't necessarily good. Skipping, turning, captivating puppet face, Danube waves in each valley of forest or meadow will be boring. You can't do anything, dear children, if you like academic or free gestures. It would all be quite good if the dancers weren't so educated, natural and whatever else.[39]

Döblin satirically refers to both the institution of academic ballet and the dances of Grete Wiesenthal. Alexandra Kolb believes "Danube waves" ("Donauwellen") alludes, not necessarily to a popular confection, a cake with cherries, cream, and cocoa shaped as waves, but rather to the Viennese waltz whose undulating movements reflected the Danube River.[40] He even engages in wordplay by referring literally to Wiesenthal as a place where her dances could take place: in a valley ("Tal"), forest, or meadow ("Wiese"). This comment suggests that Döblin may have seen her perform when she came to Berlin from 1908 to 1912. For example, with support from Hofmannsthal, Max Reinhardt included her and her sister Elsa in the 1908 Berlin production of Aristophanes' "Lysistrata," and in 1910 Reinhardt produced with Wiesenthal the pantomime "Sumurûn" by Friedrich Freska at the Berliner Kammerspielen.[41]

Wiesenthal first performed with her sisters in 1908 at the Kabarett Fledermaus where prominent writers and artists of the Vienna Secession gathered. Among them were Gertrude Barrison, Hermann Bahr, Oskar Kokoschka, Gustav Klimt, and Karl Kraus. In her most famous dance, "Danube Waltz" ("Donauwalzer"), in a fashion reminiscent of a waltz, she turned and extended "into the vertical and horizontal positions, swinging, stretching, jumping and floating to experience the limits of equilibrium."[42] While the dancer would allow the momentum to carry her turning, she would not lose complete control. These mesmerizing and *Jugendstil* movements were, of course, derived from the nineteenth-century Austrian waltz, which was itself developed as a rebellious social dance alternative to the courtly and highly structured minuet. Walter Sorrell writes:

> To waltz was an open invitation to break with the routine of the past, with the protocol of formality, with etiquette often bordering on exaggerated subtleties. In its close embrace, the waltz defied such studied politeness. It held out a personal freedom, an individual pursuit of happiness, because its intoxicating rhythm in 3/4 time and its closeness, as much as the couple chose, offered an ecstatic experience.[43]

While Döblin embraced the boundlessness and unchartered realm of modernity, one could argue that he did not like the means through which the waltz and Wiesenthal's variation achieved this aesthetic: through decadent, sweeping, intoxicating movement. These methods are reminiscent of Endell's and Fuller's movement philosophy, yet he wants to work against them. As already demonstrated in "Modern" and now in "The Dancer and the Body," Döblin preferred to depict the rebellious body as explosive and expressionistic. The discussion of this movement form is important, because it informs how one can interpret his staging of a waltz in "The Dancer and the Body."

His opening remark in "Dancers" introduces his self-reflexive humor. Döblin unabashedly writes, "I am citing a distinguished author: a certain Alfred Döblin,"[44] and he quotes from his own "Conversations with Calypso" ("Gespräche mit Kalypso"). While this continues throughout the satirical piece, he maintains a genuine agenda concerning his thoughts on dance at the time. The author quotes a conversation between two men: the older asks if the younger admires dance and then critiques the new generation's taste in dance, since it mostly involves the grace and tenderness of female dancers. The older fellow seems to recognize that women historically began to take over male roles when it became passé for men to reflect aristocratic principles on stage.[45] As Lynn Garafola has noted:

> Beginning with romanticism, a twenty-year golden age stretching from the July Revolution to about 1850, the *danseuse en travesti* [travesty dancer] usurped the position of the male danseur in the *corps de ballet* and as a partner to the ballerina. Stepping into roles previously filled by men, women now impersonated the sailor boys, hussars, and toreadors who made up "masculine" contingents of the *corps de ballet*, even as they displaced real men as romantic leads. Until well into the twentieth century, the female dancer who donned the mufti of a cavalier was a commonplace of European ballet.[46]

The older man, by way of Döblin, demonstrates his knowledge of this fundamental shift in ballet aesthetics. As a result, female dancers became subject to the heterosexual male gaze: a phenomenon that he further condemns:

> But your dance modality does not show the tame, pious body, but rather the cultured dame or the woman-turned-into-a-man; she shows your fornication. Lush; you are allowed to forget a lot. You allow dance to be taken from your hands and know only the wooing dance of the sexes, not the solitary dance, hardly the dance with many, nor the dance and fantasy of male bodies. You lush, heavy, stupid men![47]

In an argument reminiscent of his small feminist treatise in "Modern," he contends that the disproportionate representation of the female dancer has resulted in a hegemonic, heterosexual male gaze that objectifies the female body. Similarly, he implies that dance has become inundated with wooing dances solely for visual consumption. European ballet in the late nineteenth century was in decline, having lost its elite status because of waning interest, and it was being performed alongside variety and entertainment acts.[48] Kolb has ascertained that companies such as the Berlin Hofopernballett and the Hofoperntheater in Vienna emphasized light entertainment with exotic themes, fairytale motifs, and simple plots; by showcasing virtuosic dance technique, their ballets expressed little emotion.[49] Additionally, according to Garafola the largely male audience enjoyed watching the *danseuse en travesti* over the male *danseur* because the former still maintained their shapely legs, feminine hips, and buttocks in skin-tight pants: "What audiences wanted was a masculine image deprived of maleness, an idealized adolescent, a beardless she-man."[50] Döblin critiques the old man's view—more or less the author's own—by saying that one should not despise wooing dances since they depend on who performs these roles.

After this short aesthetic overview, Döblin then describes two dancers, whose performances he claimed to have seen. I believe, however, that unlike his description of Barrison's reading, his depictions in "Dancers" are fictitious precisely because they strikingly resemble Bertha from "Modern" and, as we will see, Ella from "The Dancer and the Body." With their striking distortion, expressionistic characteristics of Weimar dance continue to emerge. Interestingly, Döblin does not mention his location as he watches the two dancers, in contrast to his depictions of Bertha and Ella, and for that matter, Rilke's *Veitstänzer* and Endell's square. By eliminating a perceivable space and ambience, Döblin heightens his attention to not only the dancers' bodies and movements, but also to his own reaction. The bodily proportions and movements of both the dancers are rendered as thoroughly distorted:

> One of them is a solid, muscular human of the female sex with bones, limbs. In contrast, the other is skinny to the point that she almost wasn't pretty anymore. She seems to be just a leather-covered, feminine skeleton; sometimes I wracked my brain to think how something like that could be possible and how such a thing could happen.[51]

While the masculine dancer's appearance resembles the *danseuse en travesti*, she dances alone. Similarly, the other woman could be a ballet dancer, given her thin appearance, but she is completely devoid of beauty. Döblin's depiction demonstrates the unforeseen representation of the female dancers on stage. Until around 1900, ballet and the *Varieté* had dominated the dance scene with women almost exclusively in the limelight, attracting endless attention from often heterosexual male admirers. He probably creates such a fictitious setting to purposefully and satirically illustrate two distorted bodies, which he further polarizes by describing their dancing styles. The women's movements do not particularly correspond to traditional representations of their body types: "The Hercules danced a firm dance; it was firm, firm, very firm, with bulky elbows, massive shoulders, firm legs; the Hercules was evidently quite happy."[52] Döblin exaggerates and ridicules the masculine attributes of the first dancer by calling her Hercules, who expresses enthusiasm for her movement. A *danseuse en travesti* "may have aped the steps and motions of the male performer, but she never impersonated his nature."[53] Döblin's interest, however, lies in the other dancer:

> The masterpiece, the leather sofa, dance of the young kobold: the closing and beckoning of the hands, the ugly, sudden, dangling leg movements, the rushing and burrowing of the shoulders. She's quite something,— Like I said, I don't know what she perhaps has underneath—, plenty of dancerly ideas, correctly moving bodily and motor thoughts, motor thoughts, motor jokes, motor absurdity. They are real, serious, original and worth seeing, but I am by nature a bit drastic in expression.[54]

Döblin's fixation begins with an attempt to describe the abrupt way in which the emaciated dancer moves. His writing implies an emphatic documentation while lacking a clear purpose. Yet these impulsive thoughts and fragmented formulations—strongly reminiscent of his *Kinostil*—show a desperate attempt to not only illustrate succinctly and precisely the second dancer's mannerisms, but to demonstrate his profound desire, at that time, to express his feelings and thoughts in a verbal critique without needing to reflect in this dance text. One could read this citation as if he were actually spontaneously speaking his thoughts without a filter, thus implied by his repetition of the word "motor." Döblin begins with his own general criticism of past and current dance and continues by expressing his developing aesthetic in regard to the styles of two dancers. Instead of Wiesenthal's whirling "Danube Waltz," Döblin finds an impressive embodiment of rebellion, impulsivity, and exaggeration in the emaciated dancer's performance, which furthermore corresponds to the bodily experiences of his female literary counterparts:

Bertha and Ella. The kinesthetic experience of watching has relayed itself not necessarily in his body but assuredly through his writing style.

Given the time frame in which Döblin may have seen live dance performances, he seems to be aesthetically perceiving a new wave of expressionist dance, a movement style that tended to give in to the gravitational pull toward the ground, allowing for contracting and releasing the torso and abdomen instead of maintaining symmetry, line, and elevation as is often associated with ballet.[55] Perhaps even differentiating itself from the early-twentieth-century dances of Duncan, St. Denis, Fuller, and Wiesenthal and moving into more abrupt and angular movement as seen in performances by Nijinsky (*Afternoon of a Faun* and *Rite of Spring*) and Mary Wigman (*Witch's Dance*), Weimar dance encompasses a diverse range of movement styles between 1919 and 1933. Often called expressionist or *Ausdruckstanz*, this general term referred to, as Kate Elswit puts it, "a core experimentation with the medium's capacity to use bodies for expressive purposes."[56] The most widely known practitioners of this style included Rudolf von Laban—known for his communal festival dances and movement choirs, which highlighted egalitarianism, allowing all citizens to be dancers—and Mary Wigman, a student of Laban, whose elitist dances used dark, passionate expression to reach a transcendent space, leading to ecstasy and a loss of the self. Other dancers of the time include Anita Berber and Valeska Gert, who often danced in cabarets. Despite these varied movement practices in diverse spaces, Döblin was aesthetically in line with the darker, angular movement.

Between 1910 and 1912, when he wrote "Dancers," one could consider his perception of these movements to be early expressionistic tendencies before Weimar dance had reached its heyday. This text also demonstrates not only Döblin's interest in dance but his essential knowledge of its history, particularly the employment of *danseuse en travesti*, the demise of ballet, the rise of variety and erotically infused entertainment, and the emergence of expressionist dance. Even though space plays a far less dominant role in this depiction, he strategically focuses on the dancer's bodily movements, their aura, and his visceral reaction to establish a more succinct and radical impression. This trajectory plays a striking role in his depiction of Ella in "The Dancer and the Body."

"The Dancer and the Body"

Döblin's metropolitan dance text begins by introducing the protagonist Ella and describes the instrument with which she works: her body. The title already creates a separation between these two characters, which greatly increases throughout the narrative. While the body here seems to be tied to the human, Döblin and Ella treat it more as an object, which later attains a posthumanist life and vitality on its own, as with the *Veitstänzer*. At the age of eleven she shows great promise in her limbs:

> now she learned how to train her elastic ligaments and her double joints; she insinuated herself, cautiously and patiently, further and further, into her toes, her ankles, her knees, greedily ambushed the slender shoulders and bend of her thin arms, lurked over the play of her disciplined body. She managed to waft a chill over the most voluptuous dance.[57]

This depiction establishes the flexibility and resilience of Ella's body to create all sorts of shapes, to move in different directions, and to demonstrate that she can withstand the countless repetitions necessary to perform. While Cowan rightly acknowledges that the narrator does not expressly name her movement form as ballet—instead reading her in conjunction with Jaques-Dalcroze's rhythmical gymnastics[58]—other critics still maintain that she trains her body for ballet,[59] and I will further examine this position through a dance lens. This kind of bodily analysis applies to girls who want to pursue ballet as a career since the body, at this age, is still developing and can be molded to a specific form. Another sign pointing to ballet is the attention to the feet and leg articulation, because the movement form deals intensively with the training of these body parts. Next, her upper body is fitting for ballet because her arms and shoulders are slender instead of muscular and defined. Lastly, the narrator states that the dancer emits coldness when she dances, implying that her performance of calculated, mechanical steps leads to completeness and perfection. Kolb maintains that at the end of the nineteenth century, ballet was "a dead art. Its repetitive, symmetrical poses and graceful attitudes, for many more informed spectators, amounted to mere formula and superficial coquetry. Its limited movement repertory and aesthetic mode was tantamount to mannerism and dehumanization."[60] As shown in "Dancers," Döblin deplored the older ballet aesthetic and variety-style wooing dances and sought to represent the transition into modernity in his writing by using Ella as his pivotal figure.

When Ella turns eighteen, she seems to have developed more into her body:

her figure was a bare trace, as light as silk, her eyes dark and over-sized. Her face was sharp in profile and long, like a boy's. Unseduc-tive and unmusical, her voice was a shrill staccato; she walked briskly and impatiently. She lacked affection, threw an unpitying gaze on her untalented colleagues and bored herself stiff with their complaints.[61]

The dancer has retained her very light figure in order to appear whimsi-cal and delicate on stage. Some scholarship has called her a *femme fragile* because she retains an underdeveloped, child-like figure,[62] while Tewarson refer to her as "asexual, a child-woman but without the associated appeal so common in turn-of-the-century literary and artistic representations of the type."[63] Her physical traits, nonetheless, cement her position in ballet: dance-studies scholar Susan Stinson writes that training the body to be obedient for ballet "keeps women both physically and emotionally in a pre-pubescent state."[64] Also according to Edward Shorter, anorexia nervosa was happening before 1870, when the disorder was named,[65] and was often confused with "hysteria."[66] It is possible that Ella suffers from this eating disorder, which could point to her controlling her body by limiting the amount of food she consumes and perpetually staring at her body in the mirror. However, Döblin does not thematicize these behaviors at all in his prose text and concentrates mainly on the training of her body.

Based on Ella's interactions with other dancers, she could either be an elite dancer in a company or belong to the *corps de ballet*. For example, a typi-cal dancer from the Paris Opera Ballet in the 1840s was from the lower classes and danced mainly for wealthy heterosexual male patrons.[67] As McCarren asserts, such patrons had access to an exclusive salon:

> [T]he Opera [. . .] set up a patronage system for its corps de bal-let based more or less on prostitution. [. . .] But ironically, the legal code that puts the ballerina's prostitution, along with the courtesan's, above common prostitution, simultaneously classifies her public per-formance as a kind of common prostitution. [. . .] The dancer earns her living not "here and there," but publicly. Her performance is a public act; in a theoretical sense, she earns her living by giving herself, bodily, to many people.[68]

Döblin would have been aware of such practices, particularly given his rela-tion to the working-class woman whose meager wages meant she was always on the verge of prostitution. We have clearly seen this with Bertha in "Modern." Therefore, Ella could be also prostituting herself to wealthy patrons. Similarly, as she performs on stage, the dancer gives her body to many spectators—as she will also do with the doctors in the hospital—incurring the proverbial male gaze through visual consumption.

During her prime years of dancing, at the age of nineteen, Ella becomes afflicted with

> a wasting disease [. . .]. Her limbs became heavy, but she continued to dance. When she was alone, she stamped her foot on the ground, threatened her body and struggled with it. She spoke to nobody about her weakness. She gritted her teeth in the face of this stupid, childish thing she had just learned to overcome.[69]

Characterized by lack of appetite and lethargy, this affliction was identified by Kolb as chlorosis[70]—also called "a disease of virgins," green sickness, and hypochromic anemia—which affected young girls during puberty during the late nineteenth century.[71] Because of their rigorous, repetitive training and their impoverished state, ballet dancers often looked sick: "Their lips are parched and fevered; their cheeks hollow and pale, [. . .] their limbs nipped and wasted."[72] Dancers incur an array of acute and overuse injuries, which many learn to deal with in the same way Ella has to cope with her body. Not only does the dancer want to appear strong on stage, she does not want to seem frail in front of the female company members. Her actions of taming and punishing her body elucidate her conflict and the secret she attempts to hide from others and herself. Whereas before Ella was only learning how to use and manipulate her body into positions, now she must keep her body maintained and in good functioning order.

Expressing the theme of bodily observation in which not only Malte and the bystanders in the streets observe the afflicted man, but also the *Veitstänzer* himself, Ella undergoes the scrutiny of many people: the company, her mother, doctors, nurses, and herself. Undoubtedly while training for her profession, she has experienced life constantly under the microscope. Although Ella seems like a relatively strong dancer who fights her sickness, her grief-stricken and controlling mother decides to take Ella to the hospital. She gives her mother a hateful look—she would rather stay in her daily atmosphere instead of the unknown hospital.

Her relationship with her body up to this point has been similar to a taunting game and less like a real struggle. However, as she approaches the hospital in a carriage, her anger and defiance lead to a paralyzing fear:

> Mildly anxious, she opened her eyes and touched the limbs that no longer belonged to her. She was powerless, she was utterly powerless. They clattered over the cobblestones of the courtyard. The hospital gates closed behind her. She was aghast to see doctors and patients. The sisters lifted her gently into the bed.[73]

This scene is a turning point in the story, as it divides the two worlds in which Ella proclaims her existence—the old world of ballet and performing for bourgeois society, and the new modern frontier of science in an urban hospital. As a dancer, she has devoted her life to mastering her body to the best of her ability and in a familiar environment. But now, how can the dancer enter the terrifying grip of a hospital that should help her improve? Based on her reaction, this atmosphere creates even more anxiety about the future and worsens her condition. While approaching the hospital, her quiet fear begins to build because she can no longer keep her body under control. As the carriage turns into the courtyard and the gates close, the reader gets the foreboding feeling that she will never leave. Much like the disempowering effects of Bertha's search for a job, being immersed into the grind of Berlin, Ella is passively absorbed by the nurses and will have to spatially and socially become accustomed to her new setting. At this point, the body—as a nonhuman object—begins building its agency by distancing itself from Ella and becoming more empowered.

During Döblin's years prior to publishing "The Dancer and the Body," he had been oscillating between the metropolis Berlin and smaller cities. In 1904 he decided to study in Freiburg im Breisgau to specialize in neurology and psychiatry, but he returned to Berlin later that year, realizing how much he had missed his intellectual, artistic circle. He finished his dissertation in 1905, entitled "Gedächnisstörungen bei der Karsakoffschen Psychose," and, as Tewarson points out, began to approach "psychiatry from a psychophysiological rather than psychoanalytical perspective. In other words, he sought insight about mental problems on the basis of physiological symptoms and syndromes."[74] This approach certainly manifests itself in Ella's depiction through her physical movements. In 1905 he worked as the assistant doctor in Regensburg at the Kreisirrenanstalt Karthaus-Prüll, and in 1906 he returned again to Berlin. Döblin switched from psychiatry to internal medicine in

1908 and established his private practice along with a more stable bourgeois existence in 1911 in Kreuzberg in Berliner Blücherstraße 18.[75]

I suggest that Döblin's moving between Berlin and these smaller cities influenced his depiction by resulting in Ella being staged in a university hospital. According to Eric Engstrom, during the late nineteenth and early twentieth century, psychiatric hospitals began shifting their geographic locations; typically situated away from moral distractions and corrupt, urban influences to rural settings, large alienist asylums were designed to restore coherence in a chaotic, bourgeois life.[76] However, university psychiatric clinics also began emerging in urban environments and employing physicians who were also natural scientists. These academic doctors attempted to bring order to "unruly objects (be they specimens, patients, students, or societies) [. . .] as they would carefully and thoroughly document each patient's condition."[77] The polyclinic also emerged at many universities by the 1900s to be accessible to everyday citizens as outpatient care and without the stigma of an asylum.[78] Aware of these historical shifts in the nature of psychiatric care, Döblin was also privy to the rise of these hospitals in urban centers. Given this context, Ella's site of treatment most closely resembles a university clinic and reflects his experience of working in these mental facilities. The working-class dancer did not have the means of the bourgeoisie to seek treatment at an alienist asylum, and she also probably lived in a city or metropolitan area with a ballet company. The urban environment played a dominant role in fostering the development of the university clinic by providing patients who were being negatively affected by the city. These clinics also furthered the research possibilities of academic doctors. Thus, the cumulative force of the male doctors in "The Dancer and the Body" are products and representations of urban society: the city and university hospital continue to heavily impact Ella's performance.

In addition to being scared about the future and her health, Ella loses the ability to speak,[79] signaling her shock and inability to describe her symptoms to the doctor. The command of her voice is lost and "everything happened without her will."[80] By failing to dance and being displaced in a foreign, clinical environment, she truly loses control of her life. This inability to speak also points toward not only the male silencing of the female body, as with the nineteenth-century Romantic ballerina, but also the emerging privileged power of dance as a form of symptomatic expression during the beginning of the twentieth century.[81] Ella is under keen observation by the doctors: "Daily, almost hourly, they asked the dancer how her body was faring and wrote it all carefully down in the dossier: at first she was indignant and then she became more and more astonished by it. Soon she entered a state of black fear and groundlessness."[82] For the doctors to "help" her, they must obtain her medical history verbally and then periodically study her symptoms. Modernity and the metropolis have created an environment in which medical research has expanded and intensified. Thus, diseases such as Ella's—that would have been misdiagnosed or ignored before—are now being closely investigated. Yet, this new environment seems to slowly take away her agency, giving it, in turn, back to her body. Here we see the slow demise and decentering of a human and the posthumanist empowerment of the hospital setting and body. Unlike her mother or the ballet realm, this examination leaves her without any kind of comfort. The exposure to modern medicine and imposing doctors, via the city, has created anxiety and helplessness, leaving her unprepared for modernity.

When the doctors admit Ella into the hospital, they also allow the body to enter, and this is what they primarily treat instead of her emotional state. Unable to tame the body through her own will, the hospital environment and doctors enable the body to emerge as a powerful agent, further estranging Ella and her own body. According to McCarren, among doctors in hospitals there was "an increasing trend toward professionalization and erasure of the patient."[83] Like the streets that objectively record Bertha's demise in the city, the doctors as cumulative, posthumanist beings scientifically record her symptoms to learn more about her sickness. Döblin writes, "the body could come to its own arrangements with the doctors. 'It will all be taken down in writing.'"[84] The metropolis serves as a driving force and setting, which allows university clinics to emerge as a means to pursue progress in doctor's research—not necessarily the patient's well-being. Their cumulative behavior with Ella shows that they and the body are working together toward a similar goal: the physicians aim to further modern science through examining her symptoms, and the body desires to express itself through expressionist dance. However, even though the body might be thought to resemble a human, Döblin characterizes it as more of a posthumanist being.

The body seems accustomed to the idea of its symptoms being recorded, but "They [Ella and her body] ran separate households."[85] Ella remains trapped in her nineteenth-century, working-class mode of thinking, in which she only knows how to dance and tame her body. However, the doctors are also at fault for not informing Ella about her condition. Döblin denies the doctors the possibility of verbal communication, and therefore they treat the body like an object. This radical disconnect between her, the doctors, and the body comments on the gap between nineteenth-century thought and modernism. By treating her body like an object, they continue to feed it with their scientific curiosity and empower its ability to overtake Ella. And while one might question if this situation even warrants a posthumanist reading, I read the body as Ella's instrument being overtaken by a sickness that further estranges her from it. Her body lacks the human characteristics that the dancer exhibits. Much like highlighting the vibrancy of the Cambodian dancer's fingers and hands, thereby decentering the human, in both cases, a body or body parts become estranged from the whole human and can take on a life of their own. To this extent, then, the body gathers its own agency as a posthumanist entity.

The dancer has therefore been stripped unwillingly from her working-class life, and Ella has been infiltrated by the nagging, modern body. She and her nineteenth-century morals will continue to fight: "Then she became embittered and resisted. She lied to the doctors, refused to answer their questions, and even kept quiet about her pain. [. . .] [She] laughed in a sudden blaze of hatred in the face of the doctors, who shook their heads. She shot them a sarcastic grimace."[86] A cursory reading deems this scene unlikely because she does not cooperate but instead acts childishly with the doctors, who are in theory supposed to help her. However, a closer look reveals that not only is she frustrated about her lack of knowledge of her own condition but also by the foreign environment of the urban university hospital—a site of modernity and the metropolis. She even mocks the doctors in their attempts to help. As if playing a childish game, Ella laughs at the establishment of medical progress that threatens her values learned through ballet.

Having been isolated from her normal surroundings and the comfort of dance, one day she hears soldiers playing a march by the hospital.[87] Despite being within the confines of the isolated clinic, she manages to glimpse her past society through the medium of militant music, which promises, as Cowan puts it, to impose "disciplinary order onto the disorderly body."[88] From a Western perspective, music is the major aural medium to accompany dance, which works together with the regimented mechanics associated with the nineteenth-century body and culture. The image of soldiers suggests a group mentality of marching off to war, which inspires Ella to also "battle" her body. The music inspires Ella to produce something artistic; she wants to sew, demanding silk and a canvas. Realizing that the struggle against her body is thoroughly taxing and seemingly futile, she seeks needlework as a means of giving herself order. Döblin was aware that embroidery was one of the most widespread types of occupational therapy, prescribed in the hope of giving the patient "a sense of order over their environment."[89] However, before she begins stitching, she sketches a scene:

> With a crayon she rapidly sketched a strange picture on the white cloth. There were three figures: a round misshapen body on two legs, without arms or head, nothing more than a fat ball with two legs. Beside him stood a large meek man with giant spectacles who caressed this body with a thermometer. But while he gave his full attention to looking after the body, on his other side a little girl jumped around barefoot, thumbing her nose at him with the left hand while stabbing a pair of sharp scissors from beneath into the body with the other hand, so that it leaked out in a thick stream like a punctured barrel.[90]

At this point, instead of using her body as a means of expression and communication, Ella creates a prophetic illustration in which she tries to destroy her body. The amorphic body propped up on two legs represents the formless, unknown modernity that has gradually distanced itself from her and has become empowered through the doctor's attention. The posthumanist body is meticulously being medically examined and coddled by a man with huge glasses, probably the doctor. Interestingly, the dancer sketches a doctor who caresses his specimen of modernity with a probing thermometer, commonly used to measure body temperature. Kolb reads these enormous glasses as a hegemonic male gaze that functions as "the motif of surveillance, with the act of seeing being associated with appropriation and pleasure."[91] Ella's drawing suggests that the doctor sympathizes with the new, fascinating body and has left the little dancing girl in the picture alone. The empowered child, however, maliciously stabs the blob with a pair of scissors. The sketch of the doctor both nurturing and fetishizing the modern body exaggerates the thrill of the unexpected and shows that it has become the exclusive focus of their attention. The doctors, with their analytical minds, want in no way to destroy their specimen—or as the narrator also calls the body, the "little child" ("Kindchen")—but rather to protect and further examine it. By caring for their new "child," they will unearth new knowledge. The drawing of the scornful girl shows her revenge, because she has in no way been attended to emotionally by the doctors. In fact, she envies the affective consideration the body receives, and ruthlessly attacks it. Starved for attention and completely decentered, the dancer's indignant behavior in the hospital and while she had been dancing in the company have manifested themselves in the sketch of her embroidery.

Ella's depiction of the three figures seems to run remarkably counter her own nineteenth-century aesthetic sensibilities of codified, mechanical ballet movements. Her work, however, proves to be a strikingly modern, posthumanist manifestation. The blob seems less recognizable as a human and more as an amorphous object with humanlike features. Such deformed, disproportionate body parts can also be seen in the expressionist poetry of Gottfried Benn.[92] Since "The Dancer and the Body" is considered by most critics to be an example of early expressionistic literature,[93] one could also read Ella's embroidery as a prophetic embodiment of the immediate future in which she literally stabs herself. This image also demarcates the future epoch and the expressionist style that not only literature but also dance would assume. Döblin's staging of Ella expressing herself through drawing in this metropolitan dance text will appear again strikingly in the following two chapters, in which Lasker-Schüler feels the need to depict dance no longer in words but in illustrations.

In addition to being addressed expressionistically in the visual arts, literature, and film, dance is also depicted quite visibly in her embroidery. The little girl in the picture stabbing the amorphous blob is barefoot. Modern dancers from the United States, such as Ruth St. Denis and particularly Isadora Duncan, as well as many practitioners of contemporary dance, were known for dancing barefoot, which represents emancipation from the restrictive corsets, pointe shoes, and mechanical movement of the institution of ballet. Ella's illustration demonstrates this leap into modernity, whether she is ready or not. As already discussed in "Dancers," Döblin was also keenly aware of the aesthetic shift and the difficulty in bridging the gap between ballet and the explosive, rebellious form of expressionist dance.

Some scholars, such as Cowan, call Ella's act of embroidery a "dress rehearsal" for her final "dance"[94] in which she essentially stages the scene from the sketch:

> She wanted to dance again, to dance! [. . .] She wanted to dance a waltz, a marvelously suave waltz, with the one who had become her master: her body. With a movement of her will she could once more catch him by the hands—this body, this indolent animal, and throw him down, turn him around: he was no longer her master. A triumphant hate rose up within her; they weren't going to move, he to the right and she to the left, but both together—they were going to do a salto together. She wanted to roll this barrel, this limping manikin, along the floor, to spin him head over heels, to stuff his mouth with sand.[95]

Although her illustration shows the dancer of the future, Ella reverts back to the only dance form she knows besides ballet: the waltz, an egalitarian social dance of the past century.[96] As mentioned before, Döblin also refers to the passé waltz, when he negatively alludes to Wiesenthal in "Dancers." During the metropolitan dance text, Ella can maintain control over the body as she had been able to do while performing ballet. The smooth, fluid movements should result in a coordinated pair, but the harmony is nullified through her hate and the empowered body. In this rather perplexing act, she tries to dance with her modern body as if to give it one more chance. However, Ella actually seeks revenge. She yearns to master the body to give her nineteenth-century values an opportunity to live. For a while both of them are actually dancing in step, but their togetherness looks contrived. Cowan calls this dance "a paradoxical sort of harmony, one imposed rather than chosen by Ella herself, and one revealing the impossibility of her project to subject the nervous body."[97]

In the end of the metropolitan dance text she calls the doctor over to her: "Bent double, she looked up at his face, and saw the look of astonishment when he caught sight of her embroidery. Then she said to him quite calmly: 'You—you clown, you clown, you total wimp.' And throwing off the covers, she stabbed the sewing scissors into her left breast."[98] The doctor analyzes the embroidery, but it's too late to save her; she wants to have the last word in her fruitless battle against her modern body. Her incessant bickering ends as she stabs herself in the chest, destroying her body and will.

Döblin's fictional observation of Ella's final performance in the hospital resembles the "dream dancer" (*"Traumtänzerin"*) Madeleine, who from 1904 was a patient of doctor and psychologist Freiherr von Schrenck-Notzing in Munich, and allegedly performed dances under hypnosis. Although proof of the authenticity of her induced trances is lacking, other scientists understood the "artistic significance of expressive movement in hysteria and under hypnosis"[99] ("künstlerische Bedeutung der Ausdrucksbewegung in der Hysterie und Hypnose"), or as Brandstetter comments, "In this context, hypnosis fulfilled the task of rendering the body ecstatic, that is, liberating the ego from its socially acquired inhibitions and releasing the free creative 'natural' essence from its cultural form."[100] Similar to Madeleine, Ella is undergoing medical treatment and could also be considered to be suffering from a form of hysteria. Her emphatic drawing and final dance deserve artistic interpretation, indicating that she is a dancer who has learned to let go of her social obligations and opened herself up to her creative nature. Having destroyed herself, Ella relinquishes ballet and allows the pathos model of the early-twentieth-century dancers to not only end the story, but to symbolize a new beginning from which a modern aesthetic can be developed. This highly figurative suggestion demonstrates Döblin's mastery of using choreographic devices to suspensefully build a performance—ending in a dramatic turn of events and further illustrating Brandstetter's characterization of both a dance performance and a text.

The university hospital has become more than just the stage for Ella's final dance. Her experience there essentially encompasses an accumulation of many performances: the dancer's defiant interaction with the doctors and nurses as she arrives at the hospital and during her stay, her amorphous drawing and embroidery, and the desperate act of killing herself. The reader perceives the clinical setting in the metropolitan dance text as an interactive, performative space in the microcosm of urban space, as Bauer proposes.[101] While Malte encounters the *Veitstänzer* on the dynamic streets of Paris, the doctors and nurses form the suffocating, posthumanist atmosphere with which Ella is forced to interact. Although she tries to faithfully uphold nineteenth-century traditions, her aggregate experiences paradoxically serve as performative, expressionistic moments. Thus, her struggle further enhances the power of modernity in the form of the modern doctors who scientifically view her movements. Furthermore, Döblin and the reader marvel at these philosophical and aesthetic changes: the unraveling of ballet and the explosive emergence of expressionist dance.

Similar to the waiters, who probably do not see the aesthetic explosiveness of the *Veitstänzer*'s movements, the doctors objectively focus on Ella's motions and symptoms, ascertaining how they correspond to her internal psyche instead of perceiving them in a dancerly light. While the physicians are not depicted as becoming emotionally involved in her dance, the reader and of course Döblin react more kinesthetically to the metropolitan dance text. As we have seen, "Dancers" thoroughly expresses the author's kinesthetic experience of watching the emaciated dancer: the newness corresponds to his explosive and rebellious aesthetic. Ella's performance of herself is an interesting point to also tie in with the *Veitstänzer*, by demonstrating that the only individuals in these two narratives who understand—or at least try to—are the authors, Malte and the reader. Döblin presumes that the medical community will be dumbfounded by Ella's performance of her dancerly symptoms, just as the pedestrians and waiters in Paris are unable to comprehend the *Veitstänzer*'s movement. While they are not incapable of understanding these events, the staging of these scenes in the streets and the hospital is aesthetically radical and unexpected. Furthermore, both Ella and the *Veitstänzer* are consumed by an empowered nonanthropocentric illness that violently uses and overtakes their bodies to create new modernist forms of dance. Rilke and Döblin give dancing agency to unlikely objects and decenter the will of the human. Thus, in both their own experiences and representations in their metropolitan dance texts, Endell, Kessler, Rilke, and Döblin cultivate a specialized, confounding, posthumanist flâneur-like gaze demanding to be expressed.

With its mass industrialization and influx of people, the city itself drastically changed the way modern individuals perceived themselves and their environment, as Simmel[102] has remarked. Some of its citizens, such as Ella, are unable to adjust to these transformations and are brought to the urban hospital. The doctors are interested in investigating the new modernist body that has entered their university clinic. Finally experiencing a living specimen who has inhabited the modern, industrial world, they intently study her, experimenting with new methods. To remember and process their findings, they have to record phenomena and symptoms in writing—similar to how Malte observed the man with *Veitstanz*; how Peter Fritzsche described the way in which journalists would capture their *Momentbilder*; how Kessler depicted Fuller, St. Denis, and Nijinsky in his journal; and how Endell illustrated his urban structures and spaces. The doctors cannot be in the streets like the journalists and the flâneur—they have to stay within the confines of the hospital where the casualties of modernity enter the ward. Just as industrious with their findings as Malte, the flâneur, the journalists, and Endell are with processing their urban experiences, the researchers encounter living specimens who are just as unexpected as occurrences in the streets. Unlike the observers of the phenomena in the urban space, who only have moments to watch a particular occurrence, the doctors have the privilege of holding their specimen for sustained study, allowing them to keep a living body that has experienced modernity. Instead of transforming their findings into artistic expression, as did Döblin, Malte, Endell, and the flâneur, or producing reports for general knowledge like the journalists, the doctors use the results from their study to further their own medical advancements. While the *Veitstänzer* presents himself similarly as a medical study, Malte can only follow him once and is unable to observe the man's condition over time. The man with *Veitstanz*, however, could just as likely be under the supervision of a neurologist, who would be performing examinations similar to those that Ella undergoes in the hospital.

Using *Kinostil* to create a succinct succession of events, "Modern" establishes Döblin's objective camera of the city and develops a different mode of metropolitan dance text. The metropolis envelops and manipulates Bertha to perform her demise, in an illustration of Döblin's conceptualization and employment of urban space. Furthermore, "Dancers" properly demonstrates his knowledge of both historical and contemporary dance practices around 1900, from the hegemonic male gaze of hierarchical ballet to the emerging, explosive expressionist dance. The metropolis has created a thriving university hospital for the doctors, who through their research and imposing presence manage to incite a symbolic battle between the nineteenth and twentieth century as embodied through dance: ballet and waltz versus expressionist dance. Ella's power and control have been sapped by her own posthumanist body and the cumulative environment of the doctors: she is thus ill prepared to enter modernity. Döblin demonstrates the overpowering effect of decentering human agency.

Older forms of ballet and social dance lose their former grandeur in the frenetic and dizzying contemporary society and cannot match the explosive, rebellious style in Döblin's dance texts "Dancers" and "The Dancer and the Body." In the former, his emaciated dancer's sudden movements not only demonstrate the effect that modernity has had on her dancing body and function as a direct contrast to the mechanics of ballet, they expand the author's dance aesthetic to encompass expressionist movement. Unlike Ella, who receives puzzling looks and detects uncomfortable confusion from the doctors and nurses, Döblin greets the emaciated dancer with an overwhelmingly curious and positive reaction, vehemently supporting the new direction in which modern dance is progressing. And as McCarren has argued, the establishment of psychological theories of mental illness that took hold during the nineteenth century slowly liberated the visual movement of dance performances from the social stigma attached to hysteria.[103] These performances could now be regarded as instead commenting on its aesthetic resemblance to the illness, rather than necessarily representing it.[104] As a result, the endings of "Modern," "Dancers," and "The Dancer and the Body" point to an exhilarating territory that essentially only acts as a beginning for modern dance to emerge as a new aesthetic movement form and as a new mode for the metropolitan dance text.

Six

Cabarets, Cafés, and Cities

The Birth of Early-Twentieth-Century Dance in Lasker-Schüler's Writing and Drawings

If Döblin's *Kinostil* evokes the presentness of a performance and the cinematic image, then Else Lasker-Schüler's metropolitan dance texts and drawings pull the genre even more closely into a queerer, posthumanist pictorial actualization. Having moved to Berlin in 1894, in 1922 she wrote of Berlin's attraction to the artist in the *Vossische Zeitung*: "Our city, Berlin, is strong and tremendous, and its wings know where it wants to go. For this reason the artist returns—always back to Berlin, here the clock of art does not run slow or fast. This reality is yet mystical."[1] In this depiction, the city has a body and mind of its own; its "wings" convey a transcendent, liminal, and posthumanist quality. The "clock of art" refers to the trends of fashionable artistic production, particularly in the café scene where artists and writers networked with others and sought work. The nature of this clock evokes the city's own temporality and insistent productivity, which contrasts with the often ephemeral forms of art. Yet the frequency and seriality of her feuilleton-like work for *Der Sturm*—or more specifically, her metropolitan dance texts—point to intense interaction with the materiality of Berlin's spaces around 1900, which engage with and create dancing, hybrid figures. In many ways, urbanity can incite dance movement, as analyzed in the previous works by Endell, Fuller, Kessler, Rilke, and Döblin. Lasker-Schüler's fantastical and poetic spaces interact with the dancer in different ways throughout her written work and drawings between 1910 and 1914. This chapter investigates the author's depiction of the dancing body *in* the city space and in close relationship *with* the city space. I look at three of her works as well as her emerging drawings through the lens of the metropolitan dance text, postcolonial theory, queer theory, and posthumanist thought: "In the Neopathetic Cabaret" (1910) ("Im neopathetischen Cabaret"), "I Dance in the Mosque" (1911) ("Ich tanze in der Moschee"), and *Letters to Norway* (1911–1912) (*Briefe nach Norwegen*), the latter of which was later published as *My Heart* (1912) (*Mein Herz*). These texts represent the moving and dancing body intertwining itself with the urban spaces in Berlin and Thebes—both imagined and influenced by experience—in and around architectural structures and areas such as the cabaret, a mosque, a bazaar, the Café Kurfürstendamm, an Islamic stage at the Luna Park, and, in her drawings, the cityscape of Thebes.

Background on Lasker-Schüler

Her depictions of Berlin and images of dancers become thoroughly interwoven with a perceived Orientalism from a more Western perspective. However, due to her diverse identity as a queer, female, German-Jewish artist, she found it difficult to fit into mainstream culture, and she remained at the fringes of society. Jewish Germans as a minority became interested in the Orient because they struggled with what it meant to be German; since they had begun moving into mainstream German life after being allowed citizenship in 1871, they also feared total assimilation and losing their Jewishness.[2] For Donna Heizer, Lasker-Schüler's work does not aim at differentiating cultures—her representation of the Orient is "a contradictory, ahistorical, amorphous construct,"[3] which "reproduces many of the stereotypes about the Orient found in European literature."[4] Such discourse from her writing is also reflected in her drawings: Astrid Schmetterling notes that while the author's pictures interweave discourses on Primitivism, Orientalism, and majority Zionism, they also create liminal spaces that dissolve the barriers between self and other, Jew and Arab, and Oriental and European.[5] As Martin Buber writes, Jews played a "mediating" role between Europe and Asia that allowed them to preserve the insights of the Occident without sacrificing the original Oriental quality.[6] Homi Bhabha uses the term "third space of enunciation" to challenge the idea of a pure, original, and homogenous culture, instead claiming that cultures are contradictory, ambivalent spaces. He writes:

> enunciation may open the way to conceptualizing an *inter*national culture, based not on the exoticism of multiculturalism or the *diversity* of

cultures, but on the inscription and articulation of culture's *hybridity.*
To that end we should remember that it is the "inter"—the cutting
edge of translation and negotiation, the *in-between* space—that carries
the burden of the meaning of culture.[7]

His work articulates a space for Lasker-Schüler's creative work, which
wholly engages with the amalgamation of worlds and aesthetics. Influenced
by her physical space, contemporary society, urban phenomena, and dance in
Berlin, she fashions fantasy realms that intermingle with realism in her writing and artistic work, reflecting her hybrid identity.

Like Kessler, Lasker-Schüler maintained a queer identity and thrived
in a scene where she could intellectually and artistically carve out her own
space. Eve Sedgwick characterizes "queer" as "the open mesh of possibilities,
gaps, overlaps, dissonances and resonances, lapses and excesses of meaning
when the constituent elements of anyone's gender, of anyone's sexuality aren't
made (or can't be made) to signify monolithically."[8] One recognizes Lasker-
Schüler's queer identity not only through her dress but through her illustrations of Jussuf. As Penny Farfan has mentioned, queerness remained vital in
forming modernism and modernist performances. It provided an alternative
social and cultural space for imaginative, subversive, and experimental practices to emerge, and allowed individuals to act out queer experiences and sexual identities.[9] In *Queer Phenomenology*, Sara Ahmed investigates how bodies
move and interact with their surroundings and other people in space, and
how they are influenced by their background and negotiate lines of whiteness
and heteronormativity, conforming to or deviating from them.[10] Anna Babka
remarks that Lasker-Schüler's work can be considered colonial texts:

> the orientalized space becomes the projected area for wishes and
> desires and provides for an identity that can only be conceptualized
> and lived within and through the assumed "other." At the same time it
> becomes the stage on which the subject is being formed on the basis of
> unsolved, puzzled and conflicting aspects of identity. Within this area
> of conflict and tension, within those instants of ambivalence, moments
> of "postcolonial-queer" open up.[11]

In effect, her postcolonial and queer identity is thoroughly expanded, made
pliable, and mixed so as to therapeutically seek out many different manifestations of the dancing body with the city space.

Adding to these liminal states, the idea of performance has generally been considered a "centrally human practice," but the posthumanist condition maintains a liberated reimagining of the body, spectatorship, and performance, rethinking their traditionally conceived positionality; it becomes instead a dynamic system of interdependent parts.[12] This dehierarchicalization demands then a redefining of these parts. Posthumanism aims at decentering hegemonic Western cultural binaries—body/mind, self/other, culture/nature, global/local, human/animal, human/machine—by showing that humans are continually involved in constituting themselves in various forms through interdependent processes.[13] While much posthumanist thought has derived from Donna Haraway's "Cyborg Manifest," which addresses the hybridity of machine and organism,[14] Lasker-Schüler engages more with the human/architecture and human/plant realms. By combining posthumanist thought, queer theory, and postcolonial theory, Lasker-Schüler's metropolitan dance texts engage with a complex hybridity of the moving body and the urban environment to establish an open space to experiment with representation of her perpetually changing identity. This view decenters the human view and opens up agency for the nonanthropocentric.

I argue that by reading Lasker-Schüler's writing and illustrations chronologically from a span of four years, one can detect the thorough development of her first literary representations of the dancing body and the urban space interpenetrating each other in her metropolitan dance texts, and second, this aesthetic proclivity manifesting itself in her drawings as she attempts to move beyond the expressivity of language. More specifically, my contribution to Lasker-Schüler scholarship aims to show that her subversive depictions of city space often interweave with the dancing body and create a symbiotic and posthumanist dynamic of producing and sustaining. This interpenetration establishes each element as a porous stimulus that can give life to the other, thereby creating a new ethics by dehierarchicalizing the human and nonhuman realms. Furthermore, much in the vein of Döblin's *Kinostil* and Ella's sketch and embroidery, Lasker-Schüler's metropolitan dance texts can be interpreted as having photographic and filmic qualities whose dancerly aesthetics continually develop even after she discovers the expressive possibilities of drawing over writing. Her graphic work in particular resembles film stills, which depict an evolving aesthetic. Because of these constant developments in representation in her writing and drawings, it is paramount to read her work chronologically, relating it to the aesthetic and cinematic context of their creation. While Andreas Huyssen argues that his "metropolitan miniatures" are a literary genre that evokes the visual and the cinematic but are themselves not these other media,[15] my examples (particularly with

Lasker-Schüler) demonstrate that some authors *do* desire to move beyond the written word and into new media—in drawings, photographs, and film.

Melding into the Space of "In the Neopathetic Cabaret"

In Lasker-Schüler's metropolitan dance text "In the Neopathetic Cabaret," published on November 17, 1910, in *Der Sturm*, the narrator portrays an imaginary dance world and comments on the reading performances of the members of a cabaret club. While this scene is reminiscent of Döblin's short piece on Gertrude Barrison's reading, Lasker-Schüler's cabaret does not fit into the generalized definition. According to historian Peter Jelavich, a general commercial cabaret consisted of a small stage in an intimate hall allowing for direct eye contact between viewer and performer. Lasting five to ten minutes, short acts from various genres were usually performed: songs, monologues, skits, and sometimes pantomimes, dances, and films. Professional singers and actors and sometimes writers, dancers, and composers satirized or parodied issues related to sex (most often), contemporary fads, and politics (least often). An emcee introduced the acts, engaged with the audience, and commented on current events.[16] Jelavich calls the "Neopathetic Cabaret" "high end" because it focused more on the reading of literature than on other genres.[17] From June 1, 1910, until December 16, 1911, this early expressionist gathering, founded by Kurt Hiller and once called the New Club (*Der neue Club*), resembled a literary evening of reading from writers' works, and thus evoked the early-nineteenth-century salon tradition. Like the commercial cabaret, it integrated musical elements and the erotic for a smaller audience, but on a more artistic, philosophical, and neoromantic level.[18] The style of verse and recitation here probably derives from Otto Julius Bierbaum's anthology *Deutsche Chansons*, in which he posits the idea of "applied lyric poetry" ("angewandte Lyrik"),[19] the effort to free the aesthetic principle from the compartmentalized space of current artistic practices and to allow its totality as lively presentation to thrive through embodiment.

Lasker-Schüler's metropolitan dance text, "In the Neopathetic Cabaret," seems to fully embrace the idea of enlivened performance. She opens with the words "One thousand and one" ("Tausend und Einer"), which immediately awakens connotations of *One Thousand and One Nights* (also called *The Arabian Nights*), a collection of Middle Eastern and Indian tales. These stories, which have become part of Western folklore, appeared in German translations in the early nineteenth century and have continued to be translated. While the evocative beginning of Lasker-Schüler's dance text sets the stage for listening to narrative-driven stories, the narrator subverts this expectation by inscribing writers and performers into the prose. Instead of focusing on the contents of each author's verse or speech, she concentrates on their mannerisms, gestures, and passion: for Lasker-Schüler, the performance style and the space's overall atmosphere retain the utmost importance. For example, the actor Armin Wassermann performs his verse softly, richly, and superbly, with a boyish enthusiasm. Meanwhile, the poet Jakob von Hoddis defiantly reads his poetry. Among these *Varieté*-style displays of short acts, the narrator continues to weave and develop the theme of *One Thousand and One Nights*.

In one striking passage, she writes, "I look for a chair that blooms in seclusion—finally I find such a violet at the end of the wallpaper. I sit down. My Zobeïde, who is very curious about the Neopathetic Cabaret, has been resting tired for a while between white, purple-yellow, red and skyblue girls."[20] In contrast to the precise descriptions of the performer's movements, the narrator situates herself as an observer with a powerful imagination, who perceives a fluid, posthumanist line between human individual and object. This dichotomous perspective was also seen in Kessler's view of St. Denis's and Nijinsky's dances. Gradually the narrator's prose leads her to become part of the wallpaper: first, she desires to sit on a chair that is not in the cabaret realm, but rather in the wallpaper's poetic world—the chair is replaced by a flower, a clear reference to *Jugendstil* iconography and the nonanthropocentric. Second, one could read the need for seclusion as a desire to escape from the everyday cabaret life. While she describes the verbal performances with great fervor, she also expresses a yearning for an excursion. The narrator then introduces Zobeïde, whom she situates as an outsider to the performance. I discuss Zobeïde in the next section, but I will introduce her here. In *One Thousand and One Nights* the Sultan of ancient Persia tests the fidelity of his wife Zobeïde by pretending to go on a hunting trip; when he returns he catches her in an orgy with male slaves. In this metropolitan dance text, Zobeïde is reimagined as a curious and excited figure who is also overstimulated and tired from the evening event in the cabaret. By seeking seclusion, the narrator likewise becomes an outsider to the proceedings, joining her guest. The narrator maintains a modernist flâneur-like gaze over the performances because she remains physically and even poetically able to remove herself from the manifest space. She does not completely escape, but rather straddles both worlds: maintaining a perpetual *inter*-ness. Like the narrator who has joined her, Zobeïde is also woven into the fabric of other girls—their vibrant color palette emphasizes the girls' abstractness, as if Zobeïde blends into the wallpaper or crowd. By using the possessive pronoun "my," Zobeïde appears to belong to the narrator, who has mentally created the figure.

After commenting again on one of the writer's verbal performances, the narrator discloses that "I always have to think about money; how one is becoming destitute—if Zobeïde, my dancer, had a purse on her, I would drink a glass of lemonade to combat the heat from the crowd."[21] Here again the narrator straddles the two worlds by bringing the poetic muse Zobeïde from the wallpaper into the mundane social world. Lasker-Schüler herself lived a very frugal existence and constantly needed financial support. The narrator now names Zobeïde as her dancer, which evokes even further imagery of movement, transcendence, and intimacy. Even though the dancer does not buy the narrator a drink, the thought at least incites the possibility of transgressing both realms: the colorful, objectified dancer can interpenetrate the cabaret life, not as a dancer per se, but as an outside observer. Lasker-Schüler juxtaposes Zobeïde, who is incidentally not dancing, in this instance, with being able to support the narrator: the aesthetic crosses over into the banal.

After describing more of the performers, "In the Neopathetik Cabaret" concludes with a line set topographically apart from the rest of the paragraph: "Zobeïde, my dancer, does not want to come home yet."[22] The narrator poetically announces the presence of her dancer, whose rumination during the evening's performance further incites contemplation. Even though Zobeïde is tired, she remains intrigued by the various acts. Perhaps the narrator implies the desire to already leave the event, but the dancer prefers to remain. Zobeïde indeed does not dance in this metropolitan dance text, but rather remains an active listener and observer. Implied here is that Zobeïde, as the Sultana, does not want to go home to her husband, and indulges in the new, Western display of verse reading; similarly, the narrator seems to desire Zobeïde's "exotic" Easternness. Lasker-Schüler has rendered both Zobeïde and the cabaret space as a porous material as each is able to inhabit the traditional territory of the other.

Ballets Russes in Berlin and Leon Bakst's Set Design

While Karl Jürgen Skrodzki believes that Zobeïde is Wally Schramm,[23] an actor, dancer, and friend of Lasker-Schüler, I believe that the author had in mind not only Zobeïde from the *One Thousand and One Nights*, but possibly also the work of set designer Leon Bakst, whose scenography from the Ballets Russes was featured in Berlin five months before Lasker-Schüler wrote

"In the Neopathetic Cabaret." Novack's notion of *movement environments* could also be invoked here to explain the dispersion of these aesthetics. Her term essentially characterizes the permeation of various dance movements influencing each other and creating an atmosphere "implicitly perceived and understood by everyone."[24]

For the 1910 season, according to Bronislava Nijinska, the sister of Vaslav Nijinsky, the Ballets Russes planned to present the following ballets abroad during their European tour: *The Firebird, Scheherazade, Cleopatra, Polovetsian Dances, Carnaval, Giselle*, and *Les Sylphydes*.[25] They performed at the Theater des Westens in 1910 and 1912, the Kroll Oper in 1912, and the Theater am Nollendorfplatz in 1914. Many of these dances included Orientalist themes based largely on Mikhail Fokine's choreography. While Lasker-Schüler may have seen *Cleopatra* at the Theater des Westens on May 21 or May 23, 1910, *Scheherazade* was shown later, on January 15, 1912. Despite this speculation, strong Orientalist themes pervade Lasker-Schüler's oeuvre. The author even arranged the "Fakir von Theben," a *Varieté* number that was never became realized, although she developed it and practiced for it (fig. 5). She had planned to read verse in Arabic, even though the text had been translated by the Berlin University instructor Hamed Waly for her initial understanding. Moreover, in various letters from April until October 1910, Lasker-Schüler hints at how Wally Schramm may have assisted with and danced in the planned piece by referring to her as "meine Tänzerin,"[26] as the narrator refers to Zobeïde in "In the Neopathetic Cabaret."

The Orientalist performances of *Cleopatra* may have seeped into Lasker-Schüler's gestural imaginary. Presenting *Une Nuit d'Egypte* as a draft in the Mariinsky Theatre, St. Petersburg, on March 2, 1908, Mikhail Fokine's one-act ballet *Cleopatra*, inspired by stories by Théophile Gautier, premiered during the opening season for the Ballets Russes in Paris at the Théâtre du Châtelet on June 2, 1909. Seeking a break from the academic balletic form, Fokine explored the mysterious East and Orientalist themes, denying ballerinas their pointe shoes and exposing the expressivity of the libidinous torso. The dance was accompanied by music from such composers as Anton Arensky, Aleksandr Glazunov, Mikhail Glinka, Modest Mussorgsky, Nikolai Rimsky-Korsakov, Sergei Taneyev, and Nikolai Tcherepnin, who maintained affinities for the symphonic poem that fit the genre of the one-act ballet. Deborah Jowitt notes, "Their modal progressions, their strange and vivid key relationships, their irregular rhythms and obsessive repetition of rhythmic motifs seemed wildly exotic to Parisians brought up on the work of West-

Fig. 5. Else Lasker-Schüler dressed in an Oriental costume as her persona "Prince Yussuf" playing a reed instrument.

ern conservatory-trained musicians."[27] Such Orientalist aesthetics could have influenced Lasker-Schüler's movement imaginary.

This ballet depicts Amoun, a young hunter, who already has a beautiful partner, Ta-Hor, but nevertheless seeks the impossible love of Cleopatra, queen of Egypt. The bored femme fatale grants him one night with her, on the condition that at dawn he must die; he agrees to this plan, and it transpires accordingly. While lacking plot, this one-act indulged in sensual set design, costuming, dancers, and music that "fused into a single vivid landscape," remaining united in concept.[28] Set designer Leon Bakst's vibrant color palette of gold, malachite green, pink, lapis blue, orange, and violet pervaded the dancers' costuming, jewelry, and stage design, in keeping with an Egyptian theme. (These types of brilliant colors also appear in Chomón's film of Fuller as a choreography of attraction, discussed in the following chapter.) Jean Cocteau described one scene from *Cleopatra* spawned from

Bakst's imagination, in which the leading lady emerges like a mummy from a casket as twelve colorful layers of veil are peeled off her body by slaves: "the first veil, which was red, with silver lotuses and crocodiles; then the second veil, which was green with the history of the dynasties in gold filigree; then the third, which was orange with prismatic stripes"; the last veil, dark blue, reveals her body. She is wearing a small, blue wig.[29] The conceptual unity particularly with costuming and set design seems to meld the stimuli into one sensuous object, as in Lasker-Schüler's depiction of Zobeïde and the narrator herself, who blend into the wallpaper. The removal of Cleopatra's veils also evokes the various vibrant colors between which Zobeïde rests in "In the Neopathetic Cabaret."

In addition to *Cleopatra*, the Ballets Russes played *Scheherazade* at the Theater des Westens on January 15, 1912; however, it had premiered on June 4, 1910, in Paris at the Théâtre de l'Opéra. Based on the prologue to *One Thousand and One Nights*, this one-act ballet depicts Shahriyar, the sultan of ancient Persia, who tests the fidelity of his wife Zobeïde by pretending to go on a hunting trip; after he leaves, she and the other concubines bribe the Chief Eunuch to open the gates to where the male slaves reside. After the Sultana chooses the Golden Slave, an orgy ensues. The Sultan returns sooner than she expected, he demands that they all be killed, and the ballet ends with Zobeïde's suicide. While the one-act ends here, the story of *One Thousand and One Nights* continues with the Sultan marrying a new woman every day and beheading her in the morning. However, Scheherazade cleverly makes a deal, telling him a story each night with the promise to continue the next night. Exhausting her stories by the 1001th night, the Sultan decides to marry Scheherazade and spares her life.

Dance journalist André Levinson notices how the costumes from this ballet either blend into the scenery because of their complementary shades, or they clash completely: "It is a living scenery with interchangeable elements."[30] The author Carl Einstein remarks that Bakst's set design reflects far less a decorative aesthetic than a "mask of the drama" that enlivens the space. The theatrical landscape transforms into active, posthumanist stimuli that become actors and collaborators in the dance piece.[31] Einstein's perception is strikingly reminiscent of Gideon's idea of interpenetration: at times, the compartmentalized fabric of the set doubles as a dance costume. Brandstetter furthers Einstein's observation by analyzing how the dancers' movement, their costumes, and the scenography work in tandem. As the dancers move, their costumes correspondingly appear to be dancing: thus, the fabric abstracts itself from the movers' body to the point that it seems to disappear; the viewer is left, therefore, with the dancing costume and movement:[32] as if the human has transformed into an empowered abstract material as in Fuller's *Serpentine Dance*. Zobeïde from "In the Neopathetic Cabaret" assumes a similar aesthetic that Brandstetter maintains in Bakst's scenography of Scheherazade.

Ida Rubinstein also played the role of Zobeïde and Cleopatra in the Berlin performances. Having expressively performed the title role in Oscar Wilde's *Salomé* on November 3, 1908, to a private audience,[33] she was recruited by Diaghilev into his company. Although untrained as a dancer, she developed a penchant for performing gestures that corresponded to internal emotions, modalities that engaged with Dalcroze's concepts of rhythmic movement and Delsarte's gestural theories, which St. Denis also practiced.[34] Patricia Vertinsky sees Rubinstein's portraying Salomé as inciting a quest for self-realization and sexual freedom, which were usually prohibited for women. As with the actress Sarah Bernhardt, "her [Rubinstein's] Jewishness, her dark beauty and her sexuality were consistently coded as exuding Oriental appeal, exotic, erotic and dangerous."[35]

Even if Lasker-Schüler had not expressly seen Rubinstein perform *Cleopatra* and *Scheherazade* in the Theater des Westens, the movement environment attests to their similarities. Both were Jewish women who struggled with and worked through their identities. In many ways, "In the Neopathetic Cabaret" reflects an intellectual life at the margins. First, the narrator straddles both the cabaret world and her spatial imagination. Whether or not Zobeïde is the dancer Wally Schramm, the narrator has coded her as the Sultana of ancient Persia during the time when the Ballets Russes was touring Berlin with similar Orientalist ballets. Second, Bakst's interpenetrative scenography with the dancers, their costumes and movement, and the set background resembles the aesthetic phenomenon of how Zobeïde and the narrator blend into the wallpaper in "In the Neopathetik Cabaret." Lasker-Schüler's integration of the poetic and the imaginary in her writing constantly expressed the desire for the posthumanist beyond, which was also a contemporary thought of the Ballets Russes with their Orientalism. Lewinson's comment about contrasting or complementary colors also suggests that the narrator and Zobeïde sometimes blend into the background and at times snap back into the real world of the cabaret. Lasker-Schüler uses the cabaret space as the primary inspiration for creating her new world in which the dancer as observer melds into the surroundings. Furthermore, the performative space of the cabaret represents one small fragment that blends into the entire fabric of the metropolis. The author uses the cabaret as a dynamic space closely linked to the urban experience, which is particularly apparent if one keeps Jelavich's chapter "Cabaret as a Metropolitan Montage" in mind. Lasker-Schüler accords the dancer Zobeïde and the narrator the power to interpenetrate the cabaret space and to occupy liminal spaces and the desired beyond.

"I Dance (in) the Mosque"

Originally published in *The Nights of Tino Baghdad* (1907) (*Die Nächte von Tino Bagdad*), "I Dance in the Mosque"[36] ("Ich tanze in der Moschee") later appeared in *Der Sturm* in 1911. This reprint points to Lasker-Schüler's interest in isolating the evocation of this metropolitan dance as a stand-alone event among the variety of other texts in the publication. If one reads this piece in conjunction with her conceptualization of space in "In the Neopathetic Cabaret," one can more prominently see the relationship to how dance *produces* space, even more so than dancing *in* or *with* it; this phenomena also occurred in Endell's metropolitan dance text. Markus Hallensleben calls Lasker-Schüler's text a theatrical staging of words.[37] By evoking Döblin's *Kinostil*, he calls this reprinted version of "I Dance in the Mosque" a surreal dream text or film scene whose narrative is a virtual dance.[38] While his interpretation is in line with the performative and filmic nature of the depiction, he also highlights the dancerly nature of the movement. Sylke Kirschnick suggests that the narrator depicts a body being created through language and movement, and the event responsible is the recitation of the poem, a performative act. While she claims the representation does not depict a corresponding building or even the slightest hint of one,[39] I argue that the rhythm and the arrangement of words creates not only a dancing body, but a quasi-architectural structure—a mosque—which arises from the whirling movements. As if reciting a prayer or chanting a spell, the narrator *dances* the mosque by invoking her entire body and the organic elements around her to create the performance of the physical structure that probably ceases to exist following the conclusion of the dance.

In the text, the narrator explicitly announces the performance to the reader by urging them to come back three days after the rain, when the ground is presumably more fertile, and the Nile recedes to make room for her dance. The large blossoms remind one of the flower chair in "In the Neopathetic Cabaret," thus evoking interpenetration and recalling the posthumanist transformation of organic imagery into a physical structure. The narrator evokes general Egyptian iconography by depicting a mummy, as in Fokine's *Cleopatra*, in which Rubinstein emerged from the coffin with colorful veils being removed from her body. Similar to the fire in Rilke's poem

"Spanish Dancer" (1906), the dervish dance in Lasker-Schüler's dance text begins slowly as the body sparks a flame. While the movement begins in the extremities, it awakens the rest of the corpus, particularly the core. The narrator interpenetrates human body parts—eyes, an arm, forehead, lips, chin, feet, a shoulder, finger, ears—with natural elements such as stone circles, flowers, rain, river, star. The hybrid, posthumanist body emerges from the earth and breathes as if being born. Paths of human bodily development become interwoven with components of the natural world. The narrator gives off a scent like a flower; the body resembles a star. In one instance, her finger extends like the stalk of an Allahblume, her face fans itself from side to side, and her dance entangles itself in the stone circle of her ear: implied here is that the encircling dance continues to make trace markings with her ear. The Allahblume is probably an imagined flower holding spiritual, organic, and poetic connotations. On the one hand, the dance is a transient performance, but on the other, it manages to leave traces behind in the physical structure it creates out of the body and the earth. These amalgamations thoroughly display their characteristics, bringing them into a liminal, poetic space and challenging the limits of representation through paradoxical couplings. While a dervish dance can be performed in a mosque, Lasker-Schüler subverts this tradition, instead depicting a dancer engaging with the landscape to create a physical structure that could be interpreted as a mosque. We will see a similar birth of the dancer/dancing structure in Lasker-Schüler's drawings.

Even though the dance text begins with pain, sweet intoxication soon ensues, helping the dancer to thrive. While the melding of the body and these organic symbols may not represent urbanity directly, they do demonstrate an interpenetration with the landscape, which always holds the possibility of turning into a city through industrialization and cultivation. Similarly, in "In the Neopathetic Cabaret," the inner, metropolitan space becomes juxtaposed with organic flowers and colors. In other words, in Lasker-Schüler's writing, opposites quite often awaken each other and can become interchangeable. Additionally, her religious fervor and Orientalizing incantation "o, machmêde macheï" evoke the creation of a larger being, a mosque. While this chant appears to be in a non-Western language, perhaps an imitation of Arabic, it registers as "foreign" and "other" to the probably white, German readership of *Der Sturm*. Thus, instead of understanding the meaning of the words, the spell is performatively felt on a rhythmic and bodily level, and heightens an imaginary power of the mystical beyond. By the same token, this chant also Orientalizes and creates a wholly inauthentic language that embodies her Western imagination. According to Brandstetter, movement forms such as trance and ecstasy occupy precultural spaces and diverge from normative conceptions of dance; they attempt to restore the collective and individual unconscious that has been repressed by civilization and industrialization.[40] Avant-garde artists were preoccupied with accessing such a space and often retheatricalized such dances.[41] Practicing Islamic mysticism by performing a religious dance of ecstatic whirling, the dervishes—members of the Sufi order, and more specifically the Mevlevi—in groups of nine, eleven, or thirteen barefoot individuals, turned counter-sunwise with outreaching arms and closed eyes. Guided by the *sheikh*, the religious leader and venerated teacher, this ritual was performed on Tuesdays and Fridays in a mosque; the incessant circling movement along the body's axis represented inspiration and a transcendent mode in order to reach God.[42] The dervishes would not only circle around themselves, they would also be a part of a much larger circular pattern around the periphery of the space. The Mevlevi order performed in a *sema* or worship ceremony space—one of the most famous is Galata Mevlevihane in Istanbul—in the shape of an octagon.[43] While the main prayer hall, usually square, represented the world and the spherical dome stood for the heavens, the eight-sided sema symbolized the transitionary space for reaching God.[44] Farrin Chwalkowski maintains that these areas comprised the entire lodge or complex (*tekke*) where the Sufi brotherhood (*tarikat*) lived. The transitory nature of the sema—in terms of both the fleetingness of a performance taking place there and as a liminal space between heaven and earth—reflects Lasker-Schüler's interest in experimenting representationally with such an architectural structure and represents her own continually transitioning queer identity.

Western tourists were allowed to enter this space and observe performances; the indelible movement imagery cultivated a fascination with whirling dervishes and incited widespread dissemination of their representation in writing, art, and photography.[45] Lasker-Schüler was well aware of such depictions, which may have influenced her conceptualization of her literary dancing mosque. Thus, her perspective on these images is wholly colored by an often problematic and essentializing Western and Orientalizing imaginary. Travel writings such as the chapter "The Dancing Dervishes" in *Constantinople* by French writer Théophile Gautier attest to both the ballroom- and theater-like nature of the space;[46] at one end, the orchestra played, and around the octagon were different viewing areas based on class and gender.[47] Gautier notes the dance's resemblance to a waltz and how the persistent monotony of the movement and music could bring a "nonbeliever" in Islam to the point of ecstasy; he even perceived a "penetrating and intoxicating sweetness"[48] of the kind that Lasker-Schüler also depicts in "I Dance in the Mosque." Gautier even mentions both the animalistic nature and the objectification of one dancer: "His tunic, like a bird about to take flight, began to tremble, and slightly to rise and fall. The speed of the movement increased; the fragile tissue of the dress, lifted by the air, in which it revolved, spread itself in a circle and took the form of a bell, until at length it resembled a mere whirlwind of white, of which the dervish formed the centre."[49] This posthumanist description focuses on the transformation of the dancer into a moving, aesthetic object, a bell and a whirlwind. Such depictions evoke the movement aesthetic of Fuller's drapery dance and Lasker-Schüler's "I Dance in the Mosque." In the poet's metropolitan dance text, however, the narrator moves beyond this imagery of evoking a mere object: by amalgamating the dancing body with the organic elements in the surrounding area, she arguably creates and becomes a physical mosque. Instead of pursuing the traditional goal of attaining oneness with God, Lasker-Schüler subverts this dance by fusing the moving body with the actual space. Precisely by not mentioning the mosque, she expresses its presence by having the narrator embody its rich development. As opposed to "In the Neopathetic Cabaret," which involves more of an ambient melding of two porous worlds, "I Dance in the Mosque" invokes a spell that uses dance not only as a performative act to fuse growing body parts with active natural elements, but also to leave traces of a physical structure; this posthumanist mosque could be an element of an Orientalized metropolis as part of Lasker-Schüler's imaginary, as we will see later on in the chapter.

Luna Park and Cafés in *Letters to Norway*

The letters in *Letters to Norway* (*Briefe nach Norwegen*) were published in 20 weekly installments in *Der Sturm*, from September 1911 until February 1912. Lasker-Schüler's impetus for this series arose from a trip to Sweden and Norway taken only by her then-husband Herwarth Walden and his friend Kurt Neiman. Jakob Hessing believes that she turned her failing marriage into a public, performative display as part of her "anti-bourgeois strategy: Art had brought [Lasker-Schüler and her husband] together as partners in their struggle against philistine society, and in a work of art she notified the audience of their separation."[50] After publishing *Letters to Norway* as an epistolary novel called *My Heart* (*Mein Herz*) in 1912, she divorced Walden and began a more intense life in her drawings, with a lively exchange of postcards with Franz Marc, founding member of the German expressionist group *The

Blue Rider (*Der blaue Reiter*). Oscillating between the café life of Berlin and the fictitious Thebes, a city in Egypt that she never visited yet claimed to be from,[51] *Letters to Norway* wavers between real life and an imaginary world. Andrea Kraus characterizes this episodic prose text as a "writing of attractions" that reflects short, spectacular displays of popular mass entertainment: early cinema, cabaret, the *Varieté*, and café life.[52] Andrew Webber perceives Lasker-Schüler's texts during this time as a performance of displacement in which categories such as geography, topography, gender, sexuality, and ethnicity are subjected to switching and exchange: as in inside and outside spaces, urban and rural, male and female, homo- and heterosexual, and German and Jewish.[53] In addition to these characteristics outlined by Kraus and Webber, these interchangeable relationships occupy a space between these dichotomies: a certain *inter*-ness that Bhabha and Gideon espouse, a queerness, and a posthumanism.

Luna Park

In the first installment of *Letters to Norway* in *Der Sturm*[54] and at the very beginning of *My Heart*, Lasker-Schüler's narrator and her friend, *Varieté* dancer Getrude Barrison, visit an Egyptian exhibition at Luna Park:

[T]he day before yesterday I went to the Luna Park with Gertrude Barrison, quietly slipping into the Egyptian exhibition, as though we had a premonition of something sweet. In a coffeehouse Gertrude caught the attention of an Arab with a full beard; she was totally horrified at my suggestion to flirt with him. I had, you see, gazed at the curl of his lips, which had now stiffened in response to the coolness of my companion. Her reluctance bothered me very much. But during the belly dancing one of the miracles of my Arabian book happened; I danced with Minn, the son of the sultan of Morocco. We danced, danced like two dancing snakes, up on the Islam stage, shedding our skins to the enticing tones of the bamboo flute of the snake charmer, lured on by the dream of the ancient Pharoahs, with the eternal bells. And Gertrude also danced the croquette, but like a muse, not as Muslim-like as we; she danced with graceful, provocative arms, her fingers waving like fringes. But he and I suddenly found ourselves on the way to Tangiers, shouted war-like cries, until his mouth kissed me so gently, with such ardor, that I would have felt awkward resisting.

Ever since I have loved everyone whose skin color has a trace of his skin color, reminding me of his gold brocade.[55]

The narrator's remark at the beginning demonstrates that she and Barrison came to the exhibition with the premonition of something "sweet," thus recalling the possibility of an ecstatic dance as we have already seen in "I Dance in the Mosque." Additionally, the narrator's intuition points to their experienced city-dweller mentality of preparing themselves for the unexpected. They simply have a "feeling" that something would happen, but they will not discover it until they continue with their day at Luna Park. Like the journalists' *Momentbilder*, Malte's numerous strange incidents with people in the Parisian streets, Endell's modernist miniatures, and Döblin's university hospital doctors, modern individuals living in the metropolis had to prepare themselves for unlikely encounters.

For this scene, it seems fitting not only that the narrator attends Luna Park, one of the newest venues, to learn about Egyptian culture, but that she is accompanied by Gertrude Barrison, a prominent *Varieté* performer of the time. As a member of the ensemble Five Sisters Barrison, this dancer took part in *Varieté* acts in the 1890s in European metropolises and often in the Berliner Wintergarten.[56] Even if Barrison did not attend the park, Lasker-Schüler still writes her into the narrative to establish a dancerly quality in the scenario, as with Zobeïde "In the Neopathetic Cabaret." Both Barrison and the narrator visit an exotic exhibition, presumably because of their interest in non-Western cultures. Barrison and the Egyptian exhibition are examples of foreign importations that attempt to enlighten Western cultural hubs like Berlin about other parts of the world. However, bringing "authentic" elements as part of an exhibition paradoxically heightens their lack of authenticity by highlighting kitsch, a marked cultural essentialization and Orientalization, and an exercise in Western imperialism. Located in western Berlin near Halensee, Luna Park opened on May 14, 1910, as an amusement park. According to Paul Dobryden, it offered an arrangement of artificial environments: the parkgoer's ability to adapt to various different surroundings was key in inducing a feeling of pleasure instead of restriction.[57] During the summer of 1911, the park planned for a "Miniature Cairo" that was supposed to imitate the real city.[58] In the "Streets of Cairo" exhibition, over eighty men, women, and children—part Arab and part Indian—distributed themselves along a bazaar quarter to create typical handicrafts, prepare local dishes, serve drinks in an oriental café, give Koran lessons, and demonstrate dervish dances.[59] Before this exhibition, the Great Industrial Exposition of Berlin had taken place, from May 1 to October 15, 1896. Here, partitioned exhibits taking on the quality of display cases featured a contemporary Cairo exhibit leading the visitor from the ancient period to modernization: the Temple of Edfu, a mummy grave in a model pyramid, and a mosque.[60] Such displays of "authentic" Orientalism from a Western, imperialistic perspective were widely available to Lasker-Schüler, permeating her urban surroundings and feeding her imagination.

The accessibility of these stimulating microcosms certainly influenced Lasker-Schüler's writing. Hallensleben notes the many possible influences the author could have encountered in Berlin: posters, advertisements, architectural structures, the fantasy world of Luna Park, and fashion related to *Scheherazade*.[61] In doing so, he points less to a direct impact on her thought and more to a "space for imagination" ("Imaginationsraum"[62]), which awakens the creative mind to become aware of its surroundings. Similarly, Kirschnick uses the term "space for resonance" ("Resonanzraum"[63]), which evokes the possibility of (un)consciously recreating (in)direct manifestations of the physical stimuli around oneself. While the conceptualizations of Hallensleben and Kirschnick relate to a more general phenomenological understanding of perception, they both also evoke Novack's "movement environment," which relates even more particularly to the awareness of dance movement pervading the surroundings.

The narrator's and Barrison's observations at the exhibitions in *Letters to Norway*, which probably consisted of artifacts and displays, culminate when they encounter an "authentic" living being from the Orient: a fully bearded man named Minn, the son of the Moroccan sultan. By not naming him and by fetishizing his beard and lips, the narrator transforms the bearded Arab into a sensual object, such as Rilke wrote about when describing the hands and fingers of Rodin's *Danseuses cambodgiennes*. As a result, Minn has fewer characteristics of an actual person and becomes a mere fantasy. The realm of the less concrete creates a fluid space in which figures more easily straddle the real and the imaginary. The looseness in spatially depicting the characters allows them to more freely interact, blurring boundaries between the dancing figures and their surroundings.

While Barrison and the narrator peruse Luna Park, they assume the role of the modern individual who comes to observe the foreign displays. Observing small artifacts at the "Streets of Cairo" exhibition, the women attempt to understand the meaning of each representation, which incidentally also evokes the bazaar image that the narrator uses to describe café life. With a myriad of objects and exclusive artifacts giving them a glimpse into a world not immediately available to them, such an exhibit could be just as overwhelming to the senses as the stimuli in the urban setting, despite being located on the outskirts of the city. Yet such a place created a microcosm of a new land waiting to be discovered, just as the metropolis Berlin was being realized on a large scale. In fact, as Hallensleben argued, Lasker-Schüler's idea of Thebes substituting for Berlin only aligns these two polar opposite places, juxtaposing urban modernism with exotic Orientalism.[64] Like the modern individual and flâneur strolling the streets observing their surroundings, Lasker-Schüler's narrator has grown tired of the urban environment and seeks a new freedom and inspiration in the foreign exhibits at Luna Park. However, while she may think the exhibitions are "authentic," they actually reflect Western imperialism's Orientalist perspective. Thus, the perceived exotic thoroughly reflects and is still indebted to the metropolitan mindset.

Attending such an exhibition has situated Barrison and the narrator to not only watch others, but also to be observed. Thus, it awakens an unexpected performativity that deviates from the code of an ethnographic perspective and Bauer's concept of the urban *Schauplatz*. While much to her dismay, Barrison arouses the interest of the full-bearded Arab, the narrator meets Minn. Although the figures are not in a central-city area, such as the one where Malte began observing the man with *Veitstanz* on the Boulevard St. Michel in Paris or the one where Endell discovered structures and space in central parts of Berlin—Barrison and the narrator are at an exhibition: an "exotic" microcosm situated in Berlin. The two put themselves on display for the men they encounter, which culminates with the narrator dancing with Minn. This impromptu meeting reminds one again of the modern individual's chance encounters in the urban space. Whereas before, the flâneur-like gaze remained purely one of an outside observer, Lasker-Schüler subverts this expectation by depicting the narrator and Barrison dancing on stage. At this point the narrator and the exotic Minn come together for what she calls a "miracle" as both move like two dancing snakes on the Islam stage. Their dance together is stronger than that of one person alone, and results in a unifying process combining the narrator's European background and femininity and Minn's Orientalist masculinity. The resulting fantasy and hybridity of both worlds reach even higher transcendental proportions: "on the way to Tangiers" indicates an exotic spatial transformation through the means of dance, and the warlike cries signify a "primitive" ecstatic gesture from a Western perspective. Yet despite the kiss this unity might not necessarily need to be read wholly sexually, but rather as operating in a queer space between the male and the female.

Hallensleben points to a reason for Lasker-Schüler's use of Oriental symbolism: as being a break from the reality of Wilhelmine rule.[65] Incidentally, the surface on which Minn and the narrator are standing happens to be a stage devoted to Islam. Perhaps the exhibition took place here; however, the use of the word "stage" implies performance and spectatorship. For the exhibition and the stage to be the same is not unfathomable, as both have a performance function by displaying themselves as a spectacle. Stages tend to be traditionally conceptualized with and inside a theatrical setting. However, situating it outside exposes the space to the stimulating movement of the city. Therefore, the stage becomes more accessible to visitors and integrates itself more into the urban landscape. Like the narrator amalgamating with the organic elements in "I Dance with the Mosque," the narrator's body here melds posthumanistically not only into Minn's dancing through the objectification of his body, but also with the Islam stage. Thus, while dance remains the strongest means to reach an ecstatic state that transports the pair to Tangiers, it also becomes highly reliant on the physical, incumbent space of the microcosmic stage and the narrator's and Barrison's chance encounter with the men.

Kirschnick argues that while the passage attempts to create an ethnographic description of a historical setting at Luna Park, the depiction begins blending with an imaginary world; the bamboo flute, the drums, and the characteristics of the snake lose their cultural and geographical meaning and signify nothing more than a lack of consistency and an arbitrary selection of iconography.[66] Perhaps, then, instead of aiming for cultural authenticity and coherence in her depiction, Lasker-Schüler's goal is to focus on a subversive, ecstatic dance in an invented *inter*space, which unexpectedly involves the narrator and transports her to another world. On the contrary, according to Jennifer Ingalls, this scene in its periodical form of *Letters to Norway* appears at the end of an article describing the Agadir or Second Moroccan Crisis: Minn and the narrator lose their way to Tangiers probably because of the crisis.[67] The Orientalist stimuli of Berlin's Luna Park serve as a resonating space that influenced Lasker-Schüler's literary and gestural imagination. In this metropolitan dance text, the narrator and Barrison happen on an Islam stage that melds into the urban landscape, and they become swept up into the intoxicating spectacle with Minn.

City Spatial Imagination—Coffeehouse as Bazaar

Besides enlivening representations of liminal architectural structures such as the cabaret, the mosque, and the Luna Park Islam stage, *Letters to Norway* and *My Heart* (1912) also include various urban interpenetrations, such as the café or coffeehouse. Many scholars have agreed that in around 1438, Sufis in Yemen discovered that the new stimulant coffee could support wakefulness and alertness during religious ceremonies and performances.[68] Islamic rulers fretted about the wider implication of coffee's effect on their society's morality, but it could not be outlawed. In eighteenth- and nineteenth-century European culture, the café or coffeehouse came to be considered a space of thinking and intellectual exchange.[69] Sociologist Ray Oldenburg posits the idea of cafés as a third type of space: "human beings need a place distinct from home and work for a fully rounded and integrated life and [. . .] cafés provide an ideal space for ties overlapping and transcending those based on kinship or labor."[70] Benoît Lecoq has suggested that cafés were an "intellectual laboratory," since they and newspapers emerged in around the same time period.[71] Drawing on phenomenology, Sartre, de Beauvoir, and other novelists, Monique Membrado conceptualizes the café as a dream space, given the spatial play of light, the liminality of both inside and outside, and the nature of time and presence in the café.[72]

The intellectual laboratory, the idea of the third space, and dream models fit well into Lasker-Schüler's conceptualization of the café space in *Letters to Norway* and *My Heart*. Artists often spent time there because they had to share rooms with other lodgers, so private space was limited: the café was a refuge that fostered communication and inspiration among writers and artists. Lasker-Schüler also went to cafés to keep abreast of the latest news; it was here that one could learn about the most recent fashion in art and literature and could sign contracts with publishers.[73] The bustling Berlin coffeehouse culture served as a perpetual source of stimulation, much like Paris was for Rilke and Berlin's landscape was for Endell and Döblin. However, Lasker-Schüler's narrator also grew weary of it at times:

I am tired of the café, but that does not mean that I'm going to say farewell to it forever, or to go there in some gypsy wagon. On the contrary, I shall continue to spend time there often. All day yesterday the door opened and shut, like a bazaar; not everything is the real thing: imitation poets, false verbal embellishments, simulated thinking, cigarettes smoked as an affection. For a long time now the lawyer no longer comes in. Why is one drawn so to the café! Every evening a corpse is drawn to the upper room; it cannot rest. Why do people really stay in Berlin? In this cold, unpleasant city. Berlin is an irrefutable clock; we know that she, side-by-side with time, is always watching, always letting you know where art is on the clock. And I would like to sleep through time.[74]

In expressing disinterest in the café, the narrator expresses that she needs some distance from the intellectual environment, but she will come back for more. One could also read the general coffeehouse scene as a microcosm of the actual city, like the Egyptian exhibition in Luna Park. Although it harbored many of the same artists and intellectuals, one frequented the café at different times, and it was not always the same. As with the unexpectedness of the metropolis, new people could come and go, resulting in different amounts of excitement and rendering the café as a hybrid space: a porous, private, and public sphere like the Islam stage. Lasker-Schüler's narrator seems to have a relationship with the café similar to Rilke's mysterious attraction to Paris and simultaneously a yearning for the countryside. Referring to it as a bazaar, a term usually associated with a market in which miscellaneous goods are typically sold in the streets, her Western, Orientalized depiction also points to coincidental encounters, frequent visitors (as demonstrated by the opening and closing door), and the geographical space of the street, as if the café were outside in a large area. Lasker-Schüler's description of the café as bazaar evokes Simmel's observations in his essay "On Art Exhibitions" ("Über Kunstausstellungen") from 1890, in which he regarded world exhibitions as "symbolic representations of the modern metropolis."[75] A bazaar looks like an exhibition, and both forums display goods or objects. The author's comment about the clock of art here laments perpetual productivity demanded by fashionable standards. Her observation concerning this Tayloristic aspect of modern life reflects the opening to this chapter.

Lasker-Schüler's probably more Western and Orientalized understanding of a bazaar might not be completely different from an Eastern one. Maintaining a central role in the settlement and cultivation of a city, a bazaar typically consisted of a long, vaulted passageway with attachments to different buildings on either side; while the corridor mostly connected commercial enterprises, it also attached to government, religious, educational, and service structures.[76] Thus, the bazaar played a key role in commercial, social, political, and cultural influences, and its centrality also related to the metropolitan microcosm representative of urbanity. According to architectural and urban studies scholar Maryam Ziyaee, the elongated passageway and its numerous connections relayed a "sense of movement" and a beautiful mixing of open and closed spaces.[77] Such a description recalls images of Benjamin's Parisian arcades that bridge outside and inside spaces, and also evokes Gideon's architectural idea of interpenetration. These concepts suggest too that the idea of flânerie could also thrive in the bazaar, perhaps even more so from a Western perspective, given the Orientalist setting. In effect, while Lasker-Schüler's image of the café as bazaar is an attempt to distance herself from her surroundings, it still intimately mirrors her Western perception of the East. She uses Berlin as a geographical and spatial scaffold to espouse her imaginative ideas about the Orient.

Relaying the sentiment of wanting to remain away from the café also communicates her discontent when she calls Berlin cold and unenlightening. While many other thinkers considered the German capital around 1900 to be an intellectual and inspirational center, as it probably had been for Lasker-Schüler at times, the narrator is more inclined to portray it as passé—a place that no longer created any kind of artistic motivation for her. She realizes, however, that the café and Berlin remain her artistic lifeline, and she cannot completely abandon it. As Lasker-Schüler had done in "In the Neopathetic Cabaret," she allows her narrator's imagination to wander into an Orientalist realm of the beyond. Hallensleben remarks that Lasker-Schüler implies a substitution of the artistic capital Berlin through the artistic city of Thebes.[78] By following his line of argumentation, one observes a correspondence between the way she characterizes the café as a bazaar and how she aspires to look beyond the boundaries of her own present city. The Berlin she then describes in *Letters to Norway* and *My Heart* takes on depictions of both the city that she observes in real life and the one she wishes it to become—an exotic, boundless place with which she can transcendentally communicate: "[. . .] I speak to my city and open my soul to her people like a grove of palms they may enter. [. . .] My portrait is being distributed in Thebes."[79] This citation evokes the interpenetration between the city, its population, and the narrator in their ability to inhabit the other through movement.

While Thebes attains spiritual levels in the *Letters to Norway*, the narrator expresses negativity to Walden und Kurt concerning Berlin: "This evening I would like to say to you only: Berlin is a small city, every day it shrinks more and more. A city is big only if it offers a wide perspective. Berlin has only a peephole, a bottleneck, and generally it is corked up, even imagination suffocates. Good night!"[80] In her polemic characterization, Lasker-Schüler refers to Berlin's provinciality as one-dimensional. She also uses the image of a corked bottle as if the endlessness of one's creative imagination were being stifled. Once again the narrator expresses her dissatisfaction with Berlin, but at the same time the city has provided her with the opportunity to experience a world vastly different from her everyday life.

Barrison's Solo Dance and the Café Kurfürstendamm as Oriental Dancer

Whereas before Lasker-Schüler uses rather nontraditional dancerly aesthetics to create the idea of movement, in the following example, she features Barrison's talent as a dancer:

> Do you know who suddenly came into the room when Gertrude Barrison was dancing? Minn! But he understands Eastern dance in a way that I don't; I make an exception only of Gertrude. The last beauty of Barrison's dancers moves in an interesting and graceful manner, and her garments are silken secrets of the white-wigged days of the age of the Marquis. All of the onlookers were charmed.[81]

Although the narrator and Minn had been dancing on a stage in the previous scene, here she points to her lack of understanding of Oriental dance. This depiction of Barrison, who understands movement with more than a layperson's comprehension, sets her off as an exotic being, no longer a part of their world. Barrison has moved on from the *Varieté* performances, such as Kessler and Hofmannsthal had chronicled in describing St. Denis's pieces, and has delved into the new, modern dance, which evokes personal expression and demands intellectual contemplation from the spectator. One would think that Barrison's Danish-German ancestry would not have aided her understanding of Oriental dances, but, recalling Barrison's comments on the *transcendental language* of dance, then perhaps she remains an "exception" who can penetrate these movements. Certainly Ruth St. Denis believed she herself could, with her culturally appropriated Orientalized dances from a Western perspective. Since dance reaches beyond the limits of words, language does not come into question or work as a barrier against her in conceiving a foreign, Oriental dance. Even the way the narrator describes Barrison's costume as "silken secrets" implies that her entire moving aura remains a mystery beyond description. The narrator depicts her as a liminal dancing figure who can bridge two opposing worlds. In the following section I discuss the further development of her dancing and seek manifestations of the dancing café.

My chronological readings of these texts continually point to a gradual development in Lasker-Schüler's representation of dance movement and the body. She seems to be pushing toward the realm of drawing and illustration as a means of going beyond her perceived limitation of language. Her inching slowly toward this realization in some ways contradicts Huyssen's definition of the modernist miniature, because these texts remain highly visual but never actually become a different medium. It seems, though, that Lasker-Schüler cannot resist and has to explore. The scenes concerning the café as bazaar, the Islam stage at Luna Park, "I Dance in the Mosque," and "In the Neopathetic Cabaret" demonstrate how her metropolitan dance texts progress and aesthetically flourish once we reach the scene with the Café Kurfürstendamm as Oriental dancer:

> *You two friends!*
>
> What's going on here? Were you already waiting there, at the corner of Kurfürstendamm and Wilmersdorferstrasse, in the Café Kurfürstendamm? God, I have become so disloyal to the Café des Westens; how I have abandoned the coffee house, like a beloved to whom I pledged eternal loyalty. The Café Kurfürstendamm is a woman, an Oriental[82] dancer. She amuses me, consoles me, charms me with the many sweet colors of her clothing. There is a movement in the café, it twists mysteriously, like the gleaming body of Fatima. The small recesses of the galleries, covered with stars, are veiled hearts. O, the things one can say and hear there—violins quietly singing, blissful moods. The café is the embodiment of Lucien Bernard's poster. I shall have the order of the crescent moon bestowed upon him as a sign of my respectful admiration, appointing him pasha of Thebes.[83]

The narrator continues to use metaphors to transform the urban expanses and areas of Berlin into an Oriental fantasy. But instead of describing the café as a physical place like a bazaar, the narrator pushes the café metaphor further by describing the Café Kurfürstendamm *as* an oriental dancer. Instead of a bazaar that evokes images of people curiously wandering along lined passageways, the Café Kurfürstendamm *is* a posthumanist entity capable of sensual movement. Indeed, it comforts and amuses the narrator, amazes her with the various colors of the dancer's garb. The narrator uses a comparable image of Barrison's solo. Not only Barrison but everyone around them was enchanted by the modern dancer's movement. In a sense, Lasker-Schüler builds on the earlier example by first describing the real *Varieté* dancer Barrison on a smaller scale, who has now been transformed into an entire café. Since a dancing café does not immediately correspond to a recognizable image in real life, the narrator expresses the magnitude of her creative power by selecting a symbol that is essentially *only* conceivable through one's own imagination, much like the dancing mosque. Lasker-Schüler is constantly looking for a way to make Berlin appear small and finite while making dance and the "other" appear boundless and eternally vast. From the earlier scene with Barrison dancing at the exhibition-turned-Islam stage, this transformation is carried further to the present scene as the actual café becomes a stage as well. Hallensleben notes that the dancer and the space become interchangeable.[84] While the café has embodied the dancer and converted every facet into a stage on a large scale, a movement emanates and evolves throughout the room. Like the depiction of Barrison, whose costume contained "silken secrets," the Oriental dancer café similarly has mysterious qualities, hinting at the transcendental incomprehensibility of the movement. Instead of just one dancer on a stage captivating an audience, like Barrison, the Café des Westens dancer has taken on immense proportions and interpenetrating qualities that consume the café and imbue every inch of space with mysterious movement. In contrast to "I Dance in the Mosque," here Lasker-Schüler explicitly calls the physical structure a dancer, announcing the café *as* dancer. Until this metropolitan dance text in *Letters to Norway*, she has merely pointed toward the possibility of city and dance merging, but here Lasker-Schüler's café and dancer coalesce, as happened with Fuller's dances, PAL's poster of Fuller (see fig. 1), and Endell's square of pedestrians, all of whom create their own new space or physical being. The author already conceives of both entities as conjoined instead of as two entities that move as one or become melded: they are a symbiotic, posthumanist, hybrid moving structure from the very beginning of the dance text. Lasker-Schüler here clearly delineates and more emphatically conveys an imagined depiction as having real life. She uses these beginning sketches and letters to experiment with the limitations of language and is eager to draw as a means of expression.

The Birth of Jussuf the Dancer in Lasker-Schüler's Drawings

Lasker-Schüler's imaginative and abstract yet physical spaces began to manifest themselves in her drawings. Following *Letters to Norway*, she devoted considerably more time to working on her illustrations. Ricarda Dick has traced the experimental origins of the author's etchings beginning with stars, crescent moons, and comets; they then progress to hands, feet, and heads—often with profiles to the left. These symbols appear as pictograms, ideograms, or phonetic signs similar to ancient Egyptian hieroglyphics.[85] The isolation of these disembodied body parts as powerful agents reminds one of the hands and fingers of Rodin's Cambodian dancers and Malte's *Veitstänzer*. Writing, drawing, and creating poetry were one and the same act for Lasker-Schüler. Karla Bilang claims that the poet and artist found the drawings much more expressive than written text, and that the images from *Letters to Norway* appeared first and then the prose, with the drawings having the primary aesthetic function.[86] While the images may have had distinct significance, given her experimentation with the media, I propose that one should read them in conjunction with the corresponding text. Ingalls has argued that Lasker-Schüler's *Letters to Norway* to Herwarth Walden in *Der Sturm* continue in the form of *Letters and Images* (*Briefe und Bilder*) in *Die Aktion* addressed to Franz Marc; this caesura corresponds to her divorce from Walden and demonstrates her transition into creating more graphic art.[87] In the summer of 1909, manifestations of her literary figure Jussuf[88] began appearing in private letters. Overtly entering a performative queer space, the author experimentally dresses up as her male alter ego for a publicity photo: in profile to the left, with a short haircut, harem pants, flute, belt, dagger, and shoes. This iconic and frequently published image was supposed to have been created for a *Variété* performance, "Fakir von Theben," in 1910, but it never came to fruition (see fig. 5). Her literary figures began interpenetrating structures not only in her prose but also in her drawings. She is still at the beginning of conceptualizing who Jussuf is and developing who he will become.

For instance, in *Der Sturm* (an installment of *Letters from Norway* and in *My Heart* [vol. 2, no. 99, February 24, 1912]), the narrator depicts Richard Dehmel *as* a blood-red Oriental cityscape: not in an overcoat but in an old-fashioned city turban; his poetry flows like a blood transfusion. Beneath the text is a corresponding drawing of an Oriental cityscape with one specific building adorned with a turban-shaped roof. Like the dancing (in the) mosque and the café as Oriental dancer, Lasker-Schüler's depictions again tread the posthumanist boundary between the Western moving body and the Eastern architectural structure. Instead of merely producing an image in evocative prose, the narrator provides the reader with her black-and-white sketch. While the text and image seem to not directly correspond, they still attempt to complement the other and show the potential for interweaving both media. For example, the poetic language of blood red can merely be imagined, since the newspaper is printed in black and white. Also, the narrator decides not to render an image of Dehmel that corresponds to his physical appearance but rather chooses an Oriental symbol that wavers between his embodying the structure and its reflecting the aesthetic effects of his writing. Lasker-Schüler invents the term *Stadtturban* to humorously bring together and straddle the realms of clothing and architecture. In doing so, they seem to continually interpenetrate each other.

On the one hand, Dehmel is embedded in the architecture as a *Stadtturban*, yet he operates with the potential to emerge. Reading the image and the text together, it appears that Dehmel's poetry flows like blood throughout the body of both the reader and, on a larger scale, this cityscape: it has the force and passion to move beyond the spectators' perception and to imbue the buildings and architectural structures of a city. Following this scene, which narratively and visually establishes the landscape, the Oriental dancer as café appears as perhaps one of the images in her Oriental cityscape. While the content of both Dehmel as *Stadtturban* and the café as dancer do not correspond in terms of content, the overall idea of an urban structure creating or becoming a moving being begins to manifest itself. While her depiction evokes Bhabha's "third space of enunciation," which challenges the idea of a pure, original, and homogenous culture and instead opts for a contradictory and ambivalent space, her conceptualization seems to go beyond mere space by involving the liminality and amalgamation of object, body, and space.

Lasker-Schüler continues to develop her drawings aesthetically in a private letter to Karl Kraus. In this first drawing of Jussuf, dated April 20, 1912, he appears to meld into a cityscape of Thebes. Besides embodying an amalgamation of disparate cultures—ancient Egypt, the Arab Near East, and German-Jewish—Lasker-Schüler's figure occupies her queerness, between male and female, and also a posthumanism. Jussuf recalls the biblical Joseph who was taken from his home as a boy and learned to thrive in a foreign culture because of his unique ability to interpret dreams and manifest them into reality. These abilities perhaps loosely represent the author's desire. Given the two-dimensionality of the drawing, the figure's head falls in line at the same level as the buildings. Appearing to be stacked on each other, the three helmets serve as the drawing's focal point and architecturally fit into the space. Even though Lasker-Schüler is depicting Jussuf in her likeness, the repeated hat motif recalls Dehmel's *Stadtturban*, suggesting that a cityscape could produce or develop the image of a head. Lasker-Schüler radically decenters the power of humans and allocates agency to the nonhuman. Whereas before Dehmel was only recognizable as the urban space because of the corresponding text, this drawing of Jussuf communicates without the support of many words. To encompass her aesthetic intention, these two depictions demonstrate her transition from writing to drawing as a primary means of expression and an exercise of her own spatial existence. Here Jussuf is recognizable with his head in profile to the left, as Lasker-Schüler often portrays herself, but the helmets, which also resemble architectural domes, inextricably link him to the city. Also by bestowing Jussuf with a traditionally coded male name, he is made a queer figure because of the author's imprinting herself on him by representing him in her likeness. Once again, the urban space and the body interpenetrate each other, but this time the image conveys this amalgamation with few words. Dick refers to this particular image as the semipublic "workshop" for Lasker-Schüler to work through her developing renderings of Jussuf.[89] Indeed, her writing and drawing always maintain a constant movement and progressing dynamism, experimenting and building from previous ideas. Furthermore, my chronological reading highlights her aesthetic evolution from writing to illustration.

Webber interprets a stamp drawing of Jussuf's head wearing an exaggerated headpiece that resembles the treetops in the cityscape and two protruding skulls as aesthetically similar to Jussuf's three helmets. Interestingly, this image appears in *My Heart* but not in *Der Sturm*. Webber, however, reads this head as incapable of coexisting with the city space: the head functions as a "mock building" unable to resolve itself in the urban setting.[90] While he reads the head's inability to integrate into the urban tableau, I interpret the city as organically producing it: the hat resembles the city's architectural structure with the pointed star and trees, while the human head seems to emerge from the setting as an interweaving figure that is not completely human nor solely city. In Lasker-Schüler's imaginary and posthumanist worlds, Thebes's giving birth to a head, which in many ways represents her own eventual rebirth as a queer Jussuf, and later as a body and a dancer—is certainly plausible, given her hybrid depictions.

After this image of Jussuf's head, Lasker-Schüler develops a full body for Jussuf and herself. As if the smaller pictogram experiments begin to evolve into larger scenarios, the last image of *My Heart* features Jussuf addressing Thebes. Interestingly, this drawing is not in *Letters to Norway*.[91] While at first the artist depicts him as a rather static head melded into the city, now Jussuf maintains a full torso and a gesturing right hand that expressively moves with agency. For Lasker-Schüler, it appears that he continues to germinate and to grow accustomed to his body as the author develops confidence in her drawing skills. No longer is the head merely a part of the urbanity, now he can independently and intellectually communicate: "I speak to my city and open my soul to her people like a grove of palms they may enter. [. . .] My portrait is being distributed in Thebes"[92] (fig. 6). This citation maintains the porous nature of his body and the urban space. Not only does it seem that Thebes produces him, but the people of the city can reenter Jussuf and the author once he has developed and become independent. Thus, he does not abandon his kingdom but rather remains intrinsically indebted to Thebes. One might read her rendering of Jussuf as synonymous with the author who opens herself to her imagined city, which remains her lifeline. Both are able to interpenetrate each other. Sending his portrait seems to also signify two elements: first, a representation of a regal and reigning gesture, and second, a reflection of Lasker-Schüler's ability to draw and to have her graphic work publicly disseminated. Thebes's giving birth to Jussuf also symbolizes Berlin and its rich stimuli—the bustling urban life, café culture, and Luna Park— profoundly influencing the author and giving her a renewed life as an illustrator; through the creation of Jussuf, both he and Lasker-Schüler now have new agency and different ways of expressing themselves. While he maintains an intimate and bodily relationship with Thebes, the author-artist keeps her readers in Berlin in mind through her evolving representations of the urban space. This speech aesthetically manifests itself on a much grander scale in a later drawing, as we will see.

In the image on the title page of the first[93] and second[94] editions of *Hebrew Ballads* (*Hebräische Balladen*) (1913 and 1914)[95] is a drawing of Jussuf, who remains the focal point as the small cityscape of Thebes balances on his right forearm (fig. 7). Whereas before just his head was integrated into Thebes, now the figure has an entire body and appears to be looking over the city. Placed in a spatial void, the figure seems to be floating. Dick perceives something dancerly about the pose because the bent legs and the many contours of the costume suggest dynamic movement.[96] This drawing technique can also be seen in Rodin's *Danseuses cambodgiennes* (1906). If we read into the development of the figure Jussuf, he appears to continually grow from out of the city, and he remains intrinsically tied by watching over it. Nicole Behrmann traces Jussuf's genealogy as a lyrical figure through his instantiations in Lasker-Schüler's writing. She argues that he maintains a cinematic identity related to the mode of perceiving the *Varieté* and early silent films composed of continual motion and shifting images; these ideas highly influenced Lasker-Schüler's fantastic narrative style.[97] Indeed, Dick reaffirms that the writer was more concerned with and reacted to the fascination of perception instead of reflection.[98] Interested in experimenting with the fanciful-

Fig. 6. Drawing of Jussuf giving a religious speech to Thebes in *Mein Herz*.

ness of the aesthetic, kinetic figure, in many ways Jussuf, and by extension the author, seem to be *dancing* with Thebes in this image. The city seems to give birth and slowly imbue life to a dancing figure. I believe we can read these five images in the order in which they aesthetically and thematically appear, instead of assuming the continuity of a consistent figure. Much like Dehmel as a red Oriental cityscape, in Lasker-Schüler's posthumanist and poetic imagination, it is possible for the city to give birth to another queer being—Jussuf—who can then dance with, celebrate, and protect its maker. The order of these images demonstrates not only a growing confidence and an enjoyment in experimental creation, but a clear and persistent interpenetration of body and city.

Taking into account the scholarly work on her writing that relates to early cinema, one could further conceptualize her sketches as representing photographs or filmic stills that perpetually develop through the life of her images. In a sense, her sketches imitate the indexicality of the proto-cinematic mechanism when viewed chronologically, but they may not correspond directly to the stages in the development of a single drawing. Film is conceptualized as the succession of single frames played quickly to create the illusion of move-

Fig. 7. A drawing of Jussuf in a dancerly position in a void gently holding up Thebes on the cover of the *Hebrew Ballads*.

ment, hence the term "motion pictures." In reading these five images, even though Jussuf does not visually appear in all of them, Lasker-Schüler concentrates on the basic theme of Thebes as a city that produces and cultivates an aesthetic moving body. Subsequently, this dancer looks over the city, dances with it, and becomes absorbed into its urbanity. These images correspond strikingly to her writings in "In the Neopathetic Cabaret," "I Dance in the Mosque," and through the episodic fragments in *Letters to Norway* and *My Heart*. The stimuli-filled metropolitan atmosphere of everyday events causes the urban dwellers' perception to become comparably fragmented: thus their artistic reaction is to create work like the *Varieté*, early cinema, cabaret, and café life that structurally corresponds to their urban experiences. The city seems intent on generating not just any kind of movement, but more specifically, an aestheticized dance motion. On a more abstract level, the urban space coupled with the movement environment of dance companies like the Ballets Russes seems to give birth to dance and the dancing figure, as seen in Lasker-Schüler's drawings. And thus, much like film, which uses temporal succession of frames to convey movement, her literary depictions and drawings experiment with a simmering and pervading dance that eagerly desires to find representation. Berlin pedestrians, Fuller, the *Veitstänzer*, and Ella are also used in similar ways, as the bodily medium through which the new modern dance can express itself. Here, however, Lasker-Schüler has invented her own alter ego, slowly building and developing physical characteristics through drawing. And she explicitly stages both Jussuf's body with the city devoid of other extraneous stimuli, which seems to more explicitly interrogate their relationship. While Ella and the *Veitstänzer* depict the development from balletic or *Varieté* movement into an early-twentieth-century modern dance, Lasker-Schüler's metropolitan dance texts further chronicle their evolution into a cinematic medium.

While at first glance the themes of city space and dance may not seem to maintain a coherent relationship throughout Lasker-Schüler's written and visual work, her metropolitan dance texts function as an experimental workshop for her to expresses the intricacies and progression of both, and of her elusive, queer identity. My insistence on reading the development of Lasker-Schüler's aesthetic dynamics in a chronological continuum demonstrates that her representations of the interpenetrating dancing body and the city—ranging from the smaller fragmentary level of the Neopathetic Cabaret to the vast expanses of a Theban cityscape bearing Jussuf—can lead to a self-sufficient existence that demands a constant and profound posthumanist connection. In her writing Lasker-Schüler begins with urban structures like the quiet movement in the cabaret, which flourish later in the fully developed, enveloping café-dancer. Similarly, in her drawings the artist starts with small images of Jussuf that evolve into a thriving figure who dances with the city. In contrast to Huyssen's modernist miniature, I have argued that Lasker-Schüler expands this genre to include other media such as drawing instead of just a highly visual written text. Furthermore, dancing beings cannot be limited to merely humans or animals but can include the surrounding stimuli and the physical urban space on a macro, micro, and posthumanist level. The liveliness of the moving body and urbanity is maintained precisely because of their symbiotic relationship in dance: one needs the other in order to flourish. Lasker-Schüler's manifested and imagined hybrid existence on many levels is able to thrive and be celebrated through the playful interaction of her numerous identities: as a gender-queer woman, a German Jew, a writer, and a graphic artist. And then she advances the breadth of her various identities—by exercising and conceptually developing the city space and the dancing body as further instantiations of her personal individuality, and by carving out new physical space for creative practices. The birth of the dancer Jussuf from the city suggests that the permeating and all-encompassing stimuli of the city can incite dancerly movement. Dance is no longer a concept bound to a theatrical stage but effects the entire being and allows the dancerly mode to pervade everyday life.

Seven

From Drawings to Early Cinema

*Lasker–Schüler's Protocinematic Images
and the Experimental Films of Chomón
and the Skladanowsky Brothers*

In the mid-1890s, the German filmmaker Max Skladanowsky filmed his brother Emil on top of a roof in Prenzlauerberg with the Berlin skyline in the background. Emil performs a *battement a la seconde*, kicking his right leg to the side with both arms outstretched. In his right hand, he holds a hat. This experimental test shot originally consisted of forty-eight single frames and lasted less than three seconds, however only six of the frames remain. Despite its brief length, this performance for the camera demonstrates an acute fascination with capturing and explaining kinetic movement through the new and developing technology of film. Occupying a liminal space between photography and short film, this test shot forces the viewers' senses to slow down. Is there a connection between the genre of the metropolitan dance text from the previous chapters—particularly Lasker-Schüler's drawings—and the Skladanowskys' snippet? And why was Berlin also featured in the shot?

This chapter traces the development of Lasker-Schüler's drawings of Jussuf and Thebes—as a moving body with the city—into the photographic and cinematic medium through early filmic practices. Much like the metropolitan dance texts of Endell, Fuller, Rilke, and Döblin, which chronicle the emergence of a manifold early-twentieth-century modern dance intimately interacting with the urban environment, Lasker-Schüler's work also experiments with the form of the cinematic superimposition. This filmic technique is thus a further bridge into a new medium and demonstrates a distinct desire for a new form of medial expression, beyond text and photography and into early forms of film. To demonstrate this progression, I first compare her sophisticated image of Abigail Jussuf superimposed on Thebes[1] to black-and-white photographs of Loïe Fuller, which also approach a ghostly presence in the urban space. Second, I analyze the pioneering Spanish filmmaker Segundo de Chomón's short black-and-white film as well as his hand-painted color film of a bat "transforming" into what is presumably an imitation of Loïe Fuller. Finally, I relate these readings to the early cinematic stills of Emil Skladanowsky "dancing" against the Berlin skyline. Lasker-Schüler's experimentation in her drawings relates to Tom Gunning's idea of a "cinema of attraction," which involved early film embracing and experimenting with visual novelty before narrative took over.[2]

Her work also coincides with contemporary photographic methods capturing the moving image. Eadweard Muybridge's zoopraxiscope from the late nineteenth century, for example, famously photographically reproduced the movements of a horse being ridden by a jockey frame by frame, attesting to contemporary visual fascination with providing pleasure for the eyes as well as a rational depiction of movement. Technology developed further with Étienne-Jules Marey's chronophotography; instead of using several separate plates to show the chronology of one movement, his technique shows it in one image. Here one still sees the segmentation in each photo. And moving into a more artistic vein, Anton Giulio Bragaglia's essay "Futurist Photodynamism" renders a gesture that is not seen on the surface by highlighting the trajectory through "tiny *inter-momental* fractions" which "become an infinitesimal calculation of movement."[3] He aims to register the "the vibration of actual life" by awakening "hidden depths," for "as an image grows more distorted, it becomes less real, and hence more ideal and lyrical."[4] These various types of visualizations demonstrate the experimental nature and theoretical thought related to photography and its ability to bridge into film. This is the background for the works of Lasker-Schüler, Fuller, the Skladanowskys, and Chomón.

Their work also relates to discourses around dance at the time. Between 1894 and 1910, short dance solos had been filmed mostly for the vaudeville and burlesque genre.[5] In her book *Dancefilm*, dance and media studies scholar Erin Brannigan uses Gilles Deleuzes's reading of Henri Bergson's model of the "ancient" and "modern." She relates the "ancient" as forms and ideas that privilege poses in ballet and court dances and contrasts it with the "modern," which bypasses static postures and focuses on the importance of an endless flowing sequence and perpetual motion.[6] Brannigan argues that early-twentieth-century modern dancers like Fuller and Duncan anticipate the cinematic apparatus by developing practices that move from the pose to perpetual movement. Her argumentation could be furthered by comparing the nature of poses in photography of ballet with still images of Fuller. Brannigan's observation could also be applied to the form of the metropolitan dance text that desperately seeks a medium and style to break out of its fixed form. That is not to say that a text from words cannot convey kinetic momentum, but rather that it seeks an alternative medium to express itself differently than before.

These trends of wanting to capture movement in a new medium and of dance's progression toward perpetual movement demonstrate an ethos that Lasker-Schüler embraced and that influenced her drawings. In many ways, her move from word to image parallels a desire to transition to a more movement-based dance aesthetic, regarding both dance and film. I argue that she tries to take traditionally conceived static forms—written text and drawings—to demonstrate a progression and a desire for the medium itself to "dance." While she does not create films herself, in her metropolitan dance texts Lasker-Schuler shows a distinct enthusiasm for bridging into early film experiments being created by experimental filmmakers such as Chomón and the Skladanowsky brothers.

Abigail Jussuf's Embracing Robe over Thebes

German studies scholar Jennifer Ingalls argues that the poet and illustrator's work *The Prince of Thebes* (1914) represents an end point, for which *Letters to Norway* and *Letters and Images* functioned as aesthetic experiments that drive plot and representation to a thoroughly fantastic reality. While Berlin and Thebes are interchangeable cities in these first two works, in *The Prince of Thebes* he reigns as Prince Jussuf in his new world.[7] Jussuf continues to have a marked relationship with Thebes in her drawings, which eventually develop into color sketches. At the end of *Letters and Images*, Prince Jussuf is removed from exile in Thebes and ascends the throne as Abigail Jussuf I. Basileus during his coronation. The identity of the queer Jussuf is further expanded within the male-female spectrum by now being given a female name. In the Old Testament, Abigail became the wife of David after her first husband Nabal died. Lasker-Schüler's renaming Prince Jussuf as Abigail Jussuf here continues to evolve, carving out new space for him and representing the author's perpetually morphing artistic identity just as her media also begin to change. Beginning with text, and then progressing to small doodles and then to larger, more expressive illustrations, these evolutions are congruent with other developments in cinematic representation.

Fig. 8. Abigail Jussuf's Coronation Speech Above Thebes (1914), Courtesy of Forschungsstiftung Brenner-Archiv, Universtität Innsbruck, Nachlass von Ludwig von Ficker, SIG 041-94-17A-2.

The image shown in figure 8 is reminiscent stylistically of Jussuf's speech to Thebes at the end of *My Heart* (see fig. 6). With his hand raised to evoke a speaking gesture, the coronation speech demonstrates an overflowing of visual expression by occupying most of the page's blank space. The linear sketch of the Theban cityscape on the bottom half of the page directly contrasts with the swirling ringlets of Abigail Jussuf's robe, creating a striking superimposition: a decidedly photographic and filmic method. Whether this was her aesthetic intention or an experimental coincidence, this layering and the palimpsestic effect of these two striking images deserves to be analyzed. This graphic technique creates an interpenetrative and posthumanist representation. Both elements are intrinsically connected, and each is essential to the livelihood of the other, particularly because of the "narrative" surrounding Prinz Jussuf's visual development. Abigail Jussuf's costume also consists of a rather amorphous robe of interconnected circular patterns, which emphasizes the texture and materiality of his clothing but also demonstrates its amalgamation with the landscape. Aesthetically, this image evokes Lasker-Schüler's literary representation of the Café Kurfürstendamm as oriental dancer, described in the previous chapter, in the way that the architectural structure *is* a dancer. One could claim that her literary interpenetrating dancer and urban structure from 1912 is finally developed enough to manifest itself illustratively in 1914. While the first text relies solely on words to depict the café-dancer, her Abigail Jussuf–Thebes drawing can largely bypass language and convey meaning through the graphic imaginary as a stand-alone medium.

Furthermore, much like the numerous strokes on the cover of *Hebrew Ballads* (fig. 7) that aesthetically convey Jussuf's dancerly and perpetual leg movement, the circular, "feminine" swirls of Abigail's robe convey a dynamic intensity and demarcate his energetic superimposition over the linear, "masculine" city. But since both entities are amalgamated, they hold a spectrum of queer and posthumanist characteristics whose ideas of hierarchicalizing urban space, gender, and textiles becomes artistically redefined: suddenly, a banal robe expands and becomes engorged in order to embrace and become a part of Thebes. The drawing of Abigail Jussuf-Thebes (fig. 8) also appears to have been quickly and impulsively completed, leaving much of the top and upper-right area of the page empty, which speaks to its spontaneous performativity as it was being created. This drawing relates to expressionist style with its highly textured nature, exaggerated themes, and swift composition. Since Lasker-Schüler is still in her early years of developing as a visual artist, she has not yet started using brilliant colors. And instead of employing jagged and angular lines aesthetically more associated with the German expressionist group Die Brücke, she operates here mostly with the circular pattern aligning more with Der blaue Reiter, whose founder Franz Marc maintained a lasting artistic exchange with her. On New Year's Day, 1913, he sent her a preliminary study called the "Tower of Blue Horses," which depicts four blue horses layered on each other in a left-facing profile; three months later it appeared as an iconic, monumental painting.[8] Many of her drawings continued to use a flat, two-dimensional aesthetic, stacking posthumanist elements (human and nonhuman) together.

In many ways, her move from word to image parallels her desire to transition to a more movement-based dance aesthetic, regarding both dance and film. This, of course, reflects similar impulses in the metropolitan dance texts of Endell, Rilke, and Döblin. Furthermore, she tries to take traditionally conceived static forms—written text and drawings—to demonstrate a progression and desire for the media itself to "dance." While she does not create films herself, Lasker-Schüler shows a distinct enthusiasm in her metropolitan dance texts for the early film experiments being created by experimental filmmakers such as Chomón, the Skladanowsky brothers, and Fuller.

In addition to resembling the café-dancer, the Abigail Jussuf–Thebes drawing also visually evokes the overflowing and sweeping *Jugendstil* aesthetic of Endell's dragon-sea creature facade on the Elvira photo atelier and Fuller's theater (fig. 3). While the architect's amorphous and asymmetrical object remains rather centrally located on the building, the waves of the theater seem to go beyond the edges of the building, as if desiring to become a separate mass of movement. In particular, the Abigail Jussuf–Thebes drawing conveys an uncontainable and uncontrollable compulsiveness—a more direct source of expressivity like Endell's sea creature, instead of conveying the rational symmetry of the theater. Nonetheless, the enveloping nature of all three seeks a space beyond the given confines of the structured realm. It desires to flow out of itself, much like modern dance both uses and desperately wants to break out of the *Veitstänzer*'s body, as we saw in chapter 4. Similarly, the organic, circular, oversized robe evokes Fuller's massively flowing costume during the *Serpentintanz*, both of which turn into liminal beings between human and sensual, aesthetic object (fig. 1). Whereas on a smaller scale Fuller inspired a theater that visually integrated itself into the lively Parisian cityscape, Abigail Jussuf seems to emerge from and embrace Thebes more globally as a grander artistic being. These posthumanist amalgamations demonstrate both the macro and micro level on which the city and the moving body interpenetrate each other.

Ghostly Images of Perpetual Motion

Engaging with the superimposition of this Abigail Jussuf–Thebes image in its context also furthers my cinematic reading. Media studies scholar Simone Natale argues that superimposition from the mid-nineteenth century in stage magic, magic lantern projections, photography, and cinema "wavered between realism and fantasy, stasis and movement, fiction and belief," creating a religious or spiritual effect that was also contradictory.[9] He links spirit photography since the 1860s to early trick films, which visually attracted both spiritualists and those interested in their spectacular entertainment value. This wide, paradoxical range of perception could also apply to Lasker-Schüler's drawings. Even though the Abigail Jussuf–Thebes representation essentially does not exist, or exists only in her drawing, this fantastical image strongly suggests a wholly spiritual state. While Thebes has given birth to Abigail, he also seems to watch over the city in a godlike capacity—embracing it with a benevolent robe and a seemingly infinite propulsion of soothing stars and moons. These connotations again evoke the creation of a posthumanist plant-human-architectural structure like the mosque in "I Dance in the Mosque" from the previous chapter. In comparison to Lasker-Schüler's smaller drawings, the Abigail Jussuf–Thebes image achieves its spectacular eye-catching state with its sumptuous materiality and ambiguous rendering. In many ways, Abigail presents himself as a spiritual being in the stereotypical way in which ghosts were rendered into print. Spirit photographs were supposed to provide evidence of the existence of ghosts but could easily be exposed as fake because of the possibility of multiple exposures. Natale points to this photographic practice as a contradiction of both a realist explanation and an enjoyment of the illusion.[10] The stasis encompassed in this metropolitan dance text contradictorily relays perpetual motion through the circular marks on the robe and the falling stars and moons. While clearly influenced by the spiritualist aesthetic, the drawing represents a departure from this aesthetic in its portrayal of an opulent figure whose superimposition over Thebes functions less as entertainment and more a poetic and even religious figure. Although the spectacular image is unapologetically striking, Lasker-Schüler intends it to expand conceptualizations of space, movement, and artistic expression by questioning the spiritual and posthumanist bounds of her drawing. She dehierarchicalizes the city and the body, which benevolently care for each other.

Her aims of representation have an affinity with photographs of Loïe Fuller. In this image, Fuller appears to be in an atelier with a large painting, two busts, and various other items placed along the periphery of the room, giving her space to dance (fig. 9). Functioning as an artist's workspace, it also created a social area for collaboration and remained intrinsically part of the urban landscape. Similar to the atelier in which Rilke depicts the Spanish dancer in his journal, Fuller performs for the artist who invited her, and by extension for the posthumanist camera eye. Facing the camera in this photograph, her face blurred by perpetual motion and the inadequate lighting, she shifts her moving body and costume beyond the human realm. The camera, and by extension the inability of the naked eye to decipher such quick, continuous movements, can literally transform her visually into a posthumanist entity. Thus, due to technological limitations of the camera and lighting at the time, the image is an unexpected and even undesired ghostly, experimental depiction. Visually, the human dancer eerily becomes a spirit. The blurry image creates a spiritual aura, which slightly erases her face and creates a partial superimposition with her white costume: a fading from material existence. The right half of the image itself also appears damaged, which contributes to the spiritual ethos. Given the technological limitations of the camera at the time, Fuller's ghostly representation appears to create an apparition

Fig. 9. Blurred photograph of Loïe Fuller in an atelier space (1899–1900). Courtesy of Jerome Robbins Dance Division.

through a perpetual dance without poses. Instead of using multiple exposures, the image creates a different kind of spiritual photography by evoking the idea of continual transformation between states. Lasker-Schüler's Abigail Jussuf–Thebes draws a similar state but through the seemingly endless ringlets, gesturing, and superimposition.

In contrast to the ghostly image of Fuller shot in an atelier, another image features her dancing outside. Instead of the black background, which forms a visual contrast in a theatrical setting, some images—thought to be shot by Théodore Rivière—feature her outside in an urban park. The author of the accompanying text, who gives an overview of Fuller's artistic production and the context of these photos, discounts the "crude" lighting of these images because they are not shot in the theater. However, could the setting have also functioned as a form of natural inspiration, creating more ample space for her entire costume so that she can move as a direct inspiration of *Jugendstil*?[11] Urban parks were, indeed, built to help the modern citizen cope in an industrial, urban society. As such, I would like to argue for reading these images in their nontheatrical setting as this study has been doing. In many of these photographs, Fuller's head is not only still visible, but she faces or looks directly at the camera operator to create a human connection with the viewer, in stark contrast to the earlier image, which nearly erases her countenance. While the images capture her in motion, the camera operator waits for the most visually spectacular moment to shoot her and thus reverts slightly to the more traditional idea of "posing" for the camera.

Between 1840 and 1900 urban parks were developed in London, later inspiring Haussmann's own green spaces in Paris.[12] They arose as a response to rapid development in urban areas to combat overcrowding, poverty, sickness, and immorality.[13] Parks were conceived less as wild, romantic, or natural areas, than as organized, civilized, and tame refuges to help produce an ideal, rational society.[14] These areas were supposed to both educate, particularly the working class, and to display ennobling artistry through embellished architectural structures in various motifs: alpine, Oriental, or Roman.[15] Hilary Taylor views these parks as "gigantic stage-sets,"[16] and the park seems to invite and complement the staging of Fuller's performance. In Rivière's image of Fuller in a park, one sees a path behind her with chain-linked divider to guide the parkgoer, to educate, and to put a stamp of human intervention, rationality, and cultivation of the natural land. The photography shoot in the park constitutes a welcomed and hybridized, even liminal space for her to perform between the exhausting urbanity and wild nature. Her image instills both the perpetual motion of the individual's perception in the city and the natural, sweeping lines of *Jugendstil* architecture. In other words, her dance represents the paradoxical state of modernity: the perpetual push and pull between an overflowing influx of impressions and urban stimuli as well as a much-needed break for contemplation. Rilke's diaries and letters constantly allude to this tension. Rather than being photographed in a black box, where one might have seen her performance, Fuller's being staged in different areas of the metropolis points to an open experimentation with logistics and lighting in trying to read a performance that did not fit anywhere.

Posthumanism and "Choreographic Cinema of Attractions" in Serpentine Short Film

Using similar filmic techniques to convey otherworldliness as Fuller did, the film director Segundo de Chomón was one of many to film her imitators in an early black-and-white film as well as a hand-painted color film in 1902. Filmed with the Parisian production company Pathé, this short piece entitled *Loïe Fuller* (1902) does not feature Fuller, but rather an imposter. The film juxtaposes two frames to create the illusion of a transformation: one shows a large toy bat and another the Fuller imitator. Instilling the very technology of how early cinema and frames worked, he uses a sequence of frames first to establish the flying toy bat, then another with the play animal on the imitator's back, and then finally one of her emerging completely and beginning to twirl her recognizable draping costume. Early filmmakers at the time knew that sequencing two frames of differing content but in the same setting would display a "magical" transformation. This trick film technique, used by numerous directors, including George Méliès in *Voyage to the Moon*, implies that the wings and flying capability of the bat transform into another kind of human-object with a similar wingspan, all operating in a posthumanist spectrum. Lasting less than two minutes, this clip highlights the transformation from bat to swirling entity and lacks any real plot. In this experimental short, the dancing of the Fuller imitator is not just filmed but also integrated into current cinematic developments, techniques, and aesthetics by using the trick shot, thus showing an intentional experimentation and attempt to integrate both media. The setting here, however, appears less discernable—the background displays a landscape with a building with Roman or Greek columns, and in the foreground stands a meter-high decorated partition, behind which Fuller in her hunched-over position stands as the bat is on her back during the transformation. This partition probably belonged to a *Varieté* set. While little interaction happens between the dancer and the landscape, this short film most importantly displays the experimental dances of Fuller and explicitly uses trick framing to pull dance closer into the cinematic medium. Just as Lasker-Schüler's Abigail-Thebes image resembles a single, dynamic frame, and the two photographs of Fuller function as snapshots in time of her movement, Chomón's film acts as an extended form of multiple frames to create moving pictures.

Chomón also created a hand-painted color version of the short film discussed previously. Born in Spain in 1871, Chomón was probably exposed to the film industry in Paris through his wife Julienne Mathieu, whom he met in 1895. While he was fighting for the Spanish during the Cuban colonial war, Mathieu began working for the main cinema companies—Pathé and Georges Méliès's Star Films. On his return, Chomón started working for the former and distributed their films throughout Barcelona. As early as 1902, he had been coloring films, first in Barcelona and later back at headquarters in Paris. This expensive process, often performed by anonymous women, involved painstakingly hand-painting individual frames until stenciling became a wider practice in the 1910s. Mauveine, the first aniline dye, was developed in 1856 by William Henry Perkins, and it was widely sold, greatly influencing the color palette of textiles, art, fashion, and of course film. Art historian Joan M. Minguet Batllori remarks that Chomón's work engaged with magical and fantasy effects such as double or multiple exposure (superimposition), stop-motion, substitutions, transformation, and pyrotechnics with the intent to surprise.[17] Since early films were shot in black and white, color added to the visual novelty to create a "cinema of attraction": a term coined by film and media studies scholar Tom Gunning, whose observation draws from the exhibitionist form of short film before 1903. Afterward, however, narrative form dominated cinema. This early exhibitionist form was interested in experimenting with the potential of film as a medium that actively displayed its visibility as an attraction.[18] Gunning derives the term "attraction" from the avant-garde filmmaker Sergei Eisenstein's use of "exhibitionist confrontation rather than diegetic absorption."[19] This focus on the attractions of the medium draws from the realm of vaudeville and *Varieté*, which produced illogical and nonnarrative performances. Lasker-Schüler's writing, as Andrea Krauss argues,[20] draws on this similar aesthetic, but I extend this line of thought into her drawings and of course into Chomón's short film of Fuller.

In a different text Gunning argues that since cinema grew out of the context of the fairground and *Varieté*, taking on similar aesthetic components, Fuller's performances combining motion with light—and furthermore with kaleidoscopic effect—may have been the first to manifest cinematic impulses using color.[21] The early hand-tinted, cinematic manifestations of Fuller's serpentine dance created a phantasmagoria of moving color and imitated the filmic mechanism.[22] Her performances also began in darkness, similar to other protocinematic forms such as the diorama and magic lantern.[23] Her draping costume has been interpreted both as being a "curtain," with the implied promise of revealing theatrical action or her own body, as well as a "screen," onto which images and color could be projected.[24]

While it seems that Fuller herself may never have been filmed (even if a title includes her name), many imitators emerging from 1894 to 1908 cinematically demonstrate a contemporary fascination with the kinetic display and its physical embodiment. According to Laurent Guido, cinematic manifestations of the serpentine dance were filmed at the time in main studios such as Edison, Biograph, Lumière, Pathé, Gaumont, and Méliès;[25] they can be divided into two different groups: ones that feature a single, moving performer and the second with background scenery featuring transformations and "tricks" derived from a stage version.[26]

In regard again to color versus black and white, the Spanish philosopher Eugeni d'Ors compared the circus to the cinema: "The circus was light and color, and the cinematograph is gray and darkness. The circus was slow, elastic, and like the rhythm of a waltz, the cinematograph is restless and jittery. The circus was dreamlike and the cinematograph is an anecdotic, almost pedagogic, lesson on reality."[27] Given such contemporary views of this new media, Batllori argues that color was essential to the vibrant effects of flowers and animals transforming into people.[28] Some of Chomón's films appear as if on a theater stage with a decorative border around the cinematic frame. According to film and media studies scholar Joshua Yumibe, the aniline dyes used in early cinema before 1907 focused on high saturation levels with brilliant and obtrusive colors.[29] This practice provided great contrast against the often black-and-white background and created dimensionality in a flat, static image.[30] Chomón's vibrant palette took advantage of these new synthetic developments by using colors such as cerulean blue and viridian green, which Impressionist and Postimpressionist artists and others often used in their work.[31] Bakst also took advantage of these vivid tones for his scenography for the Ballets Russes.

The drive to move from black and white to color adds to the possible attributes of an experimental medium, just as metropolitan dance texts explored with forms of textual stylistics as well as into different media. The drawings of Lasker-Schüler also eventually appeared in color—a shift that would parallel developments in cinematic technology and aesthetics. Numerous drawings of Jussuf and Thebes appear in cobalt blue, orange, yellow, gold, and cyan.[32] Identical to the black-and-white version, Chomón's film of Fuller also appears as hand-painted frames. By including hues of cyan, yellow, peach, purple, blue, green, and a rainbow combination, strikingly similar to the color palette in Lasker-Schüler's drawings, the filmmaker is not simply haphazardly coloring the frames but rather intentionally conceptualizing a "choreographic cinema of attraction."

In the beginning Chomón uses solid colors during Fuller's larger, grander strokes, to first slowly establish the cinematic attraction and its capabilities as a blossoming medium. The jarring and intentional transition to other colors is juxtaposed—in a similar way to the bat-Fuller transformation—to make it appear that she suddenly and magically changes color. At other times, one side of her costume is painted in peach and the other side in blue-green. Lastly, when the dancer performs smaller, quicker movements, creating more ripples in her garb, Chomón applies a rainbow or kaleidoscopic effect that conveys the idea of a perpetual change and choreographic interest. The lively billowing highlights a further transformation at the end, by using multiple exposures to make Fuller appear even more like a disappearing spirit; she raises her arms, causing her head to visibly disappear behind the fabric, which choreographically signals her vanishing. Of course, this last technique evokes the discourse on and aesthetics of spirit photography, as Natale noted, emphasizing both the visually spectacular cinematic attraction but also the inherent experiments in both film and modern dance. Even though this cinematic representation of her dance does not expressly feature the city, it does strikingly resemble the Abigail-Thebes image and aligns Lasker-Schüler's and Chomón's aesthetic affinities as they engaged with the early cinematic technologies of ghostly superimposition, sudden framing changes, and multiple exposures. This colorful rendering of Fuller further conveys an other-worldliness on top of the black and white by adding to the dynamic appearance and colorful transformation, which is creatively manipulated through the use of juxtaposing the hand-painted frames. Additionally, the changes in color were also supposed to mimic how light projected through different colored gels onto her white costume during her live *Varieté* performances. Again, Chomón inventively uses both the technological developments and perceived limitations of early cinema to enhance the image in Fuller's performative likeness. While Lasker-Schüler was not able to produce film by herself in her metropolitan dance texts, her drawings valiantly drive in the direction of this experimental compulsion. Both the media and the method of filming align with Tom Gunning's term "cinema of attractions." The different colors appropriately correspond to Fuller's movement quality and a perpetual development: Chomón himself, therefore, was able to adroitly perceive the choreographic intention and enhance its meaning by creating a "choreographic cinema of attractions." In doing so, he also puts his own artistic imprint on her dance, fully making the hybrid, cinematic mode, a screen-dance.

Keeping these colorful images of Fuller as posthumanist entity in mind, I would evoke PAL's poster of Fuller for the Folies Bergère (see fig. 1) from the beginning of the book as a point of comparison. While the artist uses a stereotypical, sexualized, yet inaccurate rendering of Fuller as a mode of modern advertisement, thereby contributing to the music halls' economic gain, Lasker-Schüler conjures up an image more in line with the actual Fuller: a queer, stocky figure in a massive, vibrant robe dominating the page but in a far less symmetrical fashion and channeling raw expression and affect instead of rationalism in the poster. The Jussuf-Thebes and Abigail Jussuf–Thebes images are not strategic advertisements but rather artistic meditations and sketches for the author's own musing and use in letters. These images and

Chomón's short film demonstrate the range of metropolitan dance texts in actual text, image, and film.

The metropolitan dance texts in this chapter attempt to depict the static image as a vibrant force of movement, which tries to break out into a kinetic form not necessarily limited to dance but to generalized, often aestheticized movement. By way of photography, early cinema is a logical alternative because of its use of multiple frames to imitate motion and its resemblance to short, metropolitan miniatures. Its experimental form worked aesthetically with representation, presentation, narrative, and technology. Even before the Lumière brothers' *Arrival of a Train* and the Skladanowsky brothers' Bioskop presentation at the Wintergarten in Berlin, both of which have received significant scholarly attention, the Skladanowskys had created their first rudimentary "metropolitan dance text" of forty-nine frames, which lasted approximately two seconds. Drawing from the length of Chomón's film and the two photographs of Fuller, this section focuses on the middle ground by looking at the Skladanowskys' film. This mini short film, of which only six frames remain, depicts Emil performing a kick with both arms raised while holding a hat in his right hand. In the background is the skyline of Berlin as they stood on the roof of a building along Schönhauser Allee. His movements exemplify the compulsion of other early filmmakers to stage kinetic performances of the body—sports, dance, acrobatics, gymnastics— that related to science, physiology, and spectacle; these were chosen because of their aesthetic stylization and their condensed form.[33] This concise and compact form resembles the metropolitan dance text as it takes on a proto- cinematic manifestation.

At this time, dance was also undergoing drastic aesthetic rethinking and becoming categorized more as "movement."[34] Other movement forms focusing on health drew from anthropology, psychology, and psychoanaly- sis, including Greek dance, Delsartism, Dalcroze Eurythmics, and nude dancing in order to release the repressed desires and drives caused by indus- trialization.[35] Drawing from this discourse, film and media studies scholar Stephen Barber characterizes Emil's movements as "between gymnastics and clowning."[36] However, they could still also be understood under a dance rubric, particularly because of their balletic reference to a *grand battement à la seconde* (a kick to the side using a straight leg), which he surely had wit- nessed after watching *Varieté* dancers. Most important here is to note the desire for large movement, which demonstrates dynamic form and kinetic motion. He and his brother were of course showmen themselves. Sons of the projection artist Carl Skladanowsky, Max and his older brother Emil toured Europe from 1879 until 1895 displaying *Nebelbilder*—foggy images of historical events and landscapes in sequentially unfolding, hand-painted, nonphotographic glass frames.

Since photography did not belong to the realm of painting, it developed its own aesthetic practice and eventually began rivaling other media.[37] Toward the end of the nineteenth and the beginning of the twentieth century, pictorialists such as Alfred Stieglitz emerged who embraced the painterly qualities of the photographic medium. He paved the way for establishing photography as its own aesthetic medium. With the beginning of his journal *Camera Work* from 1903 to 1917, his goal was "to appeal to the ever-increasing ranks of those who have faith in photography as a medium of individual expression, and, in addition, to make converts of many at present ignorant of its possibilities."[38] With photography first appearing in France in 1839 using the Daguerreotype process, the technology soon traveled to Berlin. Professional photographers moved to Berlin in the 1860s to 1880s, shooting portraits, architecture, and other still life; they catered both to locals and to tourists eager for visual imagery of the city.[39] These images found physical form in postcards, illustrated newspapers, journals, tourist guidebooks, and family albums.[40] Panoramic and architectural photos of monumental urban sites constituted a "grand-style photography" to affirm the city's new and dynamically changing landscape. In the context of this study, I have called these the macro manifestations of the city. Photographers also captured boulevards, train stations, new residential areas, buildings, and street life: the micro impressions. With the proliferation of photograph work, emerging journals such as the *Berliner Leben: Zeitschrift für Schönheit und Kunst* (*Berlin Life: Journal for Beauty and Art*) were devoted primarily to featuring these images.[41] These photos conveyed images of an organic and cohesive city that was in reality fragmented and diverse,[42] recalling the short form of *Momentbilder* written by journalists in Berlin. According to Miriam Paeslack, "unlike any other European metropolis, Berlin's development into a world city coincided with the instrumentalization of photography's technological and aesthetic capacities and their ties to boosterism and historical consciousness."[43] The Skladanoswky brothers were well aware of these practices and both worked with and deviated from developing aesthetic norms.

Cinema studies scholar Livio Belloï adroitly characterizes the status of camera operators in the process of filming street scenes. At first resembling other pedestrians in the city, they soon appropriated visual stimuli by stopping their movements to set up a camera, creating a spectacle out of themselves and their new contraption.[44] Belloï argues that between the camera operator and other pedestrians a mode of *interaction* ensues in which the known presence of one party affects the other.[45] This could be tied back to Matthias Bauer's even more explicit placing of these interactions in the city space.[46] Unlike the flâneurs such as Malte (see chapter 4) or Endell (see chapter 2), who can maintain anonymity and be stimulated first aesthetically and then intellectually in response to particular urban moments, and who have to formulate their metropolitan dance texts with their "gestural imaginary," most likely at a later period, the camera operator "composes" on the spot and cannot covertly film. Informed partly by a documenting and aesthetic ethos, they allow their positioning of single-shot framing to create its magic, arguably with little human intervention, unlike with a written text. The city seems to partially negate the author or artist and highlight the agency of automation. In many ways the camera provides an extension and mechanization of the human eye, which work in a symbiotic fashion. The idea of the "camera eye" already expresses a posthumanist element by being associated with the human eye as well as the camera's. Although Benjamin discounts the artistic eye required for a camera person, "Because the achievement of the camera operator at the lens is just as little like an artwork" ("Denn die Leistung des Kameramanns am Objektiv ist ebensowenig ein Kunstwerk."),[47] filmmakers actually use a much different vocabulary and technique in conceptualizing and composing their work than authors do.

In regard to the cinematic framing, Barber notes the working-class milieu of Prenzlauerberg:

> Behind his figure, a panorama is visible of factory and brewery chimneys, and large tenements, with the distinctive pointed steeple of the nearby Zionskirche church prominent in that cityscape. A notable strategy of early filmmakers was to focus their cameras on sites in which a maximal concentration of urban traces could be registered by their potential spectator [. . .]; with the Skladanowsky Brothers' film, the gesturing human body is in the foreground of the image, with the Berlin cityscape forming a cohering framework for it.[48]

Barber notices here, of course, that the moving body and the urban backdrop together create an aesthetic synergy. But why did Max film Emil foregrounded with the Berlin skyline in the back—beyond the aesthetic framing of nineteenth- and early-twentieth-century panoramic and architectural practices? One reason could be the desire to avoid the possibility of another passerby walking into the frame. To deal with this issue the Lumière brothers and their camera operator[49] often opted for physical locations that dictated or "trapped" the movement of the people, for instance when filming individuals disembarking from a boat over a plank in single file. Belloï often views camera operators as flâneurs. However, after setting up for a shot, they no longer maintained anonymity and an ambulatory mode. Moreover, the operators and their newfangled contraption aroused the curiosity of passersby, who often blocked the view of the camera.[50] This was certainly not the case with Max and Emil's first film, which presupposes an exclusivity without stray pedestrians. However, the mode of the flâneur is nevertheless mildly evoked because of their search for space to stage this metropolitan dance text as a short film.

Rather than simply being a background while Emil moved, the two entities demand to be read in conjunction. Unlike the Abigail Jussuf–Thebes image, in which a superimposition connotates an intimate spirituality, and the park and atelier backgrounds in the two Fuller photographs, the small strip of Berlin does not necessarily have an overpowering effect on Emil's movement. In fact, the skyline is not very noticeable, due either to the limitations of camera positioning or to intentional framing. However, in contrast to Lasker-Schüler's fantastical image, Max operates more in a realistic realm of staging the city with Emil—drawing from theatrical aesthetics more than filmic ones. Still, the frames reflect a desire to read both together as having an interconnected and influencing relationship.

Another reason for this staging might be the desire to view Berlin as a visual and sensuous stimulus that influenced Emil to move in a dynamic way; this shot was initially conceptualized as a test shot. After shooting, the brothers projected their second set of films on a stage at the Wintergarten in 1895 for a wealthy, sensation-seeking audience. While the main stage featured live *Varieté* acts, the Skladanowskys showcased their Bioskop screening variety acts at the periphery of the event. According to Barber, the effect was to function as a "concertinaed, phantasmatic variant of the live performances that had just finished." This perceptual development demonstrates the connections of these two movement forms, one as an ephemeral act and the other as a repeatable cinematic representation. Performed in loops, the moving images included dancing Italian peasants, a juggler, boxing kangaroos, a gymnastics family, a wrestling match, and the two brothers—in life-sized projections, which reflected not only the aesthetic and extension[51] of a live variety act, but were also integrated into a live performance when they came out to bow at the conclusion of the screening. This gesture connects their physical showmanship to posterity by contributing to developing cinematic technologies. The acts were shot outside in direct sunlight to gain maximum contrast and visibility before black boxes with lighting came into more regular use. Some of the acts appear more as fragments, with the camera shooting in the middle of movements or ending abruptly. Clearly, drawing aesthetically from Edison's single-viewer Kinetoscopes, which had just opened two months previously at the Castans Panoptikum in Friedrichstraße showing similar kinetic displays, the eruptive and nonlinear arrangement of the fragments evoke experimental films from the 1960s avant-garde.[52]

While critics have argued that these single-shot films lack dynamics because of their frontal framing, Janelle Blankenship challenges this view. She notes that the moving bodies are not always centered as spectacle but rather compete with other visual stimuli, with both sometimes spilling outside the frame; the purposeful lack of a background creates a disorienting effect.[53] Lasker-Schüler's Abigail-Thebes and even the Loïe Fuller Theater seem to also embody this aesthetic intention by wanting to exceed their given architectural confines and to transform into a movement form. To me, the Skladanowskys' shots express a desire for experimentation before a normative filming standard had been established. Just like the brothers' physically emerging and bowing at the end of their Wintergarten show with their Bioskop, the idea of performance and staging the cinematic is integral to their aesthetic. Thus, this mixing of media expands the parameters of the metropolitan dance text, moving from literary text to drawing, then to photography and the moving image. Additionally, at times, the bodies in this genre appear to be moving in a void that lacks depth, which highlights the physicality in an "impossible space." Lasker-Schüler also seems to desire a void in her renderings of Jussuf dancing with Thebes and in the perpetual movement of the Abigail Jussuf-Thebes image precisely because of this new space for the dancer and the city.

The Skladanowskys' third project went back to city scenes stylistically similar to those of the Lumière brothers and reflected the aesthetic of Berlin "grand-style" panoramic and architectural urban photography that had begun in the mid-nineteenth century after cameras had become more widely available, and continued throughout the 1900s.[54] The photography of urban scenes thus began to develop its own style and aesthetics. Perhaps to reflect the trend of other filmic creations and to satisfy the visual desires of their audience, the Skladanowskys followed suit. One of the scenes from this third project is shot similarly to their very first film on the top of the same building where Emil kicked his leg, but this time it was filmed from the opposite direction, featuring a busy street corner and without the moving figure.[55] They only showed these films once in Stettin.

I find it fascinating that their very first film featured the Berlin skyline with Emil, and the third film the skyline without him. Overlooked in scholarly work focusing on their Wintergarten films, I perceive this change as a genuine reading of the city that is eclipsed overwhelmingly by the quality of Lumière brothers' *cinematographe*. Shying away from their natural proclivity to feature the moving dancing body in the urban space, the early cinematic forms of Max and Emil are kept more or less as separate genres. Perhaps this would have been too confusing and experimental for a general audience. It is important to remember that the short films discussed in this chapter were filmed before 1903, fitting under Gunning's rubric of the "cinema of attraction." However, during such an experimental phase of 1900 modernity—from the complex mix of success, failure and fad, to producing long-lasting aesthetic impressions—the brothers seemed to be inspired most by the city. The perpetual movement and excitement of the city demanded that the body also engage itself in physical expression. Shooting the urban skyline and the moving human body in a way that represented their bodily movements as choreography and as a representation of their identity, they were beginning to develop an experimental yet uninhibited aesthetic before the genre of the city street photograph and film began. Their first film thus reflects the form of the metropolitan dance text before the hegemony of narrative film took over cinematic aesthetics.

Lasker-Schüler's Abigail Jussuf–Thebes drawing demonstrates a branching out of the metropolitan dance text by engaging with superimposition and the aesthetics of spiritual photography of the time. Moving from written text to drawing, the author uses her images as a way to bridge into another aesthetic realm that she had not yet fully encountered or philosophically untangled; this aesthetic evolution could not have happened until later, after the phenomena of photography and its connection to film had become more established. The depiction of Abigail Jussuf–Thebes in a large robe also visually evokes the costume of Fuller and the ghostly aura in the two photographs of her. Chomón's black-and-white and then later hand-painted films furthered the developments Lasker-Schüler desired by creating a choreographic cinema of attractions. These objects focus on both the spectacular visuality of an overflowing garment and the intellectual, otherworldly, and posthumanist space they occupy, in an attempt to transgress ideas of space and movement.

The short film of Emil's kick in the skyline of Berlin connects these two examples even further, because its isolation of six frames demonstrates its singularity as an isolated image but also its continuity when viewed together. It arguably provides a transition from the Abigail-Thebes drawing into the possibility of movement by drawing attention to the cinematic mechanism, whereas Chomón's short film strings the frames more quickly, so as to seemingly erase the idea of the single frames. The Berlin cityscape inspires Emil to kinetically display his movement, inspired by dance and the *Varieté*, to reflect its vibrancy. In many ways, the impulsive and spontaneous idea of wanting to film kinetic body and city together speaks to an innocent yet prevalent and genuine desire for immediate expression, instead of being tied to a genre and attempting to provide audience appeal. Occupying the same situation yet not necessarily at the mercy of developing industry standards, Lasker-Schüler could continue her own internal and aesthetic journey. The Abigail Jussuf–Thebes image functions as a dynamic experimental image that begins the bridge into the six frames of Emil's kick and further into Chomón's Fuller short film. In a thoroughly exploratory and hybridized ethos, these three examples interrogate and thoroughly combine techniques from dance, performance, theater, photography, early experimental film, and posthumanism, thus expanding the conceptualization of a metropolitan dance text beyond the written form.

Coda

The multiplicitous and captivating urban stimuli of Berlin and Paris around 1900 as well as the experimental performances of early-twentieth-century modern dancers thoroughly enveloped the literary and movement imaginations of Endell, Kessler, Rilke, Döblin, Lasker-Schüler, Chomón, and Skladanowsky. Conceiving a new literary and artistic genre that interweaves these strands of vibrant stimulation, their metropolitan dance texts do not simply depict a moving body in the cityscape, but rather cultivate a complex, interpenetrative relationship in which each profoundly affects or enters the aesthetic realm of the other—dance becomes architectural space and vice versa, in a dehierarchicalized posthumanist form. The authors and filmmakers empowered the nonhuman on a micro and macro scale—via neurological conditions such as *Veitstanz*, as well as wallpaper, animals, plants, architectural structures, and cityscapes—giving them more agency, decentering the roles of humans and sometimes overpowering them. While dance often needs a human body, these case studies demonstrate that it can also manifest itself in the nonhuman. As a result, the authors and filmmakers began developing a new ethics through their representation of the dancing figure. Furthermore, the most radical thoughts in this study arise from using movement to create space as a transformative mode, as seen in the works of Endell, Fuller, and Lasker-Schüler. Therefore, according to some of these authors and filmmakers, dance has the power to create spatial materiality, even though it may be fleeting.

As a result of these artistic amalgamations, the writers and filmmakers sought ways either to develop new textual stylistics to reflect dance movement or to break away from this medium into a different form of representation altogether by creating drawings and moving pictures. The highly visual nature and brevity of the metropolitan dance text parallel photography's shift into early experimental cinema. I have contended this point with Huyssen, who has argued that miniatures did not compete with film and photography, but rather developed language that could do something better than those media.[1] I have agreed in large part with his observation—Döblin's and Rilke's literary form reflect a *Kinostil* but did not employ physical images. Lasker-Schüler, however, was eager to find alternative media, drawings and paintings, for her own artistic expression.

To these authors and filmmakers, the city itself became a highly experiential and performative entity, allowing it to more easily interact with the dancers they depicted. This genre also highlights a concise, visually evocative language that emphasizes presentness over drawn-out description. The authors experimented with the perceived limitations of their language to find an adaptable form, which also developed into pure drawing, imitated cinematic frames as we have seen in Lasker-Schüler's work, and entered early film with the Skladanowsky brothers and Chomón. In much the same way that modern dance wanted to break out of the *Veitstänzer*'s and Ella's bodies, it also desired to express itself in the authors' literary language and artistic representations. The metropolitan dance text also exhibits a heightened flaneur-like and queer gaze on the episodic unexpectedness of urban, dancerly encounters during strolls, and often also portrays kinesthetic empathy related to the narrative's protagonist and the author. In many ways, these dance texts allow the reader to bear witness to the performance just as much as the main characters. These scenes introduce a dancelike element to the metropolitan experience, demonstrating a colliding and intertwining of two disparate worlds. These texts and films also demonstrate the creative power of the cinematic and literary imagination, which often exceeds the possibilities of dance performances at the time.

Based on their own artistic fascinations and biographical histories, these five authors and two filmmakers experimented with and developed their metropolitan dance texts in different ways, depicting their literary and cinematic figures as displaying a range of movement qualities. Beginning with Endell's sweeping, impressionistic square scene and ending with Lasker-Schüler's Abigail-Thebes amalgamation, these two depictions of the dancerly body and the urban space show an intimate melding in which both become relatively indecipherable. For these two authors, the fluid movement of dancers like Loïe Fuller may have integrated with the perceived flowing elements of the city. Thus, their representations assumed a quality that they may have witnessed in real life and that morphed into a hybrid construction through their imaginations. They also draw parallels between the aesthetic dance world and movement of the everyday, demonstrating their interwoven qualities and affinities.

The chapter on Kessler aimed to give his single, queer perspective on early-twentieth-century modern dance as an alternative history, and to show parallels with the aesthetics of other authors at the time, such as Rilke. Döblin's and Rilke's representations work much less with the flowing, enveloping aesthetic and more with an explosive, angular, and unexpected expressivity associated with *Ausdruckstanz* and even Nijinsky's movement style. Instead of integrating the dancing body into the city space, the metropolis acts as an active, imposing, and aggregate force on the dancing body as it performs in various urban areas not often associated with theatrical stage dance. Once again, the aesthetic collides with the social world by raising the profile of nonhuman agency.

In all the texts and films in this study, the dancing figures are freed from the theater and can perform in essentially any space. For Endell, Lasker-Schüler, Chomón, and the Skladanowskys, the bodies seem to organically and willingly mesh with their surroundings. However, the figures described by Rilke and Döblin are used as vessels for enacting the new modern dance. The compulsion to dance, therefore, can derive both from a willful act and, more symbolically, from the dance's need to express itself both consciously and unconsciously, using the body as a medium.

As a result, the evolving movement of the modern city seems to have a dichotomous relationship with its early-twentieth-century dancers, harmonious and symbiotic as well as antagonistic and hostile, instilling a vigorous productivity and aesthetic vitality. The two tendencies combine to create experimental performance scenes via their gestural imaginaries and visual experiences, going beyond the staged dances of the time to generate a lively new genre. Their metropolitan dance texts expand the range of the modernist and posthumanist aesthetic by combining the divergent yet related realms of dance, literature, and urban space.

While my monograph ends with the early cinematic form, it essentially sets the stage for wider research concerning screen representations of the dancing body. With the publication of Douglas Rosenberg's book *Screendance* (2012), more scholarly and artistic attention has been brought to this new cinematic genre,[2] particularly with the work of more contemporary European choreographers and their collaboration with film and screen project directors, such as Wim Wenders with Pina Bausch,[3] William Forsythe with

Thierry de Mey,[4] and Sasha Waltz with Jörg Jeshel and Brigitte Kramer.[5] And while Erin Brannigan's book *Dancefilm* (2011) explores the connection between dance and the moving image from both historical and theoretical perspectives, little work has been done on early and Weimar film from dance and Germanic perspectives. The relationship between film and city space has a long tradition—consider Ruttmann's *Berlin: Symphony of a Great City*. Further investigation could be conducted, however, on how the dancing body interacted with the urban space in these early filmic representations, particularly if one considers the dancing robot Maria in Lang's *Metropolis*.

In addition to expanding into cinematic representations of the body and the city, one could return to text and image. As a forward-looking gesture in regard to future studies on dance and the urban space into the 1920s, for example, this book concludes with a poster—just as it began with PAL's lithograph of Loïe Fuller dancing with an abstract metropolis. On the right-hand side of this poster, which had been plastered around Berlin in 1919, we see an energetic skeleton representing death, who performs a ballroom dance with a limp female figure unable to keep up. Given the crown on her head, she resembles the bronze statue of Berolina situated on Berlin's Alexanderplatz, which became emblematic of the city. This image was modified from Louis Raemaekers's cartoon *German Tango* (1916), which featured the woman with an imperial crown of Germany, yet in the poster it appears to be the battlements of Berlin. To the left of the image stands the text "Berlin, stop and think! Your dance partner is Death!" ("Berlin, halt ein! Besinne dich. Dein Tänzer ist der Tod"), taken from the last couplet in Paul Zech's poem "Berlin, halt ein . . ." (1914/1916), which provides a contrasting perspective between the catastrophe of war and the distractions of city life. Elswit relates this power to the larger context: "Berlin became the limp woman embracing skeletal death on a dance floor of inflation, political unrest, and memories of war."[6] Here at the turn of the century the concerns of the war's aftermath and dancing with death outweigh a purely aesthetic perspective.

This poster is certainly reminiscent of Ella's futile attempt to waltz in tandem with her body. And as a poster, it also fits well into the genre of the metropolitan dance text, displaying a dynamic dancing image and being featured in the urban space like the lively lithographs of Fuller. Instead of macro and micro images of the city dancing with a protagonist, such as we have with most of the examples in this study, here Berlin is embodied by a drawing of a woman who more easily speaks to an everyday citizen walking through the city. However, it is important here to recognize the strolling individuals seeing themselves reflected in the city. In effect, they are dancing with death, too. This image still represents a posthumanist view, because the dancing woman actually refers to the city of Berlin and not to herself per se. After all, the image of Berolina emerged from the nonhuman city as inspiration. Thus, the representation of Berlin continues a sustained agency and continued presence with the dancing body even after 1914. We see here that by reflecting contemporary social and political concerns, the genre of the metropolitan dance text continues to develop as one's relationship with the city and dance progresses.

Notes

Introduction

1. Ann Cooper Albright, *Traces of Light: Absence and Presence in the Work of Loïe Fuller* (Middletown: Wesleyan University Press, 2007), 52.

2. Margareta Ingrid Christian, *Objects in Air: Artworks and Their Outside around 1900* (Chicago: University of Chicago Press, 2021), 6.

3. Christian, *Objects in Air*, 11–12.

4. Georg Simmel, "Die Großstädte und das Geistesleben," in *Die Berliner Moderne 1885–1914.* ed. Jürgen Schutte and Peter Sprengel (Stuttgart: Reclam, 1987), 125.

5. Charles Baudelaire, *Selected Writings on Art and Artists*, trans. and ed. P. E. Chavet (Harmondsworth: Penguin, 1972), 400.

6. David Frisby, "The Flâneur in Social Theory," in *The Flâneur*, ed. Keith Tester (London: Routledge, 1994), 83.

7. Stefan Zweig. *The World of Yesterday: An Autobiography* (London: Cassell and Company, 1943), 115.

8. Zweig, *World of Yesterday*, 117.

9. In dance studies, some scholars refer to dance around 1900 as "early modern dance," but in other fields such as German studies, this can be interpreted as a reference to the baroque. To maintain clarity, I will continue to refer to performances of this period as "early-twentieth-century dance."

10. Ulf Otto, "Enter Electricity: An Allegory's Stage Appearance between Verité and Varieté," *Centaurus* 57: (2015): 192–211. Here I am following Ulf Otto's usage of *Varieté* as borrowed from the French *variété* to refer to theatrical German genres like English music halls, French *café chantants*, or American vaudeville.

11. Edward Ross Dickinson, *Dancing in the Blood: Modern Dance and European Culture on the Eve of the First World War* (Cambridge: Cambridge University Press, 2017), 34.

12. Kate Elswit, *Watching Weimar Dance* (Oxford: Oxford University Press, 2014), xxx. See also Michael Cowan's *Cult of the Will: Nervousness and German Modernity* (University Park: Pennsylvania State University Press, 2008).

13. *The Cambridge Companion to Ballet*, ed. Marion Kant (Cambridge: Cambridge University Press, 2007).

14. Susan Jones, *Literature, Modernism and Dance* (Oxford: Oxford University Press, 2013), 2.

15. Isadora Duncan, *The Dance of the Future* (Eugen Diedrichs: Leipzig, 1903), 28.

16. Claudia Jeschke and Gabi Vettermann, "Isadora Duncan, Berlin and Munich in 1906: Just an Ordinary Year in a Dancer's Career," *Dance Chronicle* 18, no. 2 (1995): 217–29. Here: 217.

17. Helen Thomas, *Dance, Modernity and Culture: Explorations in the Sociology of Dance* (London: Routledge, 1995), 69.

18. Thomas, *Dance, Modernity and Culture*, 71.

19. Brygida Ochaim and Claudia Balk, *Varieté-Tänzerinnen um 1900: Vom Sinnenrausch zur Tanzmoderne* (Frankfurt am Main: Stroemfeld, 1998), 8.

20. Ochaim and Balk, *Varieté-Tänzerinnen*, 7.

21. Ochaim and Balk, *Varieté-Tänzerinnen*, 69.

22. Arthur Kahane, *Tagebuch des Dramaturgen* (Berlin: Bruno Cassirer Verlag, 1928), 207—cited by Jansen, p. 119.

23. Gunhild Oberzaucher-Schüller, "Vorbilder und Wegbreiter. Über den Einfluß der 'prime movers' des amerikanischen Modern Dance auf das Werden des Freien Tanzes in Mitteleuropa," in *Ausdruckstanz: Eine mitteleuropäische Bewegung der ersten Hälfte des 20. Jahrhunderts*, ed. Gunhild Oberzaucher-Schüller (Wilhelmshaven: Heinrichhofen-Bücher, 1992), 347–66.

24. Oberzaucher-Schüller, "Vorbilder und Wegbreiter," 347.

25. Ochaim and Balk, *Varieté-Tänzerinnen*, 10.

26. Arthur Moeller-Bruck, *Das Varieté* (Berlin: Julius Bard, 1902), 4.

27. Ernst Günther, *Geschichte des Varieté* (Berlin: Taschenbuch der Künste, 1978), 11.

28. Ernst Schur, *Der moderne Tanz* (München: Lammers, 1910), 88. Cited by Oberzaucher-Schüller, p. 358.

29. Ochaim and Balk, *Varieté-Tänzerinnen*, 11.

30. Ochaim and Balk, *Varieté-Tänzerinnen*, 11.

31. Ochaim and Balk, *Varieté-Tänzerinnen*, 70.

32. Ochaim and Balk, *Varieté-Tänzerinnen*, 14.

33. Ochaim and Balk, *Varieté-Tänzerinnen*, 69.

34. Peter Jelavich, *Berlin Cabaret* (Cambridge, MA: Harvard University Press, 1993), 21.

35. Jelavich, *Berlin Cabaret*, 22.

36. Jelavich, *Berlin Cabaret*, 23.

37. Jelavich, *Berlin Cabaret*, 26.

38. Ochaim and Balk, *Varieté-Tänzerinnen*, 15.

39. Ochaim and Balk, *Varieté-Tänzerinnen*, 27.

40. Dickinson, *Dancing in the Blood*, 31.

41. Dickinson, *Dancing in the Blood*, 31.

42. Ochaim and Balk, *Varieté-Tänzerinnen*, 71.

43. Dickinson, *Dancing in the Blood*, 47.

44. Andrea Haller, "Seen Through the Eyes of Simmel: The Cinema Programme as a 'Modern' Experience," in *Film 1900: Technology, Perception, Culture*, ed. Annemone Ligensa and Klaus Kreimeier (Bloomington: Indiana University Press, 2015), 113–24. Here: 114.

45. Kristen Hylenski, "Die 'Not Der Zeit': Modernity in Frank Wedekind's Dance Poems," *Monatshefte* 104, no. 1 (2012): 55–69. Here: 55.

46. Ole W. Fischer, "Bauen für den Übermenschen?—Peter Behrens, Henry van de Velde und der Nietzsche-Kult," *ICOMOS—Hefte des Deutschen Nationalkomitees* 64 (2018): 177–89. Here: 187.

47. Jones, *Literature, Modernism and Dance*, 44.

48. Jones, *Literature, Modernism and Dance*, 49.

49. Rainer Maria Rilke, *Briefe aus den Jahren 1902 bis 1906*, ed. Ruth Sieber-Rilke and Carl Sieber (Leipzig: Insel, 1930), 316–17.

50. Rainer Maria Rilke, *Briefe aus den Jahren 1906 bis 1907*, ed. Ruth Sieber-Rilke and Carl Sieber (Leipzig: Insel, 1930), 92.

51. Rainer Maria Rilke, *Briefe aus den Jahren 1902 bis 1906*, 106.

52. Alfred Döblin, "Tänzerinnen," *Der Sturm: Wochenschrift für Kultur und die Künste*, ed. Herwarth Walden, October 1912, 162.

53. Kate Elswit, *Watching Weimar Dance* (Oxford: Oxford University Press, 2014), xi.

54. Sabine Huschka, *Moderner Tanz. Konzepte—Stile—Utopien* (Reinbek bei Hamburg: Rowohlt, 2002), 9.

55. Lucia Ruprecht, *Gestural Imaginaries: Dance and Cultural Theory in the Early Twentieth Century* (Oxford: Oxford University Press, 2019), 36–37.

56. For a sample of dance representation in literature, see *Aufforderung zum Tanz: Geschichten und Gedichte*, ed. Gabriele Brandstetter (Stuttgart: Reclam, 1993)

57. For more information see Wesley Lim, "From Ritual Dance to Flight? Glimmers of the Fantastic in Robert Müller's *Tropen: Der Mythos der Reise*," *Journal of Austrian Studies* 48 (2), 101–20.

58. Deborah L. Parsons, *Streetwalking the Metropolis. Women, the City, and Modernity* (Oxford: Oxford University Press, 2000), 6.

59. Sara Ahmed, *Queer Phenomenology: Orientations, Objects, Others* (Durham: Duke University Press), 16.

60. Penny Farfan, *Performing Queer Modernism* (Oxford: Oxford University Press, 2017), 2–3.

61. Richard Schechner, *Performance Studies: An Introduction*, 3rd ed. (London: Routledge, 2013), 4.

62. Stephen D. Dowden and Meike G. Werner, "The Place of German Modernism," in *The Oxford Handbook of Modern German History*, ed. Helmut Walser Smith (Oxford: Oxford University Press, 2011), 4.

63. Martina Lauster, *Sketches of the Nineteenth Century: European Journals and Its Physiologies, 1830–1850* (Basingstoke, UK: Palgrave Macmillan, 2007), 2.

64. Peter Fritzsche, *Reading Berlin 1900* (Cambridge, MA: Harvard University Press, 1996), 94.

65. Fritzsche, *Reading Berlin 1900*, 8–9.

66. Susanne Scharnowski, "'Neben- und Durcheinander von Kostbarem und Garstigem' Das feuilletonistische Berliner Großstadtbild als Dokument der Moderne," *Zeitschrift für Literaturwissenschaft und Linguistik* 149 (2008): 34–50. Here: 50.

67. Susanne Scharnowski, "'Berlin ist schön, Berlin ist groß.' Feuilletonistische Blicke auf Berlin: Alfred Kerr, Robert Walser, Joseph Roth und Bernard von Brentano," in *Weltfabrik Berlin. Eine Metropole als Sujet der Literatur*, ed. Matthias Harder and Almut Hille (Würzburg: Königshausen & Neumann: 2006), 67–82. Here: 69.

68. Scharnowski, "'Neben- und Durcheinander,'" 37.

69. Scharnowski, "'Neben- und Durcheinander,'" 41.

70. Fritzsche, *Reading Berlin 1900*, 3.

71. Max Osborn, *Berlin 1870–1929* (Berlin: Mann Verlag, 1994), 151.

72. Karl Scheffler, *Paris. Notizen* (Leipzig: Insel Verlag, 1908), 47.

73. Matthias Bauer, "'Berlin ist eine ausführliche Stadt': Einleitende Bemerkungen zur Berliner Stadt-, Kultur- und Mediengeschichte," in *Berlin: Medien- und Kulturgeschichte einer Hauptstadt im 20. Jahrhundert* (Tübingen: Francke Verlag, 2007), 15. Gabriele Klein, "Urbane Bewegungskulturen. Zum Verhältnis von Sport, Stadt und Kultur," in *Bewegungsraum und Stadtkultur: Sozial—und kulturwissenschaftliche Perspektiven* (Bielefeld: transcript Verlag, 2008), 13.

74. Andreas Huyssen, *Miniature Metropolis: Literature in an Age of Photography and Film* (Cambridge, MA: Harvard University Press, 2015), 10.

75. Huyssen, *Miniature Metropolis*, 6.

76. Huyssen, *Miniature Metropolis*, 17.

77. Huyssen, *Miniature Metropolis*, 18.

78. Sabine Huschka, *Moderner Tanz. Konzepte—Stile—Utopien* (Reinbek bei Hamburg: Rowohlt, 2002), 17.

79. Gabriele Wittmann, "Dancing Is Not Writing: ein poetisches Projekt über die Schnittstelle von Sprache und Tanz," in *Tanz Theorie Text*, ed. Gabriele Klein and Christa Zipperich (Münster: Lit Verlag, 2002), 589.

80. John Martin, *Introduction to the Dance* (New York: W.W. Norton, 1939), 53.

81. Rudolf von Laban, *A Vision of Dynamic Space* (London: Falmer Press, 1984), 23.

82. Laurence Louppe, *Poetics of Contemporary Dance*, trans. Sally Gardner (Alton: Dance Books, 2010), 128.

83. Louppe, *Poetics of Contemporary Dance*, 128–29.

84. Ralf Remshardt, "Posthumanism," in *Mapping Intermediality in Performance*, ed. Sarah Bay-Cheng, Chiel Kattenbelt, Andy Lavender, and Robin Nelson (Amsterdam: Amsterdam University Press, 2010), 135–39. Here: 135.

85. Michael Mack, *Contaminations: Beyond Dialectics in Modern Literature, Science and Film* (Edinburgh: Edinburgh University Press, 2016), 192.

86. Donna Haraway, "A Cyborg Manifesto: Science, Technology, and Socialist-Feminism in the Late Twentieth Century," in *Simians, Cyborgs and Women: The Reinvention of Nature* (New York; Routledge, 1991), 149–81. Here: 150.

87. Derek Ryan, "Following Snakes and Moths: Modernist Ethics and Posthumanism," *Twentieth-Century Literature* 61, no. 3 (2015): 287–304. Here: 298.

88. Jacques Derrida, *The Beast and the Sovereign*, vol. 1., trans. Geoffrey Bennington (Chicago: University of Chicago Press, 2009), 108.

89. Ruben Borg, "Literary Modernism," in *Critical Posthumanism: Genealogy of the Posthuman*, https://criticalposthumanism.net/literary-modernism-and-the-posthuman/, November 26, 2017.

90. Walter Benjamin, "Paris, Capital of the Nineteenth Century. Exposé of 1939," in *The Arcades Project*, ed. Rolf Tiedemann, trans. Howard Eiland and Kevin McLaughlin (Cambridge, MA: Belknap Press, 1999), 15.

91. Lauster, *Sketches of the Nineteenth Century*, 12.

Chapter 1

1. My translation. "Der Strom eines täglich heftiger zirkulierenden Blutumlaufs befruchtete das Gemeinwesen in allen Äußerungen, [. . .] der ihn zum Ziel eines vorerst noch nicht deutlich empfundenen neuen Stadtorganismus hintrieb. Tag um Tag schob Berlin seine Vorposten abermals ein Stück weiter vor. Tag um Tag schwoll das Brausen seiner Straßenmusik stärker an, blitzten die Lichter neuer Ideen auf. Das Tempo der Entwicklung wurde so schnell, daß die Wege der früheren, bedächtig vorgehenden Logik meist verlassen wurden und jene Sprunghaftigkeit einsetzte, die oft schwierige Probleme heraufbeschwor." Max Osborn, *Berlin 1870–1929* (Berlin: Mann Verlag, 1994), 151.

2. Osborn, *Berlin 1870–1929*, 162.

3. Osborn, *Berlin 1870–1929*, 162.

4. Osborn, *Berlin 1870–1929*, 163.

5. Osborn, *Berlin 1870–1929*, 149.

6. *Vossische Zeitung*, October 7, 1900. Cited from Glatzer and Glatzer, *Berliner Leben 1900–1914*, 99.

7. Karl Scheffler, *Berlin. Ein Stadtschicksal* (Berlin: E. Reiss, 1910), 267.

8. Scheffler, *Berlin. Ein Stadtschicksal*, 200.

9. Lothar Müller, "The Beauty of the Metropolis: Towards an Aesthetic Urbanism in Turn-of-the-Century Berlin," in *Berlin: Culture and Metropolis*, ed. Charles W. Haxthausen and Heidrun Suhr (Minneapolis: University of Minnesota Press, 1990), 41.

10. https://commons.wikimedia.org/wiki/File:Berlins_erste_Litfa%C3%9Fs%C3%A4ule.jpg (cited from Osborn, *Berlin 1870–1929*, 60).

11. Peter Fritzsche, *Reading Berlin 1900* (Cambridge, MA: Harvard University Press, 1996), 150.

12. "Mehr Litfasssäulen," *Berliner Tageblatt*, no. 609, September 29, 1912.

13. Oscar Justinus, "Zettel," in *Berliner Pflaster*, ed. Moritz Reymond and Ludwig Manzel (Berlin: W. Pauli, 1891), 66–68.

14. Fritzsche, *Reading Berlin 1900*, 150.

15. Steffen Damm and Klaus Siebenhaar, *Ernst Litfaß und sein Erbe: eine Kulturgeschichte der Litfaßsäule* (Berlin: Bostermann und Siebenhaar, 2005), 25.

16. Damm and Siebenhaar, *Ernst Litfaß*, 90.

17. Fritzsche, *Reading Berlin 1900*, 150.

18. "Die Litfasssäule als Jubilarin," *Berliner Lokal-Anzeiger*, no. 315, July 1, 1905.

19. Edmund Edel, "Der Schrei der Litfasssäule," *Berliner Tageblatt*, no. 481, September 21, 1908.

20. Osborn, *Berlin 1870–1929*, 186. ("Jetzt erst erkannte man, daß hier willkommene Möglichkeiten lagen, vielfache dekorative Wirkungen zu entfalten. Die verfeinerte Farbendrucktechnik—denn künstlerischer und technischer Fortschritt verbanden sich hier wie in der Baukunst—drückte den älteren, süßlichen und kitschigen Buntdruck an die Wand. Die Maler fanden einen Weg, ihr Talent in den Dienst der Praxis zu stellen; die Kunstfreude begrüßten die Aussicht, guter Kunst Verbreitung zu geben und dadurch die Menge zu erziehen. Man erkannte die Aufgabe: der Fernwirkung zuliebe mit großen Linien und energischen Farbflächen einen einfachen, summarischen Ausdruck für einen leicht faßbaren Bildgedanken zu finden.")

21. Gabriele Brandstetter, "Die Tänzerin der Metamorphosen," in *Loïe Fuller: Getanzter Jugendstil* (München: Prestel, 1996), 25–38.

22. Jo-Anne Birnie Danzker, "Plakatkunst und Skultur um die Jahrhundertwende: Loïe Fuller als Modell," in *Loïe Fuller: Getanzter Jugendstil* (München: Prestel, 1996), 61.

23. David P. Jordan, "Haussmann and Haussmannisation: The Legacy for Paris," *French Historical Studies* 27, no. 1 (2004): 89–90.

24. David P. Jordan, "The City: Baron Haussmann and Modern Paris," *American Scholar* 61, no. 1 (1992): 99–106. Here: 100.

25. Stefan Zweig, *The World of Yesterday: An Autobiography* (London: Cassell and Company, 1943), 107.

26. Karl Scheffler, *Paris. Notizen* (Leipzig: Insel Verlag, 1908), 20–22.

27. My translation. "ein klargegliederter Organismus. Die Stadt beginnt zu atmen, als wäre sie ein Lebewesen" (31).

28. Alexander Eisenschmidt, "Metropolitan Architecture: Karl Scheffler and Alfred Messel's Search for a New Urbanity," *Grey Room* 65 (2014): 90–115. Here: 92.

29. My translation. Scheffler, *Paris. Notizen*, 46. ("Es wird in Paris sehr stark Das in Anspruch genommen, was Kant das »intellektuelle Interesse am Schönen« nennt" . . . "Die Phantasie rückt das Bild ins Licht einer höheren, geistigen Bedeutung, und es entsteht jenes Doppelspiel vom Schauen und Denken, das durchaus zum vollen ästhetischen Genuß gehört.")

30. My translation. Scheffler, *Paris. Notizen*, 47 ("auch die Pariser Atmosphäre hat etwas Theatralisches und Pathetisches").

31. My translation. Scheffler, *Paris. Notizen*, 48 ("Die Stadt wird zur Riesenbühne").

32. Fritzsche, *Reading Berlin 1900*, 3.

33. Fritzsche, *Reading Berlin 1900*, 3.

34. "Städte sind Kunstwerke, vielleicht die größten Kunstwerke der Menschheit überhaupt. Städte sind dynamische Kunstwerke, also nicht nur Objekte, reine Materialitäten oder unbewegliche Figuren, sondern Prozesse; Städte sind Skulpturen, die leben, die sich bewegen und [. . .] von Menschen in Bewegung gehalten werden." Gabriele Klein, "Urbane Bewegungskulturen. Zum Verhältnis von Sport, Stadt und Kultur," in *Bewegungsraum und Stadtkultur: Sozial—und kulturwissenschaftliche Perspektiven*, 13–30 (Bielefeld: transcript Verlag, 2008), 13.

35. Although for the purposes of this chapter, I make the argument more in regard to the city performing or dancing, Klein's book deals with spectator sports to a large degree. In one section, she characterizes Milton Singer, a cultural anthropologist, by stating: "Als Cultural Performance, [. . .] wird Sport zu Beginn des 20. Jahrhunderts allmählich zum Bestandteil der städtischen Alltagskultur. Er wird— vor allem als kommerzieller Zuschauersport—theatralisiert; zugleich wird es kulturalisiert, indem Konventionen, Werte, Rituale und Inszenierungspraktiken, also die kulturellen Praktiken dafür sorgen, dass die einzelnen Sportarten sozial unterscheidbar bleiben." In Milton Singer, *Traditional India—Structure and Change* (Austin: University of Texas Press, 1979). Here the process of aestheization of sports is depicted as being a product of the city and is strongly linked with performance.

36. Erika Fischer-Lichte, *The Routledge Introduction to Theatre and Performance Studies*, ed. Minou Arjomand and Ramona Mosse, trans. Minou Arjomand (Abington, UK: Routledge, 2014), 20.

37. "Ein Ort, auf den sich die gemeinsame Aufmerksamkeit von Beobachtern fokussiert, weil an diesem Ort etwas Neues geschieht bzw. zur Anschauung gelangt. Von Szenen gemeinsamer Aufmerksamkeit zu reden, impliziert freilich nicht nur, dass es in der Regel mehr als einen Beobachter gibt, weil das beobachtete Geschehen in einem öffentlich zugänglichen Raum vor sich geht. Vielmehr schließt eine solche Szene die Koordination von Blicken und Gesten, Aktionen und Reaktionen ein, so dass ihr eine *performative Dimension* zukommt. Weil das, was man tut, gleichsam auf einer Bühne geschieht, wird es in dem Bewusstsein vollzogen, dass man als Handelnder—ja sogar als teilnahmsloser Zuschauer—unter Beobachtung steht. Umgekehrt wissen die Beobachter, dass sie einer Aufführung, einem Rollenspiel, einer Inszenierung beiwohnen, die über sich hinausweist, die etwas demonstriert, exemplifiziert, manifestiert." Matthias Bauer, "'Berlin ist eine ausführliche Stadt': Einleitende Bemerkungen zur Berliner Stadt-, Kultur- und Mediengeschichte," in *Berlin: Medien- und Kulturgeschichte einer Hauptstadt im 20. Jahrhundert* (Tübingen: Francke Verlag, 2007), 15.

38. Georg Simmel, "Die Großstädte und das Geistesleben," in *Die Berliner Moderne 1885–1914*, ed. Jürgen Schutte and Peter Sprengel (Stuttgart: Reclam, 1987), 125.

39. Pricilla Parkhurst Ferguson, "The Flaneur On and Off the Streets of Paris," in *The Flâneur*, ed. Keith Tester (London: Routledge, 1994), 26.

40. Keith Tester, "Introduction," *The Flâneur*, ed. Keith Tester (London: Routledge, 1994), 2.

41. Tester, "Introduction," *The Flâneur*, 2.

42. Charles Baudelaire, *Selected Writings on Art and Artists*, trans. and ed. P. E. Chavet (Harmondsworth, UK: Penguin, 1972), 400.

43. Tester, "Introduction," *The Flâneur*, 4–5.

44. Ferguson, "The Flaneur On and Off the Streets of Paris," 28–29.

45. Bruce Mazlich, "The *Flâneur*: From Spectator to Representation," in *The Flâneur*, ed. Keith Tester (London: Routledge, 1994), 78.

46. Mazich, "The *Flâneur*: From Spectator to Representation," 75.

47. Ferguson, "The Flaneur On and Off the Streets of Paris," 31.

48. Ferguson, "The Flaneur On and Off the Streets of Paris," 32.

49. Ferguson, "The Flaneur On and Off the Streets of Paris," 35.

50. David Frisby, "The Flâneur in Social Theory," in *The Flâneur*, ed. Keith Tester (London: Routledge, 1994), 82.

51. Frisby, "The Flâneur in Social Theory," 83.

52. Fritzsche, *Reading Berlin 1900*, 15.

53. Fritzsche, *Reading Berlin 1900*, 16.

54. Fritzsche, *Reading Berlin 1900*, 94.

55. Deborah L. Parsons, *Streetwalking the Metropolis. Women, the City, and Modernity* (Oxford: Oxford University Press, 2000), 6.

56. Andreas Huyssen, *Miniature Metropolis: Literature in an Age of Photography and Film* (Cambridge, MA: Harvard University Press, 2015), 10.

57. Huyssen, *Miniature Metropolis*, 6.

58. Huyssen, *Miniature Metropolis*, 17.

59. Huyssen, *Miniature Metropolis*, 18.

60. Gabriele Brandstetter and Christoph Wulf, "Introduction," *Tanz als Anthropologie* (München: Wilhelm Fink Verlag, 2007), 9–10.

61. Susanne K. Langer, "From Feeling and Form," in *What Is Dance? Readings in Theory and Criticism*, ed. Roger Copeland and Marshall Cohen, 28–36 (Oxford: Oxford University Press, 1983). Here: 31.

62. Sabine Huschka, *Moderner Tanz. Konzepte—Stile—Utopien* (Reinbek bei Hamburg: Rowohlt, 2002), 9. "Die Avantgardströmungen in Literatur und bildender Kunst sind vom Tanz als Kunst ausgesprochener Sinnlichkeit und dynamisierter Kinetik inspiriert, da sie beinahe mystisch-konkret und doch abstrahierend das Energetische der aufbrechenden Moderne zu gestalten weiß."

63. Huschka, *Moderner Tanz*, 17. "Denn es begegnet einem ein Phänomenbereich, der—mit dem Sinnenbereich des eigenen Körpers verwoben—dem eignen Sprachvermögen fremd ist."

64. Huschka, *Moderner Tanz*, 20. "[d]ie Sprache wird seinen Phänomenbereich [vom Tanz] niemals berühren können."

65. Werner Jakob Stüber, *Geschichte des Modern Dance. Zur Selbsterfahrung und Körperaneignung im modernen Tanztheater* (Wilhelmshaven: Heinrichshofen Verlag, 1984), 17. "ein dynamisches, räumliches-zeitliches Geschehen auf 'verbale Äquivalente.'"

66. Gabriele Brandstetter, *Poetics of Dance: Body, Image, and Space in the Historical Avant- Gardes* (Oxford: Oxford University Press, 2015), 64.

67. Christina Thurner, *Beredte Körper—bewegte Seelen. Zum Diskurs der doppelten Bewegung in Tanztexten* (Bielefeld: transcript Verlag, 2009), 42. "Dabei

reichen die Vorstellung von einer generellen Unübersetzbarkeit bis hin zu jener von einer eigenen neuen Sprache, die gefunden werden müsste, um Bewegung verbal erfassen zu können."

68. Gabriele Wittmann, "Dancing Is Not Writing: ein poetisches Projekt über die Schnittstelle von Sprache und Tanz," in *Tanz Theorie Text*, ed. Gabriele Klein and Christa Zipperich (Münster: Lit Verlag, 2002), 586. "Gibt es eine Sprache, die das kinästhetische Momentum des Tanzes ausdrücken oder nachbilden kann?"

69. Wittmann, "Dancing Is Not Writing," 586.

70. Wittmann, "Dancing Is Not Writing," 587.

71. Wittmann, "Dancing Is Not Writing," 589.

72. Wittmann, "Dancing Is Not Writing," 589. "wir schlüpfen gewissermaßen *in die Haut* des anderen Wesens. In der Fantasie—oder wo auch immer dieser Prozess stattfindet—SIND wir dieses andere Wesen."

73. Wittmann, "Dancing Is Not Writing," 593. "Es müsste ein Gedicht sein. Ein Gedicht, das sich der im mimetischen Schreibprozess gefundenen Worte bedient und sie arrangiert, in Szene setzt. Die Mittel der poetischen Sprache bieten dabei immerhin Verdichtungen an, sodass sich das von der mimetischen Wahrnehmung als vertikale Zeitachse Erlebte als Verdichtetes und damit geschichtet durchwirkt arrangieren lässt. Außerdem ist Poesie eine Sprache, die für das Hören konzipiert ist. Selbst wenn der Leser still für sich liest, liest er im Allgemeinen so, als ob er laut rezitiere. Die Sprache tut also durch ihr Rauschen schon ihre Wirkung."

74. Quoted in E. G. Jones, "The Development of the 'Muscular Sense' Concept During the Nineteenth Century and the Work of H. Charlton Bastian," *Journal of the History of Medicine and Allied Sciences* 27, no. 3 (July 1972): 72.

75. Jones, "Development," 72.

76. Susan Foster, *Choreographing Empathy: Kinesthesia in Performance* (London: Routledge, 2011), 74.

77. Robert Vischer, Harry Francis Mallgrave, and Eleftherios Ikonomou, "On the Optical Sense of Form: A Contribution to Aesthetics," in *Empathy, Form, and Space: Problems in German Aesthetics, 1873–1893* (Santa Monica, CA: Getty Center for the History of Art and the Humanities; distributed by the University of Chicago Press, 1994), 104.

78. John Martin, *Introduction to the Dance* (New York: W. W. Norton, 1939), 53.

79. Rudolf von Laban, *A Vision of Dynamic Space*, compiled by Lisa Ullmann (London: Falmer Press, 1984), 23.

80. Laurence Louppe, *Poetics of Contemporary Dance*, trans. Sally Gardner (Alton, UK: Dance Books, 2010), 127.

81. Dominique Dupuy, "La danse de dedans," in *La dance, naissance d'un movement de pensée*, ed. L. Niklas (Paris: Armand Colin, 1989).

82. Louppe, *Poetics of Contemporary Dance*, 128.

83. Louppe, *Poetics of Contemporary Dance*, 135.

84. Louppe, *Poetics of Contemporary Dance*, 128–29.

85. Margareta Ingrid Christian, *Objects in Air: Artworks and Their Outside around 1900* (Chicago: University of Chicago Press, 2021), 6.

86. Janine Schulze, *Dancing Bodies Dancing Gender: Tanz im 20. Jahrhundert aus der Perspektive der Gender-Theorie* (Dortmund: Edition Ebersbach, 1999), 34.

87. Schulze, *Dancing Bodies*, 34.

88. Walter Benjamin, "Die Aufgabe des Übersetzers," in *Illuminationen*. 1. Auflage (Frankfurt: Suhrkamp, 1977), 57.

89. Benjamin, "Die Aufgabe des Übersetzers," 60.

Chapter 2

1. Georges Teyssot, "The Wave: Walter Benjamin's Lost Essay on Jugendstil," *AA Files*, no. 61 (2010): 37.

2. Cynthia J. Novack, *Sharing the Dance: Contact Improvisation and American Culture* (Madison: University of Wisconsin Press, 1990), 137.

3. Gabriele Brandstetter, "Die Tänzerin der Metamorphosen," in *Loïe Fuller: Getanzter Jugendstil* (München: Prestel, 1996).

4. Ann Cooper Albright, *Traces of Light: Absence and Presence in the Work of Loïe Fuller* (Middletown: Wesleyan University Press, 2007), 45–46.

5. Andreas Huyssen, "Modernist Miniatures: Literary Snapshots of Urban Spaces," *PMLA* 122, no. 1 (January 2007): 27.

6. Gabriele Brandstetter, *Poetics of Dance: Body, Image, and Space in the Historical Avant-Gardes* (Oxford: Oxford University Press, 2015), 232. While Brandstetter does define this term and cites texts such as Rilke's poem "Spanish Dancer" as belonging to this genre, her study does not focus primarily on the dance text, but rather on a plethora of cultural sources.

7. Rhonda K. Garelick, *Electric Salome: Loïe Fuller's Performance of Modernism* (Princeton: Princeton University Press, 2007); Albright, *Traces of Light*.

8. Felicia McCarren, *Dancing Machines. Choreographies of the Age of Mechanical Reproduction* (Stanford: Stanford University Press, 2003), 44.

9. Margareta Ingrid Christian, *Objects in Air: Artworks and Their Outside around 1900* (Chicago: University of Chicago Press, 2021), 6.

10. Alexander Eisenschmidt, "Visual Discoveries of an Urban Wanderer: August Endell's Perception of a Beautiful Metropolis," *Architectural Research Quarterly* 11 (2007): 71.

11. Helge David, *An die Schönheit. August Endells Texte zu Kunst und Ästhetik 1896 bis 1925* (Weimar: Verlag und Datenbank für Geisteswissenschaften, 2008), 13.

12. Tilmann Buddensieg, "The Early Years of August Endell: Letters to Kurt Breysig from Munich," *Art Journal* 43, no. 1 (1983): 41–49.

13. Zeynep Çelik Alexander, "Metrics of Experience: August Endell's Phenomenology of Architecture," *Grey Room* 40 (2010): 50–83. Here: 68.

14. David, *An die Schönheit*, 13.

15. August Endell, "Um die Schönheit," in *Eine Paraphrase über die Münchener Kunstausstellung* (München: Verlag Emil Franke, 1896), 29. "Wir müssen lernen zu sehen, und wir müssen lernen, daß Form und Farbe, die in uns bestimmte Gefühle hervorrufen, uns auch wirklich zu Bewußtsein kommen."

16. Laird McLeod Easton, *The Red Count. The Life and Times of Harry Graf Kessler* (Berkeley: University of California Press, 2002), 40.

17. Endell, "Um die Schönheit," 11. "eine nie versiegende Quelle ausserordentlichen und ungeahnten Genusses . . . . Es ist in der That eine neue Welt, die sich da aufthut. . . . Es ist wie ein Rausch, wie ein Wahnsinn, der uns überkommt. . . ."

18. Klaus Reichel, "Vom Jugendstil zu Sachlichkeit: August Endell (1871–1925)" (PhD diss., Ruhr Universität Bochum, 1974), 36.

19. Reichel, "Vom Jugendstil zu Sachlichkeit," 37.

20. August Endell, "Formenschönheit und dekorative Kunst," part two, *Dekorative Kunst* 2 (1898): 121. Translated by Alexander.

21. Alexander, "Metrics of Experience," 60.

22. Alexander, "Metrics of Experience," 53.

23. Alexander, "Metrics of Experience," 56.

24. Endell, "Architektonische Erstling," in *Dekorative Kunst: Zeitschrift für angewandte Kunst 3.8* (1900), ed. H. Bruckmann (München) and J. Meier-Graefe (Paris), 297. Akademie der Künste Berlin, August-Endell-Sammlung—"Hauptschattenmasse aber ein schweres, einheitliches Ornament, das den unregelmässigen freien Raum füllt."

25. Endell, "Architektonische Erstling," 300.

26. Johannes Otzen, "Das persönliche in Architektur und Kunstgewerbe," *Deutsche Bauzeitung* 34 (March 1900): 143–45. Translation from the German by Tilmann Buddensieg.

27. Josef Hartwig, *Leben und Meinungen des Bildhauers Josef Hartwig* (Frankfurt am Main: Mitteldeutscher Kunstgewerbe-Verein, 1955), 13. Quoted in Klaus-Jürgen Sembach and Gottfried von Haeseler, *August Endell. Der Architekt des Photoateliers Elvira 1871–1925* (Munich: Jugendstil Verein, 1977), 24, trans. Stacy Hand. ("Endell erklärte mir dessen Formen und Strukturen als Beziehungen zur Natur, zum Pfirsischkern, zu flatternden Bändern oder Meereswellen, sie sich am Strand kräuseln etc.")

28. Stacy Hand, "Embodied Abstraction: Biomorphic Fantasy and Empathy Aesthetics in the Work of Hermann Obrist, August Endell, and Their Followers" (PhD diss., University of Chicago, 2008), 136.

29. Hand, "Embodied Abstraction," 155.

30. Alexander, "Metrics of Experience," 61.

31. The translations of these titles are my own, since Alexander did not translate the entire text.

32. These are Alexander's translations.

33. Endell, "Die Schönheit der großen Stadt," 88–92.

34. Translation by Alexander, 119.

35. Eisenschmidt, "Visual Discoveries," 71–72.

36. Albright, *Traces of Light*, 83.

37. My own translation from Helge David, "Exkurs: Die Schönheit der großen Stadt," in *An die Schönheit. August Endells Texte zu Kunst und Ästhetik 1896 bis 1925* (Weimar: Verlag und Datenbank für Geisteswissenschaften, 2008), 227. "In dem Strom der permanenten Gegenwart versucht Endell, der impressionistischen

Flüchtigkeit des Sichtbaren durch einen Moment der Kontemplation eine neue, genießende Langsamkeit abzugewinnen, ohne freilich die Geschwindigkeit des modernen Lebens drosseln zu wollen oder zu können. Das Sichtbare geht vorüber, ist Bewegung. Die Stadt der Gegenwart hat sich der höheren Ideale entledigt und schafft sich ihre Existenz täglich neu."

38. Peter Fritzsche, *Reading Berlin 1900* (Cambridge, MA: Harvard University Press, 1996), 94.

39. Translated by Alexander, 132. "Zu dem Erstaunlichten gehört in dieser Hinsicht das Leben auf einem Platze. Der unseligen romanischen Kirche gegenüber liegt ein Café mit einer Terrasse, auf der ich oft an Sommerabenden stundenlang gesessen habe und mich nicht müde sehen konnte an dem bunten Spiele der kommenden und gehenden Menschen." Endell, "Die Schönheit der großen Stadt," 115.

40. Georg Simmel, "Die Großstädte und das Geistesleben," in *Die Berliner Moderne 1885–1914*. ed. Jürgen Schutte and Peter Sprengel (Stuttgart: Reclam, 1987), 125.

41. Eisenschmidt, "Visual Discoveries," 75.

42. Keith Tester, "Introduction," *The Flâneur*, ed. Keith Tester (London: Routledge, 1994), 2.

43. Endell, "Die Schönheit der großen Stadt," 115. "Der Platz ist töricht als Architektur, vielleicht noch schlimmer als Verkehrsanlage—wie wenn jemand die größtmöglichste Zahl gefährlicher Übergänge hätte schaffen wollen—aber als Feld mit darüber verteilten Menschen ist er ganz einzig. Die Menschenströme der benachbarten Straßen lösen sich hier nach allen Richtungen auf, und der ganze Platz scheint bedeckt von vereinzelten Menschen."

44. Translated by Alexander, 132. Endell, "Die Schönheit der großen Stadt," 114–115. "Jeder löst sich vom anderen. Zwischen ihnen breitet sich der Raum. In perspektivischer Verschiebung scheinen die entfernteren Gestalten immer kleiner, und man empfindet deutlich die weite Dehnung des Platzes. Alle Menschen sind frei voneinander, bald nahen sie sich zu größerer Dichte, bald lassen sie Lücken, fortwährend ist die Teilung des Raumes eine andere. Die Schreitenden schieben sich durcheinander, verdecken einander, lösen sich wieder ab, schreiten frei und allein, jeder aufrecht einen Platzteil betonend, verdeutlichend, und so wird der Raum zwischen ihnen ein fühlbares, ungeheures, lebendiges Wesen, [. . .]"

45. Laurence Louppe, *Poetics of Contemporary Dance*, trans. Sally Gardner (Alton, UK: Dance Books, 2010), 127.

46. Rudolf von Laban, *A Vision of Dynamic Space* (London: Falmer Press, 1984), 23.

47. Brandstetter, *Poetics of Dance*, 232.

48. Brandstetter, *Poetics of Dance*, 298.

49. Max Osborn, *Berlin 1870–1929* (Berlin: Mann Verlag, 1994), 151.

50. Walter Rathenau, "Die schönste Stadt der Welt," in *Die Berliner Moderne 1885–1914*, ed. Jürgen Schutte and Peter Sprengel (Stuttgart: Reclam, 1987), 100–104.

51. Anselm Heine, "Berlins Physiognomie," in *Ich weiß Bescheid in Berlin* (Berlin: Behr, 1908), 1–25. Cited from Glatzer, *Berliner Leben 1900–1914*, 111.

52. Peter Fritzsche, *Reading Berlin 1900* (Cambridge, MA: Harvard University Press, 1996), 3.

53. Translated by Alexander 132–33. "[. . .] was noch viel merkwürdiger wird, wenn Sonne jedem Fußgänger einen begleitenden Schatten, oder Regen ein blitzendes, unsicheres Spiegelbild unter die Füße breitet. Und in diesem seltsamen Raumleben entfaltet sich das Gewimmel der bunt gestrichenen Wagen, der farbigen Toiletten, alles vereint, verhüllt, verschönt mit den Schleiern des Tages und der Dämmerung." Endell, "Die Schönheit der großen Stadt," 116.

54. This is my translation. "Ehe sie ihre Vorstellung beginnt, werden Saal und Bühne in undurchdringliche Finsterniß gehüllt. Die Bühne stellt eine phantastich ausgestattete Höhle vor, und durch eine Felsspalte betritt Miß Fuller die Scene. Plötzlich bestrahlt elektrisches Licht ihre schöne Gestalt. Sie beginnt sich wie ein Kreisel zu drehen, die Falten ihres langen weißen, mit Schlangen und Schmetterlingen bestrickten Seidenkleides heben sich und bilden im Wirbel des Tanzes Figuren, wie unsere Zeichnungen deren etliche darstellen.

"Die stets wechselnden Reflexe und Farben des elektrischen Lichtes tragen wesentlich dazu bei, den Effect der ganzen Vorführung derartig zu erhöhen, daß die Zuschauer sich in den Glauben versetzt fühlen könnte, Miß Fuller in einer diamantenen Atmosphäre tanzen zu sehen, sodaß auch in dieser Hinsicht die Bezeichnung Serpentintänzerin vollkommen gerechtfertigt erscheint." (Gez.:) E.R., "Serpentinentanz," in *Illustrierte Zeitung*, 99/2580 (December 10, 1892): 684.

55. Gabriele Brandstetter, "Die Tänzerin der Metamorphosen," in *Loïe Fuller: Getanzter Jugendstil* (München: Prestel, 1996), 25.

56. Loïe Fuller, *Fifteen Years of a Dancer's Life* (Boston: Small, Maynard, 1913), 70.

57. John Martin, *Introduction to the Dance* (New York: W. W. Norton, 1939), 47.

58. Martin, *Introduction to the Dance*, 53.

59. Albright, *Traces of Light*, 63.

60. Albright, *Traces of Light*, 26.

61. Garelick, *Electric Salome*, 34.

62. Flitch quotes Fuller. J. E. Crawford Flitch, *Modern Dancing and Dancers* (Philadelphia: J. B. Lippincott, 1912), 88.

63. Arthur Moeller-Bruck, *Das Varieté* (Berlin: Julius Bard, 1902), 27.

64. Brandstetter, "Die Tänzerin der Metamorphosen," 27.

65. Penny Farfan, *Performing Queer Modernism* (Oxford: Oxford University Press, 2017), 27.

66. Susan Potter, *Queer Timing: The Emergence of Lesbian Sexuality in Early Cinema* (Urbana: University of Illinois Press, 2019), 110.

67. Wesley Lim, "The Aesthetics of Queer Work: Loïe Fuller's Exhausting Life as Performance Art in Stephanie Di Giusto's *The Dancer* (2016)," in *Circus and the Avant-Gardes: History, Imaginary, Innovation*, ed. Anna-Sophie Jürgens and Mirjam Hildbrand, 196–212 (Abington: Routledge, 2022).

68. Ochaim and Balk, *Varieté-Tänzerinnen*, 11. "ein permanent wechselndes, farbiges Spiel."

69. Ochaim and Balk, *Varieté-Tänzerinnen*, 70.

70. Ochaim and Balk, *Varieté-Tänzerinnen*, 15.

71. Max Horkheimer and Theodor Adorno, *Dialectic of Enlightenment: Philosophical Fragments*, ed. Gunzelin Schmid Noerr, trans. Edmund Jephcott (Stanford: Stanford University Press, 2002), 94–99.

72. Horkheiner and Adorno, *Dialectic of Enlightenment*, 106.

73. Ochaim and Balk, *Varieté-Tänzerinnen*, 27.

74. Andrew Webber, *Berlin in the Twentieth Century: A Cultural Topography* (Cambridge: Cambridge University Press, 2011), 16.

75. Huyssen, "Modernist Miniatures," 17.

76. Albright, *Traces of Light*, 23.

77. Ruth E. Iskin, *The Poster: Art, Advertising, Design, and Collecting, 1860s–1900s* (Hanover, NH: Dartmouth College Press, 2014), 187.

78. Garelick, *Electric Salome*, 171; Brandstetter, *Poetics of Dance*, 299.

79. Tom Gunning, "Loïe Fuller and the Art of Motion: Body, Light, Electricity, and the Origins of Cinema," in *Camera Obscura, Camera Lucida: Essays in Honor of Annette Michelson*, ed. Allen Richard and Turvey Malcolm, 75–90 (Amsterdam: Amsterdam University Press, 2003), 84.

80. Susan Potter, *Queer Timing*, 117–18.

81. Susan Potter, *Queer Timing*, 118.

82. Albright, *Traces of Light*, 52.

83. Albright, *Traces of Light*, 54.

84. Iskin, *The Poster*, 182.

85. Iskin, *The Poster*, 199.

86. Brandstetter, *Poetics of Dance*, 69.

87. Albright, *Traces of Light*, 87.

88. Richard Current and Marcia Ewing Current, *Goddess of Light* (Boston: Northeastern University Press, 1997), 100.

89. Buddensieg, "The Early Years," 47.

90. Buddensieg, "The Early Years," 47.

91. Georg Simmel, "The Berlin Trade Exhibition," trans. Sam Whimster, in *Theory, Culture & Society* 8 (1991): 119–23. The original article, "Berliner Gewerbeausstellung," appeared in *Die Zeit* (Wien) 7 (91) (1896): 204.

92. Hand, "Embodied Abstraction," 120.

93. Janine Schulze, *Dancing Bodies Dancing Gender: Tanz im 20. Jahrhundert aus der Perspektive der Gender-Theorie* (Dortmund: Edition Ebersbach, 1999), 34.

94. Gabriele Brandstetter and Gabriele Klein, "Bewegung in Übertragung. Methodische Überlegungen am Beispiel von *Le Sacre du Printemps*," in *Methoden der Tanzwissenschaft*, ed. Gabriele Brandstetter and Gabriele Klein (Bielefeld: transcript, 2007), 11–12.

95. Susan L. Foster, *Choreography and Narrative: Ballet's Staging of Story and Desire* (Bloomington: Indiana University Press, 1996), 197.

96. André Lepecki, "Inscribing Dance," in *Of the Presence of the Body: Essays on Dance and Performance Theory*, ed. André Lepecki (Middletown, CT: Wesleyan University Press, 2004), 127.

97. Schulze, *Dancing Bodies*, 34.

Chapter 3

1. Yvonne Hardt and Kirsten Maar, "Bewegte Räume: zur Verortung des Tanzes im Spannungsfeld von Metropole und Provinz—ein Einleitung," in *Tanz Metropole Provinz. Jahrbuch Tanzforschung* 17 (Hamburg, Lit Verlag: 2007), 1–17. Here: 1.

2. Günter Riederer, "Der Übergangsmensch—Kessler als Student, Untertan und Weltbürger," in *Harry Graf Kessler, Das Tagebuch*, vol. 2: *1892–1897*, ed. Günter Riederer and Jörg Schuster, 13–37 (Stuttgart: Klett-Cotta, 2004). Here: 13.

3. Penny Farfan, *Performing Queer Modernism* (Oxford: Oxford University Press, 2017), 2.

4. Farfan, *Performing Queer Modernism*, 3.

5. Harry Graf Kessler, *Das Tagebuch*, vol. 3: *1897–1905*, ed. Carina Schäfer and Gabriele Biedermann (Stuttgart: Klett-Cotta 2004), 435. ("Sie werden die Memoiren unserer Zeit schreiben. Das ist gerade richtig für Sie, dass Sie alle Leute, die Etwas bedeuten, in allen Lebenslägen kennen lernen müssen. Ich beneide unsere Enkel darum, dass Sie das lesen können.")

6. Annette Kolb, "Harry Graf Kessler," in *Maß und Wert* 4 (1938): 630–31.

7. Harry Graf Kessler, *Das Tagebuch 1880–1937* (Stuttgart: Klett-Cotta 2004).

8. Kessler, *Das Tagebuch 1880–1937*.

9. Harry Graf Kessler, "Lehrjahre," in *Gesichter und Zeiten. Erinnerungen*, ed. Cornelia Blasberg and Gerhard Schuster, 97–231 (Frankfurt am Main: Fischer, 1988), Here: 199. ("In uns entstand ein geheimer Messianismus. Die Wüste, die zu jedem Messias gehört, war in unseren Herzen; und plötzlich erschien über ihr wie ein Meteor Nietzsche.")

10. Kessler, "Lehrjahre," 209 ("Unsere Generation war wohl die erste, die von Nietzsche tief beeinflußt wurde. Zu Anfang war unser Gefühl eine Mischung von angenehmem Gruseln und staunender Bewunderung vor dem Monsterfeuerwerk seines Geistes, in dem ein Stück nach dem anderen unseres moralischen Rüstzeugs in Rauch aufging. [. . .] Das rauhe Klima des Jahrhundertendes erforderte eine andere Gesundheit und Härte der Seele [. . .] als das weiche und romantische deutsche Biedermeier. [. . .] Das Gleichgewicht zwischen Mensch und Milieu, das die Umwälzungen des neunzehnten Jahrhunderts gestört hatte, mußte durch eine Anpassung des Menschen an die neue Welt, die die alte immer radikaler verdrängte, wiederhergestellt werden.")

11. Friedrich Nietzsche, *Die Geburt der Tragödie*, in *Nietzsches Werke: Historischkritische Ausgabe*. Electronic edition. Kritische Gesamtausgabe; III-1.26. ("Singend und tanzend äussert sich der Mensch als Mitglied einer höheren Gemeinsamkeit: er hat das Gehen und das Sprechen verlernt und ist auf dem Wege, tanzend in die Lüfte emporzufliegen. Aus seinen Gebärden spricht die Verzauberung. Wie jetzt die Thiere reden, und die Erde Milch und Honig giebt, so tönt auch aus ihm etwas Uebernatürliches.")

12. Laird McLeod Easton, *The Red Count: The Life and Times of Harry Graf Kessler* (Berkeley: University of California Press, 2002), 60.

13. Easton, *The Red Count*, 60.

14. Elizabeth Aldrich, *From the Ballroom to Hell: Grace and Folly in Nineteenth-Century Dance* (Evanston: Northwestern University Press, 1991), xvii.

15. Aldrich, *From the Ballroom to Hell*, xvii.

16. Molly Engelhardt, *Dancing Out of Line: Ballrooms, Ballets, and Mobility in Victorian Fiction and Culture* (Athens: Ohio University Press, 2009), 5.

17. Engelhardt, *Dancing Out of Line*, 13.

18. Easton, *The Red Count*, 61.

19. Keith Tester, "Introduction," in *The Flâneur*, ed. Keith Tester (London: Routledge, 1994), 2.

20. Jörg Schuster, "Phantasie—Mittelbarkeit—Sinnlichkeit: Der Régnier-Aufsatz, Kesslers Diaristik und Ansätze zu einer Theorie der Wirkungsästhetik," in *Harry Graf Kessler, Das Tagebuch*, vol. 2: *1892–1897*, ed. Günter Riederer and Jörg Schuster, 59–68 (Stuttgart: Klett-Cotta 2004). Here: 65.

21. Zeynep Çelik Alexander, "Metrics of Experience: August Endell's Phenomenology of Architecture," *Grey Room* 40 (2010): 50–83.

22. Alexandra Kolb, *Performing Femininity: Dance and Literature in German Modernism* (Bern: Peter Lang, 2009), 52.

23. Kolb, *Performing Femininity*, 64.

24. My translation.

25. Harry Graf Kessler, "Henri de Régnier," in *PAN* 4 (1895): 243–49. Here: 244.

26. Kessler, "Henri de Régnier," 244. ("Seine Empfindungen, seine Triebe, seine Instinkte—so hört er—sind nicht sein individuelles Eigentum, sondern von seinen Vorfahren ererbt oder von seiner Umgebung bedingt.")

27. Kessler, "Henri de Régnier," 246.

28. Kessler, "Henri de Régnier," 247.

29. Schuster, "Phantasie—Mittelbarkeit—Sinnlichkeit," 60.

30. My translation.

31. Kessler, *Das Tagebuch*, vol. 2, *1892–1897*, 327. ("Man wollte die rohen und charakterlosen Bewegungen der Schauspieler oder die Bocksprünge des Ballets hierher und zur Kunst rechnen. Mir für meinen Teil bereitet oft die Art, wie ein Mädchen die Füsse beim Tanze setzt oder wie ein junger Offizier sein Pferd zwischen den Schenkeln hält, eine Freude, die mir in der Art keins von den orthodox sogenannten Kunstwerken gewährt oder gewähren kann. Ich finde im Ganzen solcher Bewegungen, von denen die Zeichnung z.B., selbst die japanische nur einen Augenblick, ein Fragment, bieten kann, und in ihrer Harmonie mit der Persönlichkeit eine heimliche Schönheit, einen unbewussten Stil, die mich mehr entzückt, wie alle Vollendung der festen Form.")

32. Harry Graf Kessler, *Journey to the Abyss: The Diaries of Count Harry Kessler, 1880–1918*, ed. and trans. Laird M. Easton (New York: Alfred A. Knopf, 2011), 113.

33. Kessler, *Das Tagebuch*, vol. 2: *1892–1897*, 244. ("Ich [war] zuerst als schwarz und weisser Pierrot [und habe] nachher im roten Frack mit weissen Escarpins bis um fünf Uhr getanzt. [. . .] hübsche Kostüme: Frau v. Mutzenbecher als schwarz-weisse Pierrette, die Greindl Dame Marie Antoinette, der alte Fürst Radziwill als

Beduine, Koscielski schwarzer Frack, Escarpins, rote Strümpfe u. Krawatte, die Peñalver als Zigeunerin, Loën als Pharao, Michel Königsmarck, Lafaille u Winterfeldts als Köche mit elektrisch-glühenden Nasen.")

34. Matthias Bauer, "'Berlin ist eine ausführliche Stadt': Einleitende Bemerkungen zur Berliner Stadt-, Kultur- und Mediengeschichte," in *Berlin: Medien- und Kulturgeschichte einer Hauptstadt im 20. Jahrhundert* (Tübingen: Francke Verlag, 2007), 15. ("Ein Ort, auf den sich die gemeinsame Aufmerksamkeit von Beobachtern fokussiert, weil an diesem Ort etwas Neues geschieht bzw. zur Anschauung gelangt. Von Szenen gemeinsamer Aufmerksamkeit zu reden, impliziert freilich nicht nur, dass es in der Regel mehr als einen Beobachter gibt, weil das beobachtete Geschehen in einem öffentlich zugänglichen Raum vor sich geht. Vielmehr schließt eine solche Szene die Koordination von Blicken und Gesten, Aktionen und Reaktionen ein, so dass ihr eine *performative Dimension* zukommt. Weil das, was man tut, gleichsam auf einer Bühne geschieht, wird es in dem Bewusstsein vollzogen, dass man als Handelnder—ja sogar als teilnahmsloser Zuschauer—unter Beobachtung steht. Umgekehrt wissen die Beobachter, dass sie einer Aufführung, einem Rollenspiel, einer Inszenierung beiwohnen, die über sich hinausweist, die etwas demonstriert, exemplifiziert, manifestiert.")

35. Kessler, *Das Tagebuch.* vol. 2: *1892–1897*, 103. ("Nachher mit Pachelbels nach Berlin zurückgefahren; die Pachelbel geht wieder von Rathenow aus. Sie tanzt seit 15 Jahren so oft sie kann, scheut keine Strapazen; Sucht zweifellos schöner Frauen, sich bewundern zu lassen; vielleicht, um ihren Mann durch Eifersucht festzuhalten, vielleicht auch, um sich selber immer wieder ihre Schönheit, an der sie dunkel zweifelt, durch Courmacher bestätigen zu lassen.")

36. Victoria Melita, Grand Duchess of Hesse and the Rhine, born Princess of Saxe-Coburg and Gotha, Princess of Great Britain and Ireland (1876–1936), was married to Ernst Ludwig, Grand Duke of Hesse and the Rhine, Kessler's exact contemporary and patron of the Jugendstil artists' colony at Darmstadt. In 1901 she sued him for divorce on the grounds of his homosexuality. "No stable boy was safe," she alleged. (Footnote from Easton's translation in *Journey to the Abyss*, 200.)

37. Kessler, *Das Tagebuch*, vol. 2: *1892–1897*, 119. ("Die Grossherzogin von Hessen steckte wieder pervers schön in einer goldgewirkten mit violetten Jettperlen dicht bestickten Brokatscheide; sie gleicht darin einer Bayadere. Suggestive Art, den Kopf und den Oberkörper zurückzuwerfen, wenn sie aufhört zu tanzen; dabei wirkt sie selbst in der äussersten Lascivität ihrer Bewegungen nie unvornehm. Sie ist wirklich ein bezauberndes Geschöpf.")

38. Abby Buchanan Longstreet, *Manners, Good and Bad* (New York: Kessinger, 1890), 52.

39. Francis Mason, *A Treatise on the Use and Peculiar Advantages of Dancing and Exercises, Considered as a Means of Refinement Physical Development, with General Remarks* (London: Sharp and Hale, 1854), 7.

40. A Lady of Distinction, *The Mirror of the Graces or The English Lady's Costume* (New York: B. Crosby and Company, 1813), 182.

41. Brett Farmer, "The Fabulous Sublimity of Gay Diva Worship," *Camera Obscura* 20, no. 2 (59) (2005): 165–95. Here: 170.

42. Farmer, "The Fabulous Sublimity," 170–71.

43. Gabriele Brandstetter, *Tanz Lektüren. Körperbilder und Raumfiguren der Avantgarde* (Frankfurt am Main: Fischer, 1995), 188.

44. Brandstetter, *Tanz Lektüren*, 192–95.

45. Harry Graf Kessler, "Kunst und Religion," in *Künstler und Nationen: Aufsätze und Reden 1899–1933*, ed. Cornelia Blasberg and Gerhard Schuster (Frankfurt am Main: Fischer), 27. ("Der Tanz gesellt die Innerlichkeit zu den mächtigen Empfindungen der Muskeln und Nerven des Körpers. [. . .]—der Tanzrhythmus zielt aber auch nicht auf einen bestimmten Gefühlston, wie auf den der Schönheit oder den der Freude. Sondern der Tanz hebt nur die Gefühlsfarbe, der sich die Seele am meisten zuneigt, zu Kraft und Klarheit empor und gestaltet an den Empfindungen des Körpers [. . .]. Daher kann der Tanz jede Schattierung der Persönlichkeit in sich aufnehmen und sie in mächtigem Fühlen von Takt zu Takt forttragen zu dem Unerreichbaren der Mystik und Liebe.")

46. Nietzsche, *Die Geburt der Tragödie*, III-1.26.

47. Nancy Reynolds and Malcolm McCormick, *No Fixed Points: Dance in the Twentieth Century* (New Haven: Yale University Press, 2003), 1.

48. Reynolds and McCormick, *No Fixed Points*, 2.

49. Reynolds and McCormick, *No Fixed Points*, 77. Although Isadora Duncan's dances and philosophy permeated German intellectual and artistic circles, Kessler did not hold her performances in nearly the same regard as those of Fuller and St. Denis. Accordingly, I will not focus on Duncan's dances.

50. Kessler, *Das Tagebuch*, vol. 3: *1897–1905*, 105.

51. While a kesa could be referring to a Buddhist robe, it does not make much sense in this context. However, it could also be referring to another performance role similar to or in line with a geisha.

52. Kessler, *Das Tagebuch*, vol. 3: *1897–1905*, 448. ("Abends mit VandeVelde Sada Yacco und Loie Fuller sehen. VandeVelde sagte sehr richtig von der Loie Fuller: C'est là la réalization de tout ce que nous avons cherché avec le Néo Impressionisme. Im Zusammenhang mit der kleinen Handlung, die dem einen Tanz zu grunde liegt (Verbrennen der Frau im Sonnenlicht): Je voudrais bien savoir si c'est là la fin ou le commencement d'un Art. En somme, c'est complet, et cependant il me semble qu'il y aurait encore la possibilité de developper ça. Die Sado Yacco spielte die Gesha und Kesa wieder mit aller Zartheit und Übergewalt ihrer Kunst.")

53. Gottfried Boehm, "Cold Fire: Figures and Landscape in Georges Seurat," in *Georges Seurat—Figur im Raum*, ed. Zürcher Kunstgesellschaft and Kunsthaus Zürich, 84–95 (Ostfildern, Germany: Hatje Cantz, 2009). Here: 89.

54. Easton, *The Red Count*, 91.

55. Ruth St. Denis, *An Unfinished Life* (New York: Harper and Bros., 1939), 40.

56. Shelley Berg, "Sada Yacco: The American Tour, 1899–1900," *Dance Chronicle* 16 (1993): 147–96. Here: 148.

57. Kristine Somerville, "The Logic of Dreams: The Life and Work of Ruth St. Denis," *Missouri Review* 36, no. 4 (2013): 123–41. Here: 126–27.

58. Jane Desmond, "Dancing Out the Difference: Cultural Imperialism and

Ruth St. Deni's 'Radha' of 1906," *Signs: Journal of Women in Culture and Society* 17, no. 1 (1991): 28–49. Here: 38.

59. Freny Mistry, "On Hofmannsthal's 'Die unvergleichliche Tänzerin,'" *Modern Austrian Literature* 10, no. 1 (1977): 32.

60. Uttara Asha Coorlawala, "Ruth St. Denis and India's Dance Renaissance," *Dance Chronicle* 15, no. 2 (1992): 123–52. Here:144.

61. Edward Said, *Orientalism* (New York: Random House, 1978).

62. Desmond, "Dancing Out the Difference," 35.

63. At the time Kessler met her, she was on a three-year tour of Europe, performing as a solo dancer in dances inspired by India, such as *Radha*. In her memoir she wrote of being taken to see "all the wonders of modern artistic Berlin." Her guide to many of these was Kessler: "I found Count Kessler a delightful companion. I knew him by reputation as a charming patron of the arts, a delightful ambassador who spoke English like an Oxford man and had a genius for bringing people together for their mutual benefit" (Easton, *Journey to the Abyss*, 381).

64. Trans. Easton, *Journey into the Abyss*, 381. ("Über die St. Denis, die ich Sonntagabend mit Schröder gesehen habe, an Hofmannsthal geschrieben: ich habe sie jetzt wieder in einer ihrer wirklich grossen Sachen gesehen und davon den stärksten Eindruck gehabt, den mir der Tanz als Kunst überhaupt gemacht hat. Ein indischer Tempeltanz, ganz nackt, aber doch in einem märchenhaften Kleid aus schwarzem Goldgeschmeide. Wie sich hier die Linien des Nackten mit dem Faltenwurf und seiner schweren Grazie vereinigen, so dass bald das Gewand und bald der Mädchenkörper zu verschwinden scheint, und doch beide immer in ihrer ganzen Fülle von Reichtum und Anmut zusammenwirken, ist wirklich Bayaderenhaft, die Wesenheit der Bayadere, in der bloss die beiden Pole: Tierschönheit und Mystik, ohne jede Zwischen-Skala geistiger oder sentimentaler Töne, vorhanden sind, geschlechtslose Gottheit und blos-geschlechtliches Weib, der Kontrast die Wirkung Beider in höchster Potenz und in Eins auslösend.") Harry Graf Kessler, *Das Tagebuch*, vol. 4: *1906–1914*, ed. Jörg Schuster (Stuttgart: Klett-Cotta-Verlag, 2005), 192.

65. Kent G. Drummond, "The Queering of *Swan Lake*: A New Male Gaze for the Performance of Sexual Desire," *Journal of Homosexuality* 23, nos. 2–4 (2003): 235–55.

66. Kessler, *Das Tagebuch*, vol. 4: *1906–1914*, 204. ("Im Lyceum Club bei Miss Smedley mit der Ruth St. Denis soupiert. Sie ist auch in Gesellschaftstoilette eine sehr auffallende Erscheinung: ein sehr kleiner Kopf auf einem sehr langen schlanken Körper, der wie eine Gerte biegsam und aufrecht ist. Aber über dem noch ganz jungen Gesicht, das kaum sechs- oder siebenundzwanzig scheint, fast graues Haar. Sie sagt ernste, tiefe Dinge und daneben plötzlich kindliche Naïvitäten. Sie sagt, ihr Wunsch wäre, in ihrem Theater schon die Türsteher indisch zu kostümieren, damit der Zuschauer gleich vom Eintritt an in die Stimmung käme; und sie sagt, dass die Wiederholung, die fortgesetzte, monotone Wiederholung die Macht und der Zauber der orientalischen Kunst sei, die geduldige, einlullende Wiederholung bis der Zuschauer wie hypnotisiert sich selbst vergisst und seine Seele ganz in die Seele des Kunstwerks hingiebt.")

67. Kessler, *Das Tagebuch*, vol. 4: *1906–1914*, 246.

68. Trans. Easton, *Journey into the Abyss*, 385–86. ("Über ihre Kunst spricht sie sehr klar und detailliert. [. . .] beim Erfinden eines neuen Tanzes müsse sie für die Einzelheiten immer auf eine Art Inspiration warten. ['I am often very long over one thing, till I find exactly what I have in mind, I was two years over Radhu; because the moment you cut away from tradition, you have to be all yourself, or else you're a hybrid, you're nothing'].") Kessler, *Das Tagebuch*, vol. 4: *1906–1914*, 204.

69. Trans. Easton, *Journey into the Abyss*, 386. ("Mit Gerhard Hauptmanns u. Ludwig von Hofmanns in die Matinee der Ruth St. Denis im Theater des Westens. Der Moment, wo sie aus der Lotosblüte aufwacht und aufsteht, ist wie ein Frühling; ich habe nie eine Kunst gesehen, die so vollkommen wie ihre Bewegungen in diesem Augenblick Dasselbe ausstrahlt wie junge Blüten, zartes Grün und der frische, reine Himmel im April. Sie ist die erste grosse Tänzerin, ein Genie der Bewegung.") Kessler, *Das Tagebuch*, vol. 4: *1906–1914*, 205.

70. Trans. Easton, *Journey into the Abyss*, 386.

71. Trans. Easton, *Journey into the Abyss*, 386.

72. Trans. Easton, *Journey into the Abyss*, 386.

73. My translation. ("Sexuelle Erregung und Kunstgenuss analoge Zustände, die sich ablösen; Kunstschaffen der Übergang zwischen Beiden, indem ein gleichwertiger Zustand zum Ersatz gesucht wird."). Kessler, *Das Tagebuch*, vol. 4: *1906–1914*, 205.

74. Karl Schlögel, *Im Raume lesen wir die Zeit: Über Zivilisationsgeschichte und Geopolitik* (Munich: Carl Hanser, 2003), 419.

75. My translation. ("Im Theater des Westens beginnt heute das erste Gastspiel des großen russischen Ballets um 8 Uhr. Das außergewöhliche an diesem Ensemble ist, daß der Star der Truppe ein Mann ist, ein kaum 20 jähriger junger Mensch, namens Nijinski, der hervorragenste Tänzer nicht nur der russischen Theater, sondern sicher auch einer der merkwürdigsten und interessantesten Tanzkünstler der Gegenwart. An Leichtigkeit, Ausdrucksfähigkeit, Elastizität nimmt es keine der gefeierten Primaballerinen Petersburgs und Moskaus mit Nijinski auf.") Gunhild Oberzaucher-Schüller, "Interlude classique: Sergei Diaghilew im Kaiserlichen Berlin," in *Spiegelungen: Die Ballets Russes und die Künste*, ed. Claudia Jeschke, Ursel Berger, and Birgit Zeidler, 93–104 (Berlin: Vorwerk 8, 1997). Here: 96.

76. Alex Ross, "Diary of an Aesthete. Count Harry Kessler Met Everyone and Saw Everything," review of *Journey to the Abyss: The Diaries of Count Harry Kessler, 1880–1918*, trans. and ed. Laird Easton, *The New Yorker*, April 23, 2012, http://www.newyorker.com/magazine/2012/04/23/diary-of-an-aesthete

77. John Derbyshire, "Slim Pickings," review of *Berlin in Lights: The Diaries of Count Harry Kessler, 1918–1937*, trans. and ed. Laird Easton, *New Criterion*, November 2000. http://www.newcriterion.com/articles.cfm/kessler-derbyshire-2319

78. Ramsay Burt, *The Male Dancer: Bodies, Spectacle, Sexualities* (London: Routledge, 1995), 79.

79. Trans. by Easton, 587. ("Ich kam letzten Samstag früh aus Berlin an und habe seit dem Abend dieses Samstag eigentlich mit Niemand anderem existiert

als mit Diaghilew und Nijinsky, Abends im Theater, frühstückend mit ihnen, sitzend und redend vom Frühstück bis wieder zum Theater—und Nachts schlecht schlafend aber vergnügt—Ballete für sie dichtend, von denen nur 2, ein tragisches, antikes und ein macabres, in diesem Hotelzimmer und an Nijinskys Krankenbett so weit gebracht wurden, dass mir fast vorkommt, als seien sie auch schon komponiert und sceniert und als könne nun garnichts Schöneres mehr kommen. Das tragische Sujet ist Orestes und die Furien, ein Ballett von 35 Minuten. Der Entwurf geht heute an Strauss, der es komponieren soll. [. . .] Das schliesst natürlich gar und ganz nicht aus, Harry, dass wir ein drittes machen.") Kessler, *Das Tagebuch*, vol. 4: *1906–1914*, 800.

80. Schuster, "Phantasie—Mittelbarkeit—Sinnlichkeit," 64.

81. Kessler, *Das Tagebuch*, vol. 4: *1906–1914*, 826.

82. Farfan, *Performing Queer Modernism*, 42.

83. My translation. ("Nach einem Vorspiel aus 'Daphnis et Chloé‹ von Ravel kam Nijinsky's' 'Après-midi-d'un Faune' zur Vorführung: archaïsch stilisierte Gebärden, die Debussy's Musik begleiten; Nijinsky moduliert so herb mit seinem jungen Körper die halb tierisch halb sentimentale Begierde, dass sie fast tragisch wirkt; man tut, halb erschrocken halb entzückt, einen Blick in den faunischen Ursprung der Tragödie. Die Wucht von Nijinsky's Leistung erdrückt allerdings die zarte komplizierte Debussysche Musik, und Baksts kitschige Decoration stört; aber trotz dieser Disharmonie bleibt der Eindruck einer Art von Wiederauferstehung antiken Heidentums.") Kessler, *Das Tagebuch*, vol. 4: *1906–1914*, 830.

84. My translation ("Russisches Ballet. Erste Aufführung des Après-midi-d'un Faune hier. Ganz Berlin dort. [. . .] Stürmischer Erfolg des Faun, der wiederholt werden musste. Nur [Oskar] Bie drehte sich herum und flüsterte: 'Daran finde ich Nichts.' Ich fast noch mehr als in Paris ergriffen. Der Faun: das Tier, das den Menschen ahnt, das ahnt, was es heisst, Mensch zu sein, ein Tier das vergleicht, das sich und die anderen vergleicht, erstes Aufflammen der Reflexion und damit der Tragik und auch der Komik; aber die Tragik überwiegend. Man meint, in allen Bewegungen von Nijinski zu fühlen, dass es ein Tier ist, das sich seiner Nacktheit schämt (Sündenfall). Äusserste Konzentration des Ausdrucks; eine solche Gewalt in der Sparsamkeit der Mittel erreicht nur das Genie.") Kessler, *Das Tagebuch*, vol. 4: *1906–1914*, 861–62.

85. Burt, *The Male Dancer*, 84.

86. Hanna Järvinen, "Dancing without Space—On Nijinsky's 'L'Après-midi d'un Faune' (1912)," *Dance Research: The Journal of the Society for Dance Research* 27, no. 1 (2009): 28–64. Here: 53.

87. Lucia Ruprecht, "Der Virtuose geht. Waslaw Nijinskys *L'Après-midi d'un faune*," *Arcadia: International Journal for Literary Studies* 43, no. 2 (2008): 235–56. Here: 242.

88. Gabriele Brandstetter, "Ritual as Scene and Discourse: Art and Science Around 1900 as Exemplified by 'Le Sacre du printemps,'" *World of Music* 40, no. 1 (1998): 37–59. Here: 41.

89. Lucia Ruprecht, *Gestural Imaginaries: Dance and Cultural Theory in the Early Twentieth Century* (Oxford: Oxford University Press, 2019), 2.

90. Kessler wrote "Delacroix" and then crossed it out.

91. Trans. Easton, *Journey to the Abyss*, 619. ("Abends 'Sacre du Printemps' Premiere. Eine ganz neue Choreographie und Musik; Nijinskis Tanzstil so verschieden von Fokines wie Gauguins Malerei von. Eine durchaus Neue Vision, etwas Niegesehenes, Packendes, Überzeugendes ist plötzlich da, eine neue Art von Wildheit in Unkunst und zugleich in Kunst: alle Form verwüstet, neue plötzlich aus dem Chaos auftauchend. Das Publikum, das glänzendste Haus, das ich in Paris je gesehen habe, Aristokratie, Diplomaten, Halbwelt, war von Anfang an unruhig lachte, zischelte, machte Witze; hier und dort standen Einige auf. Strawinski, der mit seiner Frau hinter uns sass, raste nach kaum fünf Minuten wie ein Besessener hinaus. Plötzlich rief aus der Galerie eine Stentorstimme: 'Allons, les grues du Seizieme (das 16te Arrondissement, das der eleganten Welt), allez vous bientôt nous ficher la paix?' Die Antwort kam aus einer Loge 'Les voilà ceux qui sont murs pour l'annexion.' Im selben Augenblick bekamen in Astrucs Loge d'Annunzio und Debussy Krakehl mit den Herren der Nebenloge, denen sie ins Gesicht schrieen: 'Tas d'imbéciles.' Jetzt wurde der Lärm allgemein. [. . .] Und über diesen Höllenlärm giengen immerfort wie Sturmwetter Lachsalven und gegnerisches Klatschen, während die Musik wütete und auf der Bühne die Tänzer unentwegt und emsig prähistorisch tanzten. Am Schluss der Vorstellung schlug Welt und Halbwelt aufs Haupt, ehe frenetischer Beifall siegte, so dass sich Strawinski und Nijinski zeigen und immer wieder verbeugen konnten.") Kessler, *Das Tagebuch*, vol. 4: *1906–1914*, 886.

92. Kessler, "Die Entstehung der Josephs-Legende," in *Künstler und Nationen: Aufsätze und Reden 1899–1933* (Munich: Fischer, 1988), 277–84. Here: 277.

93. Kessler, "Die Entstehung der Josephs-Legende," 278.

94. Kessler, *Das Tagebuch*, vol. 4: *1906–1914*, 850.

95. Kessler, *Das Tagebuch*, vol. 4: *1906–1914*, 868.

96. My translation. ("Vor dem Frühstück Lady Ripon zu ihrer Beruhigung einen Teil des Joseph vorgelesen. Sie ist seit Monaten in einer nervösen Aufregung wegen des Sujets, weil Joseph eine 'komische Figur' sei und sie fürchtet, Nijinsky könne lächerlich werden. Sie sagte mir nachher, sie sei beruhigt; die Figur sei ganz neu gemacht und könne nicht schockieren.") Kessler, *Das Tagebuch*, vol. 4: *1906–1914*, 868.

97. Harry Graf Kessler, "Die Handlung der Josephs-Legende," in *Künstler und Nationen: Aufsätze und Reden 1899–1933* (Munich: Fischer, 1988), 180.

98. Kessler, "Die Handlung," 181.

99. Kessler, "Die Handlung," 181.

100. Easton, *The Red Count*, 205.

101. Easton, *The Red Count*, 205.

102. Kessler, *Journey to the Abyss*, trans. Easton 129.

103. Trans. Easton 608. ("Joseph [sei] ein Träumer [. . .], die Atmosphäre des Magischen [. . .] müsse den ganzen Schluss einhüllen vom Moment der Nacktheit Josephs an. Dieser Moment der Enthüllung Josephs müsse der Höhepunkt des Werkes für Auge und Ohr sein, ein allerstärkster Effekt und Umschwung in der Stimmung. . . .") Kessler, *Das Tagebuch*, vol. 4: *1906–1914*, 853.

104. My translation.

105. Kessler, "Henri de Régnier," 244.

106. Easton, *The Red Count*, 205.

107. Kessler, *Das Tagebuch*, vol. 4: *1906–1914*, 868.

108. Schuster, "'Sehr hohe Absichten der Mimik,'" 66.

109. My translation. Schuster, "'Sehr hohe Absichten der Mimik,'" 67. ("Sehr schön namentlich das Innerliche, die Macht religiöser Extase. Er ist das genauer Gegenteil von Nij; ganz Innigkeit wie ein russisches Volkslied Nichts von Nijinskis Glanz und übermenschlicher Kraft. Er packt aber durch die Tiefe der Empfindung.")

110. Cited by Prost-Romand: "La Légende de Joseph," 544, in Schuster, "'Sehr hohe Absichten der Mimik,'" 68.

111. Schuster, "'Sehr hohe Absichten der Mimik,'" 66.

112. My translation. Schuster, "'Sehr hohe Absichten der Mimik,'" 70. ("Die *Josephslegende* ist ein später Repräsentant des Fin de Siècle mit seiner widersprüchlichen Mischung aus Historismus, Eklektizismus und einzelnen Momenten der Modernität, wie sie etwa im ekstatischen Ausdruckstanz Josephs verwirklicht wird.")

113. Drummond draws from Laura Mulvey's theory of the male gaze and applies it to a new male gaze that queers Matthew Bourne's *Swan Lake* (1995).

114. Burt, *The Male Dancer*, 79.

115. Burt, *The Male Dancer*, 86.

116. Farfan, *Performing Queer Modernism*, 2–3.

117. Kessler, "Henri de Régnier," 246.

118. Harry Kessler and Charles Kessler, *Berlin in Lights: The Diaries of Count Harry Kessler, 1918–1937* (New York: Grove Press, 2000). Here: 279.

119. Kessler and Kessler, *Berlin in Lights*, 280.

Chapter 4

1. Rainer Maria Rilke, *The Notebooks of Malte Laurids Brigge* (hereafter cited as *MLB*/Hulse), trans. Michael Hulse (London: Penguin Classics, 2009), 44. "Jetzt kam ein Straßenübergang, und da geschah es, daß der Mann vor mir mit ungleichen Beinen die Stufen des Gangsteigs hinunterhüpfte. . . . Auf den jenseitigen Gangsteig kam er einfach mit einem langen Schritt hinauf. Aber kaum war er oben, zog er das eine Bein ein wenig an und hüpfte und auf dem anderen einmal hoch und gleich darauf wieder und wieder." Rainer Maria Rilke, *Die Aufzeichnungen des Malte Laurids Brigge*, in *Werke. Kommentierte Ausgabe in vier Bänden. Prosa und Dramen*, vol. 3 (hereafter cited as *MLB*), eds. Manfred Engel, Ulrich Fülleborn, Horst Nalewski, and August Stahl (Frankfurt am Main: Insel Verlag, 1996), 501.

2. Eric Santner, *The Royal Remains: The People's Two Bodies and the Endgames of Sovereignty* (Chicago: University of Chicago Press, 2012), 193.

3. See, for example, Santner's *The Royal Remains* and Michael Cowan, *Cult of

the Will: Nervousness and German Modernity (University Park: Pennsylvania State University Press, 2008).

4. See, for example, Andreas Kramer, "Rilke and Modernism," in *The Cambridge Companion to Rilke*, ed. Karen Leeder and Robert Vilain (Cambridge: Cambridge University Press, 2010), 119–20.

5. Susan Manning and Melissa Benson, "Interrupted Continuities: Modern Dance in Germany," *TDR: The Drama Review* 30, no. 2 (1986): 31.

6. Lucia Ruprecht, "Ambivalent Agency: Gestural Performances of Hands in Weimar Dance and Film," *Seminar* 46, no. 3 (2010): 257.

7. Keith Tester, "Introduction," *The Flâneur*, ed. Keith Tester (London: Routledge, 1994), 2.

8. Giorgio Agamben, "Notes on Gesture," in *Means without End: Notes on Politics*, trans. Vincenzo Binetti and Cesare Casarino (Minneapolis: University of Minnesota Press, 2000), 49.

9. Andrew Hewitt, *Social Choreography: Ideology as Performance in Dance and Everyday Movement* (Durham: Duke University Press, 2005), 83–84.

10. Georg Simmel, "Die Großstädte und das Geistesleben," in *Die Berliner Moderne 1885–1914*, ed. Jürgen Schutte and Peter Sprengel (Stuttgart: Reclam, 1987), 125.

11. Georg Simmel, "Die Großstädte und das Geistesleben," 125.

12. Harald Neumeyer, *Der Flaneur: Konzeptionen der Moderne* (Würzburg: Königshausen & Neumann, 1999), 235.

13. Frisby, "The Flâneur in Social Theory," 83.

14. Kélina Gotman, *Choreomania: Dance and Disorder* (Oxford: Oxford University Press, 2018), 73.

15. Gotman, *Choreomania*, 71 and 77.

16. Gotman, *Choreomania*, 76.

17. Gotman, *Choreomania*, 72.

18. Hewitt, *Social Choreography*, 3.

19. Hewitt, *Social Choreography*, 19.

20. Hewitt, *Social Choreography*, 80.

21. Agamben, "Notes on Gesture," 49.

22. Hewitt, *Social Choreography*, 82.

23. Hewitt, *Social Choreography*, 83–84.

24. Felicia McCarren, *Dance Pathologies: Performance, Poetics, Medicine* (Stanford: Stanford University Press, 1998), 33–34.

25. Stefan Zweig, *The World of Yesterday: An Autobiography* (London: Cassell and Company, 1943), 114–15.

26. Zweig, *The World of Yesterday*, 115.

27. Zweig, *The World of Yesterday*, 117.

28. Stephanie Harris, "Exposures: Rilke, Photography, and the City," *New German Critique* 33, no. 3 (2006): 121–49. Here: 121.

29. Michael Pleister, *Das Bild der Großstadt in den Dichtungen Robert Walsers, Rainer Maria Rilke, Stefan Georges und Hugo von Hofmannsthals* (Hamburg: Helmut Kuske, 1990).

30. My translation. "Der Anspruch, den diese Stadt an einen macht, ist uner-meßlich und ununterbrochen. (Ich verdanke ihr das Beste, was ich bis jetzt kann.) Deshalb hilft sie einem nicht gleich und unmittelbar bei künstlerischer Betäti-gung, sie wirkt gleichsam nicht zuerst auf die Arbeit ein, die man tut,—aber sie verwandelt, steigert und entwickelt einen fortwährend, sie nimmt einem leise die Werkzeuge aus der Hand, die man bisher benutzte, und ersetzt sie durch andere, unsäglich feinere und präzisere und tut tausend unerwartete Dinge mit einem, wie eine Fee, die Lust daran hat, ein Wesen alle Gestalten annehmen zu sehen, deren Möglichkeiten in ihm verborgen sind. Man muß Paris, wenn man es zum ersten-mal um sich hat, mehr wie ein Bad wirken lassen, ohne selbst zuviel dabei tun zu wollen: als zu fühlen und es sich geschehen zu lassen." Rainer Maria Rilke, *Briefe*, Bd. 3, S. 183–29.03.1907 to Tora Holmström.

31. "in dem der Reiz zu tausen[d] Tänzen lag." Rainer Maria Rilke, *Briefe aus den Jahren 1902 bis 1906*, ed. Ruth Sieber-Rilke and Carl Sieber (Leipzig: Insel Verlag, 1930), 106. All translations from Rilke's letters are my own.

32. My translation. "Gestern war die Taufe von Zuloagas Sohn. Ich hatte keine Zeit, in die Kirche zu gehen, war aber hernach für eine Weile in seinem neuen Atelier, Montmartre, unter dreißig oder vierzig mir völlig fremden Menschen (von Cottet kannte ich wenigstens Nase und Bart, konnte aber, da er selbst dabei war, mit denen allein nicht sprechen). Man sang und tanzte. Eine Spanierin, deren Wesen es war zu singen, sang sehr schön, im Rhythmus spanischen Bluts, die Carmen und spanische Lieder; eine Gitane, mit dem gewissen schwarz-bunten Tuch, tanzte spanische Tänze. Es war ziemlich viel vom Klima in dem mittelgroßen Atelier, in dem man sich drängte. (Aber die eng von Zuschauern umstandene Tänzerin Goyas war mehr.) Zuloaga war lieb und schön, mit seinem Stolz und seinem aufglänzen-den Lächeln . . ." Rilke, *Briefe aus den Jahren 1902 bis 1906*, 316–17.

33. Gabriele Brandstetter, *Poetics of Dance: Body, Image, and Space in the His-torical Avant-Gardes* (Oxford: Oxford University Press, 2015), 64. "Die Wahl des Museums als Tanz-Bühne erfolgt dabei unter zwei Gesichtspunkten: Der eine steht im Zusammenhang mit der für die Theater- und Tanzreform der Jahrhun-dertwende aktuellen Frage des Aufführungsortes: der Suche nach anderen, von der Tradition des Illusionstheaters des 19. Jahrhunderts unbelasteten Theaterbauten und Bühnenformen. Nicht nur antike Amphitheater, Festspielstätten, Rundbauten und alle Formexperimente avantgardistischer Theaterarchitektur bezeugen dieses Streben nach einem Wandel der Institution. Auch für den Tanz besitzt die Ero-berung neuer Aufführungsräume eine vergleichbare Bedeutung. Neben Konzert-bühnen und Tonhallen, Künstlerhäusern und Park-Terrassen werden Galerien und Museumssäle zur Bühne der modernen Bewegungsdarstellung." Gabriele Brand-stetter, *Tanz-Lektüren. Körperbilder und Raumfiguren der Avantgarde* (Frankfurt am Main: Fischer, 1995), 83.

34. Rainer Maria Rilke. *Translations from the Poetry of Rainer Maria Rilke*, trans. M. D. Hrefer (New York: Norton, 1962), 177.

Wie in der Hand ein Schwefelzündholz, weiß,
eh es zu Flamme kommt, nach allen Seiten
zuckende Zungen streckt -: beginnt im Kreis
naher Beschauer hastig, hell und heiß
ihr runder Tanz sich zuckend auszubreiten.
Und plötzlich ist er Flamme, ganz und gar.
Mit einem Blick entzündet sie ihr Haar
und dreht auf einmal mit gewagter Kunst
ihr ganzes Kleid in diese Feuersbrunst,
aus welcher sich, wie Schlangen die erschrecken,
die nackten Arme wach und klappernd strecken.
Und dann: als würde ihr das Feuer knapp,
nimmt sie es ganz zusamm und wirft es ab
sehr herrisch, mit hochmütiger Gebärde
und schaut: da liegt es rasend auf der Erde
immer und ergibt sich nicht -.
Doch sieghaft, sicher und mit einem süßen
grüßenden Lächeln hebt sie ihr Gesicht
und stampft es aus mit kleinen festen Füßen.
(Rainer Maria Rilke, "Spanische Tänzerin," in *Sämtliche Werke*,
Bd. I [Wiesbaden: Insel, 1955], 531)

35. Brandstetter, *Poetics of Dance*, 232. ("Rilkes Gedicht bietet darüber hinaus eine Exposition der wichtigsten Themenbereiche, die für den Tanz und für Tanz-Texte von Bedeutung sind: die Dramaturgie eines Tanzes in Sukzession und Steigerung von Bewegungselementen; den Gegensatz von beherrschter und entfesselter Gebärde, von Disziplin und Ekstase des Tanzes als Modell von Selbstfindung und Selbstverlust des Individuums; die Dualität von Natur und Kultur, von Bewegung und Stilstand, von Augenblick und Dauer im transitorischen Prozeß der Zeichensetzung und Zeichenlöschung.") Brandstetter, *Tanz-Lektüren*, 283.

36. Rilke, *MLB*/Hulse, 42. "Heute habe ich es nicht erwartet, ich bin so mutig ausgegangen, als wäre das das Natürlichste und Einfachste. Und doch, es war wieder etwas da, das mich nahm wie Papier, mich zusammenknüllte und fortwarf, es war etwas Unerhörtes da." Rilke, *MLB*, 499.

37. Rilke, *MLB*/Hulse, 42–43. "Der Boulevard St-Michel war leer und weit, und es ging sich leicht auf seiner leisen Neigung. Fensterflügel oben öffneten sich mit gläsernem Aufklang, und ihr Glänzen flog wie ein weißer Vogel über die Straße. Ein Wagen mit hellroten Rädern kam vorüber, und weiter unten trug jemand etwas Lichtgrünes. Pferde liefen in blinkernden Geschirren auf dem dunkelgespritzten Fahrdamm, der rein war. Der Wind war erregt, neu, mild, und alles stieg auf: Gerüche, Rufe, Glocken." Rilke, *MLB*, 500.

38. Susan Leigh Foster, *Reading Dancing. Bodies and Subjects in Contemporary American Dance* (Berkeley: University of California Press, 1986), 60.

39. Foster, *Reading Dancing*, 60.

40. Foster, *Reading Dancing*, 61.

41. Matthias Bauer, "'Berlin ist eine ausführliche Stadt': Einleitende Bemerkungen zur Berliner Stadt-, Kultur- und Mediengeschichte," in *Berlin: Medien- und Kulturgeschichte einer Hauptstadt im 20. Jahrhundert* (Tübingen: Francke Verlag, 2007), 15.

42. Rilke, *MLB*/Hulse, 43. "Glattgekämmte Kellner waren dabei, vor der Türe zu scheuern. . . . Der Kellner, der ganz rot im Gesicht war, schaute eine Weile scharf hin, dann verbreitete sich ein Lachen auf seinen bartlosen Wangen, als wäre es darauf verschüttet worden. Er winkte den anderen Kellnern, drehte das lachende Gesicht ein paarmal schnell von rechts nach links, um alle herbeizurufen und selbst nichts zu versäumen. Nun standen alle und blickten hinuntersehend oder suchend, lächelnd oder ärgerlich, daß sie noch nicht entdeckt hatten, was Lächerliches es gäbe." Rilke, *MLB*, 500.

43. Rilke, *MLB*/Hulse, 43–44. "Ich erwartete, sobald mein Auge Raum hatte, irgendeine ungewöhnliche und auffallende Figur zu sehen, aber es zeigte sich, daß vor mir niemand ging als ein großer, hagerer Mann in einem dunklen Überzieher und mit einem weichen schwarzen Hut auf dem kurzen fahlblonden Haar. Ich vergewisserte mich, daß weder an der Kleidung noch in dem Benehmen dieses Mannes etwas Lächerliches sei, und versuchte schon, an ihm vorüber den Boulevard hinunterzuschauen, als er über irgend etwas stolperte. Da ich nahe hinter ihm folgte, nahm ich mich in acht, aber als die Stelle kam, war da nichts, rein nichts. Wir gingen beide weiter, er und ich, der Abstand zwischen uns blieb derselbe." Rilke, *MLB*, 501.

44. Hewitt, *Social Choreography*, 89.

45. Rilke, *MLB*/Hulse, 44. "Jetzt kam ein Straßenübergang, und da geschah es, daß der Mann vor mir mit ungleichen Beinen die Stufen des Gangsteigs hinunterhüpfte in der Art etwa, wie Kinder manchmal während des Gehens aufhüpfen oder springen, wenn sie sich freuen. Auf den jenseitigen Gangsteig kam er einfach mit einem langen Schritt hinauf. Aber kaum war er oben, zog er das eine Bein ein wenig an und hüpfte und auf dem anderen einmal hoch und gleich darauf wieder und wieder. Jetzt konnte man diese plötzliche Bewegung wieder ganz gut für ein Stolpern halten, wenn man sich einredete, es wäre da eine Kleinigkeit gewesen, ein Kern, die glitschige Schale einer Frucht, irgend etwas; und das Seltsame war, daß der Mann selbst an das Vorhandensein eines Hindernisses zu glauben schien, denn er sah sich jedesmal mit jenem halb ärgerlichen, halb vorwurfsvollen Blick, den die Leute in solchen Augenblicken haben, nach der lästigen Stelle um." Rilke, *MLB*, 501.

46. Cowan, *Cult of the Will*, 10–11.

47. Eric L. Santner, *On Creaturely Life: Rilke, Benjamin, Sebald* (Chicago: University of Chicago Press, 2006), xvii.

48. Rilke, *MLB*/Hulse, 44. "Der Kragen seines Überziehers hatte sich aufgestellt; und wie er sich auch, bald mit einer Hand, bald mit beiden umständlich bemühte, ihn niederzulegen, es wollte nicht gelingen. Das kam vor. Es beunruhigte mich nicht. Aber gleich darauf gewahrte ich mit grenzenloser Verwunderung, daß in den beschäftigten Händen dieses Menschen zwei Bewegungen waren: eine heimliche, rasche, mit welcher er den Kragen unmerklich hochklappte, und jene

andere ausführliche, anhaltende, gleichsam übertrieben buchstabierte Bewegung, die das Umlegen des Kragens bewerkstelligen sollte. Diese Beobachtung verwirrte mich so sehr, daß zwei Minuten vergingen, ehe ich erkannte, daß, im Halse des Mannes, hinter dem hochgeschobenen Überzieher und den nervös agierenden Händen dasselbe schreckliche, zweisilbige Hüpfen war, das seine Beine eben verlassen hatte. Von diesem Augenblick an war ich an ihn gebunden." Rilke, *MLB*, 501–2.

49. Santner, *The Royal Remains*, 194.

50. Rilke, *MLB*/Hulse, 44–45. "Ich begriff, daß dieses Hüpfen in seinem Körper herumirrte, daß es versuchte, hier und da auszubrechen. Ich verstand seine Angst vor den Leuten, und ich begann selber vorsichtig zu prüfen, ob die Vorrübergehenden etwas merkten. Ein kalter Stich fuhr mir durch den Rücken, als seine Beine plötzlich einen kleinen, zuckenden Sprung machten, aber niemand hatte es gesehen, und ich dachte mir aus, daß auch ich ein wenig stolpern wollte, im Falle jemand aufmerksam wurde." Rilke, *MLB*, 502.

51. Rochelle Tobias, "Rilke's Landscape of the Heart: On *The Notebooks of Malte Laurids Brigge*," *Modernism/modernity* 20, no. 4 (2013): 669–70.

52. Tobias, "Rilke's Landscape," 676.

53. Rilke, *MLB*/Hulse, 45. "Der eine, wirklich sichtbare Sprung war so geschickt angebracht . . . , daß nichts zu befürchten war. Ja, noch ging alles gut; von Zeit zu Zeit griff auch die zweite Hand an den Stock und preßte ihn fester an, und die Gefahr war gleich wieder überstanden. Ich konnte nichts dagegen tun, daß meine Angst dennoch wuchs. . . . Ich wußte, daß, während er ging und mit unendlicher Anstrengung versuchte, gleichgültig und zerstreut auszusehen, das furchtbare Zucken in seinem Körper sich anhäufte; auch in mir war die Angst, mit der er es wachsen und wachsen fühlte, und ich sah wie er sich an den Stock klammerte." Rilke, *MLB*, 503.

54. Cowan, *Cult of the Will*, 2.

55. Rilke, *MLB*/Hulse, 46. "Auf der Place St-Michel waren viele Fahrzeuge und hin und her eilende Leute, wir waren oft zwischen zwei Wagen . . . so betraten wir die Brücke, und es ging. Es ging. Nun kam etwas Unsicheres in den Gang, nun lief er zwei Schritte, und nun stand er. Stand. Die linke Hand löste sich leise vom Stock ab und hob sich so langsam empor, daß ich sie vor der Luft zittern sah; er schob den Hut ein wenig zurück und strich sich über die Stirn. Er wandte ein wenig den Kopf, und sein Blick schwankte über Himmel, Häuser und Wasser hin, ohne zu fassen, und dann gab er nach. Der Stock war fort, er spannte die Arme aus, als ob er auffliegen wollte, und es brach aus ihm wie eine Naturkraft und bog ihn vor und riß ihn zurück und ließ ihn nicken und neigen und schleuderte Tanzkraft aus ihm heraus unter die Menge. Denn schon waren viele Leute um ihn, und ich sah ihn nicht mehr." Rilke, *MLB*, 503–4.

56. Rilke's unusual formulation aims at rendering his progressive understanding of the aesthetic, dancing body into a language that could accurately describe this movement phenomenon.

57. Rilke, *MLB*/Hulse, 43. "Ich fühlte, daß ein wenig Angst in mir anfing.

Etwas drängte mich auf die andere Seite hinüber; aber ich begann nur schneller zu gehen." Rilke, *MLB*, 500.

58. Rilke, *MLB*/Hulse, 44. "Von diesem Augenblick an war ich an ihn gebunden." Rilke, *MLB*, 502.

59. Rilke, *MLB*/Hulse, 44. "kalter Stich," Rilke, *MLB*, 502.

60. Santner, *The Royal Remains*, 195.

61. Susan Foster, "Movement's Contagion: The Kinesthetic Impact of Performance," in *The Cambridge Companion to Performance Studies*, ed. Tracy C. Davis (Cambridge: Cambridge University Press, 2008), 57.

62. My translation. "Der Anspruch, den diese Stadt an einen macht, ist unermeßlich und ununterbrochen. (Ich verdanke ihr das Beste, was ich bis jetzt kann.) Deshalb hilft sie einem nicht gleich und unmittelbar bei künstlerischer Betätigung, sie wirkt gleichsam nicht zuerst auf die Arbeit ein, die man tut,—aber sie verwandelt, steigert und entwickelt einen fortwährend, sie nimmt einem leise die Werkzeuge aus der Hand, die man bisher benutzte, und ersetzt sie durch andere, unsäglich feinere und präzisere und tut tausend unerwartete Dinge mit einem, wie eine Fee, die Lust daran hat, ein Wesen alle Gestalten annehmen zu sehen, deren Möglichkeiten in ihm verborgen sind. Man muß Paris, wenn man es zum erstenmal um sich hat, mehr wie ein Bad wirken lassen, ohne selbst zuviel dabei tun zu wollen: als zu fühlen und es sich geschehen zu lassen." Rainer Maria Rilke, *Briefe*, Bd. 3, S. 183–29.03.1907 to Tora Holmström.

63. John Martin, *Introduction to the Dance* (New York: W. W. Norton, 1939), 47.

64. John Martin, *The Dance* (New York: Tudor Publishing Company, 1946), 105.

65. Jacob Haubenreich, "Text-corporeality and the Double Rend of the Page: The Specter of the Manuscript in Rilke's *Die Aufzeichnungen des Malte Laurids Brigge*," *Monatshefte* 105, no. 4 (2013): 581.

66. Cynthia J. Novack, *Sharing the Dance: Contact Improvisation and American Culture* (Madison: University of Wisconsin Press, 1990), 137.

67. Rilke, *Briefe aus den Jahren 1906 bis 1907*, 316.

68. Rilke, *Briefe aus den Jahren 1906 bis 1907*, 187.

69. "in dem der Reiz zu tausen[d] Tänzen lag." Rilke, *Briefe aus den Jahren 1902 bis 1906*, 106. All translations from Rilke's letters are my own.

70. "Es war nicht um vieles mehr als gestern, qualitativ, aber doch bemerkenswert." Rilke, *Briefe aus den Jahren 1906 bis 1907*, 92.

71. Rilke, *Briefe aus den Jahren 1906 bis 1907*, 100.

72. Hugo von Hofmannsthal, "Die unvergleichliche Tänzerin," in *Aufforderung zum Tanz*, ed. Gabriele Brandstetter (Stuttgart: Reclam, 1992), 243.

73. Hofmannsthal, "Die unvergleichliche Tänzerin," 241.

74. Hofmannsthal, "Die unvergleichliche Tänzerin," 242–43.

75. Hofmannsthal, "Die unvergleichliche Tänzerin," 243.

76. Hofmannsthal, "Die unvergleichliche Tänzerin," 243.

77. Harry Graf Kessler, *Das Tagebuch*, vol. 4: *1906–1914*, ed. by Jörg Schuster (Stuttgart: Klett-Cotta, 2005), 192. Much more involved with the pioneers of mod-

ern dance than Rilke, Kessler had witnessed the performances of Loïe Fuller, Ruth St. Denis, Isadora Duncan, and Vaslav Nijinsky and documented his experiences in exhaustive diaries. Developing a modern dance aesthetic similar to Hofmannsthal's, Kessler also interacted with St. Denis socially, visited Duncan's school on the outskirts of Berlin, and worked on the ballet *The Legend of Joseph* for Nijinsky. For more detail, see Wesley Lim, "From Spectator to Practitioner: Transforming Harry Graf Kessler's Dance Aesthetic," *KulturPoetik* 13, no. 2 (2013): 197–217.

78. Rainer Maria Rilke and Marie von Thurn und Taxis, *Briefwechsel*, ed. Ernst Zinn (Frankfurt am Main: Suhrkamp, 1986), 50.

79. Tamara Barzantny, *Harry Graf Kessler und das Theater: Author, Mäzen, Initiator 1900–1933* (Köln: Böhlau Verlag, 2002), 22.

80. Klaus Jonas, "Rilke und Clotilde Sacharoff: Ein unveröffentlichter Briefwechsel," *Monatshefte* 58, no. 1 (1966): 1–19.

81. "aus den Teilen neue Verbindungen . . . schaffen, neue, größere, gesetzmäßige Einheiten. . . . Und dieser Reichtum, diese unendliche, fortwährende Erfindung, diese Geistesgegenwart, Reinheit und Vehemenz des Aufbruchs, diese Unerschöpflichkeit, diese Jugend. . . . Das ist ohne Gleichen in der Geschichte der Menschen." Rilke, *Briefe aus den Jahren 1902 bis 1906*, 28–29.

82. "Diese Finger gespreizt, offen, strahlig oder zueinander gebogen wie in einer Jerichorose; diese Finger entzückt und glücklich oder bange ganz am Ende der langen Arme aufgezeigt: sie tanzend. Und der ganze Körper verwendet, diesen äußersten Tanz im Gleichgewicht zu halten in der Luft." Rilke, *Briefe aus den Jahren 1906 bis 1907*, 382.

83. "vibrierenden Umrisses," in Rainer Maria Rilke, *Werke: Kommentierte Ausgabe*, vol. 4, ed. Horst Nalewski, (Stuttgart: Insel, 1996), 431.

84. Jana Schuster, *"Umkehr der Räume": Rainer Maria Rilkes Poetik der Bewegung* (Freiburg: Rombach, 2011).

85. "modernen heraklitischen Existenz," in Joseph Adolph Schmoll, "Simmel und Rodin," in *Ästhetik und Soziologie um die Jahrhundertwende: Georg Simmel*, ed. Hannes Böhringer and Karlfried Gründer (Frankfurt: Vittorio Klostermann, 1976), 30.

86. Rainer Maria Rilke, *Briefe*, Bd. 3, S. 183–29.03.1907 to Tora Holmström.

87. Neumeyer, *Der Flaneur*, 220.

88. Steffan Arndal, "Sehenlernen und Pseudoskopie: Zur visuellen Verarbeitung des Pariserlebnisses," in R. M. Rilkes, *Die Aufzeichnung des Malte Laurids Brigge*, *ORBIS Literrarum* 62, no. 3 (2007): 213.

89. Rilke, *MLB*/Hulse, 44. "Auswahl und Ablehnung gibt es nicht," Rilke, *MLB*, 505.

90. David Weir, *Decadence and the Making of Modernism* (Amherst: University of Massachusetts Press, 1995), xii.

91. Rilke, *MLB*/Hulse, 11. "zwei Früchte: ein Kind und ein Tod," Rilke, *MLB*, 464.

92. Arndal, "Sehenlernen und Pseudoskopie," 212.

93. Agamben, "Notes on Gesture," 52.

94. Judith Ryan, *Rilke, Modernism and Poetic Tradition* (Cambridge: Cambridge University Press, 2016), 42.

95. Ryan, *Rilke, Modernism and Poetic Tradition*, 1.

96. Ryan, *Rilke, Modernism and Poetic Tradition*, 42.

Chapter 5

1. Michael Cowan, "Die Tücke des Körpers: Taming the Nervous Body in Alfred Döblin's 'Die Ermordung einer Butterblume' and 'Die Tänzerin und der Leib,'" *seminar* 43, no. 4 (November 2007): 483.

2. Döblin, "Mein Standort," in *Schriften zu Leben und Werk* (Olten, Switzerland: Walter-Verlag, 1986), 194.

3. Döblin, "Erlebnis zweier Kräfte," in *Schriften zu Leben und Werk* (Olten, Switzerland: Walter-Verlag, 1986), 40.

4. Döblin, "An Romanautoren und ihre Kritiker: Berliner Programm" (1913), in *Schriften zu Ästhetik, Poetik und Literatur* (Olten, Switzerland: Walter-Verlag, 1989), 119–23.

5. Peter Jelavich, *Berlin Alexanderplatz: Radio, Film and the Death of Weimar Culture* (Berkeley: University of California Press, 2006), 14–15.

6. Heidi Thomann Tewarson, "Döblin's Early Collection of Stories, *Die Ermordung einer Butterblume*: Toward a Modernist Aesthetic," in *A Companion to the Works of Alfred Döblin*, ed. Roland Dollinger, Wulf Koepke, and Heidi Thomann Tewarson (Rochester, NY: Camden House, 2004), 38.

7. Andreas Huyssen, *Miniature Metropolis: Literature in an Age of Photography and Film* (Cambridge, MA: Harvard University Press, 2015), 10.

8. Marilyn Sibley Fries, "The City as Metaphor for the Human Condition: Alfred Döblin's *Berlin Alexanderplatz* (1929)," *Modern Fiction Studies* 24, no. 1 (1978): 41–64. Here: 43.

9. David B. Dollenmayer, "An Urban Montage and Its Significance in Döblin's *Berlin Alexanderplatz*," *German Quarterly* 53, no. 3 (1980): 317–36. Here: 317.

10. Oliver Bernhardt, *Alfred Döblin* (München: Deutscher Taschenbuch Verlag, 2007), 17.

11. My translation. "Geschäftiges Leute flutete in der Leipzigerstr. Auf dem Trottoir drängte sich ein Pêle-mêle von allen Ständen, allen Berufen." Alfred Döblin, "Modern: Ein Bild der Gegenwart," *Jagende Rosse. Der schwarze Vorhang und andere frühe Erzählwerke* (Olten, Switzerland: Walter-Verlag, 1981), 7–25. Here: 7.

12. My translation. "Da trottete schweren Schritts der Bankbeamte mit seiner großen Ledermappe, [. . .] Bummler, der Deutsche nennt sie Flanuers, in der Hand die lange Cigarette, die mit der anderen einen dünnen Stock wirbelnd [. . .]. Dann konnte ganz hinten am Dönhoffsplatz ein Heuwagen, bis zum Umfallen beladen, nicht vorwärtskommen—bis zur Friedrichstraße standen die Pferdebahnen, eine hinter der andern. Und an dem Hindernisse, da nun ein Lärm! Dick alles ringsum von Menschen besät. [. . .] Und nun rollen die Pferdebahnen, alle in doppelter Eile [. . .] Die Menge löste sich sofort auf [. . .] Dann geht's langsam am Dönhoffsplatz vorbei, Schritt vor Schritt." Döblin, "Modern," 7–8.

13. Gabriele Sander, "Döblin und der Großstadtrealismus," in *Realistisches Schreiben in der Weimarer Republik*, edited by Sabine Kyora, Stefan Neuhaus (Würzburg: Königshausen & Neumann, 2006), 142.

14. David B. Dollenmayer, *The Berlin Novels of Alfred Döblin: 'Wadzek's Battle with the Steam Turbine,' 'Berlin Alexanderplatz,' 'Men without Mercy,' and 'November 1918'* (Berkeley: University of California Press, 1988), 10.

15. My translation. "hatte kein Auge für das Treiben um sich her, keinen Blick für die glänzenden Auslagen der Schaufester. [. . .] Gewohnheit stumpft ab." Döblin, "Modern," 8.

16. My translation. "Nur ab und zu griff sie zur Bibel, sie vergaß ihres Gottes in dem Drange des Lebens, der Not des Augenblicks. Sie plapperte abends lieber mit ihren Freundinnen [. . .] Die Großstadt, die Großstadt rückt dir näher,—Weh dir Armen!–" Döblin, "Modern," 9.

17. August Endell, "The Beauty of the Metropolis," trans. Zeynep Çelik Alexander, *Grey Room* 56 (2014), 132.

18. My translation. "Und so zogen sie weiter, Straße nach Straße—Leipzigerstraße—Andreasstraße, aus dem Viertel des Besitzes in den der Arbeit, oder auch der—Nichtarbeit; doch in jedem Streben danach,—wir sahen Bertha." Döblin, "Modern," 10.

19. Dollenmayer, *The Berlin Novels of Alfred Döblin*, 14.

20. My translation. "Und das ist das Entsetzliche,——aus diesem jammervollen Leben können sie sich retten; es giebt eine Rettung—eine Rettung—die Prostitution!———————" Döblin, "Modern," 18.

21. My translation. "Es darf kein Glied des Körpers vernachlässigt werden, bei Strafe der furchtbarsten Krankheiten. Und wer es wagt, der Natur zu trotzen, seine 'tierischen Triebe' zu unterdrücken, er wird in diesem Kampfe gebrochen unterliegen." Döblin, "Modern," 15.

22. My translation. "Ruhe, schwüle Ruhe lag in dem Zimmer Berthas. In sich gesunken saß sie auf dem Rande ihres Bettes; [. . .] und in den Augen eine träumende, matt gedankenlose Ruhe." Döblin, "Modern," 20.

23. My translation. "Glühendrote Strahlen kündeten den Untergang der Sonnen an, ein Bild, das selbst die Großstadt mit ihrem Fabrikrauch nicht zerstören kann." Döblin, "Modern," 21.

24. My translation. "sie ist überwältigt von der erhabenen Größe dessen, an den sie fast vergessen hatte—, an ihr verlorenes Sein." Döblin, "Modern," 24.

25. My translation.

—sie stürzt hinaus, hinaus nur aus der Stube, in fliegender Hast die Treppe hinab—auf die schweigende Straße. Gehetzt, gejagt, getrieben von der Einbildung—Straße nach Straße—ohne zu sehn wohin—bis sie stehn bleibt, heiser keuchend.

Am Wasser.

Das Engelbecken.

[. . .]

Sie fühlte, sie konnte dem Triebe, der sie durchwühlte, nicht widerstehn, sie mußte sich ihm hingeben—und sie wäre entehrt—und die Schade wäre ihr Los—Und hier der—Selbstmord—du sollst nicht töten——! O, wie sich retten aus dem Wirrsal?

[. . .]

[Ms-Rand abgerissen] wirbelt es nun wieder in ihrem Hirn. In gespenster [Ms-Rand abgerissen] Reigen umschlingen, umschweben, umkreisen sie [Ms-Rand abgerissen] stalten und bethören sie und verwirren sie [Hier bricht das Manuscript ab.] Döblin, "Modern," 24–25.

26. Dollenmayer, *The Berlin Novels of Alfred Döblin*, 13.

27. Dollenmayer, *The Berlin Novels of Alfred Döblin*, 11.

28. My translation. ("In gespenster [Ms-Rand abgerissen] Reigen umschlingen, umschweben, umkreisen sie.")

29. Elizabeth Wilson, *The Sphinx in the City: Urban Life, the Control of Disorder, and Women* (Berkeley: University of California Press, 1991), 7–8.

30. Tewarson, "Döblin's Early Collection of Stories," 48.

31. Bernhardt, *Alfred Döblin*, 29.

32. Sven Arnold, *Das Spektrum des literarischen Expressionismus in den Zeitschriften Der Sturm und Die Weissen Blätter* (Frankfurt am Main: Peter Lang, 1998), 34.

33. Georg Brühl, *Herwarth Walden und "Der Sturm"* (Leipzig: Edition Leipzig, 1983), 20.

34. My translation. ("Sie sprach volltönend, alle Register aufgezogen: hart, wild, zart, mit Leidenschaft und Fülle.") Alfred Döblin, "Gertrude Barrison," *Der Sturm: Wochenschrift für Kultur und die Künste*, ed. Herwarth Walden (October 1911), 4.

35. My translation. "es trat jener Umschwung hervor, der aus dem Strengen, Lyrischen, Theoretischen, Abrupten in die Masse der Empirie, in den Reichtum der Erlebnisse, der Sturz in das ausgebreitete Leben. Auch hier: Reife,—ich will das Vorangegangene damit nicht Unreife genannt haben. Es waren nicht sechs Kerzen wie früher in dem Saal, aber diese beiden Kerzen leuchteten hell genug." Döblin, "Gertrude Barrison," 4.

36. My translation. "Im Hinterzimmer eines Cafes in der Potsdamer Str. ist eine seltsame kleine Gesellschaft versammelt. Ganz junge Menschen, Maler, Literaten, Dichter—darunter Else Lasker-Schüler und der andere Arzt-Dichter Gottfried Benn. Ein behender, kleiner Mann mit rötlichem Spitzbart und scharfen Augengläsern springt an das Pult, liest lebhaft und nie ermüdend aus einem Manuskript "Gespräche mit Kalypso. Über die Musik," liest mit großer Leidenschaft, halb belehrend, halb verkündend, Denker und Dichter zugleich. Es ist Alfred Döblin." Rudolf Kayser, "Alfred Döblin. Zu seinem 50. Geburstag," in *Berliner Tageblatt*, Jg. 57, Nr. 374–9.8.1928.

37. Kirchner often depicted dancers, primarily female, ranging in number from one to six. He also painted a portrait of Döblin in 1912.

38. Alfred Döblin, "Tänzerinnen," *Der Sturm: Wochenschrift für Kultur und die Künste*, edited by Herwarth Walden (October 1912), 162.

39. My translation. "Wir haben genug von den schlechten Tänzerinnen. Eine Tanzkunst, die nicht akademisch ist, ist darum noch nicht gut. Hupfen, Drehen, entzücktes Puppengesicht, Donauwellen in jedem Wald- und Wiesental wird nachgerade fad. Ihr könnt nichts, liebe Kinder, mögt Ihr Euch akademisch oder frei gebärden. Es wäre alles ganz gut, wenn die Tänzerinnen nur nicht so gebildet, naturfroh und sonst was wären." Döblin, "Tänzerinnen," 162.

40. Alexandra Kolb, *Performing Femininity: Dance and Literature in German Modernism* (Bern: Peter Lang, 2009), 126.

41. Jarmila Weissenböck, "Gertrud Bodenwieser: Dance for the Theater," *Gertrud Bodenwieser and Vienna's Contribution to Ausdruckstanz*, ed. Betinna Vernon-Warren and Charles Warren (Abington, UK: Routledge, 1999), 40.

42. Mary Fleischer, *Embodied Texts: Symbolist Playwright-Dancer Collaborations* (Amsterdam: Rodopi, 2007), 123.

43. Walter Sorrell, *Dance in Its Time* (New York: Columbia University Press, 1981), 204.

44. My translation. ("Ich zitiere einen hervorragenden Autor, einen gewissen Alfred Döblin") Döblin, "Tänzerinnen," 162.

45. Kolb, *Performing Femininity*, 52.

46. Lynn Garafola, "The Travesty Dancer in Nineteenth Century Ballet," *Dance Research Journal* 17 no. 2/18 no. 1 (1985–1986): 35–40. Here: 35.

47. My translation. "Aber Eure Tanzkunst zeigt nicht den gezüchteten frommgewordenen Körper, sondern das gezüchtete Weib oder den [sic] Frau gewordenen Mann; sie zeigt Eure Unzucht. üppig; Ihr dürftet vieles vergessen. Ihr ließt Euch den Tanz aus den Händen reißen, kennt nur den Locktanz der Geschlechter, nicht den Eintanz, kaum den Vieltanz, den Tanz und die Phantasie der Männerkörper. Ihr Ueppigen, Schweren, Blöden!" Döblin, "Tänzerinnen," 162.

48. Kolb, *Performing Femininity*, 52.

49. Kolb, *Performing Femininity*, 67.

50. Garafola, "Travesty," 37.

51. My translation. "Die eine ist ein solider, muskelöser Mensch weiblichen Geschlechts, mit Knochen, Gliedern. Dagegen und hinwiderum die andere dünn, wie das beinah nicht mehr schön ist. Sie scheint nur ein lederüberzogenes Klappergestell weiblicher Signatur; manchmal zerbrach ich mir den Kopf, wie so was möglich sein kann, wie derartiges stattfinden kann." Döblin, "Tänzerinnen," 162.

52. My translation. "Der Herkules tanzte einmal einen 'Festtanz'; fest war es, fest, ganz fest, mit wuchtigen Ellenbogen, massiven Schultern, trittfähigen Beinen; der Herkules freute sich ersichtlich." Döblin, "Tänzerinnen," 129.

53. Garafola, "Travesty," 37.

54. My translation. "Das Meisterstück der einen (Led.-sof.) [Ledersofa], Tanz der jungen Koboldin: das Klappen und Winken der Hände, die unschönen, plötzlichen, schlenkernden Beinbewegungen, das Rasen und Wühlen der Schultern. Sie kann etwas,—ich weiß wie gesagt nicht, was sie vielleicht von da unten hat -, reichlich tänzerische Einfälle, richtig gehende körperliche motorische Gedanken, motorische Gedanken, motorische Witze, motorische Absurdität. Sie sind

wirklich, ernsthaft, originell und sehenswert, aber ich bin von Natur im Ausdruck etwas drastisch." Döblin, "Tänzerinnen," 162.

55. Susan Jones, *Literature, Modernism, and Dance* (Oxford: Oxford University Press, 2013), 6.

56. Kate Elswit, *Watching Weimar Dance* (Oxford: Oxford University Press, 2014), xxv.

57. Alfred Döblin, "The Dancer and the Body," trans. Iain Bamforth, in *British Journal of General Practice* 59 (2009): 959–60. Here: 959. "[sie] lernte [. . .] jetzt ihre federnen Bänder, ihre zu glatten Gelenke zwingen, sie schlich sich behutsam und geduldig in die Zehen, die Knöchel, die Knie ein und immer wieder ein, überfiel habgierig die schmalen Schultern und die Biegung der schlanken Arme, wachte lauernd über dem Spiel des straffen Leibes. Es gelang ihr, über den üppigsten Tanz Kälte zu sprühen." Alfred Döblin, "Die Tänzerin und der Leib," in *Jagende Rosse. Der schwarze Vorhang und andere frühe Erzählwerke*, ed. Christina Althen (Olten, Switzerland: Walter-Verlag, 1981), 18.

58. Michael Cowan, "Die Tücke des Körpers: Taming the Nervous Body in Alfred Döblin's 'Die Ermordung einer Butterblume' and 'Die Tänzerin und der Leib,'" *seminar* 43, no. 4 (November 2007): 490.

59. See Erwin Kobel, *Alfred Döblin: Erzählkunst im Umbruch* (Berlin: De Gruyter, 1985). Kolb, *Performing Femininity*.

60. Kolb, *Performing Femininity*, 68.

61. Trans. by Bamforth, 959. "[sie] hatte [. . .] eine seidenleichte Figur, übergroße schwarze Augen. Ihr Gesicht fast knabenhaft lang und scharfgeschnitten. Die Stimme hell, ohne Buhlerei und Musik, abgehackt; ein rascher, ungeduldiger Gang. Sie war lieblos, sah klar auf die unbefähigten Kolleginnen und langweilte sich bei ihren Klagen." Döblin, "Die Tänzerin und der Leib," 18.

62. Stephanie Catani, "Die Geburt des *Döblinismus* aus dem Geist des Fin die Siecle: Döblins frühe Erzählungen im Spannungsfeld von Ästhetik, Poetik und Medizin," in *Alfred Döblin: Paradigms of Modernism*, ed. Steffan Davies and Ernest Schonfield (Berlin: Walter de Gruyter, 2009), 40. Alexandra Kolb also mentions this.

63. Tewarson, "Döblin's Early Collection," 44.

64. Susan Stinson, "Places Where I've been: Reflections on Issues of Gender in Dance Education, Research and Administration," *Choreography and Dance* 5, no. 1 (1998): 117–27. Here: 118.

65. Edward Shorter, "The First Great Increase in Anorexia Nervosa," *Journal of Social History* 21, no. 1 (1987): 69–96. Here: 70.

66. Shorter, "The First Great Increase in Anorexia Nervosa," 71.

67. Felicia McCarren, *Dance Pathologies. Performance, Poetics, Medicine* (Stanford: Stanford University Press, 1998), 171.

68. McCarren, *Dance Pathologies*, 73–76.

69. Trans. by Bamforth, 959. "ein[em] bleiche[n] Siechtum [. . .] Ihre Glieder wurden schwer, aber sie spielte weiter. Wenn sie allein war, stampfte sie mit dem Fuße, drohte ihrem Leib und mühte sich mit ihm ab. Keinem sprach sie von ihrer

Schwäche. Sie knirschte mit den Zähnen über das Dumme, Kindische, das sie eben zu besiegen gelernt hatte." Döblin, "Die Tänzerin und der Leib," 18.

70. Kolb, *Performing Femininity*, 81.

71. Helen King, *The Disease of Virgins: Green Sickness, Chlorosis, and the Problems of Puberty* (Abington, UK: Routledge, 2004), 1–5.

72. Albert Smith, *The Natural History of the Ballet Girl* (London: Dance Books, 1996 [1847]), 19.

73. Trans. by Bamforth, 959. "In leiser Angst öffnete sie die Augen, als sie die Glieder betrachtete, die sich ihr entzogen. Wie machtlos sie war, o wie machtlos sie war. Sie rasselten über das Pflaster des Hofes. Die Tore des Krankenhauses schlossen sich hinter ihr. Die Tänzerin sah mit Abscheu Ärzte und Kranke. Die Schwestern hoben sie weich ins Bett." Döblin, "Die Tänzerin und der Leib," 19.

74. Tewarson, "Döblin's Early Collection," 33.

75. Oliver Bernhardt, *Alfred Döblin* (Munich: Deutscher Taschenbuch Verlag), 30–40.

76. Eric J. Engstrom, *Clinical Psychiatry in Imperial Germany: A History of Psychiatric Practice* (Ithaca: Cornell University Press, 2003), 1–2.

77. Engstrom, *Clinical Psychiatry*, 6–7.

78. Engstrom, *Clinical Psychiatry*, 175.

79. Döblin, "Die Tänzerin und der Leib," 19.

80. Trans. by Bamforth, 959. "es geschah alles ohne ihren Willen." Döblin, "Die Tänzerin und der Leib," 19.

81. McCarren, *Dance Pathologies*, 23.

82. Trans. by Bamforth, 959. "Täglich, fast stündlich fragten sie die Tänzerin nach seinen Dingen, schrieben es sorgfältig in Akten auf, so daß sie erst darüber unwillig wurde, dann sich immer tiefer verwunderte. Sie trieb bald in eine dunkle Angst und Haltlosigkeit hinein." Döblin, "Die Tänzerin und der Leib," 19.

83. McCarren, *Dance Pathologies*, 28.

84. Trans. by Bamforth, 960. "der Leib konnte sehen, wie er sich mit den Doktoren abfand. 'Es wird schon protokolliert werden.'" Döblin, "Die Tänzerin und der Leib," 20.

85. Trans. by Bamforth, 959. "Sie [Ella and her body] führten getrennte Wirtschaften." Döblin, "Die Tänzerin und der Leib," 20.

86. Trans. by Bamforth, 959. "Jetzt wurde sie erbittert und wehrte sich. Sie belog die Ärzte, beantwortete ihre Fragen nicht, ihren Schmerz verheimlichte sie. [. . .] [Sie] lachte in plötzlich aufloderndem Hasse den Ärzten, die den Kopf schüttelten, ins Gesicht und schnitt ihnen eine höhnische Fratze." Döblin, "Die Tänzerin und der Leib," 20.

87. Döblin, "Die Tänzerin und der Leib," 20.

88. Cowan, "Die Tücke des Körpers," 496.

89. Cowan, "Die Tücke des Körpers," 497.

90. Trans. by Bamforth, 960. "Mit einem Bleistift warf sie rasch auf das weiße Tuch ein sonderbares Bild. Drei Figuren standen da: ein runder unförmiger Leib auf zwei Beinen, ohne Arm und Kopf, nichts als eine zweibeinige, dicke Kugel. Neben ihm ragte ein sanftmütiger großer Mann mit einer Riesenbrille, der den

Leib mit einem Thermometer streichelte. Aber während er sich ernst mit dem Leib beschäftigte, machte ihm auf der anderen Seite ein kleines Mädchen, das auf nackten Füßen hüpfte, eine lange Nase mit der linken Hand und stieß mit der rechten eine spitze Schere von unten in den Leib, so daß der Leib wie eine Tonne auslief in dickem Strahl." Döblin, "Die Tänzerin und der Leib," 21.

91. Kolb, *Performing Femininity*, 88.

92. Benn's poem "Nachtcafe" displays varying body parts such as "Grüne Zähne, Pickel im Gesicht," "Doppelkinn," "Fettleibigkeit."

93. Tewarson, "Döblin's Early Collection," 37.

94. Cowan, "Die Tücke des Körpers," 497.

95. Trans. by Bamforth, 960. "Sie wollte wieder tanzen, tanzen. [. . .] Sie wollte einen Walzer, einen wundersüßen, mit ihm tanzen, der ihr Herr geworden war, mit dem Leib. Mit einer Bewegung ihres Willens konnte sie ihn noch einmal bei den Händen fassen, den Leib, das träge Tier, ihn hinwerfen, herumwerfen, und er war nicht mehr der Herr über sie. Ein triumphierender Haß wühlte sie von innen auf, nicht er ging zur Rechten und sie zur Linken, sondern sie,—sie sprangen mitsamt. Sie wollte ihn auf den Boden kollern, die Tonne das hinkende Männlein, Hals über Kopf es hintrudeln, ihm Sand ins Maul stecken." Döblin, "Die Tänzerin und der Leib," 21.

96. Ruth Katz, "The Egalitarian Waltz," *Comparative Studies in Society and History* 15, no. 3 (1973): 368–77.

97. Cowan, "Die Tücke des Körpers," 494.

98. Trans. by Bamforth, 960. "Über sich gebeugt, sah sie ihm von unten ins Gesicht, wie er erstaunt die Stickerei betrachtete, sagte dann mit ruhiger Stimme zu ihm auf: 'Du,—Du Affe,—Du Affe, Du Schlappschwanz.' Und stieß sich, die Decke abwerfend, die Nähschere in die linke Brust." Döblin, "Die Tänzerin und der Leib," 21.

99. Brandstetter, *Poetics of Dance*, 204.

100. Brandstetter, *Poetics of Dance*, 204. "Die Hypnose erfüllt in diesem Zusammenhang die Aufgabe, den Körper zu ekstatisieren; mithin das Ich aus seinen sozial erworbenen Hemmungen zu befreien und das kreative 'Natur'-Wesen aus der Kultur herauszulösen." Brandstetter, *Tanz-Lektüren*, 251.

101. Matthias Bauer, "'Berlin ist eine ausführliche Stadt': Einleitende Bemerkungen zur Berliner Stadt-, Kultur- und Mediengeschichte," in *Berlin: Medien- und Kulturgeschichte einer Hauptstadt im 20. Jahrhundert* (Tübingen: Francke Verlag, 2007), 15.

102. Simmel, *Die Großstädte und das Geistesleben*.

103. McCarren, *Dance Pathologies*, 27.

104. McCarren, *Dance Pathologies*, 47.

Chapter 6

1. My translation. "Unsere Stadt Berlin ist stark und furchtbar, und ihre Flügel wissen, wohin sie wollen. Darum kehrt der Künstler—doch immer wieder zurück nach Berlin, hier ist die Uhr der Kunst, die nicht nach, noch vor geht. Diese

Realität ist schon mystisch." Else Lasker-Schüler, "Die kreisende Weltfabrik," *Die kreisende Weltfabrik: Berliner Ansichten und Porträts*, ed. Heidrun Loper (Berlin: Transit, 2012). First published in *Vossische Zeitung*, April 16, 1922.

2. Donna Heizer, *Jewish-German Identity in the Orientalist Literature of Else Lasker-Schüler, Friedrich Wolf, and Franz Werfel* (Columbia, SC: Camden House, 1996), 8.

3. Heizer, *Jewish-German Identity*, 42.

4. Heizer, *Jewish-German Identity*, 45.

5. Astrid Schmetterling, "'I am Jussuf of Egypt': Else Lasker-Schüler's Orientalist Drawing," *Ars Judaica* 8 (2012): 81–98. Here: 98.

6. Martin Buber, "The Spirit of the Orient and Judaism," trans. Eva Jospe, in Martin Buber, *On Judaism*, ed. Nahum N. Glatzer, 56–78 (New York: Schocken, 1967).

7. Homi K. Bhabha, *The Location of Culture* (London: Routledge, 1994), 38.

8. Eve Kosofsky Sedgwick, "Queer and Now," in *Tendencies* (Durham: Duke University Press, 1993), 8.

9. Penny Farfan, *Performing Queer Modernism* (Oxford: Oxford University Press, 2017), 2–3.

10. Sara Ahmed, *Queer Phenomenology: Orientations, Objects, Others* (Durham: Duke University Press), 16.

11. Anna Babka, "Orientalistische Miniaturen im literarischen Expressionismus: Fremdheit und Geschlecht in Else Lasker-Schülers *Der Prinz von Theben. Ein Geschichtenbuch* (1914)—eine postkoloniale und queertheoretische Perspektivierung," *Estudios Filológicos Alemanes* 21 (2011): 146.

12. Ralf Remshardt, "Posthumanism," in *Mapping Intermediality in Performance*, ed. Sarah Bay-Cheng, Chiel Kattenbelt, Andy Lavender, and Robin Nelson (Amsterdam: Amsterdam University Press, 2010), 135–39. Here: 135.

13. Michael Mack, *Contaminations: Beyond Dialectics in Modern Literature, Science and Film* (Edinburgh: Edinburgh University Press, 2016), 192.

14. Donna Haraway, "A Cyborg Manifesto: Science, Technology, and Socialist-Feminism in the Late Twentieth Century," in *Simians, Cyborgs and Women: The Reinvention of Nature* (New York; Routledge, 1991), 149–81. Here: 150.

15. Andreas Huyssen, *Miniature Metropolis: Literature in an Age of Photography and Film* (Cambridge, MA: Harvard University Press, 2015), 7.

16. Peter Jelavich, *Berlin Cabaret* (Cambridge, MA: Harvard University Press, 1993), 2.

17. Jelavich, *Berlin Cabaret*, 3.

18. Peter Sprengel, "Literarische Avantgarde und Cabaret in Berlin—Erotik und Moderne," in *Hundert Jahre Kabarett: Zur Inszenierung gesellschaftlicher Identität zwischen Protest und Propaganda*, ed. Joanne McNally and Peter Sprengel (Würzburg: Königshausen & Neumann, 2003), 35.

19. Otto Julius Bierbaum, *Deutsche Chansons* (Brettl-Lieder) (Berlin: Schuster & Loeffler, 1900), X.

20. My translation. "Ich suche nach einem Stuhl, der im Verborgenen blüht— endlich finde ich so ein Veilchen abseits am Tapetenrand; ich setze mich. Meine

Zobeïde, die sehr neugierig auf das Cabaret der Neopathetik ist, ruht schon lange müde zwischen weißen, lilagelben, roten und himmelblauen Mädchen;" Else Lasker-Schüler, "Im neopathetischen Cabaret," in *Der Sturm: Wochenschrift für Kultur und die Künste*, ed. Herwarth Walden, November 1910, 304.

21. My translation. ("Ich muß immer ans Geld denken; wie man so runterkommt—wenn Zobeïde, meine Tänzerin, ein Portemonnaie bei sich hätte, würde ich doch zu der Menschenhitze ein Glas Limonade trinken.") Lasker-Schüler, "Im neopathetischen Cabaret," 305.

22. My translation. "Zobeïde, meine Tänzerin, will noch nicht mit nach Hause kommen." Lasker-Schüler, "Im neopathetischen Cabaret," 305.

23. Karl Jürgen Skrodzki, "Freundschaft mit Else Lasker-Schüler. Widmungen, Porträts, Briefe. Ein quellenkundliches Verzeichnis zu den Werken und Briefen der Dichterin," accessed September 11, 2023, http://www.kj-skrodzki.de/Dokumente /Text_048s.htm

24. Cynthia J. Novack, *Sharing the Dance: Contact Improvisation and American Culture* (Madison: University of Wisconsin Press, 1990), 137.

25. Bronislava Nijinska, *Bronislava Nijinska: Early Memoirs*. ed. and trans. Irina Nijinska and Jean Rawlinson (Durham: Duke University Press, 1992), 292.

26. Else Lasker-Schüler, *Briefe 1893–1913*, ed. Ulrike Marquardt (Berlin: Jüdischer Verlag, 2003). Letters 239 and 240 to Jethro Bithell on April 21 and May 7, 1910, respectively; Letters 247 and 254 to Friedrich Andreas Meyer on July 1 and August 4, 1910, respectively; Letters 251 and 386 to Paul Zech on July 30, 1910, and September 19, 1912; Letters 261 and 262 to Richard Dehmel in October; Letter 344 to Paul Lindau on May 20, 1912.

27. Deborah Jowitt, *Time and the Dancing Image* (Berkeley: University of California Press, 1988), 117–18.

28. Jowitt, *Time and the Dancing Image*, 113.

29. Jean Cocteau and Arsène Alexandre, *The Decorative Art of Léon Bakst*, trans. Adrienne Foulke (Mineola, NY: Dover, 1973), 37.

30. André Levinson, *Bakst: The Story of the Artist's Life* (New York: Benjamin Bloom, 1971), 158.

31. Carl Einstein, "Léon Bakst," in *Werke*, vol. 2, 1919–1928, ed. Marion Schmid in cooperation with Henriette Beese and Jens Kwasny (Berlin: Medusa Verlag, 1981), 341–68. Here: 354–56.

32. Gabriele Brandstetter, *Poetics of Dance: Body, Image, and Space in the Historical Avant-Gardes* (Oxford: Oxford University Press, 2015), 287–89.

33. Charles S. Meyer, "Ida Rubinstein: A Twentieth-Century Cleopatra," *Dance Research Journal* 20, no. 2 (1989): 47.

34. Patricia Vertinsky, "Ida Rubinstein: Dancing Decadence and 'The Art of the Beautiful Pose,'" *Nashim: A Journal of Jewish Women's Studies & Gender Issues* 26 (2014): 122–46. Here: 126.

35. Vertinsky, "Ida Rubinstein," 124.

36. Else Lasker-Schüler, "Ich tanze in der Moschee," in *Der Sturm: Wochenschrift für Kultur und die Künste*, ed. Herwarth Walden, February 25, 1911, 414.

37. Markus Hallensleben, *Else Lasker-Schüler: Avantgardismus und Kunstinszenierung* (Tübingen: Francke, 2000), 76.

38. Hallensleben, *Else Lasker-Schüler*, 79–80.

39. Sylke Kirschnick. *Tausend und ein Zeichen: Else Lasker-Schülers Orient und die Berliner Alltags- und Populärkultur um 1900* (Würzburg: Königshausen und Neumann, 2007), 71–75.

40. Gabriele Brandstetter, *Poetics of Dance: Body, Image, and Space in the Historical Avant-Gardes* (Oxford: Oxford University Press, 2015), 199.

41. For more information consult chapter 3, "Delirium of Movement and Trance Dance," in Brandstetter's *Poetics of Dance*.

42. Brandstetter, *Poetics of Dance*, 209.

43. Raymond Lifchez, "The Lodges of Istanbul," in *The Dervish Lodge: Architecture, Art, and Sufism in Ottoman Turkey* (Berkeley: University of Californina Press, 1991), 73–129. Here: 108.

44. Farrin Chwalkowski, *Symbols in Arts, Religion and Culture: The Soul of Nature* (Newcastle upon Tyne, UK: Cambridge Scholars, 2016), 86–87.

45. Nancy Micklewright, "Derwish Images in Photographs and Painting," in *The Dervish Lodge: Architecture, Art, and Sufism in Ottoman Turkey* (Berkeley: University of California Press, 1991), 269–83. Here: 270.

46. Théophile Gautier, *Constantinople*, trans. Robert Howe Gould (New York: Henry Holt and Company, 1875), 129.

47. Gautier, *Constantinople*, 129.

48. Gautier, *Constantinople*, 131–33.

49. Gautier, *Constantinople*, 133.

50. Jakob Hessing, "My Heart: An Introduction," *My Heart: A Novel of Love, with Pictures and Real, Living People*, trans. Sheldon Gilman and Robert Levine (Amsterdam: November Editions, 2016), xiv.

51. In Kurt Pinthus's anthology of expressionist poetry *Menschheitsdämmerung: Symphonie jüngster Dichtung* (1920), Lasker-Schüler proclaimed, "I was born in Thebes (Egypt), even though I also came into the world in Elberfeld in the Rheinland. I went to school until 11, became Robinson, and lived for five years in the Orient, and since then I have been vegetating." ("Ich bin in Theben (Ägypten) geboren, wenn ich auch in Elberfeld zur Welt kam im Rheinland. Ich ging bis 11 Jahre zur Schule, wurde Robinson, lebte fünf Jahre im Morgenlande, und seitdem vegetiere ich.") Else Lasker-Schüler, ed. Kurt Pinthus. *Menschheitsdämmerung: Symphonie jüngster Dichtung* (Reinbeck bei Hamburg: Rowohlt, 1997), 149.

52. Andrea Krauss, "Writing of Attractions: Else Lasker-Schüler's Avant-Garde Techniques," trans. Nils F. Schott, *Modern Language Notes* 132, no. 3 (2017): 602–24. Here: 611. She borrows Tom Gunning's term "cinema of attractions," which brings about an aesthetics of surprise by highlighting the visibility of images through exhibition. Tom Gunning, "The Cinema of Attractions: Early Film, Its Spectator and the Avant-Garde," *Early Cinema: Space—Frame—Narrative*, ed. Thomas Elsaesser (London: BFI, 1990), 56–62. Here: 56.

53. Andrew Webber, "Inside Out: Acts of Displacement in Else Lasker-Schüler," *Germanic Review* 81, no. 2 (2006): 143–62. Here: 143.

54. "Briefe nach Norwegen," *Der Sturm* 2, no. 77 (September 16, 1911): 615.

55. Lasker-Schüler, trans. Sheldon Gilman and Robert Levine, *My Heart*, 3–4. "Vorgestern war ich mit Gertrude Barrison in den Lunapark gegangen, leise in die ägyptische Ausstellung, als ob wir so etwas Süßes vorausahnten. Gertrude erweckte dort in einem Caféhaus die Aufmerksamkeit eines Vollbartarabers, mit ihm zu kokettieren, auf meinen Wunsch, schlug sie mir entsetzt ab, ein für allemal. Ich hätte nämlich gerne den Lauf seiner sich kräuselnden Lippen beobachtet, die nun durch die Reserviertheit meiner Begleiterin gedämmt wurden. Ich nahm es ihr sehr übel. Aber bei den Bauchtänzerinnen ereignete sich eines der Wunder meines arabischen Buches, ich tanzte mit Minn, dem Sohn des Sultans von Marokko. Wir tanzten, tanzten wie zwei Tanzschlangen, oben auf der Islambühne, wir krochen ganz aus uns heraus, nach den Locktönen der Bambusflöte des Bändigers, nach der Trommel, pharaonenalt, mit den ewigen Schellen. Und Gertrude tanzte auch, aber wie eine Muse, nicht muselhaft wie wir, sie tanzte mit graziösen, schlankhaften Armen die Craquette, ihre Finger wehten wie Fransen. Aber der und ich verirrten uns nach Tanger, stießen kriegerische Schreie aus, bis mich sein Mund küßte so sanft, so inbrünstig, und ich hätte mich geniert, mich zu sträuben. Seitdem liebe ich alle Menschen, die eine Nuance seiner Hautfarbe an sich tragen, an sein Goldbrokat erinnern." Lasker-Schüler, *Mein Herz*, 7–8.

56. Kirschnick, *Tausend und ein Zeichen*, 172.

57. Paul Dobryden, "The Institution of Pleasure: From Display to Environment at the Berlin Lunapark," *Studies in European Cinema* 10, nos. 2/3 (2013): 157–78. Here: 157.

58. Kirschnick, *Tausend und ein Zeichen*, 168. (*Berliner Tagesblatt* 13.03.1911).

59. Kirschnick, *Tausend und ein Zeichen*, 169.

60. Kirschnick, *Tausend und ein Zeichen*, 28–30.

61. Hallensleben, *Else Lasker-Schüler*, 77.

62. Hallensleben, *Else Lasker-Schüler*, 77.

63. Kirschnick, *Tausend und ein Zeichen*, 54.

64. Hallensleben, *Else Lasker-Schüler*, 155.

65. Hallensleben, *Else Lasker-Schüler*, 75–76.

66. Kirschnick, "Tausend und ein Zeichen," 173–74.

67. Jennifer Ingalls, "Else Lasker-Schüler's Collaborative Avant Garde: Text & Image in Berlin c. 1910" (PhD diss., UC Berkeley, 2017), 41.

68. W. Scott Haine, "Introduction," *The Thinking Space: The Café as a Cultural Institution in Paris, Italy and Vienna*, ed. Leona Rittner, W. Scott Haine, and Jeffrey H. Jackson (Abingdon, UK: Routledge, 2013), 3.

69. Haine, "Introduction," 2.

70. Ray Oldenburg, *The Great Good Place: Cafes, Coffee Shops, Bookstores, Bars, Hair Salons, and Other Hangouts at the Heart of a Community* (Boston: Da Capo Press, 1999)

71. Benoît Lecoq, "Le Café," in *Les Lieux de mémoire*, ed. Pierre Nora (Paris: Gallimard, 1992), vol. 3, 878; *Rethinking France: Les Lieux des mémoire*, trans. Mary Trouille and David P. Jordan, ed. Pierre Nora (Chicago: University of Chicago Press, 2001).

72. Monique Membrado, *Poétique des cafes*, preface by Pierre Sansot (Paris: Publisud, 1989).

73. Sigrid Bauschinger, "The Berlin Moderns: Else Lasker-Schüler and Café Culture," in *Berlin Metropolis: Jews and the New Culture, 1890–1918*, ed. Emily D. Bilski, 58–101 (Berkeley: University of California Press, 2000). Here: 79.

74. Lasker-Schüler, *My Heart*, 24. "Ich habe das Café satt, aber damit will ich nicht behaupten, daß ich ihm Lebewohl für ewig sage, oder fahre dahin Zigeunerkarren. Im Gegenteil, ich werde noch oft dort verweilen. Gestern ging es Tür auf, Tür zu, wie in einem Bazar; nicht alles dort ist echte Ware: Imitierte Dichter, falsches Wortgeschmeide, Similigedanken, unmotivierter Zigarettendampf. Der Rechtsanwalt kommt schon lange nicht mehr hin. Warum es einen so ins Cafe zieht! Eine Leiche wird jeden Abend dort in die oberen Räume geführt; sie kann nicht ruhen. Warum man überhaupt in Berlin wohnen bleibt? In dieser kalten unerquicklichen Stadt. Eine unumstößliche Uhr ist Berlin, sie wacht mit der Zeit, wir wissen, wieviel Uhr Kunst es immer ist. Und ich möchte die Zeit so gern verschlafen." Else Lasker-Schüler, *Mein Herz: Ein Liebesroman mit Bildern und wirklich lebenden Menschen*. Mit Zeichnungen der Autorin aus der Ausgabe von 1912 (Berlin: Suhrkamp Verlag, 1989), 34–35.

75. David Frisby, "The City Interpreted: Georg Simmel's Metropolis," in *Cityscapes of Modernity*, 100–58 (Cambridge: Polity Press, 2001). Here: 100.

76. Kambiz Haji Qassemi, *Ganjnameh; Cyclopaedia of Iranian Islamic Architecture*, vol. 9, *Bazaar Buildings* (Tehran: Rowzaneh Press, 2005).

77. Maryam Ziyaee, "Revitalization of Cultural and Aesthetical Assets of Iranian Traditional Bazaar," *International Journal of Architecture & Planning* 5, no. 2 (2017): 234–51. Here 241.

78. Hallensleben, *Else Lasker-Schüler*, 155.

79. Lasker-Schüler, *My Heart*, 99. "[. . .][ich] spreche [. . .] zu meiner Stadt und öffne ihren Menschen meine Seele wie einen Palmenhain, den sie betreten dürfen. [. . .] Mein Bildnis wird verteilt in Theben." Lasker-Schüler, *Mein Herz*, 164.

80. Lasker-Schüler, *My Heart*, 26–27. "Ich möchte Euch heut abend nur sagen: Berlin ist eine kleine Stadt, täglich schrumpft sie mehr und mehr ein. Groß ist eine Stadt nur, wenn man von ihr aus groß blicken kann. Berlin hat nur ein Guckloch, einen Flaschenhals, und der ist auch meist verkorkt, selbst die Phantasie erstickt. Gute Nacht!" Lasker-Schüler, *Mein Herz*, 38.

81. Lasker-Schüler, *My Heart*, 31. "Wißt Ihr, wer plötzlich in den Saal trat, als Gertrude Barrison tanzte? Minn! Aber er versteht die Tänze des Abendlandes wie ich nicht; nur bei Gertrude mache ich eine Ausnahme. Die letzte Schöne der Tänzerinnen Barrisons bewegt sich interessant und anmutig, und ihre Gewänder sind seidene Geheimnisse weißer Marquisperückenzeiten. Alle Schauenden waren entzückt." Lasker-Schüler, *Mein Herz*, 44.

82. The translator uses "Asian," but I have changed this to "Oriental."

83. Lasker-Schüler, *My Heart*, 92–93. "*Ihr beiden Freunde!* Was ist das? Wart ihr schon dort, Ecke Kurfürstendamm und Wilmersdorferstraße, im Café

Kurfürstendamm? Ich bin zum Donnerwetter dem Café des Westens untreu geworden; wie einen Herzallerliebsten hab ich das Caféhaus verlassen, dem ich ewige Treue versprach. Das Café Kurfürstendamm ist eine Frau, eine orientalische Tänzerin. Sie zerstreut mich, sie tröstet mich, sie entzückt mich durch die vielen süßerlei Farben ihres Gewands. Eine Bewegung ist in dem Café, es dreht sich geheimnisvoll wie der schimmernde Leib der Fatme. Verschleierte Herzen sind die sternumhangenen, kleinen Nischen der Galerien. O, was man da alles sagen und lauschen kann—leise singen Violinen, selige Stimmungen. Das Café ist das lebendig gewordene Plakat Lucian Bernhards. Ich werde ihm einen Mondsichelorden, der ihn zum thebanischen Pasche ernennt, und meine huldvollste Bewunderung übermitteln lassen." Lasker-Schüler, *Mein Herz*, 148–51.

84. Hallensleben, *Else Lasker-Schüler*, 94.

85. Ricarda Dick, "Else-Lasker-Schüler als Künsterlin," in *Else Lasker-Schüler: Die Bilder*, 117–58 (Berlin: Jüdischer Verlag im Suhrkamp Verlag, 2010). Here: 120–23.

86. Karla Bilang, "'. . . ich habe ein Geschöpf hingesetzt' ELSE LASKER-SCHÜLER. Der STURM und die Bildkunst," in *STURM-Frauen: Künstlerinnen der Avantgarde in Berlin 1910–1932*, ed. Max Hollein and Ingrid Pfeiffer, 212–15 (Köln: Wienand, 2015). Here: 212–13.

87. Ingalls, "Else Lasker-Schüler's Collaborative Avant Garde," 84–85.

88. The Arabian prince Jussuf from the city of Thebes was based on the story of Joseph from the Old Testament and also played a large role in the Koran. He was a figure of exile, a survivor, and a dreamer.

89. Dick, "Else-Lasker-Schüler als Künsterlin," 129.

90. Webber, "Inside Out," 152.

91. The last installment appears in vol. 3, nos. 113–114, June 8, 1912.

92. Lasker-Schüler, *My Heart*, 99. "[. . .][ich] spreche [. . .] zu meiner Stadt und öffne ihren Menschen meine Seele wie einen Palmenhain, den sie betreten dürfen. [. . .] Mein Bildnis wird verteilt in Theben." Lasker-Schüler, *Mein Herz*, 164.

93. Else Lasker-Schüler, *Hebräische Balladen* (Berlin-Wilmersdorf: A. R. Meyer, 1913). Includes fifteen poems.

94. Else Lasker-Schüler, *Hebräische Balladen*. Zweite, vermehrte Auflage (Berlin-Wilmersdorf: A. R. Meyer, 1914). Includes seventeen poems.

95. This collection first appeared in 1912 as an engagement present for Lucie Goldschmidt-Rotschild in a completely handwritten and drawn version. *Versöhnung* is the first ballad (1912), which had appeared earlier in *Der Sturm* 1910. She published different subsets of *Hebräische Balladen* in 1913, 1914, and 1920. In the 1914 version, the title page features Jussuf holding Thebes.

96. Dick, "Else-Lasker-Schüler als Künsterlin," 129.

97. Nicole Behrmann, "Varieté, Telefon, Kino: Die Entstehung des Prinzen von Theben," *Modern Language Notes* 132, no. 3 (April 2017) (German Issue): 639–57. Here: 642.

98. Dick, "Else-Lasker-Schüler als Künsterlin," 132.

Chapter 7

1. This image is different from the Jussuf-Thebes image.

2. Tom Gunning, "The Cinema of Attraction[s]: Early Film, Its Spectator, and the Avant-Garde," *Wide Angle* 8, nos. 3–4 (1986): 63–70. Here: 64.

3. Anton Giulio Bragaglia, "Futurist Photodynamism (1911)," trans. Lawrence S. Rainey. *Modernism/modernity* 15 (2008): 363–79. Here: 367–70.

4. Bragaglia, "Futurist Photodynamism," 365–70.

5. Erin Brannigan, *Choreography and the Moving Image* (Oxford: Oxford University Press, 2011), 19.

6. Brannigan, *Choreography*, 27–28.

7. Jennifer Ingalls, "Else Lasker-Schüler's Collaborative Avant Garde: Text & Image in Berlin c. 1910" (PhD diss., UC Berkeley, 2017), 107.

8. Ricarda Dick, ed., *Else Lasker-Schüler–Franz Marc: eine Freundschaft in Briefen und Bildern: mit sämtlichen privaten und literarischen Briefen* (München: Prestel, 2012), 26.

9. Simone Natale, "A Short History of Superimposition: From Spirit Photography to Early Cinema," *Early Popular Visual Culture* 10, no. 2: 125–45. Here: 128.

10. Natale, "Short History," 129.

11. For a look at this photograph under discussion, see https://www.metmuseum.org/art/collection/search/287806

12. Frank Clark, "Nineteenth-Century Public Parks from 1830," *Garden History* 1, no. 3 (1973): 31–41. Here: 38.

13. Hilary A. Taylor, "Urban Public Parks, 1840–1900: Design and Meaning," *Garden History* 23, no. 2 (1995): 201–21. Here: 202.

14. Taylor, "Urban Public Parks, 1840–1900," 204.

15. Taylor, "Urban Public Parks, 1840–1900," 206.

16. Taylor, "Urban Public Parks, 1840–1900," 213.

17. Joan M. Minguet Batllori, "Segundo De Chomón and the Fascination for Colour," *Film History* 21, no. 1 (2009): 7–103. Here: 97.

18. Gunning, "The Cinema of Attraction[s]," 64.

19. Gunning, "The Cinema of Attraction[s]," 66.

20. Andrea Krauss, "Writing of Attractions: Else Lasker-Schüler's Avant-Garde Techniques," trans. Nils F. Schott. *Modern Language Notes* 132, no. 3 (2017): 602–24. Here: 611.

21. Tom Gunning, "The Attraction of Motion: Modern Representation and the Image of Movement," in *Film 1900: Technology, Perception, Culture*, ed. Annemone Ligensa and Klaus Kreimeier, 165–74 (Bloomington: Indiana University Press, 2015), 167.

22. Tom Gunning, "Loïe Fuller and the Art of Motion: Body, Light, Electricity, and the Origins of Cinema," in *Camera Obscura, Camera Lucida: Essays in Honor of Annette Michelson*, ed. Allen Richard and Turvey Malcolm, 75–90 (Amsterdam: Amsterdam University Press, 2003), 87.

23. Gunning, "Loïe Fuller and the Art of Motion," 85–86.

24. Susan Potter, *Queer Timing: The Emergence of Lesbian Sexuality in Early Cin-

ema (Champaign: University of Illinois Press, 2019), 106; and Rhonda K. Garelick, *Electric Salome: Loïe Fuller's Performance of Modernism* (Princeton: Princeton University Press, 2007), 52–54.

25. Laurent Guido, "Between Paradoxical Spectacles and Technical Dispositives: Looking Again at the (Serpentine) Dances of Early Cinema," in *Cine-Dispositives: Essays in Epistemology Across Media*, ed. François Albera and Maria Tortajada, 249–74 (Amsterdam: Amsterdam University Press, 2015), 252. This article goes into much more detail.

26. Guido, "Between Paradoxical Spectacles and Technical Dispositives," 254.

27. Eugeni d'Ors, "Elegia," *Obra Catalana Completa. Glosari 1906/1910* (Barcelona: Editorial Selecta, 1950), 790–92.

28. Batllori, "Segundo De Chomón," 98.

29. Joshua Yumibe, "The Color Image," in *The Image in Early Cinema: Form and Material*, ed. Joshua Yumibe, Scott Curtis, Philippe Gauthier, and Tom Gunning, 142–50 (Bloomington: Indiana University Press, 2018), 144.

30. Joshua Yumibe, *Moving Color: Early Film, Mass Culture, Modernism* (New Brunswick, NJ: Rutgers University Press, 2012), 77–79.

31. John Gage, *Color and Culture: Practice and Meaning from Antiquity to Abstraction* (Berkeley: University of California Press, 1999), 221–24.

32. See more in Ricarda Dick, *Else Lasker-Schüler–Franz Marc: eine Freundschaft in Briefen und Bildern: mit sämtlichen privaten und literarischen Briefen*, 26.

33. Laurent Guido, "'Auf die Bühne gezaubert, dass man erstaunt': cinéma, danse et music-hall au tournant du 20e siècle," *Seminar: A Journal of Germanic Studies* 46, no. 3 (2010): 205–22. https://muse.jhu.edu/ (accessed May 23, 2019), 206.

34. Susan Jones, *Literature, Modernism and Dance* (Oxford: Oxford University Press, 2013), 70.

35. Jones, *Literature, Modernism and Dance*, 70.

36. Stephen Barber, "The Skladanowsky Brothers: The Devil Knows," *Senses of Cinema* 56 (2010): http://sensesofcinema.com/2010/feature-articles/the-skladanowsky-brothers-the-devil-knows/

37. Miriam Paeslack, *Constructing Imperial Berlin: Photography and the Metropolis* (Minneapolis: University of Minnesota Press, 2019), xvi.

38. Alfred Stieglitz, *Camera Work: The Complete Illustrations 1903–1917* (Köln: Taschen, 1997), 104.

39. Paeslack, *Constructing Imperial Berlin*, xvi.

40. Paeslack, *Constructing Imperial Berlin*, xvi.

41. Paeslack, *Constructing Imperial Berlin*, 15–18.

42. Paeslack, *Constructing Imperial Berlin*, 33.

43. Paeslack, *Constructing Imperial Berlin*, xviii.

44. Livio Belloï, "Lumière and His View: The Cameraman's Eye in Early Cinema," *Historical Journal of Film, Radio and Television* 15, no. 4 (1995): 463.

45. Belloï, "Lumière and His View," 464.

46. Matthias Bauer, "'Berlin ist eine ausführliche Stadt': Einleitende Bemerkungen zur Berliner Stadt-, Kultur- und Mediengeschichte," in *Berlin: Medien- und*

Kulturgeschichte einer Hauptstadt im 20. Jahrhundert (Tübingen: Francke Verlag, 2007), 15.

47. Walter Benjamin, "Das Kunstwerk im Zeitalter seiner technischen Reproduzierbarkeit," *Gesammelte Schriften*, ed. Rolf Tiedemann and Hermann Schweppenhäuser (Frankfurt am Main: Suhrkamp, 1991), 448.

48. Barber, "The Skladanowsky Brothers."

49. Belloï, "Lumière and His View," 466.

50. Belloï, "Lumière and His View," 462.

51. Guido, "'Auf die Bühne gezaubert, dass man erstaunt,'" 213–14.

52. Barber, "The Skladanowsky Brothers."

53. Janelle Blankenship, "To Attract/to Alternate: The Skladanowsky Experiment," *Cinema & Cie: International Film Studies Journal* no. 9 (2007): 61–79. Here: 68–70.

54. Miriam Paeslack, *Berlin im 19. Jahrhundert. Frühe Photographien 1850–1914* (*Berlin in the 19th Century. Early Photographs 1850–1914*) (Munich: Schirmer-Mosel Verlag, 2015).

55. Barber, "The Skladanowsky Brothers."

Coda

1. Andreas Huyssen, *Miniature Metropolis: Literature in an Age of Photography and Film* (Cambridge, MA: Harvard University Press, 2015), 7–8.

2. Douglas Rosenberg, *Screendance: Inscribing the Ephemeral Image* (New York: Oxford University Press, 2012).

3. Wesley Lim, "The Specter of Pina Bausch: Enhancing the Possibilities of *Tanztheater* through Film in Wim Wenders's *Pina* (2011)," *Studies in European Cinema* 17, no. 1 (2020): 4–19. https://doi.org/10.1080/17411548.2018.1498609

4. Wesley Lim, "Reimagining the Brown Body: Contact Improvisation and an Alternative Masculinity in *Alignigung*, William Forsythe's Screendance," *TDR: The Drama Review* 65, no. 3 (2021): 78–90. https://doi.org/10.1017/S1054204321000320

5. Wesley Lim, "Bodies in Color, Black and White, and in Piles: The Dichotomy of Concentration Camp Aesthetics and Somatic Dance Practices in Sasha Waltz's Screendance *Körper* (2000)," *German Studies Review* 44, no. 2 (2021): 335–58. https://doi.org/10.1353/gsr.2021.0042

6. Kate Elswit, "Berlin Your Dance Partner Is Death," *TDR: The Drama Review* 53 (2009): 73–92. https://doi.org/10.1162/dram.2009.53.1.73

Bibliography

Agamben, Giorgio. "Notes on Gesture." In *Means without End: Notes on Politics*, translated by Vincenzo Binetti and Cesare Casarino, 49–61. Minneapolis: University of Minnesota Press, 2000.

Ahmed, Sara. *Queer Phenomenology: Orientations, Objects, Others*. Durham: Duke University Press, 2006.

Albright, Ann Cooper. *Traces of Light: Absence and Presence in the Work of Loïe Fuller*. Middletown, CT: Wesleyan University Press, 2007.

Aldrich, Elizabeth. *From the Ballroom to Hell: Grace and Folly in Nineteenth-Century Dance*. Evanston: Northwestern University Press, 1991.

Alexander, Zeynep Çelik. "Metrics of Experience: August Endell's Phenomenology of Architecture." *Grey Room* 40 (2010): 50–83.

Arndal, Steffan. "Sehenlernen und Pseudoskopie: Zur visuellen Verarbeitung des Pariserlebnisses in R. M. Rilkes *Die Aufzeichnungen des Malte Laurids Brigge*." *ORBIS Literrarum* 62, no. 3 (2007): 210–29.

Arnold, Sven. *Das Spektrum des literarischen Expressionismus in den Zeitschriften Der Sturm und Die Weissen Blätter*. Frankfurt am Main: Peter Lang, 1998.

Babka, Anna. "Orientalistische Miniaturen im literarischen Expressionismus: Fremdheit und Geschlecht in Else Lasker-Schülers *Der Prinz von Theben. Ein Geschichtenbuch* (1914)—eine postkoloniale und queertheoretische Perspektivierung." *Estudios Filológicos Alemanes* 21 (2011): 145–54.

Barber, Stephen. "The Skladanowsky Brothers: The Devil Knows." *The Senses of Cinema* 56 (2010). http://sensesofcinema.com/2010/feature-articles/the-skladanowsky-brothers-the-devil-knows/

Barzantny, Tamara. *Harry Graf Kessler und das Theater. Author, Mäzen, Initiator 1900–1933*. Köln: Böhlau Verlag, 2002.

Batllori, Joan M. Minguet. "Segundo De Chomón and the Fascination for Colour." *Film History* 21, no. 1 (2009): 7–103.

Baudelaire, Charles. *Selected Writings on Art and Artists*, translated and edited by P. E. Chavet. Harmondsworth, UK: Penguin, 1972.

Bauer, Matthias. "'Berlin ist eine ausführliche Stadt': Einleitende Bemerkungen zur Berliner Stadt-, Kultur- und Mediengeschichte." In *Berlin: Medien- und*

Kulturgeschichte einer Hauptstadt im 20. Jahrhundert. Tübingen: Francke Verlag, 2007.

Bauschinger, Sigrid. "The Berlin Moderns: Else Lasker-Schüler and Café Culture." In *Berlin Metropolis: Jews and the New Culture, 1890–1918*, edited by Emily D. Bilski, 58–101. Berkeley: University of California Press, 2000.

Behrmann, Nicole. "Varieté, Telefon, Kino: Die Entstehung des Prinzen von Theben." *Modern Language Notes* 132, no. 3 (2017): 639–57.

Belloï, Livio. "Lumière and His View: the Cameraman's Eye in Early Cinema." *Historical Journal of Film, Radio and Television* 15, no. 4 (1995): 461–74.

Benjamin, Walter. "Die Aufgabe des Übersetzers." In *Illuminationen*. 1. Edition. Frankfurt am Main: Suhrkamp, 1977.

Benjamin, Walter. "Das Kunstwerk im Zeitalter seiner technischen Reproduzierbarkeit." In *Gesammelte Schriften*, edited by Rolf Tiedemann and Hermann Schweppenhäuser. Frankfurt am Main: Suhrkamp, 1991.

Benjamin, Walter. "Paris, Capital of the Nineteenth Century. Exposé (1939)." In *The Arcades Project*, edited by Rolf Tiedemann, translated by Howard Eiland and Kevin McLaughlin, 14–26. Cambridge: Belknap Press, 1999.

Berg, Shelley. "Sada Yacco: The American Tour, 1899–1900." *Dance Chronicle* 16 (1993): 147–96.

Bernhardt, Oliver. *Alfred Döblin.* München: Deutscher Taschenbuch Verlag, 2007.

Bhabha, Homi K. *The Location of Culture.* London: Routledge, 1994.

Bierbaum, Otto Julius. *Deutsche Chansons* (Brettl-Lieder). Berlin: Schuster & Loeffler, 1900.

Bilang, Karla. "'. . . ich habe ein Geschöpf hingesetzt' ELSE LASKER-SCHÜLER. Der STURM und die Bildkunst," *STURM-Frauen: Künstlerinnen der Avantgarde in Berlin 1910–1932*, edited by Max Hollein and Ingrid Pfeiffer, 212–15. Köln: Wienand, 2015.

Blankenship, Janelle. "To Attract/to Alternate: The Skladanowsky Experiment." *Cinema & Cie: International Film Studies Journal* no. 9 (2007): 61–79.

Boehm, Gottfried. "Cold Fire: Figures and Landscape in Georges Seurat." In *Georges Seurat—Figur im Raum*, edited by Zürcher Kunstgesellschaft and Kunsthaus Zürich, 84–95. Ostfildern: Hatje Cantz, 2009.

Borg, Ruben. "Literary Modernism." In *Critical Posthumanism: Genealogy of the Posthuman*, November 26, 2017. https://criticalposthumanism.net/literary-modernism-and-the-posthuman/

Bragaglia, Anton Giulio. "Futurist Photodynamism (1911)," translated by Lawrence S. Rainey. *Modernism/modernity* 15 (2008): 363–79.

Brandstetter, Gabriele. *Aufforderung zum Tanz: Geschichten und Gedichte*, edited by Gabriele Brandstetter. Stuttgart: Reclam, 1993.

Brandstetter, Gabriele. *Poetics of Dance: Body, Image, and Space in the Historical Avant- Gardes.* Oxford: Oxford University Press, 2015.

Brandstetter, Gabriele. "Ritual as Scene and Discourse: Art and Science Around 1900 as Exemplified by 'Le Sacre du printemps.'" *World of Music* 40, no. 1 (1998): 37–59.

Brandstetter, Gabriele. "Die Tänzerin der Metamorphosen." In *Loïe Fuller: Getanzter Jugendstil.* München: Prestel, 1996.

Brandstetter, Gabriele. *Tanz Lektüren. Körperbilder und Raumfiguren der Avantgarde.* Frankfurt am Main: Fischer, 1995.

Brandstetter, Gabriele, and Gabriele Klein. "Bewegung in Übertragung. Methodische Überlegungen am Beispiel von *Le Sacre du Printemps.*" In *Methoden der Tanzwissenschaft*, edited by Gabriele Brandstetter and Gabriele Klein, 9–24. Bielefeld: transcript, 2007.

Brandstetter, Gabriele, and Christoph Wulf. Introduction to *Tanz als Anthropologie*, edited by Gabriele Brandstetter and Christoph Wulf, 9–13. München: Wilhelm Fink Verlag, 2007.

Brannigan, Erin. *Choreography and the Moving Image.* Oxford: Oxford University Press, 2011.

Brühl, Georg. *Herwarth Walden und 'Der Sturm.'* Leipzig: Edition Leipzig, 1983.

Buber, Martin. "The Spirit of the Orient and Judaism." In *On Judaism* by Martin Buber, edited by Nahum N. Glatzer, translated by Eva Jospe, 56–78. New York: Schocken, 1967.

Buddensieg, Tilmann. "The Early Years of August Endell: Letters to Kurt Breysig from Munich." *Art Journal* 43, no. 1 (1983): 41–49.

Burt, Ramsay. *The Male Dancer: Bodies, Spectacle, Sexualities.* London: Routledge, 1995.

Catani, Stephanie. "Die Geburt des *Döblinismus* aus dem Geist des Fin die Siecle: Döblins frühe Erzählungen im Spannungsfeld von Ästhetik, Poetik und Medizin." In *Alfred Döblin: Paradigms of Modernism*, edited by Steffan Davies and Ernest Schonfield, 28–46. Berlin: Walter de Gruyter, 2009.

Christian, Margareta Ingrid. *Objects in Air: Artworks and Their Outside around 1900.* Chicago: University of Chicago Press, 2021.

Chwalkowski, Farrin. *Symbols in Arts, Religion and Culture: The Soul of Nature.* Newcastle, UK: Cambridge Scholars Publishing, 2016.

Clark, Frank. "Nineteenth-Century Public Parks from 1830." *Garden History* 1, no. 3 (1973): 31–41.

Cocteau, Jean, and Arsène Alexandre. *The Decorative Art of Léon Bakst*, translated by Adrienne Foulke. Mineola, NY: Dover Publications, 1973.

Coorlawala, Uttara Asha. "Ruth St. Denis and India's Dance Renaissance." *Dance Chronicle* 15, no. 2 (1992): 123–52.

Cowan, Michael. *Cult of the Will: Nervousness and German Modernity.* University Park: Pennsylvania State University Press, 2008.

Cowan, Michael. "Die Tücke des Körpers: Taming the Nervous Body in Alfred Döblin's 'Die Ermordung einer Butterblume' and 'Die Tänzerin und der Leib.'" *seminar* 43, no. 4 (2007): 482–98.

Current, Richard, and Marcia Ewing Current. *Goddess of Light.* Boston: Northeastern University Press, 1997.

Damm, Steffen, and Klaus Siebenhaar. *Ernst Litfaß und sein Erbe: eine Kulturgeschichte der Litfaßsäule.* Berlin: Bostermann und Siebenhaar, 2005.

Danzker, Jo-Anne Birnie. "Plakatkunst und Skultur um die Jahrhundertwende: Loïe Fuller als Modell." In *Loïe Fuller: Getanzter Jugendstil*. München: Prestel, 1996.

David, Helge. *An die Schönheit. August Endells Texte zu Kunst und Ästhetik 1896 bis 1925*. Weimar: Verlag und Datenbank für Geisteswissenschaften, 2008.

Derbyshire, John. "Slim Pickings." Review of *Berlin in Lights: The Diaries of Count Harry Kessler, 1918–1937*, translated and edited by Laird Easton. *The New Criterion*, November 2000. http://www.newcriterion.com/articles.cfm/kessler-derbyshire-2319

Derrida, Jacques. *The Beast and the Sovereign*, vol. 1, translated by Geoffrey Bennington. Chicago: University of Chicago Press, 2009.

Desmond, Jane. "Dancing Out the Difference: Cultural Imperialism and Ruth St. Denis' 'Radha' of 1906." *Signs: Journal of Women in Culture and Society* 17, no. 1 (1991): 28–49.

Dick, Ricarda. "Else-Lasker-Schüler als Künsterlin." In *Else Lasker-Schüler: Die Bilder*, edited by Ricarda Dick, 117–58. Berlin: Jüdischer Verlag im Suhrkamp Verlag, 2010.

Dick, Ricarda, ed. *Else Lasker-Schüler–Franz Marc: eine Freundschaft in Briefen und Bildern: mit sämtlichen privaten und literarischen Briefen*. München: Prestel, 2012.

Dickinson, Edward Ross. *Dancing in the Blood: Modern Dance and European Culture on the Eve of the First World War*. Cambridge: Cambridge University Press, 2017.

Döblin, Alfred. "The Dancer and the Body," translated by Iain Bamforth. In *British Journal of General Practice* 59 (2009): 959–60.

Döblin, Alfred. "Erlebnis zweier Kräfte." In *Schriften zu Leben und Werk*, edited by Walter Muschg, 40–45. Olten, Switzerland: Walter-Verlag, 1986.

Döblin, Alfred. "Gertrude Barrison." In *Der Sturm: Wochenschrift für Kultur und die Künste*, no. 11, edited by Herwarth Walden (October 1911), 4.

Döblin, Alfred. "Mein Standort." In *Schriften zu Leben und Werk*, edited by Walter Muschg, 193–94. Olten, Switzerland: Walter-Verlag, 1986.

Döblin, Alfred. "Modern: Ein Bild der Gegenwart." In *Jagende Rosse, der schwarze Vorhang und andere frühe Erzählwerk*, edited by Walter Muschg, 7–25. Olten, Switzerland: Walter-Verlag, 1981.

Döblin, Alfred. "An Romanautoren und ihre Kritiker: Berliner Programm." In *Schriften zu Ästhetik, Poetik und Literatur*, edited by Walter Muschg, 119–23. Olten, Switzerland: Walter-Verlag, 1989.

Döblin, Alfred. "Tänzerinnen." *Der Sturm: Wochenschrift für Kultur und die Künste*, no. 129, edited by Herwarth Walden (October 1912), 162.

Dobryden, Paul. "The Institution of Pleasure: From Display to Environment at the Berlin Lunapark." *Studies in European Cinema* 10, no. 2/3 (2013): 157–78.

Dollenmayer, David B. *The Berlin Novels of Alfred Döblin: "Wadzek's Battle with the Steam Turbine," "Berlin Alexanderplatz," "Men without Mercy," and "November 1918"*. Berkeley: University of California Press, 1988.

Dollenmayer, David B. "An Urban Montage and Its Significance in Döblin's *Berlin Alexanderplatz*." *German Quarterly* 53, no. 3 (1980): 317–36.

Dowden, Stephen D., and Meike G. Werner. "The Place of German Modernism." In *The Oxford Handbook of Modern German History*, edited by Helmut Walser Smith. Oxford: Oxford University Press, 2011.

Drummond, Kent G. "The Queering of *Swan Lake*: A New Male Gaze for the Performance of Sexual Desire." *Journal of Homosexuality* 23, no. 2–4 (2003): 235–55.

Duncan, Isadora. *The Dance of the Future*. Eugen Diedrichs: Leipzig, 1903.

Easton, Laird McLeod. *The Red Count. The Life and Times of Harry Graf Kessler*. Berkeley: University of California Press, 2002.

Edel, Edmund. "Der Schrei der Litfasssäule." In *Berliner Tageblatt* no. 481 (September 21, 1908).

Einstein, Carl. "Léon Bakst." In *Werke*, vol. 2, *1919–1928*, edited by Marion Schmid in cooperation with Henriette Beese and Jens Kwasny, 341–68. Berlin: Medusa Verlag, 1981.

Eisenschmidt, Alexander. "Metropolitan Architecture: Karl Scheffler and Alfred Messel's Search for a New Urbanity." *Grey Room* 65 (2014): 90–115.

Eisenschmidt, Alexander. "Visual Discoveries of an Urban Wanderer: August Endell's Perception of a Beautiful Metropolis." *Architectural Research Quarterly* 11 (2007): 71–80.

Elswit, Kate. "Berlin Your Dance Partner Is Death." *TDR: The Drama Review* 53 (2009): 73–92.

Elswit, Kate. *Watching Weimar Dance*. Oxford: Oxford University Press, 2014.

Endell, August. "Architektonische Erstling." In *Dekorative Kunst: Zeitschrift für angewandte Kunst* 3, no. 8 (1900), edited by H. Bruckmann (München) and J. Meier-Graefe (Paris), 297.

Endell, August. "The Beauty of the Metropolis." *Grey Room* 56 (2014), translated by Zeynep Çelik Alexander.

Endell, August. "Formenschönheit und dekorative Kunst," part two, translated by Zeynep Çelik Alexander. *Dekorative Kunst* 2 (1898): 121.

Endell, August. "Um die Schönheit." In *Eine Paraphrase über die Münchener Kunstausstellung*, 5–29. München: Verlag Emil Franke, 1896.

Engelhardt, Molly. *Dancing Out of Line: Ballrooms, Ballets, and Mobility in Victorian Fiction and Culture*. Athens: Ohio University Press, 2009.

Engstrom, Eric J. *Clinical Psychiatry in Imperial Germany: A History of Psychiatric Practice*. Ithaca: Cornell University Press, 2003.

Farfan, Penny. *Performing Queer Modernism*. Oxford: Oxford University Press, 2017.

Farmer, Brett. "The Fabulous Sublimity of Gay Diva Worship." *Camera Obscura* 20, no. 2 (59) (2005): 165–95.

Ferguson, Pricilla Parkhurt. "The Flaneur On and Off the Streets of Paris." In *The Flâneur*, edited by Keith Tester. London: Routledge, 1994.

Fischer, Ole W. "Bauen für den Übermenschen?—Peter Behrens, Henry van de Velde und der Nietzsche-Kult." *ICOMOS—Hefte des Deutschen Nationalkomitees* 64 (2018): 177–89.

Fischer-Lichte, Erika. *The Routledge Introduction to Theatre and Performance Studies*, edited by Minou Arjomand and Ramona Mosse, translated by Minou Arjomand. Abington, UK: Routledge, 2014.

Fleischer, Mary. *Embodied Texts: Symbolist Playwright-Dancer Collaborations*. Amsterdam: Rodopi, 2007.

Flitch, J. E. Crawford. *Modern Dancing and Dancers*. Philadelphia: J. B. Lippincott, 1912.

Foster, Susan. *Choreographing Empathy: Kinesthesia in Performance*. London: Routledge, 2011.

Foster, Susan. *Choreography and Narrative: Ballet's Staging of Story and Desire*. Bloomington: Indiana University Press, 1996.

Foster, Susan. "Movement's Contagion: The Kinesthetic Impact of Performance." In *The Cambridge Companion to Performance Studies*, edited by Tracy C. Davis. Cambridge: Cambridge University Press, 2008.

Foster, Susan. *Reading Dancing. Bodies and Subjects in Contemporary American Dance*. Berkeley: University of California Press, 1986.

Fries, Marilyn Sibley. "The City as Metaphor for the Human Condition: Alfred Döblin's *Berlin Alexanderplatz* (1929)." *Modern Fiction Studies* 24, no. 1 (1978): 41–64.

Frisby, David. "The City Interpreted: Georg Simmel's Metropolis." In *Cityscapes of Modernity*, 100–158. Cambridge: Polity Press, 2001.

Frisby, David. "The Flâneur in Social Theory." In *The Flâneur*, edited by Keith Tester. London: Routledge, 1994.

Fritzsche, Peter. *Reading Berlin 1900*. Cambridge, MA: Harvard University Press, 1996.

Fuller, Loïe. *Fifteen Years of a Dancer's Life*. Boston: Small, Maynard, 1913.

Funkenstein, Susan. *Marking Modern Movement: Dance and Gender in the Visual Imagery of the Weimar Republic*. Ann Arbor: University of Michigan Press, 2020.

Gage, John. *Color and Culture: Practice and Meaning from Antiquity to Abstraction*. Berkeley: University of California Press, 1999.

Garafola, Lynn. "The Travesty Dancer in Nineteenth Century Ballet." *Dance Research Journal* 17, no. 2/18, no. 1 (1985–1986): 35–40.

Garelick, Rhonda K. *Electric Salome: Loïe Fuller's Performance of Modernism*. Princeton: Princeton University Press, 2007.

Gautier, Théophile. *Constantinople*, translated by Robert Howe Gould. New York: Henry Holt and Company, 1875.

George, Alys X. *The Naked Truth: Viennese Modernism and the Body*. Chicago: University of Chicago Press, 2020.

Girdwood, Megan. *Modernism and the Choreographic Imagination: Salome's Dance after 1890*. Edinburgh: Edinburgh University Press, 2021.

Glatzer, Dieter, and Ruth Glatzer. *Berliner Leben 1900–1914. Eine historische Reportage aus Erinnerungen und Berichten*. Band 1 & 2. Berlin: Rütten & Loening, 1986.

Guido, Laurent. "Auf die Bühne gezaubert, dass man erstaunt': cinéma, danse et music-hall au tournant du 20e siècle." *Seminar: A Journal of Germanic Studies* 46, no. 3 (2010): 205–22.

Guido, Laurent. "Between Paradoxical Spectacles and Technical Dispositives: Looking Again at the (Serpentine) Dances of Early Cinema." In *Cine-*

Dispositives: Essays in Epistemology Across Media, edited by Albera François and Tortajada Maria, 249–74. Amsterdam: Amsterdam University Press, 2015.

Gunning, Tom. "The Attraction of Motion: Modern Representation and the Image of Movement." In *Film 1900: Technology, Perception, Culture*, edited by Ligensa Annemone and Kreimeier Klaus, 165–74. Bloomington: Indiana University Press, 2015.

Gunning, Tom. "The Cinema of Attraction[s]: Early Film, Its Spectator and the Avant-Garde." In *Early Cinema: Space—Frame—Narrative*, edited by Thomas Elsaesser, 56–62. London: BFI, 1990.

Gunning, Tom. "Loïe Fuller and the Art of Motion: Body, Light, Electricity, and the Origins of Cinema." In *Camera Obscura, Camera Lucida: Essays in Honor of Annette Michelson*, edited by Allen Richard and Turvey Malcolm, 75–90. Amsterdam: Amsterdam University Press, 2003.

Günther, Ernst. *Geschichte des Varieté*. Berlin: Taschenbuch der Künste, 1978.

Haine, W. Scott. "Introduction." to *The Thinking Space: The Café as a Cultural Institution in Paris, Italy and Vienna*, edited by Leona Rittner, W. Scott Haine, and Jeffrey H. Jackson. Abingdon, UK: Routledge, 2013.

Hallensleben, Markus. *Else Lasker-Schüler: Avantgardismus und Kunstinszenierung*. Tübingen: Francke, 2000.

Haller, Andrea. "Seen Through the Eyes of Simmel: The Cinema Programme as a 'Modern' Experience." In *Film 1900: Technology, Perception, Culture*, edited by Annemone Ligensa and Klaus Kreimeier, 113–24. Bloomington: Indiana University Press, 2015.

Hand, Stacy. "Embodied Abstraction: Biomorphic Fantasy and Empathy Aesthetics in the Work of Hermann Obrist, August Endell, and their Followers." PhD diss., University of Chicago, 2008.

Haraway, Donna. "A Cyborg Manifesto: Science, Technology, and Socialist-Feminism in the Late Twentieth Century." In *Simians, Cyborgs and Women: The Reinvention of Nature*, 149–81. New York: Routledge, 1991.

Hardt, Yvonne, and Kirsten Maar. "Bewegte Räume: zur Verortung des Tanzes im Spannungsfeld von Metropole und Provinz—ein Einleitung." In *Tanz Metropole Provinz. Jahrbuch Tanzforschung* 17, 1–17. Hamburg: Lit Verlag, 2007.

Harris, Stephanie. "Exposures: Rilke, Photography, and the City." *New German Critique* 33, no. 3 (2006): 121–49.

Hartwig, Josef. *Leben und Meinungen des Bildhauers Josef Hartwig*. Frankfurt am Main: Mitteldeutscher Kunstgewerbe-Verein, 1955.

Haubenreich, Jacob. "Text-corporeality and the Double Rend of the Page: The Specter of the Manuscript in Rilke's *Die Aufzeichnungen des Malte Laurids Brigge*." *Monatshefte* 105, no. 4 (2013): 565–92.

Heine, Anselm. "Berlins Physiognomie." In *Ich weiß Bescheid in Berlin*, 1–25. Berlin: Behr, 1908.

Heizer, Donna. *Jewish-German Identity in the Orientalist Literature of Else Lasker-Schüler, Friedrich Wolf, and Franz Werfel*. Columbia, SC: Camden House, 1996.

Hessing, Jakob. "My Heart: An Introduction." In *My Heart: A Novel of Love, with*

Pictures and Real, Living People, translated by Sheldon Gilman and Robert Levine, vii–xix. Amsterdam: November Editions, 2016.

Hewitt, Andrew. *Social Choreography: Ideology as Performance in Dance and Everyday Movement*. Durham: Duke University Press, 2005.

von Hofmannsthal, Hugo. "Die unvergleichliche Tänzerin." In *Aufforderung zum Tanz*, edited by Gabriele Brandstetter, 238–45. Stuttgart: Reclam, 1992.

Horkheimer, Max, and Theodor Adorno. *Dialectic of Enlightenment: Philosophical Fragments*, edited by Gunzelin Schmid Noerr, translated by Edmund Jephcott. Stanford: Stanford University Press, 2002.

Huschka, Sabine. *Moderner Tanz. Konzepte—Stile—Utopien*. Reinbek bei Hamburg: Rowohlt, 2002.

Huyssen, Andreas. *Miniature Metropolis: Literature in an Age of Photography and Film*. Cambridge, MA: Harvard University Press, 2015.

Huyssen, Andreas. "Modernist Miniatures: Literary Snapshots of Urban Spaces." *PMLA* 122, no. 1 (January 2007): 27–42.

Hylenski, Kristen. "Die 'Not Der Zeit': Modernity in Frank Wedekind's Dance Poems." *Monatshefte* 104, no. 1 (2012): 55–69.

Ingalls, Jennifer. "Else Lasker-Schüler's Collaborative Avant Garde: Text & Image in Berlin c. 1910." PhD diss., University of California at Berkeley, 2017.

Iskin, Ruth E. *The Poster: Art, Advertising, Design, and Collecting, 1860s–1900s*. Hanover, NH: Dartmouth College Press, 2014.

Järvinen, Hanna. "Dancing without Space—On Nijinsky's 'L'Après-midi d'un Faune' (1912)." *Dance Research* 27, no. 1 (2009): 28–64.

Jelavich, Peter. *Berlin Alexanderplatz: Radio, Film and the Death of Weimar Culture*. Berkeley: University of California Press, 2006.

Jelavich, Peter. *Berlin Cabaret*. Cambridge: Harvard University Press, 1993.

Jeschke, Claudia, and Gabi Vettermann. "Isadora Duncan, Berlin and Munich in 1906: Just an Ordinary Year in a Dancer's Career." *Dance Chronicle* 18, no. 2 (1995): 217–29.

Jordan, David P. "The City: Baron Haussmann and Modern Paris." *American Scholar* 61, no.1 (1992): 99–106.

Jordan, David P. "Haussmann and Haussmannisation: The Legacy for Paris." *French Historical Studies* 27, no. 1 (2004): 87–113.

Jonas, Klaus. "Rilke und Clotilde Sacharoff: Ein unveröffentlichter Briefwechsel." *Monatshefte* 58, no. 1 (1966): 1–19.

Jones, E. G. "The Development of the 'Muscular Sense' Concept During the Nineteenth Century and the Work of H. Charlton Bastian." *Journal of the History of Medicine and Allied Sciences* 27, no. 3 (July 1972): 298–311.

Jones, Susan. *Literature, Modernism and Dance*. Oxford: Oxford University Press, 2013.

Jowitt, Deborah. *Time and the Dancing Image*. Berkeley: University of California Press, 1988.

Justinus, Oscar. "Zettel." In *Berliner Pflaster*, edited by Moritz Reymond and Ludwig Manzel, 66–68. Berlin: W. Pauli, 1891.

Kahane, Arthur. *Tagebuch des Dramaturgen*. Berlin: Bruno Cassirer Verlag, 1928.

Kant, Marion. *The Cambridge Companion to Ballet*, edited by Marion Kant. Cambridge: Cambridge University Press, 2007.

Katz, Ruth. "The Egalitarian Waltz." *Comparative Studies in Society and History* 15, no. 3 (1973): 368–77.

Kayser, Rudolf. "Alfred Döblin. Zu seinem 50. Geburstag." In *Berliner Tageblatt*, Jg. 57, Nr. 374–9.8.1928.

Kessler, Harry Graf. "Die Entstehung der Josephs-Legende." In *Künstler und Nationen: Aufsätze und Reden 1899–1933*, edited by Cornelia Blasberg and Gerhard Schuster, 277–79. Munich: Fischer, 1988.

Kessler, Harry Graf. "Die Handlung der Josephs-Legende." In *Künstler und Nationen: Aufsätze und Reden 1899–1933*, edited by Cornelia Blasberg und Gerhard Schuster, 180–85. Munich: Fischer, 1988.

Kessler, Harry Graf. "Henri de Régnier." *PAN* 4 (1895): 243–49.

Kessler, Harry Graf. *Journey to the Abyss: The Diaries of Count Harry Kessler, 1880–1918*, edited and translated by Laird M. Easton. New York: Alfred A. Knopf, 2011.

Kessler, Harry Graf. "Kunst und Religion." In *Künstler und Nationen. Aufsätze und Reden 1899–1933*, edited by Cornelia Blasberg and Gerhard Schuster, 9–47. Frankfurt am Main: Fischer 1988.

Kessler, Harry Graf. "Lehrjahre." In *Gesichter und Zeiten. Erinnerungen*, edited by Cornelia Blasberg and Gerhard Schuster, 97–231. Frankfurt am Main: Fischer, 1988.

Kessler, Harry Graf. *Das Tagebuch*, vol. 2, *1892–1897*, edited by Günter Riederer and Jörg Schuster. Stuttgart: Klett-Cotta, 2004.

Kessler, Harry Graf. *Das Tagebuch*, vol. 3, *1897–1905*, edited by Carina Schäfer and Gabriele Biedermann. Stuttgart: Klett-Cotta 2004.

Kessler, Harry Graf. *Das Tagebuch*, vol. 4, *1906–1914*, edited by Jörg Schuster. Stuttgart: Klett-Cotta, 2005.

Kessler, Harry, and Charles Kessler. *Berlin in Lights: The Diaries of Count Harry Kessler, 1918–1937*. New York: Grove Press, 2000.

King, Helen. *The Disease of Virgins: Green Sickness, Chlorosis, and the Problems of Puberty*. Abington, UK: Routledge, 2004.

Kirschnick. Sylke. *Tausend und ein Zeichen: Else Lasker-Schülers Orient und die Berliner Alltags- und Populärkultur um 1900*. Würzburg: Königshausen und Neumann, 2007.

Klein, Gabriele. "Urbane Bewegungskulturen. Zum Verhältnis von Sport, Stadt und Kultur." In *Bewegungsraum und Stadtkultur: Sozial—und kulturwissenschaftliche Perspektiven*, 13–30. Bielefeld: transcript Verlag, 2008.

Kobel, Erwin. *Alfred Döblin: Erzählkunst im Umbruch*. Berlin: De Gruyter, 1985.

Kolb, Alexandra. *Performing Femininity: Dance and Literature in German Modernism*. Bern: Peter Lang, 2009.

Kolb, Annette. "Harry Graf Kessler." *Maß und Wert* 4 (1938): 630–31.

Kramer, Andreas. "Rilke and Modernism." In *The Cambridge Companion to Rilke*, edited by Karen Leeder and Robert Vilain, 113–30. Cambridge: Cambridge University Press, 2010.

Krauss, Andrea. "Writing of Attractions: Else Lasker-Schüler's Avant-Garde Techniques," translated by Nils F. Schott. *Modern Language Notes* 132, no. 3 (2017): 602–24.

Laban, Rudolf von. *A Vision of Dynamic Space*. London: Falmer Press, 1984.

A Lady of Distinction. *The Mirror of the Graces or The English Lady's Costume*. New York: B. Crosby and Company, 1813.

Langer, Susanne K. "From Feeling and Form." In *What Is Dance? Readings in Theory and Criticism*, edited Roger Copeland and Marshall Cohen, 28–36. Oxford: Oxford University Press, 1983.

Lasker-Schüler, Else. *Briefe 1893–1913*, edited by Ulrike Marquardt. Berlin: Jüdischer Verlag, 2003.

Lasker-Schüler, Else. "Briefe nach Norwegen." In *Der Sturm: Wochenschrift für Kultur und die Künste*. 1911/1912.

Lasker-Schüler, Else. "Die kreisende Weltfabrik." In *Die kreisende Weltfabrik: Berliner Ansichten und Porträts*, edited by Heidrun Loper. Berlin: transit, 2012. First published in *Vossische Zeitung*, April 16, 1922.

Lasker-Schüler, Else. *Hebräische Balladen*. Berlin-Wilmersdorf: A. R. Meyer, 1913.

Lasker-Schüler, Else. *Hebräische Balladen*. Zweite, vermehrte Auflage. Berlin-Wilmersdorf: A. R. Meyer, 1914.

Lasker-Schüler, Else. "Ich tanze in der Moschee." In *Der Sturm: Wochenschrift für Kultur und die Künste*, no. 52, edited by Herwarth Walden (February 25, 1911), 414.

Lasker-Schüler, Else. "Im neopathetischen Cabaret." In *Der Sturm: Wochenschrift für Kultur und die Künste*, no. 38, edited by Herwarth Walden (November 1910), 304.

Lasker-Schüler, Else. *Mein Herz: Ein Liebesroman mit Bildern und wirklich lebenden Menschen*. Mit Zeichnungen der Autorin aus der Ausgabe von 1912. Berlin: Suhrkamp Verlag, 1989.

Lasker-Schüler, Else. *My Heart*, translated by Sheldon Gilman and Robert Levine. Amsterdam: November Editions, 2016.

Lauster, Martina. *Sketches of the Nineteenth Century: European Journalism and Its Physiologies, 1830–1850*. Basingstoke, UK: Palgrave Macmillan, 2007.

Lecoq, Benoît. "Le Café." In *Les Lieux de mémoire*, vol. 3, edited by Pierre Nora, 878. Paris: Gallimard, 1992.

Lecoq, Benoît. *Rethinking France: Les Lieux des mémoire*. Translated by Mary Trouille and David P. Jordan (Chicago: University of Chicago Press, 2001).

Lepecki, André. "Inscribing Dance." In *Of the Presence of the Body: Essays on Dance and Performance Theory*, edited by André Lepecki, 124–39. Middletown, CT: Wesleyan University Press, 2004.

Levinson, André. *Bakst: The Story of the Artist's Life*. New York: Benjamin Bloom, 1971.

Lifchez, Raymond. "The Lodges of Istanbul." In *The Dervish Lodge: Architecture, Art, and Sufism in Ottoman Turkey*, edited by Raymond Lifchez, 73–129. Berkeley: University of California Press, 1991.

Lim, Wesley. "The Aesthetics of Queer Work: Loïe Fuller's Exhausting Life as Performance Art in Stephanie Di Giusto's *The Dancer* (2016)." In *Circus and the Avant-Gardes: History, Imaginary, Innovation*, edited by Anna-Sophie Jürgens and Mirjam Hildbrand, 196–212. Abington, UK: Routledge, 2022.

Lim, Wesley. "Bodies in Color, Black and White, and in Piles: The Dichotomy of Concentration Camp Aesthetics and Somatic Dance Practices in Sasha Waltz's Screendance *Körper* (2000)." *German Studies Review* 44, no. 2 (2021): 335–58. https://doi.org/10.1353/gsr.2021.0042

Lim, Wesley. "From Ritual Dance to Flight? Glimmers of the Fantastic in Robert Müller's *Tropen: Der Mythos der Reise*." *Journal of Austrian Studies* 48, no. 2 (2015): 101–20.

Lim, Wesley. "Reimagining the Brown Body: Contact Improvisation and an Alternative Masculinity in *Alignigung*, William Forsythe's Screendance." *TDR: The Drama Review* 65, no. 3 (2021): 78–90. muse.jhu.edu/article/807609

Lim, Wesley. "The Specter of Pina Bausch: Enhancing the Possibilities of *Tanztheater* through Film in Wim Wenders's *Pina* (2011)." *Studies in European Cinema* 17, no. 1 (2020): 4–19. https://doi.org/10.1080/17411548.2018.1498609

"Die Litfasssäule als Jubilarin." *Berliner Lokal-Anzeiger*, no. 315. July 1, 1905.

Longstreet, Abby Buchanan. *Manners, Good and Bad*. New York: Kessinger, 1890.

Louppe, Laurence. *Poetics of Contemporary Dance*, translated by Sally Gardner. Alton, UK: Dance Books, 2010.

Mack, Michael. *Contaminations: Beyond Dialectics in Modern Literature, Science and Film*. Edinburgh: Edinburgh University Press, 2016.

Manning, Susan, and Melissa Benson. "Interrupted Continuities: Modern Dance in Germany." *TDR: The Drama Review* 30, no. 2 (1986): 30–45.

Manning, Susan, and Lucia Ruprecht, eds. *New German Dance Studies*. Champaign: University of Illinois Press, 2012.

Martin, John. *Introduction to the Dance*. New York: W. W. Norton, 1939.

Mason, Francis. *A Treatise on the Use and Peculiar Advantages of Dancing and Exercises, Considered as a Means of Refinement and Physical Development, with General Remarks*. London: Sharp and Hale, 1854.

Mazlich, Bruce. "The *Flâneur*: From Spectator to Representation." In *The Flâneur*, edited by Keith Tester. London: Routledge, 1994.

McCarren, Felicia. *Dance Pathologies: Performance, Poetics, Medicine*. Stanford: Stanford University Press, 1998.

McCarren, Felicia. *Dancing Machines. Choreographies of the Age of Mechanical Reproduction*. Stanford: Stanford University Press, 2003.

"Mehr Litfasssäulen." *Berliner Tageblatt*, no. 609. Sept. 29, 1912.

Membrado, Monique. *Poétique des cafes*, preface by Pierre Sansot. Paris: Publisud, 1989.

Meyer, Charles S. "Ida Rubinstein: A Twentieth-Century Cleopatra." *Dance Research Journal* 20, no. 2 (1989): 33–51.

Micklewright, Nancy. "Derwish Images in Photographs and Painting." In *The Dervish Lodge: Architecture, Art, and Sufism in Ottoman Turkey*, edited by Raymond Lifchez, 269–83. Berkeley: University of California Press, 1991.

Mistry, Freny. "On Hofmannsthal's 'Die unvergleichliche Tänzerin.'" *Modern Austrian Literature* 10, no. 1 (1977): 31–42.

Moeller-Bruck, Arthur. *Das Varieté.* Berlin: Julius Bard, 1902.

Müller, Lothar. "The Beauty of the Metropolis: Towards an Aesthetic Urbanism in Turn-of-the-Century Berlin." In *Berlin: Culture and Metropolis,* edited by Charles W. Haxthausen and Heidrun Suhr. Minneapolis: University of Minnesota Press, 1990.

Natale, Simone. "A Short History of Superimposition: From Spirit Photography to Early Cinema." *Early Popular Visual Culture* 10, no. 2 (2012): 125–45.

Neumeyer, Harald. *Der Flaneur: Konzeptionen der Moderne.* Würzburg: Königshausen & Neumann, 1999.

Nietzsche, Friedrich. *Die Geburt der Tragödie.* In *Nietzsches Werke: Historisch-kritische Ausgabe.* Electronic edition. Kritische Gesamtausgabe; III-1.26. http://www.nietzschesource.org/#eKGWB/GT

Nijinska, Bronislava. *Bronislava Nijinska: Early Memoirs,* edited and translated by Irina Nijinska and Jean Rawlinson. Durham: Duke University Press, 1992.

Novack, Cynthia J. *Sharing the Dance: Contact Improvisation and American Culture.* Madison: University of Wisconsin Press, 1990.

Oberzaucher-Schüller, Gunhild. "Vorbilder und Wegbreiter. Über den Einfluß der 'prime movers' des amerikanischen Modern Dance auf das Werden des Freien Tanzes in Mitteleuropa." In *Ausdruckstanz: Eine mitteleuropäische Bewegung der ersten Hälfte des 20. Jahrhunderts,* edited by Gunhild Oberzaucher-Schüller, 347–66. Wilhelmshaven, Germany: Heinrichhofen-Bücher, 1992.

Ochaim, Brygida, and Claudia Balk. *Varieté-Tänzerinnen um 1900: Vom Sinnenrausch zur Tanzmoderne.* Frankfurt am Main: Stroemfeld, 1998.

Oldenburg, Ray. *The Great Good Place: Cafes, Coffee Shops, Bookstores, Bars, Hair Salons, and Other Hangouts at the Heart of a Community.* Cambridge, MA: Da Capo Press, 1999.

d'Ors, Eugeni. "Elegia." In *Obra Catalana Completa. Glosari 1906/1910,* 790–92. Barcelona: Editorial Selecta, 1950.

Osborn, Max. *Berlin 1870–1929.* Berlin: Mann Verlag, 1994.

Otto, Ulf. "Enter Electricity: An Allegory's Stage Appearance between Verité and Varieté." *Centaurus* 57 (2015): 192–211. https://doi.org/10.1111/1600-0498.12091

Otzen, Johannes. "Das persönliche in Architektur und Kunstgewerbe." *Deutsche Bauzeitung* 34 (March 1900): 143–45.

Paeslack, Miriam. *Berlin im 19. Jahrhundert. Frühe Photographien 1850–1914* [*Berlin in the 19th Century. Early Photographs 1850–1914*]. Munich: Schirmer-Mosel Verlag 2015.

Paeslack, Miriam. *Constructing Imperial Berlin: Photography and the Metropolis.* Minneapolis: University of Minnesota Press, 2019.

Parsons, Deborah L. *Streetwalking the Metropolis: Women, the City, and Modernity.* Oxford: Oxford University Press, 2000.

Pinthus, Kurt. *Menschheitsdämmerung: Symphonie jüngster Dichtung,* edited by Kurt Pinthus. Reinbeck bei Hamburg: Rowohlt, 1997.

Pleister, Michael. *Das Bild der Großstadt in den Dichtungen Robert Walsers, Rainer Maria Rilke, Stefan Georges und Hugo von Hofmannsthals*. Hamburg: Helmut Kuske Verlag, 1990.

Potter, Susan. *Queer Timing: The Emergence of Lesbian Sexuality in Early Cinema*. Urbana: University of Illinois Press, 2019.

Qassemi, Kambiz Haji. *Ganjnameh; Cyclopaedia of Iranian Islamic Architecture*, vol. 9, *Bazaar Buildings*. Tehran, Iran: Rowzaneh Press, 2005.

Rathenau, Walter. "Die schönste Stadt der Welt." In *Die Berliner Moderne 1885–1914*, edited by Jürgen Schutte and Peter Sprengel, 100–104. Stuttgart: Reclam, 1987.

Reichel, Klaus. "Vom Jugendstil zu Sachlichkeit: August Endell (1871–1925)." PhD diss., Ruhr Universität Bochum, 1974.

Remshardt, Ralf. "Posthumanism." In *Mapping Intermediality in Performance*, edited by Sarah Bay-Cheng, Chiel Kattenbelt, Andy Lavender, and Robin Nelson, 135–39. Amsterdam: Amsterdam University Press, 2010.

Reynolds, Nancy, and Malcolm McCormick. *No Fixed Points: Dance in the Twentieth Century*. New Haven: Yale University Press, 2003.

Riederer, Günter. "Der Übergangsmensch—Kessler als Student, Untertan und Weltbürger." In *Harry Graf Kessler, Das Tagebuch*, vol. 2, *1892–1897*, edited by Günter Riederer and Jörg Schuster, 13–37. Stuttgart: Klett-Cotta, 2004.

Rilke, Rainer Maria. *Die Aufzeichnungen des Malte Laurids Brigge*. In *Werke. Kommentierte Ausgabe in vier Bänden. Prosa und Dramen*, vol. 3, edited by Manfred Engel, Ulrich Fülleborn, Horst Nalewski, and August Stahl. Frankfurt am Main: Insel Verlag, 1996.

Rilke, Rainer Maria. *Briefe*, Bd. 3, S. 183–29.03.1907 to Tora Holmström.

Rilke, Rainer Maria. *Briefe aus den Jahren 1902 bis 1906*. Leipzig: Insel, 1930.

Rilke, Rainer Maria. *Briefe aus den Jahren 1906 bis 1907*, edited by Ruth Sieber-Rilke and Carl Sieber. Leipzig: Insel Verlag, 1930.

Rilke, Rainer Maria. *The Notebooks of Malte Laurids Brigge*, translated by Michael Hulse. London: Penguin Classics, 2009.

Rainer Maria Rilke. *Translations from the Poetry of Rainer Maria Rilke*, translated by M. D. Hrefer. New York: Norton, 1962.

Rilke, Rainer Maria. *Werke. Kommentierte Ausgabe*, vol. 4, edited by Horst Nalewski. Stuttgart: Insel, 1996.

Rilke, Rainer Maria, and Marie von Thurn und Taxis. *Briefwechsel*, edited by Ernst Zinn. Frankfurt am Main: Suhrkamp, 1986.

Rosenberg, Douglas. *Screendance: Inscribing the Ephemeral Image*. New York: Oxford University Press, 2012.

Ross, Alex. "Diary of an Aesthete. Count Harry Kessler Met Everyone and Saw Everything." Review of *Journey to the Abyss: The Diaries of Count Harry Kessler, 1880–1918*, translated and edited by Laird Easton. *The New Yorker*, April 23, 2012. http://www.newyorker.com/magazine/2012/04/23/diary-of-an-aesthete

Ruprecht, Lucia. "Ambivalent Agency: Gestural Performances of Hands in Weimar Dance and Film." *Seminar* 46, no. 3 (2010): 255–75.

Ruprecht, Lucia. *Gestural Imaginaries: Dance and Cultural Theory in the Early Twentieth Century*. Oxford: Oxford University Press, 2019.

Ruprecht, Lucia. "Der Virtuose geht. Waslaw Nijinskys *L'Après-midi d'un faune*." *Arcadia: International Journal for Literary Studies* 43, no. 2 (2008): 235–56.

Ryan, Derek. "Following Snakes and Moths: Modernist Ethics and Posthumanism." *Twentieth-Century Literature* 61, no. 3 (2015): 287–304.

Ryan, Judith. *Rilke, Modernism and Poetic Tradition*. Cambridge: Cambridge University Press, 2016.

Said, Edward. *Orientalism*. New York: Random House, 1978.

Sander, Gabriele. "Döblin und der Großstadtrealismus." In *Realistisches Schreiben in der Weimarer Republik*, edited by Sabine Kyora and Stefan Neuhaus, 139–50. Würzburg: Königshausen & Neumann, 2006.

Santner, Eric L. *On Creaturely Life: Rilke, Benjamin, Sebald*. Chicago: University of Chicago Press, 2006.

Santner, Eric. *The Royal Remains: The People's Two Bodies and the Endgames of Sovereignty*. Chicago: University of Chicago Press, 2012.

Scharnowski, Susanne. "'Neben- und Durcheinander von Kostbarem und Garstigem' Das feuilletonistische Berliner Großstadtbild als Dokument der Moderne." *Zeitschrift für Literaturwissenschaft und Linguistik* 149 (2008): 34–50.

Scharnowski, Susanne. "'Berlin ist schön, Berlin ist groß.' Feuilletonistische Blicke auf Berlin: Alfred Kerr, Robert Walser, Joseph Roth und Bernard von Brentano." In *Weltfabrik Berlin—Eine Metropole als Sujet der Literatur*, edited by Matthias Harder and Almut Hille, 67–82. Würzburg: Königshausen & Neumann, 2006.

Schechner, Richard. *Performance Studies: An Introduction*. 3rd ed. London: Routledge, 2013.

Scheffler, Karl. *Berlin. Ein Stadtschicksal*. Berlin: E. Reiss, 1910.

Scheffler, Karl. *Paris. Notizen*. Leipzig: Insel Verlag, 1908.

Schlögel, Karl. *Im Raume lesen wir die Zeit: Über Zivilisationsgeschichte und Geopolitik*. Munich: Carl Hanser, 2003.

Schmetterling, Astrid. "'I am Jussuf of Egypt': Else Lasker-Schüler's Orientalist Drawing." *Ars Judaica* 8 (2012): 81–98.

Schmoll, Joseph Adolph. "Simmel und Rodin." In *Ästhetik und Soziologie um die Jahrhundertwende: Georg Simmel*, edited Hannes Böhringer and Karlfried Gründer, 18–43. Frankfurt: Vittorio Klostermann, 1976.

Schulze, Janine. *Dancing Bodies Dancing Gender: Tanz im 20. Jahrhundert aus der Perspektive der Gender-Theorie*. Dortmund: Edition Ebersbach, 1999.

Schur, Ernst. *Der moderne Tanz*. München: Lammers, 1910.

Schuster, Jana. *"Umkehr der Räume": Rainer Maria Rilkes Poetik der Bewegung*. Freiburg: Rombach, 2011.

Schuster, Jörg. "Phantasie—Mittelbarkeit—Sinnlichkeit: Der Régnier-Aufsatz, Kesslers Diaristik und Ansätze zu einer Theorie der Wirkungsästhetik." In *Harry Graf Kessler, Das Tagebuch*, vol. 2, *1892–1897*, edited by Günter Riederer and Jörg Schuster, 59–68. Stuttgart: Klett-Cotta 2004.

Sedgwick, Eve Kosofsky. "Queer and Now." In *Tendencies*. Durham: Duke University Press, 1993.

Sembach, Klaus-Jürgen, and Gottfried von Haeseler. *August Endell. Der Architekt des Photoateliers Elvira 1871–1925*. Munich: Jugendstil Verein, 1977.

"Serpentinentanz." In *Illustrierte Zeitung*, 99/2580 (December 10, 1892): 684.

Shorter, Edward. "The First Great Increase in Anorexia Nervosa." *Journal of Social History* 21, no. 1 (1987): 69–96.

Simmel, Georg. "The Berlin Trade Exhibition," translated by Sam Whimster. In *Theory, Culture & Society* 8 (1991): 119–23.

Simmel, Georg. "Berliner Gewerbeausstellung." *Die Zeit* (Wien) 7 (91): 204.

Simmel, Georg. "Die Großstädte und das Geistesleben." In *Die Berliner Moderne 1885–1914*, edited by Jürgen Schutte and Peter Sprengel, 124–30. Stuttgart: Reclam, 1987.

Singer, Milton. *Traditional India—Structure and Change*. Austin: University of Texas Press, 1979.

Skrodzki, Karl Jürgen. "Freundschaft mit Else Lasker-Schüler. Widmungen, Porträts, Briefe. Ein quellenkundliches Verzeichnis zu den Werken und Briefen der Dichterin." Accessed September 11, 2023. http://www.kj-skrodzki.de/Dokumente/Text_048s.htm

Smith, Albert. *The Natural History of the Ballet Girl*. London: Dance Books, 1996 [1847].

Somerville, Kristine. "The Logic of Dreams: The Life and Work of Ruth St. Denis." *Missouri Review* 36, no. 4 (2013): 123–41.

Sorrell, Walter. *Dance in Its Time*. New York: Columbia University Press, 1981.

Sprengel, Peter. "Literarische Avantgarde und Cabaret in Berlin—Erotik und Moderne." In *Hundert Jahre Kabarett: Zur Inszenierung gesellschaftlicher Identität zwischen Protest und Propaganda*, edited by Joanne McNally and Peter Sprengel, 29–50. Würzburg: Königshausen & Neumann, 2003.

St. Denis, Ruth. *An Unfinished Life*. New York: Harper and Bros., 1939.

Stieglitz, Alfred. *Camera Work: The Complete Illustrations 1903–1917*. Köln: Taschen, 1997.

Stinson, Susan. "Places Where I've Been: Reflections on Issues of Gender in Dance Education, Research and Administration." *Choreography and Dance* 5, no. 1 (1998): 117–27.

Stüber, Werner Jakob. *Geschichte des Modern Dance. Zur Selbsterfahrung und Körperaneignung im modernen Tanztheater*. Wilhelmshaven: Heinrichshofen Verlag, 1984.

Taylor, Hilary A. "Urban Public Parks, 1840–1900: Design and Meaning." *Garden History* 23, no. 2 (1995): 201–21.

Tester, Keith. "Introduction," to *The Flâneur*, edited by Keith Tester. London: Routledge, 1994.

Tewarson, Heidi Thomann. "Döblin's Early Collection of Stories, *Die Ermordung einer Butterblume*: Toward a Modernist Aesthetic." In *A Companion to the Works of Alfred Döblin*, edited by Roland Dollinger, Wulf Koepke, and Heidi Thomann Tewarson, 23–54. Rochester, NY: Camden House, 2004.

Teyssot, Georges. "The Wave: Walter Benjamin's Lost Essay on Jugendstil." *AA Files*, no. 61 (2010): 23–37.

Thomas, Helen. *Dance, Modernity and Culture: Explorations in the Sociology of Dance.* London: Routledge, 1995.

Thurner, Christina. *Beredte Körper—bewegte Seelen. Zum Diskurs der doppelten Bewegung in Tanztexte.* Bielefeld: transcript Verlag, 2009.

Tobias, Rochelle. "Rilke's Landscape of the Heart: On the Notebooks of Malte Laurids Brigge." *Modernism/modernity* 20, no. 4 (2013): 667–84.

Vertinsky, Patricia. "Ida Rubinstein: Dancing Decadence and 'The Art of the Beautiful Pose.'" *Nashim: A Journal of Jewish Women's Studies & Gender Issues* 26 (2014): 122–46.

Vischer, Robert, Harry Francis Mallgrave, and Eleftherios Ikonomou. "On the Optical Sense of Form: A Contribution to Aesthetics." In *Empathy, Form, and Space: Problems in German Aesthetics, 1873–1893,* edited by Harry Francis Mallgrave and Eleftherios Ikonomou, 89–122. Santa Monica, CA: Getty Center for the History of Art and the Humanities; distributed by the University of Chicago Press, 1994.

Vossische Zeitung. October 7, 1900. Cited from Glatzer, *Berliner Leben 1900–1914,* 99.

Webber, Andrew. *Berlin in the Twentieth Century: A Cultural Topography.* Cambridge: Cambridge University Press, 2011.

Webber, Andrew. "Inside Out: Acts of Displacement in Else Lasker-Schüler." *Germanic Review* 81, no. 2 (2006): 143–62.

Weir, David. *Decadence and the Making of Modernism.* Amherst: University of Massachusetts Press, 1995.

Weissenböck, Jarmila. "Gertrud Bodenwieser: Dance for the Theater." In *Gertrud Bodenwieser and Vienna's Contribution to Ausdruckstanz,* edited by Betinna Vernon-Warren and Charles Warren, 39–50. Abington, UK: Routledge, 1999.

Wilson, Elizabeth. *The Sphinx in the City: Urban Life the Control of Disorder, and Women.* Berkeley: University of California Press, 1991.

Wittmann, Gabriele. "Dancing Is Not Writing: ein poetisches Projekt über die Schnittstelle von Sprache und Tanz." In *Tanz Theorie Text,* edited by Gabriele Klein and Christa Zipperich, 585–96. Münster: Lit Verlag, 2002.

Yumibe, Joshua. "The Color Image." In *The Image in Early Cinema: Form and Material,* edited by Joshua Yumibe, Scott Curtis, Philippe Gauthier, and Tom Gunning, 142–50. Bloomington: Indiana University Press, 2018.

Yumibe, Joshua. *Moving Color: Early Film, Mass Culture, Modernism.* New Brunswick, NJ: Rutgers University Press, 2012.

Ziyaee, Maryam. "Revitalization of Cultural and Aesthetical Assets of Iranian Traditional Bazaar." *International Journal of Architecture & Planning* 5, no. 2 (2017): 234–51.

Zweig, Stefan. *The World of Yesterday: An Autobiography.* London: Cassell and Company, 1943.

Index